Personal Injury Practice

The guide to litigation in the
County Court and the High Court

Fifth edition

Andrew Buchan
Cloisters, Temple

Jenny Kennedy
Partner, Anthony Gold Solicitors

Eliot Woolf
Barrister, Outer Temple Chambers

Tottel publishing

Published by
Tottel Publishing Ltd
Maxwelton House
41–43 Boltro Road
Haywards Heath
West Sussex
RH16 1BJ

ISBN 978 1 84766 108 1
© Tottel Publishing Ltd 2008
Formerly published by LexisNexis Butterworths
Fifth edition published by Tottel Publishing Ltd 2008.

British Library Cataloguing-in-Publication Data
A catalogue record for this book is available from the British Library

Typeset by Etica Press Ltd, Malverrn
Printed and bound in Great Britain by CPI Antony Rowe Limited, Chippenham, Wiltshire

Personal Injury Practice

Preface to the fifth edition

This fifth edition updates the changes since the fourth edition which was dated 27 October 2003.

Besides the usual updating there has been major re-writing to Chapter 6 (Funding), 12 (Instructing Experts), 13 (Part 36 Offers), 25 (Handling the Award and Periodical Payments), and 31 (Occupational Stress).

We would like to thank Victoria Oliver (Anthony Gold & Co) for all her hard work.

Once again we hope that this book will be of assistance to the personal injury practitioner, the DIT claimant or defendant as well as students of practice and procedure.

Andrew Buchan

Jenny Kennedy

Eliot Woolf

28 April 2008

Contents

PART I

Preparation

CHAPTER 1

Case Management – in House   3

CHAPTER 2

Case Management – by the Courts   11

CHAPTER 3

Small Claims Track   17

CHAPTER 4

Fast Track and the Protocols   25

CHAPTER 5

Multi Track   35

CHAPTER 12

Evidence – Expert Evidence on Liability and Quantum   107

CHAPTER 13

Negotiations, Offers and Payments In   127

PART II

Issue to Trial

CHAPTER 14

Alternative Dispute Resolution ('ADR')   143

CHAPTER 15

Issue and Service   147

CHAPTER 19

Non-Compliance with Court Orders   211

CHAPTER 20

Disclosure and Inspection   215

CHAPTER 23

The Trial   267

CHAPTER 24

Costs   279

CHAPTER 28

Fatal Accidents   319

CHAPTER 29

Claimants Under a Legal Disability   327

CHAPTER 30

Disease Cases   335

CHAPTER 31

Claims for Injury Caused by Stress at Work   341

PART IV

Appendices

APPENDIX C

Specimen Schedules of Special Damages   461

APPENDIX D

Useful Addresses   477

Table of statutes

Table of statutory instruments

EUROPEAN LEGISLATION

INTERNATIONAL CONVENTIONS

Table of cases

L

M

X

Y

EU CASES

Preparation

CHAPTER 1

Case Management – in House

With the Civil Procedure Rules 1998, the courts entered an era of pro-activity. The rules provide powers for a judge (at whatever level) to strike out, summarily dismiss and penalise with costs on the spot a solicitor's failure to comply with relatively simple matters such as payment of a required fee on time. The abiding message was that no longer will delay and failure to comply with orders be tolerated.

The system consists of three 'tracks' for the pursuit of a claim; the *small claims track* which is for all cases where the overall award is likely to be less than £5,000 and in which the personal injury element of the claim is less than £1,000; the *fast track* where the whole claim, including the personal injury award, is less than £15,000 and where the issues arising are fairly simple and trial of the matter is likely to last less than one court day. All other cases are allocated to the *multi track*.

The timetable for all litigation is rigorously controlled by the court in all cases – small claims, fast track and multi track. It is likely that most solicitors avoid large amounts of small claim litigation, but it is in fast track where the problems of time management and date entry really lie.

COMPUTERISATION

Any firm that wishes to litigate any volume of work through the personal injury fast track will need a computerised case management package. Such packages are provided by a variety of firms and are tailored to the purchaser's needs. While not infallible (you can lead a horse to water but you cannot make a solicitor heed a computer warning), they will certainly reduce the fear of missing dates or tasks.

The Rules envisaged the increased use of technology, but computerised packages must still be tailored to need. They do not remove the skill from litigation and they certainly do not remove the volumes of paper that exist in every lawyer's office! In an era where a solicitor may not get paid if the case is lost, it is the solicitor and not the computer who will have to make the careful analysis of the risks involved in litigating a particular claim.

PANELS AND FRANCHISES

Practitioners who are intent upon gaining entry to the Law Society's Personal Injury Panel or who (whilst public funding for personal injury work continues to exist in a limited way) are intending to apply for or have gained a franchise for personal injury work from the Legal Aid Board, or who wish to be included on the panel of a legal expense insurers are obliged to devise procedures and ensure compliance with the strict criteria laid down for the administration of cases. The requirements of the two structures are onerous and it is not the purpose of this book to replicate what is set out in great detail in the documents provided to applicant solicitors.

ADMINISTRATIVE SYSTEMS

In order to keep the initiative, to remain on top of the case, and to run it hard and fast, whether or not a computer management package is used, all lawyers must have in place efficient administrative systems. Such systems differ from solicitor to solicitor and it is not within the scope of this book to indicate a 'best buy'. The best systems will be those with which the solicitor feels comfortable and which work effectively and quickly. The size of the firm is a major determinant of the resources available. What is vital is that each file must be maintained at all times in good order. The test is 'could a colleague who knows nothing of the case pick it up and continue it without difficulty if I dropped dead tomorrow?'

Files should be returned to the filing cabinet when not in use, rather than piled on the floor in random order; documents and letters must be filed *daily*. All this is commonplace for any branch of solicitors' work, but the successful personal injury lawyer, in particular, needs this discipline because of the high number of ongoing cases that must be handled at any one time. An expert fast track personal injury practitioner with an effective staff and the full range of efficient administrative systems often handles 350 cases at any one time; some handle up to 500. Dealing with a smaller number does not excuse using all the administrative systems available; they are as effective and as useful for five cases as for 500.

Crucial to success is a faultless system of keeping future dates recorded. If a computerised system is not used, this must be in the form of a paper diary (a lot of practitioners with computer systems keep a parallel paper diary), or on a wall chart. It is vital that the date recording system is kept outside the file and is checked and updated daily. A good case management computer system will highlight key diary dates at pre-programmed times; thus one week's notice of an important deadline will be given with the deadline date repeated at strategically programmed times. The date will 'ping' up on the screen in the morning when the machine is switched on. Most, if not all, specialist personal injury firms use two different systems simultaneously in order to ensure that dates are not missed.

One aspect of personal injury practice which must be systematic is periodic review of each and every file. This is obligatory for franchised or expense panel solicitors, but is vital for all personal injury lawyers. Indeed, the authors consider, in addition, that, whenever a client's file is considered for whatever reason, important or trivial, the practitioner should mentally review all aspects of the case to ensure that every appropriate step is being taken and that no time limit is approaching.

A further practice required of franchised solicitors, and increasingly of expense panels too, is a regular audit of the files of one fee-earner by another. A small but fixed percentage of files is sufficient, but the audit should be applied to the files of all fee-earners including the senior partner. This should occur regularly and should be diarised.

FILE MANAGEMENT

In all types of legal work, a practitioner should keep well-ordered files, but for the personal injury lawyer it is particularly important. For the great majority of personal injury cases, little more than 20 hours' work will be spent over what is likely to be a one- or two-year period. Cases often have many similarities, and the more cases there are, the more difficult it becomes to remember the stage which each has reached. It is, therefore, important that files are kept in a logical order so that the current position can be quickly assessed. The guiding principle is to keep each category of document on a separate tag and, usually, in reverse chronological order (so as to add to the top of each pile).

The correspondence between the Claimant's and Defendant's representatives ('party and party' correspondence) must be kept separate from the rest. The current state of the proceedings is quickly revealed by the progress of party and party correspondence. Pleadings, medical reports, statements, special damage documents and other expert evidence should each be kept separately. Large cases may warrant keeping each category of document in a separate ring binder or lever arch file. This also facilitates copying to counsel preparing court bundles. All surplus copies of documents, together with papers that are no longer relevant to the current running of the case, should be held together at the back of the file and kept out of the way.

IMPORTANT DATES

For any lawyer handling a heavy caseload, it is impossible to remember every crucial date in all the cases. Within the rules all deadlines are important and failure to comply with them may lead to the claim being dismissed. The solicitor will then have to take a positive step to have the claim reinstated with the associated anxiety of the same. However, no deadline is as important as the date on which the statutory limitation period expires (see Chapter 8 on Urgent action). The Limitation Act 1980 provides that personal injury actions (apart from those at sea or in the air for which difference time scales apply) must be commenced no later than three years from the date of the accident or the date when the Claimant first knew, or ought to have known, the facts which could give rise to a claim, or, if the Claimant is a minor, three years from his 18th birthday. If the action is commenced after that period, the Defendant can apply to have it struck out. Unless the court can be persuaded to exercise its discretion – usually if the Defendant is not prejudiced – this is very likely to succeed. One of the most common negligence claims against solicitors is for failing to issue proceedings in this limitation period.

The basic principle for statutory limitation periods should be: when in doubt issue. There will be times when the expiry of the three-year period is approaching and it appears that there is little chance of the case succeeding. If there are still enquiries being made, it is better to issue proceedings even with the front-end-loading obligations that are contained in the Civil Procedure Rules than to face the possibility of a negligence action. However, careful consideration needs to be given to the funding position of such clients.

There will be many important dates in every personal injury case to be kept in the recording systems: issue dates, service dates, dates to return the allocation questionnaire, dates following a case management conference, dates for the trial window, the listing questionnaire receipt and return dates, dates for any applications. There will be dates for checking replies to queries that have been received and for reminder letters to be sent, dates on which time is to be set aside for special damage calculations, dates for inspections, dates for conferences with counsel, and so on.

It helps to have a checklist on the inside of each file with the standard steps of an action set out. Against this, the practitioner can insert the dates when each task is completed as a quick reminder of the stage the case has reached.

FILE REVIEWS

There will be times when, for a period, nothing further can be done to progress a case. A doctor's report, for example, might be awaited. Without regular review, a case may lie dormant. Consequently, each file must be checked regularly. Consideration should be given to see if any steps can be taken to push the case forward and to ensure that no dates have been, or are about to be, missed. The file review should take place at least once every six weeks. Time to carry out file reviews must be set aside and noted in the diary without fail.

File review is time consuming and contrasts with the speed and efficiency which marks all the personal injury practitioner's other work. It is, however, an essential tool.

STANDARD PAPERWORK

A significant proportion of a personal injury solicitor's correspondence is repetitious. If a computerised case management system is used, the standard documentation will be entered at the point of setting the system up. It will all be ready and waiting for use when needed. If an automatic management computer system is used, then standard letters and documents ought to be kept on hard disk, and by inserting information specific to each where needed, a great deal of time and money can be saved. Standard documents include correspondence as well as frequently used court forms. Part IV of this book contains a set of standard form documents, the use of which is referred to in each relevant chapter. These are not intended to be finite; they are for guidance only, and of course standard documentation must be reviewed at regular intervals and updated when necessary.

TIME RECORDING

In litigation, time is money. At present, the only 'fixed' costs regime applies to pre-issue fast track road traffic accident cases. However, it is likely that in the future there will be fixed costs attached to other work. It is a matter of the greatest importance to the financial viability of personal injury litigation to ensure the development of a good time/costs recording system. An automatic case management system will do this for the practitioner. However, for those that have no such system, making a note of every telephone call and every attendance on the case, with time spent, must become a matter of habit if a solicitor wishes to stay in business. Further, with an automatic system, the solicitor or her secretary must enter the data. If data is not entered by way of timed notes, then the matter will not be recorded! Attendances on clients, witnesses and experts, conferences with counsel, perusing and preparing documents should all be rigorously timed and recorded. Where there are no fixed costs, because of the standard nature of a lot of personal injury work, there is a rough kind of tariff of charges, depending on the size and complexity of the case; neither the costs assessing judge nor the insurance companies will be impressed by, or pay for, a lot of needless work. The question of whether a particular piece of work will be paid for should never be far from the practitioner's mind.

A benefit of a computerised time recording system, whether linked to a case management package or not, is that the practice obtains an estimate of work in progress and the practitioner gains an overview of her efficiency in respect of fee-earning hours. Such a system may also be a franchising requirement of legal expense insurers who may require the solicitor to report back to them when certain costs levels have been reached for permission to continue working the case. Computer time entry is a supplement, but never a substitute for the diligent recording of time against each piece of work on the file.

A system which gives a warning as accumulated costs on a case near any limit imposed by a legal aid certificate or a legal expense insurer is a necessity for those doing work where there are financial ceilings on the work allowed to be done, as do many legal expense insurance contracts. It is essential to know what costs have been expended on each file.

Costs in personal injury cases are described in detail in Chapter 24.

COMMUNICATING WITH CLIENTS

A client who is regularly kept informed and who has confidence that the case is being vigorously pursued will be more likely to accept unpalatable advice than one whose faith in the solicitor has ebbed away with the passing of time. Clients should be systematically informed of significant steps in the case. If no step is being taken for some reason, the client should be told at least every six weeks that the case is under review and the reason for any lack of progress. Every six months, the client should be sent a statement of costs incurred in the case as required under the Solicitors Conduct Rules.

It is wise to obtain written authority for all steps involving significant outlay since the client may have to pay in the end. So written authority to issue proceedings or to obtain or disclose a specialist's report should normally be sought. Such practice also makes the client feel he is taking the important decisions and is being kept in touch.

Many clients have an impression of what their cases are worth, based on stories from the press or friends with a 'similar' injury. In many instances, that opinion is totally wrong. Hence, the lawyer must not only explain the true position and the strengths and weaknesses at the outset, but also communicate all developments which may affect the amount of damages recoverable. Then, when discussions about a settlement eventually take place, the client is more likely to understand the true value of the claim.

The complexity of legal issues and jargon places an obligation on all lawyers to communicate clearly, without being pompous or patronising. A significant number of people have difficulty reading and writing, and few will have any familiarity with lawyers or litigation. Plain, simple English, short sentences and no unexplained legal jargon are three vital rules.

The Solicitors Conduct Rules put special emphasis on letters to clients and make specific requirements of the initial letter to the client.

REMUNERATION

A key part of a profitable law practice is to ensure that there is a good system of billing, obtaining payments on account and paying disbursements promptly. As mentioned above, accurate time recording is essential. Modern technology facilitates all these tasks.

The greater majority of personal injury claims are now run under a 'no win no fee' agreement and risk managing those claims is essential. The firm will need to know exactly how much money is being expended on a regular basis. Details of losses over the years will hone the practice's risk management skills. Meticulous records need to be kept of such claims, the levels of success fees recovered and details of disbursement expenditure. An order for the Claimant's solicitor to pay from her office account the Defendant's costs within 14 days of a failed application, provokes careful thought for each and every risky application.

In a private case, the client should receive regular invoices for work done and disbursements paid. Payments on account should be regularly requested, so that the solicitor maintains a proper cash flow.

With the few remaining public funding certificates (apart from those cases that fall within group action where legal aid continues), payment for disbursements can be sought either when the invoice is received or when it is quantified but not yet received. There is a standard legal aid form (CLA 28) by which applications for payment can be made. The Board now requires that details of disbursements paid to date are given, as is an estimate of updated profit costs expended. There are stringent financial limits on certificates, the details of which have to be kept. Increase of the limits cannot be applied for retrospectively.

Except in legal aid cases, or in claims where counsel is agreeing to defer fees or is advising under a 'no win no fee' contract, counsel's fees must be paid within three months of the delivery of the fee note to the solicitor, unless otherwise agreed in writing. Counsel is under a professional duty to write to the solicitor, and thereafter to report the facts to the Chairman of the Bar Council, if the fees are not paid within three months and no satisfactory explanation is received. Therefore, solicitors must ensure that they have money on account in privately funded cases. In legally aided cases, counsel should apply for interim payments to the Legal Aid Board. Counsel must have a record of the legal aid number and date of issue of the certificate for the case. There is a strict period of time during which applications can be made.[1]

---

[1]   Civil Legal Aid (General) Regulations 1989, reg 100. See, further, reg 101(1)(b) in cases of hardship, and reg 101(2) for payments outstanding for at least six months after an event giving rise to a right of cost assessment.

CHAPTER 2

Case Management – by the Courts

Over the years, the courts have been given increasing powers to case manage personal injury litigation. The original opportunity for judicial case management was the summons for directions, but automatic directions allowed parties to successfully circumnavigate the directional summons, and in any event, most directions were agreed by consent.

The Civil Procedure Rules ('CPR') provide a framework for the management and progress of personal injury work. Essentially, the progress of a claim is dependant upon its value. Very small value claims are allocated to a *small claims track* where there is a limited allowance for costs. Medium value claims are allocated to a *fast track* in which it is intended that the case will progress within a very short timetable to trial. All other personal injury claims are allocated to a *multi track* where highly interventionist judicial case management will tailor directions appropriate to the nature and complexity of the claim.

THE 'OVERRIDING OBJECTIVE' (RULE 1.1)

The CPR are underpinned by what is called 'the overriding objective'. This objective is part of the rules and is intended to be the framework within which the rules are interpreted.

The overriding objective is simply stated as follows:

'(2) Dealing with a case justly includes, so far as is practicable—
(a) ensuring that the parties are on an equal footing;
(b) saving expense;
(c) dealing with the case in ways which are appropriate
 (i)   to the amount of money involved;
 (ii) to the importance of the case;
 (iii) to the complexity of the issues; and
 (iv) to the financial position of each party;
(d) ensuring that it is dealt with expeditiously and fairly; and
(e) allotting to it an appropriate share of the court's resources, while taking into account the need to allot resources to other cases.'

The court must apply the overriding objectives when it exercises any power given to it or interprets any rule and the court will generally rely upon it whenever it justifies the broad exercise of a particular discretion. All the players in an action, from the Claimant, their solicitor, and witnesses both lay and expert, are required to help the court to further the overriding objectives. However, the overriding objective is not applicable where legal rights are involved[1] and it cannot confer jurisdiction if there is none.

The historical purpose of the overriding objectives involved changing the role of the court from one of facilitation of the process of litigation, to that of an active 'case manager'. Active case management involves encouraging the parties to co-operate with each other in the conduct of the proceedings. The rules promote the early identification of the issues in a claim as early in the process as possible, for example, it is no longer acceptable for the Defendant to an action to serve a 'negative' defence which simply denies everything (sometimes even that an accident happened); the defence is expected to answer fully the statement of claim and put forward reasons for refusing to accept liability. The court is given the active power to decide which issues need a full investigation and trial and dispose quickly of those that do not. The parties are encouraged to use Alternative Dispute Resolution and the court is to help the parties to settle the whole, or part of, the case.

The court fixes timetables and controls the progress of the case and considers at each stage whether the benefit of taking a particular step (for example, instructing an expert witness) justifies the cost of taking it. Telephone conferences for interlocutory hearings (outside of London at any rate) have become commonplace and there is an expectation that the parties should not attend court if it is possible to deal with the matter in their absence, but that if they do have to attend, as many outstanding matters should be dealt with as possible on the day. The aim of all directions given is to ensure that the case proceeds quickly and efficiently to trial.

The CPR envisaged a positive promotion of the use of technology through video conferencing facilities, interlocutory applications dealt with by conference telephone and e-mail. The timetable to progress claims is such that, in a busy personal injury firm, carrying a large fast track caseload can probably only be safely operated with the benefit of an in-house automated case management computer package.

THE TRACKS

In order to deal with the rules, and to understand how claims proceed under them, it is essential to have a thorough understanding of which claim is likely to fall into which track and what 'being in track' actually means. There are, below, separate chapters for fast track and multi track claims. What follows is a brief outline.

When deciding to which track to allocate a claim, the court must consider various factors. In practice, the overriding factor is likely to be the financial value of the claim. Other factors are the nature of the remedy being sought, the likely complexity of the facts, law or evidence, the number of parties (or likely parties), the value of

---

[1]   *Dicker v Scammell* [2003] EWHC 1601.

any counterclaim or other associated claim, the degree to which expert evidence may be required, the importance of the claim to parties not involved, and the views and circumstances of the parties who are involved.

While the track allocation of a run-of-the-mill personal injury claim will usually be obvious, the unusual case may require thought. Take, say, a claim for alleged abuse of a patient in a residential home where the likely damages were perhaps £7,000 for a fractured arm. It could be more appropriate to argue that the matter was heard in the multi track. To support this argument it could be said:

(i)   a large amount of oral evidence is likely to be needed. Inappropriate to use paper evidence. Need to call lots of past employees, relatives, etc;
(ii) this is a claim of importance to persons not parties to the proceedings; ie other residents;
(iii) these other residents may become parties themselves.

When assessing the financial value of the claim the court must disregard any amount of damages not in dispute. So in a road traffic accident, damage to the Claimant's vehicle and clothing which has been agreed by the insurer will be disregarded in the personal injury claim. The financial valuation must disregard any claim for interest and costs. It also disregards any likely reduction for contributory negligence. So although a deduction for contributory negligence would reduce a multi track level award to one within the fast track range, there will be no penalty for remaining in the multi track.

These provisions are of great importance in assessing the appropriate track at the outset. In a claim for personal injuries, where the value of the claim as a whole is not more then £5,000 but the element of damage for the injury itself is less then £1,000, then the matter must proceed by way of the small claims procedure.

The court's case management powers

The whole of the CPR confirm the powers of the court. At every section, there is an affirmation of the power of the court to strike out or penalise the parties in terms of costs.

Part 3 specifically deals with the court's case management powers. This control extends to striking out a claim where it thinks it unmeritorious. The powers arise not only upon application, but of the court's own motion. There are even powers to strike out for the Claimant's failure to pay a court fee by a required time (rule 3.7(4)). These sanctions are effective unless a party applies for relief from them and the penalty on relief (assuming that the solicitor can get the case in track again) is likely to result in costs orders either against the client or personally against the solicitor.

Apart from the court's general case management powers, there are more specific management duties at strategic points in the claim; on allocating the case to track after service on the defence, in multi track cases at the case management and, more generally again, at every interlocutory application the court has a power to review, assess and attempt to control the progress of the claim.

It is useful to overview the three tracks. These are dealt with in more detail later.

The small claims track (CPR Part 27)

This is the normal track for a claim where the personal injury element will not exceed £1,000 and the total value of the claim will not exceed £5,000. There is, for the purpose of the litigation process, a separation between the value of general damages and special damages. The most significant feature of the small claims track is that costs will not normally be paid by the winner to the loser. The importance of this is that the client who has a small claim cannot retain the services of a solicitor and expect the Defendant, at the end of the day, to pay their legal costs. This means that in practice most solicitors will not accept small claims work. A potential client's injuries must be carefully evaluated.

The fast track (CPR Part 28)

All personal injury claims worth between £1,000 and £15,000 will normally fall into the fast track. The valuation is a global valuation – taking into account general damages for personal injury, the sums under the various heads of special damage and any recovery of benefits paid out by the state under the Compensation Recovery Regulations.

The fast track is the normal track for claims where the trial is unlikely to last for longer then one day (five hours) (rule 26.6(5)(a)). Oral expert evidence is normally limited to one expert per party in relation to any expert field and to two expert fields (CPR, r 26.6(5)(b)). There are a set of pre-issue 'protocols' that must generally be complied with in all work that proceeds in the fast track. Failure to comply may well lead to some costs sanction.

It is possible to transfer matters between tracks and litigators must be vigilant to ensure that if it becomes apparent that a claim ought to be transferred up from fast track to multi track – this is done. If not, it is almost certain that the judge will transfer the claim when it is next before the court. It is possible under certain circumstances to hear a higher value claim in fast track but as there are likely to be fixed costs at some point in the future for the whole of fast track claims (at present there are only fixed costs for the trial process) it is advisable to transfer if possible. The rules do not specify the sort of margins that will apply for transfer – it is likely that a claim that is worth in the region of £15,000 will remain in fast track and that the solicitor will have to clearly demonstrate a likely higher recovery to make a successful transfer application.

In any event, fast track work is expected to be exactly what it says it is. Fast. The rules state that the standard period between the giving of directions and the trial will not be more then 30 weeks.

The multi track (CPR Part 29)

The court will allocate any claim worth in excess of £15,000 to the multi track. It will also allocate to the multi track claims for which 'the small claims track or the fast track is not the normal track' (CPR, r 26.6(6)).

After allocation, the court will give directions for the management of the case and set a timetable for the steps to be taken between directions and trial, or fix a case management conference, or both. The intention of multi track work is that the court can be case sensitive. This means that directions can be tailored to the actual case rather than given as standard. The protocols for fast track litigation do not formally apply in the multi track, but their spirit is intended to prevail and the litigator must be aware of this and be prepared to explain why they have not been used, if they have not. Finally, the principles embodied in the overriding objectives may be used to the Claimant's advantage. There will be many occasions upon which the solicitor will wish to take a certain step in her client's case that needs the approval and sanction of the court. For example, the court's power to restrict expert evidence almost certainly provides ample opportunity for argument over why the client needs to be seen by a psychiatrist or neuro-surgeon. The way to argue for the client's needs is to utilise the language of the overriding objectives. Words such as 'unfair' and 'unjust' or 'importance to the case' should be relied on. The solicitor should be prepared, when attending on an application, to provide the court with details of dates upon which the expert could see the client to deal with any argument based on delay. The solicitor should be ready with an explanation of the likely benefit in the value of the claim of the additional expert evidence.

CHAPTER 3

Small Claims Track

This chapter gives an overview of the small claims track procedure which is primarily governed by CPR Part 27. It is exclusive to the county court and hearings will almost always be conducted by district judges. It is intended to provide an informal procedure where it is possible for a litigant to conduct his or her own case without legal representation. Accordingly, costs are strictly limited. Owing to the unique nature of the small claims track, little reference is made to other chapters of this book which deal with specific topics which are necessary to cross-refer to when reading the chapters on fast track and multi track.

ALLOCATION

Cases suitable for the small claims track are commenced in the county court under the same forms and procedures as cases of higher value. They are then assigned to the small claims track when the court considers allocation of the claim as part of its preliminary case management procedure. CPR, r 26.6(1) specifies that the small claims track is the normal track for any claim for personal injuries where the financial value does not exceed £5,000 and the damages for pain, suffering and loss of amenities do not exceed £1,000.

However, the financial limits only *indicate* the normal track, the final decision remains at the discretion of the court. If the court does not have enough information to allocate the claim, it will generally make an order under rule 26.5(3) requiring one or more parties to provide further information within 14 days. In deciding the track, the court should have regard to the following (rule 26.8(1)):
(i)   the financial value;
(ii)   the nature of the remedy sought;
(iii)   the complexity of the facts, law or evidence;
(iv)   the number of parties;
(v)   the value of any counterclaim or other Part 20 claim and the complexity of matters relating to it;
(vi)   the amount of oral evidence required;
(vii)   the importance of the claim to non-parties;

(viii) the views of the parties; and

(ix)   the circumstances of the parties.

The financial value of the claim is assessed by the court when it decides upon allocation. Although the value of a counterclaim is relevant when determining the track, the fact that a counterclaim is over £5,000 does not preclude the claim from the small claims track. Any amount not in dispute, interest, costs and contributory negligence is disregarded (rule 26.8(2)). The 'amount not in dispute' is limited in its application. The supplemental practice direction to Part 26 (PT 26 PD), sets out certain guidelines (rule 7.4). In particular, if a Defendant does not admit liability, the amount is still in dispute even if the value is agreed. The only occasion an amount is not in dispute is when a Defendant is indisputably liable to pay a specific amount by way of judgment, admission or agreement.

Furthermore, although the track is designed to deal with cases which are straightforward, small value cases will often still be assigned to the small claims track even where they deal with comparatively complex issues of law and fact such as consumer disputes, holiday claims and accidents at work.

Even if the value of the claim is outside the limit, the parties may mutually consent to the case being assigned to the small claims track (rule 26.7(3)), although, even where the parties agree, the court has to be satisfied that the case is suitable for that track (PD para 8.1(2)(b)).

In the absence of allocation to the small claims track for disposal, costs remain at the discretion of the trial judge.[1]

SMALL CLAIMS TRACK PROCEDURE

The small claims track is intended to provide appropriate and speedy procedure for the most straightforward and financially moderate claims. It is therefore important to remove the need for substantial pre-hearing preparation and the general formality associated with the other tracks.

The application of other rules

Due to the desire for informality in proceedings, a number of the new rules are expressly *excluded* from being applicable to the small claims track (rule 27.2):

(i)   Part 25 – interim remedies except interim injunctions;

(ii)   Part 31 – disclosure and inspection;

(iii) Parts 32 and 33 – evidence – except the power of a court to control the evidence remains;

(iv)   Part 35 – experts – except the duty to restrict expert evidence (rule 35.1), the overriding duty of the court (rule 35.3) and instructions to a single joint expert (rule 35.8) all remain;

---

[1]   *Panechal v Maguire* [2006] 1 CL 59.

(v)   Part 18 – further information, although the court may, of its own initiative, order a party to provide further information if it considers it appropriate to do so (rule 27(2)(3));

(vi)   Part 36 – offers to settle and payments in; and

(vii) Part 39 – the hearing – except the general rule remains that hearings are to be in public.

The disclosure rules are replaced by a standard direction referred to below. Most importantly, the use of experts is limited and cannot be adduced either in writing or orally without prior permission of the court (rule 27.5). Summary judgment is not excluded, but in view of the costs limitations and speed with which such cases are concluded, it is a rarely used procedure.

All the other parts of the rules do apply where appropriate (subject to certain specific limitations). The court in a small claims track case does, however, have the same powers to impose any final remedy available to a court on the fast or multi track (rule 27.3).

Initial options of the court (rule 27.4)

When a case has been allocated to the small claims track, the court has five options regarding the future conduct of the claim:

(i)   to give standard directions and fix a date for the final hearing;

(ii)   to make special directions and fix a date for the final hearing;

(iii) to make special directions and direct that the court will consider further directions within 28 days;

(iv)   to fix a date for a preliminary hearing (see below); or

(v)   issue notice that the court intends to deal with the claim without a hearing and invite the parties to agree[2] within a specified date.

If a final hearing date is fixed, the parties must be given 21 days' notice unless they agree to less and the court should inform the parties of the length of time allowed for the hearing.[3]

The standard directions mentioned in (i) above are shown at Appendix B to the practice direction. Each party, 14 days before the hearing, must serve copies of all documents relied upon on the other parties and the court. An example of standard information and documentation to be provided in a road accident claim is contained in Appendix A to the practice direction. This specifies certain documents to be served.[4] The original documents of the copies served should be taken to court on the day of the hearing. Any direction made may be revoked, added to or varied by the court (rule 27.7).

---

[2]   Rule 27.10 allows the court to deal with a claim without a hearing if both parties consent.

[3]   Practice Direction PT 26 PD states that the maximum usually allowed is one day (para 8(2)(c)).

[4]   Namely experts' reports, witness statements, invoices and estimates for repairs, documents relating to other loss and sketch plans or photographs.

Experts (rule 27.5)

No expert evidence may be given, whether in writing or oral at a hearing without the permission of the court. The permission must be obtained in advance and the costs recovered for the use of such evidence is very restricted by the limit on costs imposed by rule 27.14(3)(d), namely £200. However, the content of such report can be much more informal than under the other tracks as the rigours of most of Part 35 are excluded.

Preliminary hearing (rule 27.6)

Generally, claims will be given directions towards final determination without the need for an interim hearing. However, on allocation to the small claims track, a court may, instead of issuing directions of its own motion, order a preliminary hearing in limited circumstances (rule 27.6(1)):
(i)   where special directions are required and the court believes it is necessary for a party to attend to ensure s/he understands what s/he is required to do;
(ii)   to enable the claim to be immediately disposed of due to there being no real prospect of success of one party at any final hearing; or
(iii)   to enable the court to strike out a party's statement of case because it discloses no reasonable grounds for bringing or defending the claim.

For instance, if the parties intend to use experts at the hearing, the judge may call a hearing to restrict the extent of such evidence. However, even if one of these situations exist, the court must take account and give consideration to the parties' expense in attending the preliminary hearing (rule 27.6(2)). Further, the parties must be given 14 days' notice of the hearing (rule 27.6(3)) and if the parties so agree, the hearing may be treated as final (rule 27.6(4)).

If the court has not already done so (or unless the preliminary hearing has been treated as final) a date should be fixed for the final hearing at or after the preliminary hearing (rule 27.6(5)). The parties must be given 21 days' notice, informed of the amount of time allowed for the hearing and any appropriate directions may be made.

The hearing (rule 27.8)

Any hearing conducted in a small claims track case will be on an informal basis and is usually conducted in the district judge's room with the parties sitting around the tables provided in front of the judge's desk. The strict rules of evidence will not apply. Particular emphasis is placed on the judge's control of evidence and judges will generally be flexible when it comes to admitting hearsay evidence. In order to make proceedings more user friendly for the unrepresented party the judge is in control of the extent of cross-examination. He may refuse to allow any cross-examination until all witnesses have given their evidence in chief and may limit the duration of the cross-examination. The judge may also undertake to ask questions of the witness before any parties are allowed to do so.[5] The court may, in effect, adopt

---

[5]   See Practice Direction PT 27 PD, para 4.

any method of proceeding it considers fair, the only limit being that reasons must be given for the final decision.

Where the parties are not legally represented, the case law applicable to the conduct of CICB hearings may be analogous.[6] The parties may present their own case or a lawyer or lay representative[7] may act on the party's behalf.[8]

One further restrictive rule in a small claims track case is that no expert may give evidence (either oral or written) without the permission of the court.

The hearing is in public unless the judge decides that a private hearing is appropriate by the parties' agreement or where the matters in rule 39.2(3) apply.[9]

The judge may direct that all or any part of the proceedings will be tape recorded and will otherwise make a note of the central points of the oral evidence.[10]

Non-attendance of a party (rule 27.9)

If, for whatever reason, a party cannot or does not wish to attend the hearing, s/he may give seven days' notice of this absence and request the court to decide the claim in their absence (rule 27.9(1)). The party is required simply to give the notice and the court will then take that party's statement of case and other documents into account when deciding the case. Thus a party may produce a comprehensive argument on paper and avoid time-consuming attendance at the hearing. This is useful in strong cases but presents obvious risks, particularly the possibility of unforeseen issues arising at the trial.

If a Claimant does not attend or does not give the seven days' notice, the court may strike out the claim (rule 27.9(2)). Alternatively, if the Claimant does attend or give notice but the Defendant does not, then the court may decide the claim on the evidence of the Claimant alone (rule 27.9(3)). It should be noted that this does not mean the Claimant automatically obtains judgment. The Claimant must still prove their claim, although this will usually be easy without opposition.

If neither party attends or gives notice, the court may strike out the claim and any defence and counterclaim (rule 27.9(4)).

Disposal without a hearing (rule 27.10)

The court may, if all parties agree, deal with the claim without a hearing (rule 27.10). However, this would be extremely rare in practice.

---

[6]   The court should assist an unrepresented party, but this does not extend to asking every question a skilled advocate may have asked: *R v CICB, ex p Pearce* [1994] COD 235.

[7]   Only if the party is present, the representative is employed by the party or the court gives permission.

[8]   PT 27 PD, para 3.

[9]   For example, where publicity would defeat the object of the hearing, national security, confidential information, interests of a child or patient, unjust to any respondent in an application without notice, administration of trusts or a deceased's estate or necessary in the interests of justice.

[10]   PT 27 PD, para 5.1.

Setting aside (rule 27.11)

If a party fails to attend the hearing or give notice of non-attendance (as above), then he may apply to the court to set aside any judgment. However, the provision will not apply to a party who attended the hearing, was represented at the hearing or requested the court to decide the claim in his absence. The party must apply within 14 days of the notice of judgment and the court has the power to order a re-hearing. However, the court will only grant a re-hearing if it is satisfied that there was a good reason for the failure to attend or give notice of non-attendance and that the party has a reasonable as opposed to a fanciful prospect of success. An example of no good reason would be, for instance, where a party has deliberately chosen to be absent from a hearing.[11]

If a judgment is set aside, the court must fix a new hearing date. The hearing may take place immediately after the application to set aside and be conducted by the same judge.

A judgment cannot be set aside if there was consent to it being made without a hearing under rule 27.10.

Appeals

The grounds and procedures for bringing an appeal against a small claims decision are now the same as those for cases allocated to the fast track and multi track (see Chapter 26). The appeal court will allow an appeal where a decision was wrong or unjust because of a serious or other procedural irregularity in the proceedings (rule 52.11(3)). A party needs permission to appeal, which can be sought at the hearing or afterwards by application. There is a reduced court fee for an appeal against a small claims decision.

PD 52, para 5.8A additionally provides that the appellant must file with his notice:
(i)   a sealed copy of the order being appealed;
(ii)   any order giving or refusing permission to appeal, together with a copy of the reasons for that decision; and
(iii)   a suitable record of the reasons for judgment of the lower court.

Provisions of additional documentation set out in para 5.6 is discretionary.

As noted below, costs incurred by the appeal are covered by the usual small claims limitation on costs.

Costs

The costs recoverable in the small claims track, including those relating to an appeal, are limited, but there are a number of costs orders that the court can make (rule 27.14(2)):
(i)   the fixed costs attributable to issuing the claim which are payable under Part 45; and

---

[11]   *Shocked v Goldschmidt* [1998] 1 All ER 372 (a case decided under the previous rules).

(ii)   any such further costs assessed by summary procedure paid by a party who has behaved unreasonably.

Therefore, the court has the discretion to order costs against any party they consider to have acted in an unreasonable way. Examples are cases where a Claimant has brought a pointless case or has persisted with a claim when information has been provided which makes it abundantly clear that the result of the claim is a foregone conclusion; a party has fabricated a claim or defence or has failed to comply with procedural orders of the court; or if a party has increased the costs of an action by delay, late and avoidable applications for adjournments of the final hearing or failure to co-operate with the other side.

A further order may be made for a party to pay the whole or part of the following (rule 27.14(3)):
(i)   the court fees paid by another party, for example, the issue fee and an allocation fee if paid;
(ii)   expenses incurred by a party or witness in attending court; this includes the cost of traveling to and from a hearing and any overnight expenses. There is no upper limit;
(iii) the loss of earnings of a party or witness;[12] and
(iv)   experts' fees if any.[13]

Further, a case may have been allocated to the small claims track, with the consent of the parties under rule 26.7(3), despite the fact that the claim is over the financial limit. In such circumstances, the costs should be treated as if the case were in the small claims track unless the parties agree that the fast track costs provisions are to apply. However, the trial costs are at the discretion of the court and can not exceed the amount set out in rule 46.2 (ie £500 for £3,000 to £10,000 claims).

When a case is reallocated out of the small claims track under rule 26.10, the costs rules of the newly allocated track apply as of the date of transfer (rule 27.15). Small claims track cost rules apply up to that date.

Note that infant approval hearings are treated as allocated to the multi track and the costs assessed accordingly even if the amount of the award might otherwise have justified an allocation to the small claims track.[14]

---

[12]   PT 27 PD, para 7.3 limits this to £50 per day.
[13]   PT 27 PD, para 7.3, limits this to £200 per expert.
[14]   *W (a child) v Robinson* [2002] 4 CL 50.

CHAPTER 4

Fast Track and the Protocols

This chapter gives an overview of the fast track procedure. It begins by summarising the effect of the protocols since they apply directly to the fast track procedure. Many aspects of the overview in this chapter are necessarily dealt with in more detail in later chapters.

THE PROTOCOLS

In his final report,[1] Lord Woolf recommended that a series of protocols be developed to 'build on and increase the benefit of early but well informed settlement which genuinely satisfies both parties to (the) dispute'.

Accordingly, a series of pre-action protocols were developed for, in the first place, personal injury and clinical negligence claims and subsequently disease and illness claims. The protocol for clinical negligence claims is not considered in this book. The disease protocol is considered further in Chapter 30.

The personal injury protocol applies mainly to fast track claims and was primarily designed for straightforward road traffic, tripping and slipping claims. The court expects practitioners to use the protocols, but will not be concerned over minor infringements of them. If they are not used, then a reason must be given for not doing so and the court will look at the effect of non-compliance on the other party when deciding whether to impose costs sanctions.

However, a word of warning. The spirit of the personal injury protocol is expected to be followed for multi track claims. The court will expect the solicitor to have regard for the 'all cards on the table' approach to the litigation process, which is central to the CPR. Furthermore, regardless of the existence of a specific protocol the court expects reasonable pre-action behaviour in all cases.[2]

The aims of the protocols are:
(i)   to encourage more contact between the parties before the issue of proceedings;

---

[1]   Access to Justice Report, July 1996.
[2]   CPR protocols – notes of guidance.

(ii)   for a better and earlier exchange of information;

(iii) for better pre-action investigation by both sides;

(iv)   to put the parties in a position where they may be able to settle cases fairly and early without litigation; and

(v)   to enable proceedings to run to the court's timetable and efficiently, if litigation does become necessary.[3]

In the spirit of the overriding objectives, the protocols encourage the use of standardised letters requesting relevant information. There is a comprehensive set of notes of guidance to be found in the CPR's practice direction on the protocol. It describes the protocol as kept deliberately simple to promote its ease of use and general acceptability.

The protocols themselves are simple; there is nothing complex apart from ensuring that time limits are kept to (these can be varied, but an explanation of why this was necessary may be required) and the case driven onwards to resolution. The allocation questionnaire served after defence contains a question which has to be answered to confirm whether or not the protocols apply to the case in hand and, if they do, whether they have been complied with. If the protocols apply but there has been no or only been limited compliance, a written reason has to be given.

In the notes of guidance to the personal injury protocols, a distinction is drawn between a letter notifying the insurers of a possible claim, and the actual claim itself (at para 2.6 of the personal injury protocol). The 'letter of claim' will start the protocol timetable but a letter putting the Defendant on notice of a claim will not. The protocols anticipate the Defendant receiving three months in which to investigate the claim although it accepts that there will be times when proceedings need to be issued early (for example to deal with an approaching limitation bar). There will be times when the solicitor will want to put the Defendant's insurers on early notice so that they can start early investigation and there will be times when she will not. The protocols do not encourage such tactical considerations. The premise is that the letter of claim will be sent as soon as sufficient information is available to substantiate a realistic claim, even before issues of quantum are addressed in detail.

An explanation of the relevant protocol must be given to all clients. The client must understand that there is an expectation that he may have to submit to a joint medical examination and his consent to this, and the release of his medical notes obtained.

Protocol procedure

Once the client's instructions have been accepted, funding arrangements have been agreed and the necessary professional conduct information (the client care and costs letters) preliminary investigations into the claim will take place. As soon as sufficient information is available then the letter of claim should be prepared. The protocol recommends a standard format be used. The protocol standard letters of claim can be found below at Appendix B – Specimen correspondence (see also Chapter 9 on Preliminary correspondence and letter of claim). Before sending the letter to the

---

3   Protocols, para 1.2.

other side, it is sensible to send a draft to the client to check its accuracy and for confirmation that the client is happy to proceed.

Two copies of the letter of claim are to be sent to the proposed Defendant, one being intended for the Defendant's insurers. Best practice will probably be to identify the insurers as quickly as possible and to write to them directly as well as to the Defendant. This is current best practice, of course. In a road traffic accident claim where the police report is not available, the police process department can be telephoned and, provided insurance details have been produced by the Defendant to the police, they will be given over the telephone.

The personal injury protocol provides that the letter of claim should ask for insurance details and request that the accompanying copy letter be forwarded to the insurers. If the insurers have been written to, the proposed Defendant should be informed that a letter has been sent to Insurer X and if Insurer X is not the relevant insurer, they should let the relevant insurer know of the claim at once.

The letter of claim must contain a clear summary of the facts on which the claim is based, together with an indication of the nature of any injuries suffered and of any financial loss incurred. In cases of road traffic accidents, the letter should provide the name and address where treatment has been obtained and the Claimant's hospital reference number. Notification should be given of the existence of a conditional fee agreement. The emphasis is on plain English. Speculation should be avoided and details limited to the facts asserted by the client. Sufficient information should be given in order to enable the Defendant's insurer/solicitor to put a broad valuation on the risk of the claim.

After the letter of claim has been sent, the Defendant or their insurer has 21 days to acknowledge the letter of claim and a further three months thereafter to investigate the matter and comment on whether liability is accepted or not. If they make an admission of liability after investigation, the presumption is that they will be bound by the admission for all claims with a value of up to £15,000. For this reason, it is sensible to tell the Defendant whether or not it is envisaged that the claim is proceeding in the fast or multi track (paras 3.6–3.9).

The protocol states that the letter of claim is not intended to have any status as a pleading and that sanctions should not apply if it is the nature of the claim in the future. However, any discrepancies will provide ammunition for cross-examination as well as a basis for a costs application on the basis that the Defendant was not given early opportunity to deal with the true basis of the claim. So accuracy is very important.

Once the letter of claim has been sent, the Defendant (or insurer) must reply within 21 days identifying the insurer. This date must be entered into the solicitor's diary (an automatic case management system should automatically diarise it). If no reply is received after 21 days, then the claim may proceed without risk of costs penalisation.

The letter of claim includes a provision for disclosure of standard documents relevant to the type of incident complained of. If the Defendant denies liability, it should enclose in its letter of reply copies of these documents, and copies of others in its possession which are clearly relevant to the issues between the parties. The documents to be disclosed are those which will be likely to be ordered as disclosed by the court, either on an application for pre-action disclosure, or on disclosure during the proceedings.

Special damages (personal injury protocol, para 3.14)

The protocol provides that a schedule with supplementary documents should be submitted as soon as possible. In practice, outline details of special damages should be given in the letter of claim. A full schedule should be provided if the Defendant admits liability and/or an early interim payment is requested. In any event, if the case is capable of settlement before proceedings because the Claimant's prognosis is certain, it is best to provide a full schedule, together with the medical evidence and a Part 36 offer to settle the claim before proceedings are issued.

Expert evidence (personal injury protocol, paras 3.15–3.21)

The protocols envisage the use of joint expert evidence with no oral evidence at fast track trials. It is quite likely that the solicitor will want to obtain expert evidence – certainly from a medical expert, reasonably early on in the claim. The medical records should be sought and at least one, and preferably two, alternative experts in the same specialty identified. The Defendant should then be written to (see Chapter 9 on Preliminary correspondence and letter of claim and Chapter 12 on Expert evidence; see also Appendix B – Specimen correspondence) and given the names of the proposed experts. The Defendant then has 14 days to accept or reject and put forward other named experts. If the Defendant does not respond, or if the Defendant objects to all the experts then the parties may instruct experts of their own choice and the court will decide if proceedings are issued, and whether either party had acted unreasonably.

If the Defendant does not object to the expert, then it will not be entitled to rely on its own expert evidence unless the Claimant agrees, or the court directs, or the first party's expert report has been amended and the first party is not prepared to disclose the original report (para 3.18).

If it is intended to rely on a medical agency to arrange a medical report then the protocol guidelines suggest that the solicitor obtains the Defendant's prior consent to this action. The Defendant is entitled to write to the agency to find out the specific name(s) of the doctor(s) to be instructed.

Written questions

Where an agreed expert is instructed, either party may send to the expert written questions on the report, relevant to the issues, via the first party's solicitors. The expert should send answers to the question(s) separately and directly to each party (para 3.20).

The protocol provides that the cost of a report from an agreed expert will usually be paid by the instructing first party; the costs of the expert replying to questions will usually be borne by the party which asks the questions.

Rehabilitation (personal injury protocol, paras 4.1–4.4)

The protocol directs that the Claimant or Defendant or both should consider as early as possible whether the Claimant has reasonable needs that could be met by rehabilitation treatment or other measures and annexes a rehabilitation code to be followed. The provision of any report obtained for the purposes of assessment of provision of a party's rehabilitation needs is to be used in litigation arising out of the accident save by consent and is exempt from the provisions of the protocol dealing with expert evidence.

Timetable

(i)   Protocol letter of claim is sent;

(ii) Defendant replies within 21 days of identifying insurer;

(iii) insurer investigates and replies accepting or denying liability within three months of expiration of the 21 days at (ii) above and disclosing relevant documents;

(iv) if either party wishes to instruct an expert he gives other party 14 days' notice of the expert(s)' name;

(v)   other party then has 14 days to object or accept that expert or experts. If parties cannot agree on expert to instruct they may instruct experts of their own choice.

It can only be in exceptional cases where the time limits contained in the protocol can be disobeyed. If the time limits cannot be complied with or are varied, then a careful note of why this has happened must be made and the solicitor will have to explain to the court when asked.

Issue of proceedings

If the solicitor is dealing with insurers rather than solicitors, the protocols provide that the insurers should be written to 7–14 days prior to the issue to allow for solicitors to be nominated to accept service. The protocols provide that the parties should consider carrying out a 'stock take' of issues in dispute and the evidence that the court may need to decide those issues before commencement of proceedings (personal injury protocol, para 2.20).

If a joint medical report has been obtained but not yet received, and liability is admitted, proceedings must not be issued until the Defendant has had 21 days after receipt to consider the report and make, if desired, a settlement offer (personal injury protocol, para 5.1).

THE FAST TRACK (CPR PART 28)

The fast track – issue of proceedings

In the assumption that the protocols have been complied with but no offer of settlement has been received the matter will go forward to issue of proceedings. There is no essential difference between issue of proceedings in the fast track or multi track claim.

The solicitor should give careful consideration to whether or not the client's claim is capable of immediate resolution. She should give careful consideration to the valuation of the claim. The solicitor should see the client and advise on the likely value, taking into account the liability risks, and any percentage for contributory negligence and consider making a Part 36 offer (see Chapter 13 on Negotiations) to settle the claim. Advice on quantum and on the advisability of making a Part 36 offer and the amount of the offer should be clear and unambiguous. The client's clear consent – preferably in writing – to offer to settle the claim must be obtained. The solicitor should send a covering letter with her letter of advice for the client to sign and return – 'I confirm that I have read and understood the contents of your letter to me dated 00 and accept your advice as set out above' (see Appendix B – Specimen correspondence). See also Chapter 13 on Negotiations and Part 36 offers to settle.

If the Part 36 letter does not yield an acceptable settlement offer, proceedings should be issued. This will concentrate the Defendant's mind and provoke a settlement – the only other resolution is trial. The solicitor must ensure that she has both the client's consent to issue and the authority (if necessary) from the case funder and complied with any notifications required by any insurer to a 'no win no fee' contract.

Careful thought must be given to risk management prior to issue of proceedings. It is at this point that some after-the-event insurance policies come on risk (of having to pay out if there is a loss). Careful notes ought to be made on file when making the decision to issue proceedings and any in house risk management process complied with.

If the solicitor is not funding disbursements, the issue and setting down fees that the client may have to pay should be requested in good time and placed in the firm's client account. If the solicitor is not in funds and defaults on paying a fee when it is due the claim is likely to be automatically struck out.

For the process of issue and service, see Chapter 15 on Issue and service. After issue and service of the documentation the court will send the parties a case allocation questionnaire (see Chapter 22 on Preparing for trial). It is at this point possible to ask the court to stay proceedings for initially one month so that settlement can be explored. It is usually unwise to agree to a blanket request by the Defendant at this time unless there is clear evidence that a settlement offer is forthcoming. Once the court has received the returned questionnaires, if the case is suitable to fast track, it will then be allocated to the fast track. Note that on filing the allocation questionnaire the solicitor must also comply with Part 43 PD 4.5(1) and file an estimate of costs and serve the same on every other party unless the court directs otherwise.

The fast track – allocation

The procedure governing allocation to the fast track is considered in Chapter 2.

CPR Part 28 deals with fast track claims. Judicial case management of a claim allocated to the fast track will generally be by directions given at two stages in the case; at the point of allocation to the fast track, where automatic directions will usually apply, and on the filing for listing of trial questionnaires. The court's aim is to give directions without the need for a hearing and it expects the co-operation of the parties. A degree of consent on the directions to be given is expected in the rules. Time is of the essence bearing in mind the overall expected length of time between allocation to fast track and trial is only 30 weeks.

Once directions are given any variation must be made with the consent of the court. If the rules allow a variation (and they do not if it involves anything that threatens the trial timetable), it must be by way of written agreement between the parties.

At the point of giving directions, the court will normally set a trial window. Much here is dependant upon local court practice – the rules envisage that some courts will fix an actual date, and others a window of time in which the trial is listed to be heard (the specific date itself being fixed after filing of the listing questionnaire). For this reason, it is essential for the solicitor to familiarise herself with the local court's practice. If the matter is issued away from the solicitor's own local court for any reason, she should ask the court about local listing practice at the point of issue (see Appendix B – Specimen correspondence).

Directions (CPR, rr 28.3 and 28.6(b))

(See also 28 PD at paras 3, 4 and 7.)

In order to save time and costs, the court will attempt to deal with directions in the absence of the parties. It will only hold a directions hearing if it appears 'necessary or desirable' to do so. If the case is simple, and the evidence is ready then standard directions will suffice. However, if the client has an uncertain prognosis, or perhaps where the solicitor has had to issue without full preparation because instructions were received almost at the time bar, then a request may have to be made for a directions hearing. A hearing should always be requested if the solicitor suspects that she will be unable to comply with the tight directions timetable. It is quite clear from the rules that the court wants to be appraised of problems early.

The CPR provide standard pro formas for directions (although local court practice should also be considered). The pro forma should be put on computer and consideration given to what directions are likely to be needed in the particular case as soon as the defence is received. The Defendant should be written to with suggested directions and attempts made to agree them. Draft consent directions should be returned with the allocation questionnaire which the court will send out with the defence or shortly afterwards. As the allocation questionnaire should normally be returned to the court no sooner than 14 days of receipt (CPR, r 26.3), once again time is of the essence (see Appendix B – Specimen correspondence).

When the court makes directions, it will consider what steps have already been taken. The solicitor should inform the court of these when the allocation questionnaire is returned. It is at this point that the court considers whether or not the protocols have been complied with. So, for example, if disclosure has already taken place prior to issue, then the directions (usually) need not include a provision for disclosure.

Agreed directions must set out with calendar dates a timetable of steps for preparing the case, including a date or period for the trial. Provision should be made for disclosure of documents and factual and expert evidence. So far as expert evidence is concerned, the directions must state whether it is to be joint or not and whether it is to be by simultaneous or sequential exchange. Provision should be made for the amendment of the pleadings if necessary. Dates are required for everything.

The pro forma directions provide for limitation of evidence, both oral and written, and a limitation on the time allowed for each party to present evidence at trial. Acceptance of time limits on the presentation of evidence requires caution; the Claimant with a small value but complex injury case could be put in difficulties in proving the nature and severity of injuries if limited significantly by time in the witness box.

What directions will and will not be allowed are likely to depend on local court practice and the particular idiosyncrasies of the local judges.

The pro forma practice directions provide for a typical fast track court timetable where the court gives directions itself:
(i)   disclosure – four weeks;
(ii)   exchange of witness statements – 10 weeks;
(iii) exchange of experts' reports – 14 weeks;
(iv)   listing questionnaires sent by the court – 20 weeks;
(v)   filing of completed listing questionnaires – 22 weeks;
(vi)   hearing – 30 weeks.

The time period runs from the date of the notice of allocation.

It is possible to appeal or ask the court to reconsider directions given by the court in the parties' absence; steps to do so must be taken as soon as possible within 14 days of the service of the order. If the parties were not present, the court will usually be prepared to reconsider the order. A reconsideration will be heard by the same judge who gave the directions, or a judge of the same level. If the parties were present, then the matter proceeds by way of an appeal to another judge (28 PD, para 4.3).

Interlocutory hearings

There are obviously going to be times – even in fast track cases – where one party needs to make an interlocutory application. It may be that there has been a default on a directions requirement, or where further information is sought that has not been forthcoming by consent. It may be that the client's recovery is delayed for some good reason – further surgery may be necessary, or an important witness is going to be out of the country on the trial date. Once again, the whole emphasis is on time. If the solicitor becomes aware of a problem, she must make an application to the court as early as possible.

The rules state that it is only in exceptional circumstances that a failure to comply with directions will lead to the postponement of the trial. Postponement of the trial is described in the practice directions as an order of last resort. In some instances, it is possible that the court will order a party seeking postponement of the trial to be present at court when the application is heard (28 PD, para 5.4).

The pre-trial checklist

The pre-trial check list, formerly named listing questionnaire, will be sent by the court to the parties in Forms N170 and N171 (see Appendix C). These forms will be sent to the parties no later than two weeks before the date specified in the notice of application or in any later direction of the court and not more than eight weeks before the trial date or trial window. The parties are encouraged to exchange copies of the questionnaires before they are filed to avoid the court being given conflicting or incomplete information. The pre-trial checklist (Part 43 PD 4.5 (2)) requires the filing of an estimate of costs and service of the same on every other party, unless the court otherwise directs. This estimate must be divided into parts to show the costs already incurred by the party separately from those which will be incurred by that party if the case proceeds to trial.

The pre-trial checklist must be filed no more than eight weeks before the trial date or the beginning of the trial period. Best practice is to check the local court's practice directions to see if this has been varied.

If neither party files a pre-trial checklist by the date specified by the court, the court will order that unless they are filed within seven days from service of the order, the claim, defence and any counterclaim will be struck out without any further order of the court. Accordingly, the strike out provisions are automatic (Part 28.5(3)). A party in default will have to take the step of applying for relief from sanctions under rule 3.9 if it wishes its case to be reinstated with a witness statement dealing with each of the grounds set out under that provision and the reason for the default. The onus is on the Claimant to file his questionnaire because if one party files but the other does not, the court will normally give listing directions suitable to the party who filed (28 PD, para 6.5(2)).

Listing directions (28 PD, para 7)

The prime object of the listing directions (which are given in Form N172) is the fixing of the trial date. It may be that a date has already been fixed or a trial window set. Either way, or if (as is the usual case) no date or window has been determined, the court will at this stage fix the precise date of trial as one of the listing directions. It will specify the trial venue and the duration of the trial. It will give all other directions required for the conduct of the trial.

There is a specific provision that the parties can agree directions as to the conduct of the trial and this option should be used as far as possible to avoid the court imposing unwanted directions. The directions will include directions on evidence and the lodging of trial bundles. The listing directions include provision for the court to approve or disapprove the use of oral expert evidence. Directions on oral evidence may well have been given at the original directions stage. The listing directions provide an opportunity for the court to look again at the matter. Oral evidence from an expert will not normally be allowed unless the court considers that it is in the interests of justice to do so (see Chapter 12 on Expert evidence). The court may grant permission to allow oral expert evidence conditional upon a without prejudice meeting between the experts prior to the trial date, and on the reports being filed for trial.

Fast track trial (28 PD, para 8)

Note that at present the only area of fast track to be subject to fixed costs is the trial (see Chapter 24 on Costs for further details).

The trial will normally take place at the court where the case is being managed. The trial bundle must be lodged in good time prior to the trial – the listing directions will deal with this. The practice direction anticipates the judge having read the papers and therefore a direction may be given to dispense with the opening speech. The judge is given a discretion to vary the directed timetable.

If the trial is not completed on the day(s) fixed, it 'will normally' continue over to the next court day for completion. If the case is not reached on the listed day, the parties will normally bear their own costs rather than the loser paying both sides' costs (and certainly the costs will not be borne by the court!) – see Chapter 24 on Costs.

The judge will certainly exercise his powers to control the giving of evidence and this may involve the exclusion of certain evidence and limitation of cross-examination (see Chapter 12 on Evidence and Chapter 23 on The trial). A witness statement will stand as the evidence in chief of that witness and expert evidence may be ordered to be taken on paper alone.

CHAPTER 5

Multi Track

This chapter gives an overview of the multi track procedure. Many aspects are dealt with in more detail in later chapters. The protocols provide general guidance for multi track cases (see below) and reference should be made to the preceding chapter for the detail of the protocols.

Any claim where damages are likely to exceed £15,000 will be allocated to the multi track, though claims below that value may also be allocated in the light of other factors which the court will take into consideration. The general rules are set out in CPR, rr 26.7 and 26.8. Factors other than the value of the claim include the nature of the remedy being sought, the likely complexity of the facts, law or evidence, the number of parties or likely parties, the value of any counterclaim or other associated claim, the amount of expert evidence which may be required, the importance of the claim to parties not involved, and the views and circumstances of the parties who are involved.

Thus, multi track cases will range from those which are likely to proceed fairly simply through the system and be of fairly modest value through to those of the highest value and complexity.

The rules stress the need for the court's flexibility in the multi track. Judicial case management is intended to control and oversee the progress of the claim, but the Claimant's solicitor should find no real difficulty in securing the support of the case management judge in progressing the case, provided she takes a realistic view of the necessary evidence, a firm grip on the timetable, and prepares the case properly in advance.

Many cases that are suitable for the multi track will also be suitable for early settlement and this should be in the solicitor's mind from the very beginning. Unless she has to issue proceedings to protect the client from a time bar or for any of the other very valid reasons to issue, consideration must be given as to whether the claim can or should be settled prior to issue of proceedings (see Chapter 15 on Issue and service). In particular, a Part 36 offer must be considered (see, for a summary, Chapter 4 on Fast track and Chapter 13 on Negotiations).

Once it is clear that settlement cannot be reached, then proceedings should be issued and served.

The client's authority to issue proceedings must be obtained, as must any necessary agreements from relevant funding sources (such as legal expense insurers). If the client is being advised under a 'no win no fee' agreement with after-the-event insurance, consideration must be given against the risk that is being accepted when issuing proceedings. The solicitor may have her own in-house risk management protocol; there will almost certainly be a requirement that the insurers are notified of the issue of proceedings as the risk now includes Defendant's potential costs since, of course, it is from issue that the Defendant's costs become payable by the Claimant if the claim is lost.

THE ALLOCATION QUESTIONNAIRE

The decision on which track the case is allocated to is made after service of defence when the parties complete and return Form 150 – the allocation questionnaire. This form contains a section for the solicitor to complete to say which track is most suitable for the claim. If it is thought that the claim ought to be in a specialist list (eg clinical negligence) there is a space for this to be stated. If the solicitor wants the case to be heard in the multi track for other reasons then again there is a section for her to complete. CPR, r 26.8 details the matters that the court will consider relevant when allocating a case to a particular track. In every case thought should be given as to whether there are special circumstances that may make it more appropriate that the matter is dealt with in the multi track. The multi track is more attractive since costs are not fixed for trial and the solicitor has more influence over the pre-trial procedure.

The idea that a claim allocated to the multi track should, in principle, travel slower than a claim allocated to the fast track is wrong. The rules anticipate that multi track cases should also pass speedily through the system. However, the CPR anticipate that there may be more problems in a large value claim and that therefore directions should be more tailor made in multi track cases than in fast track cases.

A claim allocated to the multi track outside the area of the High Court of the Royal Courts of Justice in London will normally be dealt with and managed at a Civil Trial Centre of the local District Registry. The CPR anticipate that in exceptional circumstances the matter will be retained and managed at the feeder court (ie the court from which the claim was referred to the local District Registry). Essentially, if a judge in the feeder court considers it appropriate to retain and manage any part of the case other then a pre-allocation hearing such as a strike out application, he must consult a designated civil judge before so ordering.

If a claim is issued in the High Court of the Royal Courts of Justice and it has an estimated value of less then £50,000 it will (normally) be transferred to the Claimant's local county court. It is within the High Court's power to transfer claims worth more then £50,000 to the county court; so in a claim where liability and quantum appear uncomplicated (even if the value is large) the claim may well be transferred to a local county court. If the solicitor considers the case should be managed and tried at the High Court reasons must be given in the allocation questionnaire. Professional negligence and Fatal Accident Act claims may provide such reasons. If a case remains in the Royal Courts, it will be case managed by a Master in the Queen's Bench Division.

Note that on filing the allocation questionnaire the solicitor must file an estimate of costs to date and serve a copy on all involved parties. The estimate must be in the style of Form 1.

DIRECTIONS ON ALLOCATION

Prior to returning the allocation questionnaire, consideration must be given as to what directions would be sensible in the particular claim. The opponents should be written to and attempts made to agree directions. The Claimant's solicitor will then be in a position to send a draft consent order for directions to the court with the allocation questionnaire. The CPR encourage parties to agree directions. Under CPR, r 29.4, where directions and a window for a trial date can be agreed, the court may approve them without a hearing. If directions cannot be agreed, or if the court does not think that it can give directions of its own initiative in the absence of the parties, it will fix a case management conference (PD Part 29 4.12(1)).

At the time the claim is allocated to the multi track the judge will either give directions for its management (with or without a hearing), or fix a case management conference. When giving directions the judge, in an uncomplicated claim, will certainly fix a trial date or trial 'window' (ie dates between which the trial will come on). The court will wish to fix a trial date, or a trial window as quickly as possible. The court will direct (and hence the parties will try to agree in advance) all necessary directions for the case up to and including trial. Each step must be given a calendar date.

The court has the power to hold an allocation hearing and will do so on its own initiative if it considers that it is necessary to do so giving the parties at least seven days' notice of the hearing. The legal representative who attends the hearing must, if possible, be the person responsible for the case and have knowledge of the claim. She must have the authority to deal with any issues (including timetabling) likely to arise in the giving of directions or the making of the decision on allocation. There are significant sanctions imposed for default in connection with the allocation procedure. These include a summary assessment of the costs of the other party who has attended the hearing and a forthwith order to pay the same against the party in default.

Prior to the multi track directions, the solicitor will have to have applied her mind to many matters. She will have thought about whether or not disclosure of documents should be limited (see Chapter 20 on Disclosure and inspection). She will have considered whether separate or joint expert evidence should be used and, if separate, whether or not there should be a without prejudice expert discussion or meeting (see Chapter 12 on Expert evidence). Consideration will have been given as to whether there should be exchange of evidence sequentially or simultaneously. It is clear from the practice direction that the court will usually support the simultaneous exchange of liability evidence, but evidence that goes to quantum will usually be disclosed sequentially, first by the Claimant.

If the proposed consent directions fail to comply with the requirements of the CPR or the court, then the draft order will not be approved and the court will fix a meeting on directions, or will give directions on its own initiative.

There are occasions where the court will order a case management conference. One such occasion will be where it anticipates directions that expert evidence be given on an issue by a single joint expert. This direction cannot be made unless the parties agree to it in writing. If a case management conference is to be fixed, it will be listed as promptly as possible.

THE CASE MANAGEMENT CONFERENCE

A case management conference pre-supposes an invitation to the parties (ie their representatives) to be present. Directions, however, may, as has been noted, be given in the absence of the parties and of the court's own volition and, increasingly, these hearings take place by telephone.

The case management conference will take place before the judge managing the case. In the Royal Courts of Justice, this will be a Master, and in the District Registry or county court a District Judge.

It is essential to prepare properly for a case management conference. The person who attends must be personally involved in the conduct of the claim and have the authority and information to properly deal with matters that may reasonably be expected to be dealt with such as listing timetables (Part 29 PD 5.2 (2)). It is very important that the person with conduct of the matter attends themselves. If the person attending does not have the authority to deal with the matter or cannot properly answer questions raised, then it is possible that the conference will be adjourned and a wasted costs order made against the solicitor in person (Part 29 PD 5.2(3)).

At the time of receiving notice of the case management conference date, the opponents should be sent a draft of a case summary for their approval. The aim of this is to assist the court to understand and deal with the questions before it. It should not be longer than 500 words and attempt must be made to agree it with the other parties if possible. The summary must set out a short chronology of the claim and list the issues of fact which are agreed or in dispute and the evidence needed to decide them. So, for example, if a medical expert has reported that he cannot report further until a medical expert from another specialty has examined and reported, this must be made clear in the case summary.

The claim as a whole must be considered prior to the conference. Any non-routine application (such as for an interim payment) can be dealt with at the conference and should be applied for in advance. Sufficient time for the conference and applications to be heard must be secured. The court listing for the conference should be checked. If there is insufficient time, the court should be asked to extend time, or to re-list the matter so that sufficient time is allowed. If this is not done, and there is insufficient time to hear the matter the solicitor may once again find a costs sanction imposed.

The solicitor must take to the conference all the documents that the court is likely to want to see. In practice it will be convenient to take the whole file. At the least, the following will be necessary: documentation to show that the pre-action protocols have been complied with, the statement of claim and defence and other pleadings, any documents that have been disclosed already such as witness statements and expert reports. The topics that the court will typically want to consider are:

(i)   any amendments to the pleadings;
(ii) disclosure of documents;
(iii) exchange of lay and expert witness evidence;
(iv) putting of questions to experts and discussions between the experts for each side;
(v)   the trial date and whether a split trial is appropriate.

Client attendance

The client has always had the right to attend all hearings. In the past it has been sensible to take clients to certain applications (for example, for an interim payment). However, as a matter of routine practice the client has not attended interlocutory hearings.

The new rules anticipated increased client involvement at certain stages, and the case management conference is one of them. Whilst it is not yet commonplace for clients to attend case management conferences, there are indications in the rules that the court expects the solicitor to bring the client to court when there have been significant breaches of procedure; for example if a trial date is to be put off.

Essentially, there is an element of 'solicitor bashing' attached to the times when the court may expect the client to be produced. However, it is not really clear how the court expects the client to be involved at the case management stage and perhaps the best practice, in the absence of any local practice direction that states that the court expects the client to attend, will be to take the client to a case management conference where the solicitor needs them to understand why she may have difficulty in getting the court to allow her to utilise the evidence she wishes. So, in a complex claim where it is considered that several experts are needed to report, and where there is uncertainty as to whether the court will allow it all, it may well be sensible to take the client so that he can see the attempts to put the evidence in, and understand why the evidence in his claim is being limited.

In any event, it is expected that the application of the Rules will vary from court to court and the solicitor must keep herself fully appraised of, at least, her own local court's practice.

The court expects a case management conference to be pro-active. The practice direction envisages that the court will ensure that as much agreement as possible be reached and recorded about the matters in issue and the conduct of the claim. What the status of agreements not subsequently embodied in an order will be is not altogether clear. However, it may be anticipated that the court will lean towards enforcing them whether before or at trial. At the least, non-compliance with an agreement may usually be expected sound in costs. It is obvious that no agreement should be reached on a matter of significance unless the solicitor has given it careful consideration (and if necessary, the client's instructions obtained.)

Varying directions

Time limits may be varied by agreement, and without asking for the court's consent, but only if another rule or court order does not specify that the court's consent is required. An application must be made to the court if a party wishes to vary the date which the court has fixed for a case management conference, a pre-trial review, the return of a pre-trial checklist, the trial or trial period (CPR Part 29.5).

If the court's consent is needed, then a consent order should be sought. A draft of the order should be filed together with a statement agreed with the other party(ies) as to why the variation is sought. The court may make the order in terms or varied, or direct that a hearing on the matter be listed.

As in fast track, the rules provide that the courts consider postponement of the fixed trial date as an 'order of last resort'. It is possible that the court may well order that the trial proceeds on certain issues alone rather then delay it.

COMPLIANCE WITH DIRECTIONS BY THE OTHER SIDE

If the opponent does not comply with any of the case management directions then they should be written to and told that an application will be made for an order that they comply, and for a sanction to be imposed for their failure to do so. Give the opponents clear notice of the intention to issue the application and allow them to remedy their delay; if they do not within a day or two, make the application. Failure to do so may be a source of criticism by the court.

The Claimant's solicitor should remember that what works one way, often works the other way too. It is usually sensible to build some give and take into a relationship with the opponent. It is clear from the Rules that delays and failures to comply will not be tolerated by the court but while aggression may well be called for on occasion, reasonableness should temper firmness.

THE PRE-TRIAL CHECKLIST

When the court fixes the trial date or trial period, it will make a provision in the direction for the filing of the pre-trial checklist (formerly named listing questionnaire) – Form N170 (see Chapter 22). This checklist must be filed no later than eight weeks prior to the trial date or trial window. The court will serve the checklist on the parties at least 14 days before they are due to be sent back completed.

In a claim of any size, it is almost certain that prior to completing the pre-trial checklist a conference with counsel will be needed, or the advocate's views obtained if other than the solicitor handling the case. The evidence in the case will have had to be considered in detail prior to completing the checklist. Thus the necessary conference must be held in good time prior to the return date for the checklist so that any further necessary work can be done prior to filing the checklist.

The checklist is simple to complete, but care is required. Certain steps have to have taken place prior to completing it. So, for example, no statement can be made as to whether any of the witness statements are agreed if they have not been served or the Defendants asked to agree them. Information is sought on how many pages the trial bundles will consist of. A schedule of costs must be filed with the pre-trial checklist. This schedule must separate out those costs incurred to date, and those that will be incurred if the matter goes to trial. If this schedule is materially inaccurate (for example the actual costs are substantially more then set out in the checklist), then the solicitor may well have considerable difficulty recovering the difference at costs assessment. On completion, the checklist should be sent to the other side for agreement. The court expects as much agreement as possible and if there is not agreement, it expects to be able to see clearly where the disagreements lie and why.

Failure to return the checklist by the due date may cause the court to strike the case out, or order a listing hearing and make the solicitor pay, personally and at once, the other party's costs of attending. If no party files a pre-trial checklist, the court will ordinarily make a conditional order striking out the proceedings unless a pre-trial checklist is filed within seven days of service of the order (29.6(3)).

Further directions for trial

Further directions may be needed to provide a timetable for the trial and a time estimate for the trial. The solicitor may need to ask the court to approve that an expert gives oral evidence if, for example, the original directions order did not approve the giving of oral evidence from that expert. The client's medical condition may have deteriorated; extra expert evidence may be needed. Directions may be needed to deal with preparation and filing of the trial bundle. See Chapter 22 on Preparing for trial.

If further directions are needed, then, as always, the Defendant's agreement should be sought to a draft consent order with the listing questionnaire. If the Defendant does not agree, then application will have to be made to the court.

Pre-trial review

After filing of the listing questionnaire the court considers whether or not further directions are needed prior to trial even where neither side has requested any. The court will make such directions as it thinks fit and will, of course, consider any draft agreement for further directions. It can make further directions without a hearing or fix a pre-trial review to do so. If either party thinks a pre-trial review is necessary, perhaps because of the nature of further directions needed, or there is a problem with the speed of progress of the claim (perhaps the client is still very unwell and the prognosis remains uncertain) then application should be made for a review.

Multi track trials

Multi track trials are expected to take place in the court which has been managing the case. There remains a power to transfer a case to another court for hearing in appropriate cases.

At the trial, the expectation is that the judge will have read the papers. In simpler cases, the opening address may be dispensed with. Parties will ordinarily be expected to have filed skeleton arguments in advance of the hearing and will ordinarily have given a direction to that effect.

As before, the judge may control or exclude the giving of evidence and may limit cross examination. Witness statements will usually stand as evidence in chief and expert evidence may be given on paper alone if the directions so order (see Chapter 23 on The trial).

Once the trial has begun the judge will usually sit until its completion – so there should be none of the adjournments that have been common in county courts under the old rules.

If the case is not reached in the list for the fixed day, it will be listed, normally, for the next day.

CHAPTER 6

Funding

THE FIRST INTERVIEW

The first full interview with the client forms the bedrock of the case, in terms of both the information given by and to, and the relationship developed with, the client. It is, therefore, a meeting to which ample time should be given and which should not be squeezed in between other important events. It is important that the person handling the case is introduced at this meeting, if the interviewer will not be the person in day-to-day charge. There are many matters that need to be sorted out at this first meeting, as well as much information that must be understood and assessed. In some cases, a preliminary interview may be necessary before the first full interview, just to consider whether the case is worth proceeding to full interview or not. A precedent telling a client he has no prospect of success can be found at Appendix B – Specimen correspondence.

For most clients, the whole issue of the funding of a case weighs very heavily before even the first meeting. The normal first point of contact is by way of telephone and most clients will ask whether or not the first meeting will be free. With the growth of TV advertisement by personal injury claims companies, most clients will be aware of the existence of 'no win no fee' arrangements and may expect to be offered risk free litigation from the start. It is very important that at the first meeting – whether by telephone or in person – they are told what funding arrangements can be put in place to enable them to litigate a claim without fear of a large costs bill at the end of the day.

Whether or not a solicitor offers the first meeting for free is, of course, a matter of the firm's choice, but it is suggested that very few personal injury solicitors expect to charge for the first meeting now, and if the first meeting is not offered free of charge, the prospective client is likely to look elsewhere for legal advice.

It is important that the client leaves the meeting with a full understanding of how the case can be funded and the extent of his financial commitment to it. Whether that discussion takes place at the beginning or end of the interview is a question of style, but time must be spent on this subject before the client leaves the office. The position should be set out clearly in a letter immediately after the interview.

LEGAL AID

Legal aid was largely withdrawn for personal injury cases on 1 April 2000. There remains a limited form of funding for assault cases, some housing claims and certain complex high value claims, multi-party claims and clinical negligence work.

Private funding

From the solicitor's point of view, the easiest way for a case to be funded is for the client to pay personally. However, with conditional fee agreements ('CFAs') becoming increasingly widespread, clients privately funding their claims are rare and are only likely to occur where the case is easy and the client takes the view that the risks of losing are too small to warrant the cost of the insurance premium and the success fee. In those cases it is usual for the solicitor to defer charging costs until the end of the case rather then ask for payments on account as the case progresses. Other times when the client may consider funding the claim personally is where the case is too risky for the lawyer to take under a CFA.

Cases that are directly funded by the client are easiest in the sense that decisions on the case are made by the client and the solicitor without the involvement of a third party. The need to refer matters to funding bodies always creates a delay in running a case.

As in all other cases, in a privately-funded case the solicitor will need to send to the client a letter detailing the charging arrangements. It is often convenient to set out the detailed terms in one document and send it under a covering letter. The client must be given a clear estimate of the likely overall costs if he wins and if he loses, at what stages payments will be required, and how much each demand is likely to be. The efficient solicitor should ask for payment on account, particularly for disbursements such as experts' reports and counsel's fees, which are payable within three months.

Legal expense insurance

A surprising number of people have legal expense insurance without knowing it. Legal expense insurance can attach to motor vehicle insurance, household insurance, holiday insurance cover and even credit cards, and will provide for solicitors' costs and expenses to a preset level generally to investigate any type of claim that the insurance covers.

At the point of first contact with a client, if there is an intention to enter into a 'no win no fee' agreement, it is imperative to ask whether or not they have such cover and to ask them to bring to any meeting, or forward to the solicitor, a copy of any policies confirming cover. This requirement should be incorporated into the letter confirming interview and should recommend that the client brings along any relevant motor insurance policy (in road traffic accident claims), any household policy in force at the time of the accident and any other 'before the event' insurance policies if they exist.

Legal expense insurance is not limited to policies held by the client. The solicitor should consider whether the potential Defendant to the action may carry expense insurance that may benefit the Claimant, for example, the driver of a vehicle in which the Claimant was injured as a passenger – whether that be a normal car or public transport.

Failure to investigate the existence of legal expense insurance properly could result in the solicitor failing to recover the cost of any subsequent 'after the event' insurance premium and success fee. It could also be a breach of the solicitors conduct rules leaving the solicitor possibly open to disciplinary procedure.

The policy (or policies if there are more then one) should be checked carefully and the client asked to put the insurer on notice of a claim, to ask if cover will be extended to the claim and to ensure that the insurer is happy to instruct the solicitor of the client's choice (see *Sarwar v Alam*[1] where the Court of Appeal said that the solicitor should refer the client to the insurer without further ado if the claim were worth more then £5,000).

It is often the case that the insurers have their own panel solicitors. Whilst, as a generality, the insurers are entitled to nominate their own solicitors pre-issue of proceedings, the client is entitled to freedom of choice of solicitor post-issue. Further, an ombudsman decision established that where there are issues of complexity, the client is entitled to take advice from a solicitor of their own choice. It is worth noting that the insurance will never pay for legal expenses incurred before the claim is accepted and the choice of solicitor approved. Therefore if work is done prior to the insurance confirmation, it is either done for nothing, or the client must pay privately. If the indemnity principle is not to be breached, then the client must be put on proper notice of the intention to charge them for the work done by way of a proper client costs letter.

Legal expense insurance typically comes with a financial ceiling – normally £25,000 or £50,000 worth of cover. It is increasingly common for the insurer to expect the solicitor and their nominated barrister to run the case on a CFA leaving the level of indemnity for disbursements and possible adverse costs orders.

The insurer has the right to refuse the claim should it be thought that it is without merit, and if this happens and the case is not to be considered for a 'no win no fee' agreement then the client should be given careful advice on the likely time bar in the claim and if relevant referred elsewhere. It is not normal for legal expense insurers to deduct any money from the client's damages at the end of the day and most policies prohibit the solicitor levying a 'solicitor and own client' charge.

Where the insurers do not demand that the solicitor enters into a CFA, they will negotiate hourly rates and expect to be kept appraised of the progress of the case, any changes of risk in respect of the claim, and normally work cannot be done without specific permission. It is very important for the solicitor to familiarise herself with the policy terms attached to the insurance as, in the event of the claim failing, the insurers may well not pay out the solicitor's costs if the policy terms have been breached.

---

[1]   [2002] 1 WLR 125.

If the legal expense insurers will not nominate a particular solicitor, and that solicitor enters into a 'no win no fee' agreement with the client, then the Claimant will not normally recover a risk success fee if legal expense insurance was available but not used. The solicitor should put the legal expense insurers on notice of their intention to ask the insurer to indemnify the claim and the client's choice of solicitor at the point of issue of proceedings – to avoid having to purchase 'after the event' insurance to protect against adverse costs.

Once the extent of the insurance is used up, it is normal to consider transferring the claim to a 'no win no fee' agreement. For this reason it is important that a careful eye is kept on mounting costs so a sensible decision on when a 'no win no fee' agreement is offered can be made.

Trade union funding

Most trade unions offer free legal advice and representation to members who are injured at work. Sometimes accidents on the way to and from work are also covered. Some extend the service to other legal problems. Some have a scheme for paying for a member to have a half-hour consultation with a solicitor on any matter. Unions appoint firms of solicitors and it is almost invariably a requirement of the union's support that the member obtains legal advice from a nominated firm. About eight million people are trade union members entitled to this form of help. They include retired and unemployed members who may have claims in respect of injury or ill-health sustained while at work.

The role of the union is dependant upon its terms of agreement but generally the union has the right to refuse to support a case if it is not satisfied that there is a reasonable chance of success. If that happens, solicitors acting for unions usually advise the client to go elsewhere if she wishes to continue the case privately. It is essential to couple that advice with a warning about the limitation period. This should always be given in writing in case of any future dispute.

The advantage to the Claimant of a union-backed case is that there are no financial eligibility criteria, apart from the requirement of keeping union subscriptions up to date. The member does not have to worry about the costs of the case under any circumstances. There is no deduction from the damages in respect of solicitor and own client costs; all costs shortfalls will be paid so that the member receives every penny of the damages. Union cases give the opportunity for the nominated solicitors to build up a body of expertise round the particular kinds of work and workplaces and the particular kinds of accident and ill health with which they frequently deal.

In the past, union solicitors have charged unions for their services and for disbursements and for the Defendant's costs ordered to be paid by the Claimant. Nowadays that is no longer the practice. Competition between union firms has resulted in solicitors not charging the union of the Claimant anything. The solicitors make their money by the assured volume of cases coupled with their own efficiency. The result has been to concentrate union work in the hands of a very few high volume firms. These firms have adopted sophisticated computerised case management systems and 'bottom heavy' supervisory systems to make the CPR procedures cost effective.

Conditional fee agreements

The CFA is a contingency style arrangement which means that the Claimant's solicitor takes the case on the basis that she will be allowed to charge the client a 'success fee' if the Claimant wins, but no fee at all if the client loses, ie 'no win no fee'.

The benefit to the solicitor of taking the case on is that she is allowed to charge a premium on the costs of running the case, from the date that the contract is signed, against both the Defendant and the Claimant should she choose to do so.

The Rules do not allow the success fee to exceed the sum of 100% of the profit cost figure incurred since entering into the agreement; plus VAT.

For example, Mrs Smith enters into a CFA with Solicitor A. Profit costs from the date of the agreement until final order are £10,000 and the success premium is 50%. Solicitor A is therefore entitled to charge £5,000 as the success fee element in respect of the agreement.

Whilst a 'no win no fee' agreement protects a Claimant from paying his own solicitor costs in the event of the case being lost, the normal rule that the loser pays the winner's costs still remains, and the Claimant continues to be at risk of having to pay the Defendant's costs if he loses the case, or abandons the case.

In order to protect the Claimant against this risk, it is usual for a solicitor to purchase an insurance policy which will pay out, at least, the Defendant's costs in the event of the case being lost. Depending on the type of policy, it will typically indemnity the Claimant to the sum of £50,000 or £100,000 and pay out for the Defendant's costs, disbursements, solicitor's disbursements (normally from the date the contract is signed but some policies can be retrospective) and VAT.

There are a number of insurers who provide cover in various ways, including cover for clinical negligence claims and insurance products have undoubtedly become more sophisticated as the years have progressed.

The CFA has now become the usual funding base for personal injury solicitors.

The success fee

Fixed success fees

CPR Part 45 fixed the success fee for road traffic accident claims and some employers' liability claims that are worth less then £500k on a full liability basis to 12.5% if the case settles before trial, and 100% where the matter is actually heard at trial.

Other success fees

There are two types of 'no win no fee' agreements in existence: the longer form agreement allowed under the Conditional Fee Agreement Rules 2000 and the shorter form, simpler agreement allowed under the Conditional Fee Agreement Rules (Miscellaneous Amendment) Regulations 2003.

The more common agreements – because of their simplicity, they are less likely to be the subject of challenge at the end of the day – are made under the 2003 Amendment Regulations.

The Conditional Fee Agreement Rules 2000

The success fee attached to a 'no win no fee' contract is set at a percentage of the solicitor's basic charges and cannot be more than 100% of the basic charges. The percentage reflects the following:
(i)   the fact that if the case is won, the solicitor will not be paid their basic charges until the end of the claim;
(ii) the fact that the solicitor may (or may not) agree to fund the expenses as the case proceeds;
(iii) the fact that if the case is lost, the solicitor will not be paid.

The Defendant is expected to pay the risk element of the success fee, and the solicitor is entitled to charge the Claimant the remaining elements, that of delayed charges and funding expenses.

In practice, a company that is still using the 'long form' CFA will have its own rules about whether or not the Claimant should fund any of the expenses herself and it is normal for the client to be charged nothing and for the risk element to be the contentious element in respect of recovery of the success fee.

For example, Mrs Smith enters into a CFA with Solicitor A. The case is very complex and Solicitor A decides, after risk management, to charge her as follows:
(i)   in respect of the delayed payment element, 2.5% per annum and it is calculated that the case will take two years to complete;
(ii) in respect of funding expenses, nothing because Solicitor A will fund expenses themselves;
(iii) in respect of the risk element, ie that the case will not be won, 80%.

Therefore the total success fee is 85% of which the client is expected, if the case is won, to pay 5% and the Defendant 80%. If the costs, at the end of the day, were £10,000 and the client recovered £50,000 then out of the £50,000 she would be charged £500 (5% of £10,000) and the Defendant would be charged the £10,000 plus 80% of the same, ie £8,000. Total costs £18,000 plus VAT.

In order to recover the success fee element from the Defendant, the Claimant has to satisfy the Assessing Master that the correct rules have been complied with at the point of entry into the agreement, and that the percentage levied in respect of the success fee itself is reasonable. The test of reasonableness is the risk perceived at the point of entry into the contract.

There has been a lot of satellite litigation in respect of success fees and their recovery and in respect of procedural anomalies in respect of entry into the contract.

It is recommended that in order to ensure that the solicitor recovers the success fee element, and that the contract is not declared void or not enforceable because the correct procedures were not followed when entering into the same, that great care is taken to ensure that the rules are complied with.

The 2003 Amendment Regulations

The Conditional Fee Agreements (Miscellaneous Amendments) Regulations 2003 permit the entry into a more simple CFA than that provided for under the 2000 Rules. This CFA, colloquially known as a 'CFA light', avoids the majority of the procedural requirements of the 'standard' CFA. The entry into a CFA light will not permit the solicitor to charge the client anything by way of success fee, and the only charge permitted will be against the Defendant in respect of the risk element. It must briefly set out the reasons for setting the percentage increase at the level set, and the circumstances in which the client becomes liable to pay the solicitor's charges and provides that before the agreement is entered into the solicitor has to tell the client when they may be liable to pay their charges. In comparison to the 'normal' CFA, the requirements are far less onerous and it is likely that in the future CFA light will be preferred to the more cumbersome standard agreements. The difficult issues associated with proving compliance of the requirements connected with signing the agreement are thus avoided and the solicitor should be more assured that at the end of the day her agreement is unlikely to be the subject of a successful challenge at a detailed assessment for procedural anomalies.

Entering into the contract

The contract itself must have complied with the relevant CFA in place at the time of signature. As above, current CFAs are governed by Regulations made in 2000[2] and amended in 2003. If the CFA does not comply with the relevant Regulations, then it will not be enforceable. Further, the conditions contained within the contract must be complied with; in particular, the client must have a verbal explanation (either face to face or by telephone) at the point of signing the same or immediately before signing the same of the following:

(i)   the circumstances in which he may be liable to pay the solicitor's disbursements and charges;
(ii) the circumstances in which he may seek assessment of the solicitor's charges and disbursements and the procedure for doing so;
(iii) whether the solicitor considers that the client's risk of becoming liable for any costs in these proceedings is insured under an existing contract of insurance;
(iv) other methods of financing those costs, including private funding, community legal service funding, legal expenses insurance, trade union funding.

They must be told about after the event insurance and declare any interest (financial or otherwise) in any particular product recommended.

It is good practice to see the client face to face when signing the contract, and to ensure that a careful file note is prepared of the circumstances surrounding the signing of the same. Further, it is good practice to ensure that the client has a written explanation of the above issues as well as a verbal explanation to avoid any misunderstanding or confusion at a later date over advice given.

---

[2]   SI 2000/692.

THE RISK MANAGEMENT PROCESS

Most firms who undertake a substantial amount of 'no win no fee' work have in place a clear risk management structure, normally by way of nominated people, or a committee, who can review applications for 'no win no fee' agreements and authorise entering into a contract.

A draft risk management form is normally developed within the practice, setting out the likely areas of strengths of the case and the areas of weakness and then arriving at a careful, and documented, reason for entering into the percentage recommended.

There are very real difficulties in arriving at a reason for justifying the percentage recommended. Litigation has established that very simple fast track shunting accidents should probably not attract a higher risk percentage . In *Halloran v Delaney*[3] it was said that in simple claims settled without commencing proceedings, success fees should ordinarily be 5% of costs. What constitutes simple remains in debate!

However, there are all sorts of reasons that may well be valid, for increasing the percentage sought. These may include:

(i)   risk of losing the case – are there witnesses who confirm the client's version of events – in an road traffic accident, is there a danger that a conflict of evidence will seriously weaken the Claimant's case perhaps to the point of loss?

(ii)   danger of failing to beat an offer to settle/payment into court/ offer on apportionment of liability;

(iii) difficulty/complexity of liability issues or causation of injury issues;

(iv)   value/importance of the case to the client – is this a claim of high value which will cost a significant amount to litigate and so the risk of losing is of more financial importance to both the client and the solicitor;

(v)   danger of the client dying and so the case being (perhaps) abandoned.

The risk management process must be clearly documented on the file; it will need to be produced at the end of the day for the assessment officer at the costs hearing. It forms the bedrock of the analysis for why the success fee has been set at the level it has been set at. It cannot be stressed that a full and frank risk analysis is of great importance if the solicitor wants to recover her success fee in full; a few lines vaguely setting out general difficulties in litigating personal injury claims is generally insufficient to ensure recovery of the success fee.

Since the case of *Callery v Gray*, it is usual for a two-stage success fee to be entered into; the first initial stage of the CFA being the highest (because of the greater risk on accepting the agreement) and with a provision contained within the contract for a reduced success fee if a certain circumstance (ie an admission of liability being made or settlement prior to trial) is achieved.

SERVICE OF INFORMATION OF ENTRY INTO A CONTRACT

The Defendant should be put on notice of entry into a 'no win no fee' agreement at the point of signing the same. The solicitor should not, under any circumstances, tell

---

[3]   [2003] 1 All ER 755.

the Defendant of the success fee percentage charged. Some insurers persist in asking these questions – they do so to find out what level of risk the solicitor perceives the claim to attract. The Defendant should also be told whether or not there is after the event insurance attached to the agreement.

It is a matter of individual practice whether or not the solicitor chooses to attempt to flush out an admission of liability from the Defendant before entering into such an agreement.

Some clients will require 'no win no fee' agreements at the point of entry into the firm; for these clients the risk management process is much harder – it is difficult to give a logical evaluation of the likely risks of running a case where the only version of events that the solicitor has is the clients and there is no other supporting documentation. These clients are often given a two-stage success fee with a very high first-stage fee – often 100% – and any reduction from 100% argued at the point of detailed assessment or costs negotiation.

At the point of issue of proceedings, a notice of funding must be served with the court documentation.

If the above disclosure is not complied with then the solicitor is at serious risk of not recovering any risk element of the success fee from the Defendant, who is entitled to be told that he is facing a much higher costs bill at the end of the day if he persists in fighting the claim.

CONDITIONAL FEE AGREEMENTS AND CHILDREN AND PATIENTS

It is possible to enter into a CFA on behalf of a child or a person who is under a disability (a patient). The litigation friend has the authority to sign the agreement for the child/patient and if there is to be any deduction from the client's damages at the end of the day this will be subject to the usual rule that you cannot charge a child or a patient without the court's approval. It is for this reason that careful thought must be given to any success fee that it is intended to levy against the child/patient and in respect of any charge that may be made in respect of after the event insurance premiums.

If the Court of Protection is involved, for example there is a receivership or deputyship order in place at the point of entry into the agreement, then it is wise to seek the authority of the Court of Protection prior to signing the agreement.

It is essential to remember that when the client attains the age of 18 years, or if a patient attains capacity, then he will have to sign the CFA again. At this point, it would be wise to reassess the issues of risk at the point of entry into the agreement and to give the statutory explanations to the person signing the agreement to comply with the relevant rules.

CONDITIONAL FEE AGREEMENTS AND BARRISTERS

Whilst there are insurance packages that are prepared to treat counsel's fees as disbursements, the majority of after the event insurance policies in existence for standard personal injury litigation require the solicitor to ensure that if the solicitor is advising the client by way of a 'no win no fee' agreement, then any counsel instructed is also acting under the same basis.

Barristers are used to dealing with 'no win no fee' agreements and accepting the risk to themselves that this type of litigation involves.

The Bar Council and APIL have issued guidance on the Bar entering into agreements, and most sets of chambers have a risk management process and standard chambers agreement.

The Agreement will be between the solicitor and counsel (although it is imperative that the client's full consent, and understanding of the nature of any extra charge that may be incurred as a result of the agreement is explained) and the cab-rank rule (by which, essentially, a barrister was duty bound to accept a brief within his area of expertise) has gone for conditional fees. The rule only applies to cases where counsel is being offered a proper professional fee and does not apply when counsel is not promised any fee. It is for this reason most solicitors establish relationships with counsel's chambers to ensure that there is a 'bank' of acceptable counsel with whom they can work. This is necessary in case the counsel nominated to deal with the case cannot – for reasons of alternative booking – deal with an interlocutory application or even accept the brief for trial.

AFTER THE EVENT INSURANCE

There are a plethora of insurance products that provide after the event insurance that attaches to CFAs.

Firms that carry out a substantial volume of CFA work generally enter into arrangements with specific insurers in relation to bulk provision of policies. The advantage of these arrangements is multifold; often there is a degree of delegated authority which means that the solicitor can enter into the agreement without the insurance company's direct approval, provided certain provisions have been complied with. For the extremely valuable and complex personal injury claims, it is usual to negotiate directly with the insurance provider who will individually underwrite the policy.

In particular, it is important to know that claims run under the Motor Insurers Bureau ('MIB') uninsured driver scheme may benefit from 'free' after the event insurance negotiated directly by the MIB with a major insurance company. Failure to apply for this insurance (details of which can be found on any application made to the MIB or on their website) will almost certainly cause the MIB at the end of the day to refuse to fund the premium.

Most solicitors have found over the years that it is beneficial to establish a good relationship with an insurance provider. Not all cases will be won, and it can be very helpful when making a claim on the policy to know that the insurer will pay out without difficulty. After all, insurance is purchased, at a cost, specifically for this reason.

Most insurers now offer what is called a 'deferred premium'. In the early days of after the event insurance, it was difficult for a client to find the often substantial sum to pay for the insurance premium, but now most insurers will defer charging the premium until the end of the case, and waive the charge if the claim is lost or abandoned on advice. However, it is worth remembering that nearly all policies cause the client to remain liable to pay for the premium at the end of the day, and if the premium is not recovered from the Defendant then the client will normally have to pay for the same out of their damages. If the client has been promised that no money will be taken from their damages, then the solicitor herself will have to pay for an unrecoverable element of the insurance premium.

The solicitor must familiarise herself with the contractual requirements of the after the event insurers. There are normally a serious of reporting dates to update the insurers on the nature and extent of the risk that they are under, and in particular most insurers set priority report requirements when the nature of the risk within a case changes. Most insurers require to be told when the case has been issued, when payments into court have been made but not accepted and when the trial date is fixed. Failing to keep the insurers informed may well void the policy.

As with CFA contracts, the client's conduct throughout the case remains under scrutiny. A client who fails to comply with the requirement of the contract will find himself with a policy that is voided.

At the end of the day, the insurance premium should be recoverable from the Defendant provided it can be shown that the insurance was purchased at a reasonable cost; the word 'reasonable' is not defined, but generally interpreted as competitive costs to that in the open marketplace. For this reason, where there is a substantial risk, a valuable claim and the insurance premium likely to be substantial, it is important to get several quotes from different insurers on behalf of the client so that a comparison between the level of cover and protection offered can be made before a decision made on which quote to accept. By taking this precaution, the solicitor will almost certainly recover the premium at the conclusion of the claim.

Contingency fee agreements are arrangements under which a lawyer is entitled to a percentage of moneys recovered by his client. These are common in the US. Such arrangements have always been regarded as contrary to public policy in the UK in the majority of cases. There are exceptions – it is possible to enter into a contingency fee agreement in respect of applications to the Criminal Injuries Compensation Authority.

CHAPTER 7

The Initial Interview and the Claimant's Proof

The Claimant's proof of evidence is the core of the case. It should, therefore, be well ordered, concise, clear and accurate. Getting it right from the start will save time and effort (often unrecoverable in costs) later.

In most claims, a proof will be taken in outline at the initial client interview. The solicitor's first contact with a client is of vital importance. The client may be wary and may well never have spoken to a solicitor before. They are almost certain to be anxious and they are often in pain. The solicitor should aim to make the initial interview as easy as possible and it is not unusual to take instructions at the client's home or perhaps even in hospital.

The development of client care skills has been acknowledged over the years as being of prime importance by the Law Society. Communications and video interviewing technique now forms part of the Legal Practice final course for training solicitors, and in continuing professional development courses.

Establishing good communications skills is essential, especially when dealing with people who are sick or injured. At some point in the case the solicitor will probably have to give unpalatable advice – whether this is to deflate a client's expectations on what the claim is worth or to explain that the claim ought to settle or be abandoned. At this point, a client who has confidence in her lawyer is more likely to accept this advice than one who does not.

Excessive and unnecessary telephone calls and letters from a client can be avoided, generally by prompt, comprehensive and routine explanations of what is happening. However, some clients have unreasonable expectations of what the lawyer can do for them and the busy personal injury lawyer will certainly come across clients who are mentally unwell. The solicitor must develop acceptable methods for dealing with these clients or else she will find herself unnecessarily burdened by their demands. The newly qualified lawyer ought to constantly evaluate her own progress in client handling skills and never shrink from asking the advice of a more experienced colleague if getting into difficulty in handling a client.

It is at the first interview that the client will form an opinion on the solicitor. It is not unusual for a client to 'shop around' and see more then one lawyer before deciding which to appoint especially where the initial interview is free. The other side of this coin is that in an era where the majority of work is to be carried out on the basis of 'no win no fee', and where the firm's office account may well be burdened with paying the client's disbursements, the solicitor's initial assessment of the client, and the value of the claim, will be crucial in making a risk assessment as to whether to take on the case.

The newly qualified practitioner must attempt to assess the strengths and weaknesses not only of the client's accident as it is recounted, but also of the client, his accuracy, memory skills, presentation as a witness, proneness to exaggerate or minimise, and how he will be as a client.

In turn, the solicitor should seek to impress the potential client with quiet confidence in her knowledge of the law and the legal process, able to explain in simple language the progress of the claim, able to listen to the client, assimilate the facts as given and then give an educated and intelligent account of what will be necessary to succeed in a claim.

At the initial interview there must be discussion on funding arrangements and advice given in detail on these. A clear note should be taken of the advice as given and, very importantly, advice given and noted on the limitation period.

The initial interview must also investigate the value of the claim, at least insofar as it can be investigated at that stage, so as to discover which track is appropriate. If the claim is likely to be small claims track, then it may not be worth the solicitor taking the case – see Chapter 3.

The initial proof of evidence is one of the documents that the solicitor will use as part of the risk assessment of the case. It is essential that it tests out all aspects of the client's claim, both the issues of liability and of damages, as well as those of pre-accident problems and illnesses that may affect those issues and any contributory negligence.

All of these matters will be relevant when considering the success fee uplift (see Chapter 6 on Case funding and Chapter 24 on Costs). At costs assessment, the solicitor's risk assessment documentation must not only be served with the bill, but will be closely scrutinised by the court when considering the reasonableness of the CFA uplift (where there is not a fixed uplift); the test is the risk as perceived at the time of entering into the agreement. The initial proof will be considered (with others) by the assessing officer.

A 'proof' should be distinguished from a 'witness statement'. The proof of evidence should contain all the relevant evidence of the Claimant or witness. It might include hearsay, gossip about other witnesses and a whole variety of matters that are relevant because they relate to the issues in the case and may assist the solicitor and, subsequently, the advocate, but are not necessarily intended for disclosure to the Defendant or the court. The 'witness statement', under CPR, r 32.4[1] on the other

---

[1]   The old RSC Order 38, r 2A and CCR Order 20, r 12A.

hand, now has a strict legal format and is for disclosure to the Defendant and the court. It should therefore contain only that information which is necessary to prove the Claimant's case and not contain any information that is likely to harm the Claimant (unless essential). Witness statements are dealt with in Chapter 10.

This chapter looks at the three main problems dealt with in the proof: the description and cause of the accident or ill health; the nature of the injuries or illness; and financial losses. A specimen proof of evidence, and a specimen witness statement ready for exchange can be found at Appendix A.

The client may wish to recount details which are more extensive than the essential information required for the case. This requires careful handling since for the solicitor time is money (especially in fast track cases) yet often important facts are revealed in inconsequential conversation and letting the client tell his story in his own way.

The solicitor who regularly takes witness statements becomes skilled at getting to the heart of the problem whilst controlling the client and stopping him from excessively diverting to other stories. More complex claims involve more detailed facts and are often likely to be claims of greater value so more time can be spent on multi track than on fast track cases. A rough valuation needs to be established in the solicitor's mind, therefore, in the early part of the interview, but spending time on the initial proof often saves time later in almost every kind of case and provides the best opportunity to evaluate the client as a witness, as well as eliciting all the necessary information and getting the 'feel' of the case.

It can be useful to dictate the proof in the client's presence. Mistakes and misunderstandings can then be corrected as the solicitor goes along. When an account is particularly long and rambling, it may be better to take notes during the interview and later dictate the proof in an ordered form.

In some discreet way, the solicitor should endeavour to discover the client's level of literacy. Knowing this will affect communication with the client, and may require more meetings in the solicitor's office than correspondence to the client's home, where an intermediary of unknown skill may be interpreting the solicitor's request and answering on the client's behalf. If the client has literacy issues, this must be borne in mind when getting the client to sign a statement of truth and the statement may need to be read to the client and verifed by a witness under PD 22. Also, knowledge of a client's literacy will be relevant to counsel at trial, if the client is asked to read a document in the witness box.

It is also important to ensure that the client's command of English is sufficient to ensure that the solicitor is being understood; if not, the interview ought to be terminated as tactfully as possible and reorganised to a time when an interpreter can attend.

While every case is unique and requires different details to be noted, the nature of the information required is fairly common to each case. A standard format for the proof of evidence should be used to ensure that all basic matters are covered. Always presenting information in the same way saves valuable time when looking in the proof for particular details. Such a format needs to deal with the following:

THE ESSENTIALS

The required basics are: the client's full name, date of birth, address, telephone number, national insurance number, hospital reference number, marital status, children, employer's name and address, client's occupation and position. Every proof should bear the solicitor's name and case reference. A guide to the substantive information required in the Claimant's proof of evidence is outlined below.

The accident (or ill health)

The date, time and place of the accident (or the cause of the ill health) are the starting point. Then will follow the explanation of the accident and why the Defendant was at fault. Details of witnesses, their names and addresses if known, and not how they can be contacted, must be recorded. Details of injuries and the way they affect the Claimant's life will be followed by details of past, present and future losses. The most common types of accident have similarities from which some basic lines of guidance can be drawn.

Road accidents

The basic question is – how did the accident happen? The answer must be set out fully and clearly, without ambiguity.

A road map should be available (and can be downloaded from the Internet) to pinpoint the accident spot. Model cars and lorries can also be helpful. The directions of the vehicles and/or pedestrians should be clarified – a sketch plan with the client indicating the route of all relevant participants should be drawn. Traffic signals and signs should be noted, as well as the width of the road, the lighting, parked cars, and other relevant features in the area.

Registration numbers of vehicles should be recorded, as should names and addresses of all the parties and witnesses involved. Scraps of paper on which numbers and names were originally noted must be saved. If the client has taken down details of the insurers of the likely Defendant, this may save some time in the earlier stages of the case.

The solicitor should next try to ascertain, from all the information, who was legally liable for the accident and the basis of that liability. Blame in a road accident case is generally a matter of common sense. However, compared with a lay person, the courts look more critically at the standard of care required of a professional driver. Where the Claimant has no recollection of the accident, witnesses are more important and the possibility of *res ipsa loquitur* may be applicable.[2]

The client should be asked whether anything was said about blame by the proposed Defendant or any of the witnesses at the time of the accident.

The solicitor should always be alive to the possibility of a conflict of interest; one such situation calling for alertness is where driver and passenger wish to instruct the

---

[2]   *Widdowson v Newgate Meat Corpn* [1997] 47 LS Gaz R 31 (pedestrian Claimant succeeded by absence of plausible explanation by car driver).

same solicitor. There will be a conflict unless the solicitor is sure the driver cannot realistically be held liable to any extent for the passenger's injuries.

The courts are keen to do justice to injured parties in road accident cases, since it is recognised that insurance companies, rather than the Defendant in person, will be footing the bill. Road accident cases should, therefore, be approached with a certain robustness. The Claimant's solicitor should not be too put off if it appears that the client contributed to, or was even the major cause, of the accident. Damages are still recoverable, even if there is contributory negligence. As a part of taking the initial statement, the sources of corroborative evidence for the client's story should immediately be sought. These may include witnesses' names and addresses and, usually, the identification of the police officers who attended the scene of the accident. All road accidents involving personal injury should have been reported to the police, so their official report can be obtained, and the outcome of any prosecution can be ascertained.

The exact nature of the weather can be important in a road accident case. The police report usually notes it, but the accuracy must be checked with the client. Where the client is unable to recollect, or if the issue is likely to be contested and the claim is likely to be a valuable one, the Meteorological Office should be asked for a weather report on the precise area at the particular time. The Office will make a charge for giving the information, but it is usually able to give accurate information in writing relatively speedily. A precedent for such a request is at (Appendix B – Specimen correspondence). In cases where costs are an issue, it may be more cost effective to get the client to obtain this information directly from the Metrological Office, as the charges can be less.

Photographs should be taken as soon as possible of all relevant aspects of the scene. This can be done by the client, by a friend, or by someone from the solicitor's practice. A professional photographer is not usually necessary at this stage. A useful dating technique is to place the day's newspaper in a corner of the frame of at least the first photograph of the series if the camera does not have an automatic dating facility.

Tripping

With the local government expenditure cuts of recent years, the poor condition of many pavements[3] and roads has given rise to an increasing number of accidents. The great majority of clients are elderly people who, having lost the agility of youth, trip over uneven pavements or road works. Their claim is usually against the highway authority under the Highways Act 1980, s 41,[4] although many claims are made against a utility company or sub-contractor which created the danger.

---

[3] The absence of a footway may found an action: *R v Norfolk County Council, ex p Thorpe* (1998) 96 LGR 597.

[4] The highway authority, usually the district council or metropolitan borough, is under a duty to maintain the highway. The Claimant has to show that the highway was not reasonably safe and that it caused the accident. The burden then shifts to the Defendant authority to satisfy the statutory defence, ie that it had 'taken such care as in all the circumstances was reasonably required to secure that the part of the highway to which the action relates was not dangerous'. If the highway authority arranges for a competent person to maintain the highway, it must show that proper instructions were given and that the person carried out those instructions: Highways Act 1980, s 58(1) and (2). See also *Pridham v Hemel Hempstead Corpn* (1970) 69 LGR 523, CA.

The courts have held that members of the public must accept that pavements will not be perfectly level.[5] Pedestrians are under a duty to keep a look out and must accept some risks. By and large, claims where the difference in levels is less than one inch are unlikely to succeed, whereas claims where the difference in levels is greater than one inch are likely to do so. Claims depend on the nature and position of the defect and on surrounding conditions including lighting.[6] The best defence for the local authority is that it regularly checked the particular street and that the proof of the defect is a crucial part of winning tripping cases. This is all the more important since authorities are often remarkably fast in repairing defects following notification of an accident. A camera and measuring tape should always be available at the office so that, if necessary, a clerk can be sent out with the client to the locus in quo immediately after the interview to take photographs. It is crucial to identify the actual paving stone or obstruction that caused the accident. The exact nature of the defect and, most particularly, the depth or height of the defect must be measured and photographed. Prior to taking the photographs, a ruler or coin should be placed in the hole or against the obstruction, so that the dimensions of the defect are quite clear. Including the day's newspaper in one shot is a convenient way of showing the date of the photographs.

As before, the possibilities of corroborative evidence from witnesses should be pursued. These are often quite easy to come by if there is a major defect; the solicitor can send somebody to interview the local shopkeepers or consider putting a notice in a local shop window to ask people to contact her to confirm the state of disrepair.

Work

Many areas of employment are closely regulated by statute. This high degree of statutory protection together with the developed state of the law of negligence in relation to employers' liability put the Claimant in a strong position in relation to illness or accident at work. These factors, and the court's discernible sympathy for the injured worker, allow the solicitor to take a robust attitude to these cases.

In cases of accidents and ill health arising at work, it is particularly important to understand the nature of the tasks carried out by the client. First, a feel for the workplace should be obtained by asking questions about its size and location, the nature of the work carried out, the number of employees, the nature of the tasks undertaken by the client and the process which gave rise to the accident.

Once a picture of the working environment has emerged, details need to be obtained of the accident itself. If the accident involves machinery, the client might draw the relevant piece. The sketch is only for the Claimant's advisers and should not be released to the Defendant. This is because a machine can often be misrepresented, albeit innocently, in the client's memory. Only when the workplace and equipment are fully understood can the solicitor ask the questions which will give a clear picture of how the accident or ill health occurred and what or who caused it.

---

[5]   *Littler v Liverpool Corpn* [1968] 2 All ER 343n.

[6]   *Griffiths v Liverpool Corpn* [1967] 1 QB 374; *Meggs v Liverpool Corpn* [1968] 1 WLR 689; *Mills v Barnsley Metropolitan Borough Council* [1992] PIQR P292; *Misell v Essex County Council* (1994) Times, 16 December.

It is far more likely in a work case than any other that there will have been witnesses to the accident, witnesses who are traceable and who are happy to help with the case. Their names and home addresses should be obtained. Because of co-workers' frequent fear of being penalised by the employer for giving evidence against the employer, the solicitor's approach to the client's work colleagues should be discussed with the client. It may be best if the client makes the initial approach.

The client should be asked whether there is a shop steward or safety representative and, if so, statements must be obtained from him, even if he did not witness the actual accident. They often have useful information, particularly about the system of work, previous accidents and previous complaints. If the accident involved machinery or equipment, it should be ascertained whether there is a witness, shop steward or safety representative in the maintenance section who can say something about the machine or piece of equipment, its maintenance, previous similar occurrences, or repairs after the accident.

For many work cases, a sure understanding of the accident is really only possible from photographs or even from a visit (lay inspection). Often an expert engineer needs to be instructed (see Chapter 12) and the photographs can be left to him/her. It is almost always helpful to attend the inspection with the engineer and the client. The Defendant will have to be put on notice of the claim by way of a letter of claim and inspection facilities may not be organised for some time. Check with the client whether the machinery or the workplace is likely to be changed or moved in the meantime. If there are any doubts, the client and/or workmates should attempt to get photographs at once. The possibility of video recording of the scene of the accident at the time of the accident should be considered. The solicitor should seek from the Defendant's insurers facilities for immediate inspection and photographs (by the solicitor, if an engineer cannot be instructed in time) and an undertaking to preserve any piece of equipment pending the trial. If the other side refuses to co-operate, the court can be requested to order inspection, photography, preservation, custody and detention of property which may become the subject matter of subsequent proceedings (see CPR Part 25[7] and Chapter 20).

Consideration must be given to the documentation that is disclosable under the relevant pre-action protocol. There are a wealth of regulations that apply to workplace claims and the protocol assists by listing the main regulations in respect of which documentation should be available.[8]

The solicitor may need to see the client to discuss and update the statement in the light of documentation disclosed after the protocols have been complied with. The duty of early disclosure (if complied with by the Defendant) should not dissuade the

---

[7]   Formerly the Supreme Court Act 1981, s 33(1)(a); County Courts Act 1984, s 52(1)(a) and RSC Ord 29, r 7A(1); CCR Ord 13, r 7(1)(g).

[8]   Workplace (Health Safety and Welfare) Regulations 1992, Provision and Use of Work Equipment Regulations 1992, Personal Protective Equipment at Work Regulations 1992, Manual Handling Operations Regulations 1992, Health & Safety (Display Screen Equipment) Regulations 1992, Control of Substances Hazardous to Health Regulations 1988, Construction (Design & Management) Regulations 1994, Pressure Systems and Transportable Gas Containers Regulations 1989, Lifting Plant and Equipment (Records of Test and Examination Etc) Regulations 1992, Noise at Work Regulations 1989, Construction (Head Protection) Regulations 1989, Construction (General Provisions) Regulations 1961.

solicitor from questioning the client about his knowledge of what documentation the employer may keep. If, on complying with the protocol, the employer fails to disclose certain documents, the client's knowledge of their existence will enable a speedy application to be made, to the embarrassment of the Defendant.

The client must be asked whether details of the accident were entered in the firm's accident book. This document is required to be kept in offices, factories, mines, quarries and many other workplaces as well as all premises where ten or more persons are employed in a trade or business.[9] Despite the expectation of the protocols that documentation is kept by employers, it is often the case that it is not. Such a failure may, in fact, assist the Claimant since it may imply a lax attitude to the regulations or, worse, deliberate destruction of relevant evidence. The Health & Safety Executive should be contacted for the results of any investigation that they have carried out into the accident.

The client should be asked whether any other evidence relating to the accident may be available from the employer, such as an investigation carried out by the employer or the safety committee, or a report in a complaints book or at the first aid centre.

The client may be entitled to disablement benefit, if the accident occurred at work and if national insurance has been paid. The benefit may be claimed up to six months from the date of the accident. If a claim has been made, copies of the application forms, which are partly completed by the employers and contain a description of the accident (possibly with useful statements or information relevant to liability), should be requested from the DSS.

INJURIES AND ILLNESS

The client should be asked to describe the circumstances immediately after the accident, including what happened and who was involved by way of rescue and treatment.

A clear description of the injuries should be obtained, together with details of the treating hospital(s), general practitioner, and any other treatment or therapy (for example, osteopathy or acupuncture) received. Many clients pay for these therapies or payment is funded by way of a private insurance plan. Details of the costs must be obtained and copies of receipts, if relevant, provided. The hospital number is also needed, to facilitate correspondence with hospital medical records officers.

---

[9]   Social Security (Claims and Payments) Regulations 1979, reg 25. Also, under Reporting of Injuries, Diseases and Dangerous Occurrences Regulations 1985, regs 3 and 5 and Sch 3, employers must keep the following records: (a) for accidents: the date and time of the accident or dangerous occurrence; the full name and occupation of the person affected; the nature of the injury or condition; the place where the accident or dangerous occurrence happened; and a brief description of the circumstances. This applies to all accidents requiring admission to hospital for more than 24 hours or incapacity from work for more than three consecutive days, (b) in disease cases: the date and diagnosis of the disease; the occupation of the person affected; and the name or nature of the disease. Diagnosis of the disease must be made by a GP. The information must be kept in relation to employees, self-employed persons, persons undergoing training, visitors, customers and other invitees: *Woking Borough Council v BHS plc* (1994) 93 LGR 396, 159 JP 427.

Brief information is also needed about the number of hospital visits, operations performed, time spent in the hospital, physiotherapy sessions, time at home convalescing, and, most importantly, time off work. The client should also be asked for details of all current symptoms and any long-term prognosis given by the client's medical advisers. The client should be asked for any personal records of the effects of the accident, for example, in the form of a diary or notes. If symptoms continue, the client should be asked to keep a diary as a nearly contemporaneous record of the impact on daily life.

The client should be asked carefully and sympathetically what effect the accident has had on his/her life. This includes details of social life, sex life, sporting activities, hobbies, housework, DIY and so on. Questions should be asked about relevant pre-existing injuries (if any) and whether any symptoms were persisting at the time of the accident.

The client should be asked about any pre-accident illnesses or problems that may affect this present claim. Consideration needs to be given to whether there is any background history that may affect liability or the value of the matter. This is particularly important when considering, for example, back injury claims and the client should be asked whether he has a history of back problems. Often clients feel awkward about acknowledging that they had previous problems; the solicitor should carefully explain that previous problems will not necessarily have an adverse effect on the claim; however, a failure to admit known previous problems can show the client in a bad light.

The client should be asked to sign a consent form for disclosure of his/her medical records. The solicitor will usually prepare a consent form seeking disclosure of medical records in relation to the accident injuries and treatment. It is always sensible to gather in all of the medical records to ensure that no pre-accident condition has been exacerbated – or that a pre-existing condition cannot be blamed on the client's continuing difficulties.

FINANCIAL LOSSES

For the great majority of cases, the most important potential area of loss is that of earnings. For the Claimant who was in work at the time of the accident, details should be obtained of the type of work, the gross and net earnings, overtime, bonuses, the name and address of the employer, any sick pay received during the period of absence, DSS benefits paid, details of the DSS office and reference number and national insurance number. Any question of contractual liability to repay moneys received while sick will need to be investigated with the client and employer. Details of the client's tax office should be obtained, including the client's reference number, if known. If not, the NI number will suffice. The client should be asked at this time to sign a consent to disclosure of earnings details. The Defendant (who may not be the employer) is entitled to employment and earnings details if loss of earnings is claimed, and it is a protocol requirement that these are given in the letter of claim so it is inefficient not to put them on file at the earliest opportunity. It is to be noted that, the fast track protocols provide that if the client is suing his employer, part of the documents that the employer must disclose after service of the letter of claim include earnings details.

If the client was in long-term employment before the accident and the period of absence was relatively short, the above information will probably be sufficient. Where the client is unable to return to work on a longer-term basis, a fuller work history needs to be established, with the names and addresses of previous employers, job details and wages earned. If there is any hint that loss of earnings may be difficult to calculate (because not on a fixed and ascertainable salary, for instance), then details of comparable earners should be taken forthwith in case they subsequently move away or lose track of their earnings. If, in the first interview, there is a suggestion that there may be a sizeable future loss claim, an outline of the client's career should be obtained.

All other expenses incurred by the client should be recorded, including travelling expenses to and from hospitals, doctors and so on. Damage to clothing, with an estimate of its value, should be noted. For some cases, there will also be the cost of health care. A client is not under any obligation to use the National Health Service and, if treatment obtained under the private health scheme can be justified, the Defendant has to pay the costs. The solicitor should make sure that the client is aware that costs of private treatment will not be recovered (unless there is also private medical insurance) if the case loses or the court does not accept that it was reasonable to seek private treatment. Also, where there is likely to be an issue of contributory negligence the solicitor should make sure that the client is aware that any sums expended on private health treatment will be subject to a reduction.

An increasing number of people are covered by private health care insurance. It is usual for the policy to include a contractual obligation to repay the insurance company in the event of a successful claim by the client in respect of treatment for which the insurance company has paid. This should be checked and a copy of the policy obtained and the health insurers notified in due course.

Damages in tort are intended to restore the Claimant to the financial position that he would have been in but for the accident. However, the law, of course, requires the Claimant to mitigate his losses. The client must be reminded of this. If the client loses employment, it is imperative that all reasonable efforts are made (and recorded) to find alternative work. All job adverts, all letters seeking work and rejection letters must be retained. A note of all visits to job centres and other employment agencies and all telephone calls in connection with the search for work should be kept.

A major area of financial loss to be considered is that of care and treatment. Many people who are injured may not need professional nursing care but may well require a relative to carry out a caring role during the period of recuperation or rehabilitation. The nature and extent of such assistance, and whether gratuitous or paid, should be noted and added to the claim. Any payments or gifts made by the client must be noted, as should the nature, times and duration of the carer's work, so that a commercial valuation can be made later. Any loss of wages the client thinks the carer may have incurred should be noted for later confirmation with the carer and the carer's employer.[10] If the client has received care or help from the local authority,

---

[10]   *George v Pinnock* [1973] 1 WLR 118; *Donnelly v Joyce* [1974] QB 454. The commercial valuation of care provided by a relative as an item of allowable special damages was confirmed in *Roberts v Johnstone* [1989] QB 878. This does not apply, however, if the services are provided by the tortfeasor: *Hunt v Severs* [1994] 2 AC 350, HL.

that authority may be entitled to recover their past outlay[11] and details should be taken of the care received and the local authority's name should be noted for reference so they can be contacted and asked to confirm whether or not they are seeking recovery, how much they assess it at and precisely what services it covers, on what dates.

The client should also be told to make a note of all further expenses incurred during the course of the case and, where possible, to back up expense claims with documentary proof (ie receipts for taxis, bus tickets, etc). It is an unusual case where every part of the financial loss claim can be substantiated by documentary evidence but, the smaller the unsubstantiated aspects of the claim, the greater the chance the client will be fully compensated for all the losses incurred.

FURTHER POINTS

The Claimant's proof and subsequently his witness statement should bring out points which will enhance the Claimant's standing in the judge's eyes: military or community service, charitable work, sporting achievements and the like – even if not, apparently, directly relevant.

Every client should be warned that Defendants' insurers often resort to private detectives and surreptitious video-taping. This way any video served in the later stages of a case should not come as a surprise.

The proof when typed must be sent to the client. It must bear the date when it was taken by the solicitor, with provision on every page for the Claimant's signature and date of signing when he comes to read and agree or amend the typescript. It is remarkable how frequently these dates are omitted from proofs. Such omissions, coupled with use of phrases such as 'up until six months ago' and references to his age without stating his date of birth, can render the proof frustratingly defective in the months or years ahead.

The proof should contain a statement verifying its truth to be signed and dated by the Claimant at the very end of the proof.

The need to record the exact date when the proof of evidence was dictated and when it was subsequently signed by the client can be important if he dies during the action before a witness statement can be prepared. In such a case the proof may be required to be put in evidence under the Civil Evidence Act 1968. If it is not signed, it may be served as a witness summary under CPR, r 32.9, but it will not have the same force as a signed statement.

By the time the proof of evidence is completed, the solicitor must be satisfied that the whole case is understood. The advantage of dictating the proof in the client's presence is that fewer errors and misunderstandings are likely. After the proof has been dictated, the client must be told in the firmest way that any part of the typescript that is unsatisfactory must be corrected and amended. This must be repeated in writing

---

[11]   Health and Social Service and Social Security Adjudications Act 1983, s 17: *Avon County Council v Hooper* [1997] 1 WLR 1605.

when the typed proof is sent out (see Appendix B – Specimen correspondence). Reticent clients often feel that it is an impertinence to correct the solicitor's draft.

The solicitor must make every effort to ensure that the statement is put as far as possible in the client's own words and in plain English. This will help the client to feel that the statement is his own and to avoid errors arising perhaps from phraseology with which the client is unfamiliar and which might thus be perpetuated, with dangers for the future of the case. On certain occasions it will be necessary to have an officially verified translation of the proof from a reputable translation agency.

PRELIMINARY MEDICAL ASSESSMENT

After the proof has been taken, it is worth discussing with the client the nature of the medical evidence needed, since an early medical report will always be advisable prior to issue of proceedings. At the same time as explaining the likely track that the claim will proceed in (see below), the various rules on joint instruction of medical experts should be explained to the client. It is important that the client understands that the court may restrict medical evidence, both in costs and quantity and that it is unlikely that oral expert evidence will be allowed in fast track claims.

Usually an orthopaedic consultant will be required but the client should be told about other specialties which the solicitor feels may be necessary at some stage, even if not initially. Most people are upset at the suggestion that they might need to see a psychiatrist, neurologist or clinical psychologist and need reassurance that such skills are essential if there is to be recovery of damages in respect of emotional upheaval or personality change. In fact, a psychiatric or psychological opinion ought normally to be sought where the solicitor suspects adverse emotional or mental consequences of the accident. Such consequences should be probed, particularly if there has been a head injury. Even if there has not, it may still be worthwhile to question the client, since treating hospitals often overlook such subjective symptoms as headache, dizziness, anxiety, sleep disorder, depression, phobias, lack of concentration, irritability or loss of memory. The client should be warned about the nature of the (many) medical examinations likely during the course of the proceedings. At this time, the client should be told about the expectations under the protocol of joint expert instruction with the proposed Defendant.

INITIAL ASSESSMENT OF CASE

At the end of the initial interview, it should be possible to make an initial assessment of whether the case is winnable, where its weaknesses lie, the possibilities of contributory negligence and, in rough terms, the level of damages recoverable.

This will enable (i) a provisional view of the likely track; (ii) a preliminary decision on whether the case is worth taking; and (iii) a provisional risk assessment for the purposes of funding arrangements.

If the case is to be handled by the solicitor, funding will require discussion with the Claimant. Most clients, who do not have legal expense insurance, will expect the solicitor to be in a position to take their case on a 'no win no fee' basis. The firm's particular protocols in this respect will have to be explained to the client. The assessment of the likely value of the claim and the principles of valuation will need to be explained to the client. It is often helpful to have a copy of the Judicial Studies Board guidelines to quantum in personal injury claims for reference, and showing the clients this booklet often helps them to understand the likely valuation of their claim.

Other funding options will need explanation.

Where consideration is being given to a 'no win no fee' agreement, the full implications of this must be discussed. If the agreement is to be signed during the initial interview the relevant statutory provisions and any provisions required by the firm's particular after the event Insurance complied with; if the agreement is to be signed after risk assessment, arrangements need to be made for the funding of the investigation while the risk is being assessed. The possible use of counsel and the CFA arrangements for use of counsel will need to be explained.

The client should be told in outline the stages of the progress of the case, what work needs to be done by the solicitor and in what order, and at what stages reassessment of the merits of the case will occur. The duration of the case will have been discussed in relation to the tracks. A letter summarising the above matters should be sent to the client. A specimen letter can be found in Appendix B.

At this stage, the solicitor should emphasise that most contact in the future will be by correspondence or by appointment by telephone (if the client expresses a preference to telephone conference). Speedy and legible responses by the client are required, as delay in responding to queries from the solicitor may be damaging to the case. Many solicitors supply a sheet of paper and a prepaid envelope when writing to clients or witnesses. If the client has difficulty reading or writing, arrangements must be made for a reader/writer to be quickly available. Further meetings to discuss matters of importance may be arranged but it should be stressed that telephone calls, except on matters of real urgency, are unhelpful. While the solicitor can give a considered response to a letter, when there is time to think, a telephone call is likely to find her busy with other cases and without the facts to hand.

Clients need to feel committed to their case and it is, therefore, important that they fully understand the process and can properly weigh up the pros and cons of proceeding. Properly explaining procedures at the beginning helps to gain client confidence and also helps to avoid subsequent telephone calls demanding to know what is happening.

If the client decides to go ahead and the solicitor agrees to handle the case, the next job is to list the tasks requiring immediate attention by the client and by the solicitor and to set a timetable for these to be done. Tactics on writing the letter of claim (see Chapter 9) need to be considered; so for example if the claim is likely to be a small one, with a good prospect of success and easily quantifiable, it may well be better to gather all of the evidence before writing to the Defendant so that the claim can be very speedily progressed after the letter of claim has been sent.

CHAPTER 8

Urgent Action

At the first interview, the solicitor must identify any step needing urgent or immediate attention. Some particular points to be aware of are given below.

PROTECTIVE PROCEEDINGS

The solicitor must be alert to the expiry date of the three-year limitation period for commencing proceedings from the very first contact with the client. A surprising number of clients have an unhappy knack of turning up at the office with only days to go before the limitation period expires. The subject of limitation in a personal injury action is complex and is addressed more fully in Chapter 27. Basically, proceedings must be issued within three years of the accrual of the cause of action or, if later, the 'date of knowledge', though this may, in some circumstances, be extended.

Where the limitation date is fast approaching, a decision has to be made speedily about whether 'protective proceedings' should be issued. Funding arrangements will have to have been discussed in detail with the client – some after the event insurers will not cover a client where proceedings have already been issued and this should be checked so that if the matter is to proceed by way of a 'no win no fee' agreement coupled with after the event insurance, then the policy must generally be in place prior to the issue of protective proceedings.

The issue of proceedings is expensive and the client needs clear advice on the likely costs of the same. However, where there is a potential limitation problem, immediate steps should be taken to issue the proceedings and if appropriate, to defer service within the four-month period whilst further investigations are undertaken. Even where there are good grounds for contending for a later 'date of knowledge', proceedings should wherever possible be issued within three years of the accrual of the cause of action unless the other side agrees a later date for the purposes of issue of proceedings.

Under the old rules, there was often a problem in getting the county court to actually deal expeditiously with the issue of proceedings. Some courts would fail to deal with the matter on an 'over the counter' basis, and papers would sit waiting for the court to seal them with consequent arguments between parties on whether or not the matter had become time barred in the interim period.

Paragraphs 5.1–5.4 of the practice direction to Part 7 are helpful in explaining that where there is a dispute as to when the claim was actually issued by the court (it being acknowledged that it is expected that on occasions the form will arrive at the court some time before the court actually seals it) then the claim is 'brought' for the purpose of the Limitation Act 1980 when the court actually received it. For this reason at 5.4 it is suggested that the parties take care in ensuring that the court records the actual date on which the form was delivered to it. It is probably best, if there is likely to be any dispute over delivery date to take the claim form to the court by hand and obtain a receipt for it signed by a member of the court staff.

The claim form must be served within four months of issue; six months if service is to take place out of the jurisdiction (Part 7.5). There are provisions for extension of time (see Chapter 18 on Applications), but this only applies in the prescribed circumstances set out in Part 7.6. If further time is required beyond the four months and the case does not fall within Part 7.6, proceedings should be served and wherever possible, an extension of time agreed with the Defendant. Within the four months, the solicitor should beware of putting the Defendant on notice of the issue of a claim form because they are entitled to demand service.

As the particulars of claim do not have to be served until 14 days after service of the claim form (but always within the four-month validity of the claim form), there should be sufficient time in which to investigate the claim within the four months after issue.

The deadline for service needs to be entered in the solicitor's diary (both computer and, if used, paper) and filing systems. Quick work is required to consider whether the claim is worth pursuing, and, if so, to obtain all the necessary information to formulate the particulars of claim. The client should be told in writing that the claim has been issued and given details of when the claim has to be served.

The client should be advised against issuing proceedings only if there is no reasonable prospect of success on the information available, and either an attempt to find further information is clearly unlikely to be successful, or such information as may reasonably be found is unlikely to have a material impact on the chance of success. In these circumstances, oral advice should be given clearly, plainly and immediately, and reiterated speedily in writing, specifying the time limit within which the proceedings have to be issued or served.

Where the claim appears to have a prospect of success but the solicitor cannot afford to undertake it (for example, because of the costs position in a small claim track case), the Claimant must be told immediately and an explanation sent in writing speedily, advising him to go to his county court to issue his claim form within the time limit, and suggesting other sources of advice (for example, Citizen's Advice Bureau or Law Centre).

PRESERVING EVIDENCE

There will be times when it is imperative that the solicitor acts immediately to ensure that a piece of evidence remains available at trial. For example, in 'tripping' accidents, it is important for photographs to be taken before the relevant road or pavement is

.

repaired. There are other cases where vital evidence may also disappear very quickly. Preservation of the evidence, whether by photograph, authoritative report or retention of the object or document, should be in the forefront of the solicitor's mind at the initial interview.

Crucial witnesses who it is thought may die, emigrate, disappear or change their evidence, may need to be interviewed. The statements of such witnesses when written, should be signed, dated and preferably witnessed.

With an accident at work, it may take too long for consent to be obtained for a site inspection by the solicitor – let alone an engineer – in order for photographs to be taken. The client, or a colleague or shop steward, may need to take photographs at the work place. Occasionally, the client may feel it will be impossible to do this, other than surreptitiously. The solicitor should not encourage any conduct contrary to any express or implied term in the contract of employment.

Though (for example) scaffolding structures or buildings in the course of demolition cannot be preserved until the trial, the Defendant can be asked for an undertaking to preserve smaller things, such as a vehicle, machinery or documents, at least until inspection. An order for such inspection may be obtained. It may be necessary to obtain an expert's report urgently where there is concern that the relevant equipment or building may be altered, removed or demolished. This will require telephoning around the lawyer's own list of experts to find one with time available.

In exceptional circumstances, where there is strong prima facie evidence that the Defendant will destroy or materially alter relevant evidence if put on notice of a claim for inspection, consideration should be given to asking the court to make an order to preserve machinery, equipment, documents and other tangible items.

URGENT PRE-ACTION DISCLOSURE/INSPECTION OF PROPERTY

Sometimes, proceedings cannot be commenced until further documentary evidence is obtained. Where the documents are in the hands of a potential Defendant, this evidence may be obtained by an order for pre-action disclosure.[1] The Defendant must first be asked to provide the documents voluntarily, usually in the initial letter of claim. If the documents are not forthcoming within a reasonable time – usually four to six weeks though this can be foreshortened in an urgent case, depending on the number and complexity of the documents – an application should be taken out in accordance with the provisions of Part 23 (see Chapter 18) and served together with a supporting witness statement. It must be made to the court where it is likely the claim to which the application relates will be started unless there is good reason not to.[2] A similar application can be made for pre-action inspection of property.[3]

---

[1]   See CPR Parts 23 and r 31.16 and the Supreme Court Act 1981, s 33(2) and County Courts Act 1984, s 52(1)(s). For an example of the need for pre-action discovery of the medical records in a personal injury case, see *Seecharran v Streets of London Ltd*, Kemp, vol 2, V4–O17. The Defendant can be ordered to verify their list of documents by affidavit if there are grounds for believing that inadequate disclosure has been given: *M v Plymouth Health Authority* [1993] PIQR P223.

[2]   CPR, r 23.2(4).

[3]   CPR, r 25.5.

The court will order the production of the documents only where it is satisfied that both parties are likely to be parties to subsequent proceedings and if proceedings had started, the respondent's duty by way of standard disclosure would extend to the classes of documents being sought, and pre-action disclosure is desirable to dispose fairly of the anticipated proceedings, assist the dispute to be resolved without proceedings or to save costs. The words 'likely to' means no more than 'may well' be a party to proceedings and the threshold is not high.[4] The court should be hesitant to embark upon any determination of substantive issues in the case. It will normally be sufficient to found an application if the substantive claim pursued is properly arguable and has a real prospect of success.[5]

The witness statement supporting the application should go into some detail about the reasons for anticipating that there is likely to be a claim, why the documentation is necessary to assist with making the decision whether to claim them, need for urgency if such is the case, and why it is believed that the Defendant has the documents in their power, possession or control. There is no need to disclose more of the Claimant's case than is necessary at this early stage.

Where the documents are in the hands of a 'non-party' (ie a party who is not a potential Defendant), there is usually no way of enforcing the production of the evidence prior to the issue of the claim form. Exceptionally, if the non-party though innocent, has in some way facilitated the wrong in question, the court can order pre-action disclosure.[6] Once a claim form has been issued, a non-party application for specific disclosure may be made provided that the court is satisfied that the non-party is likely to have in his possession, custody or power any documents which are relevant to an issue arising out of the claim.[7] The Claimant's solicitor should first write to the non-party to request the evidence without having to use legal proceedings. The court will only make an order where the documents are likely to support the case of the applicant or adversely affect the case of one of the other parties to the proceedings and disclosure is necessary in order to dispose fairly of the claim or to save costs. Again, the application must be supported by a witness statement and specify the documents or the classes of documents which the respondent must disclose.[8]

Costs

The Claimant usually has to pay the costs of non-party or pre-action disclosure.[9] Accordingly, the Claimant's solicitors should only use this procedure when it is considered absolutely necessary.

[4]   *Black v Sumitomo Corpn* [2002] 1 WLR 1562.
[5]   *Rose v Lynx Express* [2004] EWCA Civ 447, [2004] 1 BCLC 455.
[6]   *Norwich Pharmacal Co v Customs and Excise Comrs* [1974] AC 133, HL.
[7]   RSC Ord 24, r 7A(2); CCR Ord 13, r 7(1)(g).
[8]   CPR, r 31.17.
[9]   CPR, rr 48.1 and 48.2.

INQUESTS

Where there is an inquest pending in a fatal case, it is almost always desirable to have the client represented by counsel or a solicitor. This will ensure that as much information as possible emerges from the hearing.

Legal services funding is now provided in limited and exceptional cases, but the majority of inquests will be privately funded. If a case for damages is subsequently successful, representation at the inquest should be allowable on assessment. If an inquest is to be held, the coroner should be contacted and told that the client will be represented. This can be done through the coroner's officer whose telephone number is that listed for the coroner's court.

It is occasionally useful to obtain a second opinion on the cause of death recorded in the post mortem report prepared for the inquest. For example, it might be thought that the pathologist is in error (perhaps if death by a rare industrial disease is recorded as death from some more innocent cause).

More commonly, a second opinion is a useful step if the pathologist's report is correct, but the cause of death (for example, mesothelioma) may be disputed in the civil proceedings. An independent pathologist should be instructed to make an immediate second post mortem and will supply a report which may be fuller than the original. This is obviously an urgent step which must be carried out before burial or cremation.

The law on inquests is developing fast, but it beyond the bounds of this book. It is worth noting that pre-action disclosure is available prior to, and for use in, an inquest.[10]

---

[10] *Stobart v Nottingham Health Authority* [1993] PIQR P259. There is a useful charity for those needing help, 'Inquest', Tel: 020 8802 7430.

CHAPTER 9

Preliminary Correspondence and the Letter of Claim

Most of the conduct of a personal injury case is by correspondence. In the main, the correspondence will be with lawyers and institutions familiar with the language and procedure of litigation. Clients and lay witnesses will not usually have the same familiarity with legal language and it is very important in writing to them that clear, straightforward English is used that is free from legal jargon.

The first letter to the client after the interview is of vital importance. It should annex or contain the necessary material to comply with professional standards, and state who will be dealing with the client and who is in charge of the case ultimately and to whom any complaints should be made.[1] In this letter, the solicitor should repeat her view of the prospects of success of the claim and the basis on which the court will value the claim if successful.

The way the claim is to be funded must be explained in detail and any available options discussed. Because of the stringent requirements surrounding entering into a CFA, it is sensible that correspondence concerning the issue and signing of CFA contracts and after the event insurance is kept separate from the initial client care letter, but the provisions of the agreement can be summarised in the initial letter. If the client is to be assisted under the very limited remit of the Legal Help Scheme, the statutory charge should be explained and other features summarised. The requirements of money laundering legislation should be explained, and the necessary documents proving the clients identify requested, if they have not already been obtained.

If possible, the anticipated track allocation and implications needs to be summarised.

The draft proof taken at the first interview should be enclosed with instructions given to correct and return, signed.

The correspondence will list the tasks that the solicitor intends to undertake (obtain witnesses' details, etc) and will contain a resumé of the solicitor's plan of action. A summary of the estimated costs of the case must be given to all clients in the initial letter. An initial draft of the letter of claim may be sent to the client at this stage if enough information is available to formulate the same.

---

[1] Solicitors Practice Rules 1990, r 15.

THE LETTER OF CLAIM

The letter of claim effectively 'starts' the timetable for personal injury cases although it does not have the status of a pleading. The pre-action protocol for personal injury claims envisages it being sent out to the proposed Defendant 'immediately sufficient information is available to substantiate a realistic claim and before issues of quantum are addressed in detail'.

The letter of claim, whether in the fast track or the multi track, is one of the most important letters in a personal injury action. It cannot be prepared in a hurry. Certainly, there is a balance to be struck before timely informing the probable Defendant of the claim in accordance with the protocol requirement and gathering sufficient information to formulate the letter of claim in accordance with the protocol standards.

There are occasions when a letter of claim should not be the first letter. The protocols indicate that the Claimant 'may' wish to notify a potential Defendant of the possibility of the claim without launching the formal 'letter of claim'. The protocols suggest that this may occur if substantial expenditure is likely and the Claimant hopes that the Defendant will pay for this, or when the Defendant is unlikely to know that an accident has happened. A letter indicating the possibility of a claim is not a letter of claim and, according to the protocol, will not start the timetable running.

A letter intimating the possibility of a claim and asking for further information may be appropriate where it is unclear who might be at fault, or whether the Defendant is insured, or still traceable, or indeed still exists. If the solicitor intends to notify a potential Defendant early of a possible claim then this should be done by a standard non-claim letter giving details of the date, time and location of the incident, giving basic details of why negligence is alleged, and asking for the further information required.

In some cases, the Defendant may carry legal expenses insurance that could cover the Claimant, for example, in a road traffic accident claim, the Defendant's policy may cover passengers. It is obviously sensible to ask this question in the first correspondence with the Defendant or his insurers.

FAST TRACK CASES

Where it is clear that the claim is one to proceed on the fast track, then the relevant protocols must be complied with. If they are not, then the court will expect to be given a good reason for why they have not been or adverse costs orders may be imposed (see Chapter 4 on Fast track and the protocols).

In the majority of cases, any letter from the Claimant's solicitor will be passed on to the Defendant's insurers. An early response from them will confirm their interest and many of the questions raised. If a response is received, the solicitor will have to consider a letter of claim to the most likely potential Defendant. The reality is that it is unlikely that the insurers will deal expeditiously or fully with anything other than a formal letter of claim and even then a formal decision on liability is unlikely to be forthcoming.

The protocol envisages a standard letter of claim in a pro forma format (see Appendix B – Specimen correspondence). To comply with the protocol standards it must contain a clear summary of facts on which the claim is based, together with an indication of the nature of any injuries suffered and financial loss incurred. Until medical evidence is available it is not necessary to go into great detail as to injuries and their *sequelae* – a summary rather than a thesis is what is required.

The protocols state that sufficient information should be given to enable the insurers to broadly value their risk. Details of the client's employment and loss of earnings are therefore expected to be given. If a police report has been or is to be obtained, the letter should offer to provide a copy if the Defendant pays half the fee for obtaining it.

In the letter of claim, the solicitor should list the documents she expects the Defendant to disclose. The protocol provides a standard disclosure list.

If the claim is being dealt with under a CFA, then the Defendant should be notified of this in the letter of claim as well as notification of any after the event policy.

The Defendant must be told that the letter begins a timetable and that an acknowledgement of receipt of the letter is expected within 21 days. The letter must be sent in duplicate and the Defendant requested to send the copy to his insurers. It is good practice for the solicitor to herself send a copy to the insurers if they are known.

MULTI TRACK

Although the strict nature of the protocols do not formally apply to multi track cases, the spirit of them is expected to be followed and the rules say that the court will expect to see the 'spirit of reasonable pre-action behaviour applied in all cases, regardless of the existence of a specific protocol'. Accordingly, a letter of claim should be sent in a similar format to that of the fast track letter, but with the added information that it is envisaged that the claim will proceed in the multi track.

The status of the letter of claim and response is not intended to be that of a pleading. The notes of guidance to the personal injury protocol stress that it would not be consistent with the spirit of the protocol for a party to take a point on any mistake in the letter, provided that there was no obvious intention by the party who changed their position to mislead the other party. Nonetheless, it is foreseeable that any error in the letter of claim may be the subject of cross-examination at trial on the basis of alleged lack of frankness or inaccurate memory.

The solicitor will explain to the client (usually at the first interview), preferably confirmed in writing, the effect of the letter of claim so that the client understands the importance of it. A copy of the letter of claim should be sent to the client to confirm its accuracy or amend it before it is sent to the Defendant.

CHAPTER 10

Collecting Evidence

The gathering of evidence will be in the mind of the solicitor from the moment of first contact with the client. The evidence in a personal injury action falls into two parts: that on liability and that on quantum. Some evidence will be lay evidence and some will be expert evidence. This book has been arranged to deal first with the form in which the evidence will appear at trial, ie primarily by way of a witness statement. Thereafter it deals with non-expert evidence on liability and quantum (Chapter 11); then expert evidence on liability and quantum (Chapter 12).

WITNESS STATEMENTS

The CPR dictate that evidence must be given in a witness statement which has been disclosed in advance to the other side. Consequently the drafting of witness statements is a matter of the greatest importance.

A witness statement must be signed, verified with a statement of truth and exchanged before or in accordance with an order of the court to do so (CPR, rr 22.1(c) and 32.4). A failure in one or more of these respects will usually bar the party seeking to call the witness at trial from doing so (CPR, r 32.10).

Guidelines for preparing a witness statement can be found at PD 32. The witness statement must be set out under the court heading (see Appendix A – Specimen witness statement). It must be on A4 paper with a 3.5cm margin. It should be typed on one side of the page only and where possible bound in a manner which does not hamper filing in the court. Each page ought to be marked with the case number and be initialled or signed by the witness. It should be page numbered and there is a specific provision that any numbers (including dates) must be expressed in figures. If any documents are referred to, their reference must be stated in the margin and copies annexed if not served separately.

In the top right hand corner of the first page must appear: the name of the party on whose behalf the statement is made, the initials and surname of the witness, the number of the statement in relation to that witness, the date the statement was made and the identifying initials and numbers of each exhibit referred to.

The statement must set out the witness's name, address, occupation and his/her relationship to the proceedings. It must be in the first person, be in a clear, straightforward narrative form and as far as possible follow the language of the witness (the practice direction says 'the witness's own words'). It should follow a chronological sequence and indicate which statements are made from the witness's own knowledge and which are matters of information or belief.

Each paragraph should be confined if possible to a distinct portion of the witness's evidence and paragraphs should be numbered consecutively.

The statement must be dated and (except for good reason) signed by the intended witness and it must contain a statement of truth to verify it: 'I believe that the facts stated in this witness statement are true'.

A witness statement exchanged should only deal with issues of fact to be adduced at the trial. A witness statement represents (unless the court orders otherwise) what the witness will say 'in chief' at the trial (CPR, r 32.5(2)).

Accordingly, the statement should contain only statements of material fact of which the witness has direct knowledge. The rules on hearsay evidence were relaxed by the Civil Evidence Act 1995, s 2(1)(a) (see Chapter 11).

Service of a witness statement on the other parties, together with a notice of intention to rely on specific hearsay evidence within the witness statement will satisfy the requirements of the section.

The statement must contain all the evidence that it is intended the witness will give. There is a specific power under rule 32.5(3) that the witness, at trial and with the court's permission, may amplify his witness statement and/or give new evidence that has arisen since the service of the witness statement. However, permission will only be given if the court considers that there is good reason to do so. If the solicitor becomes aware of additional material on which she will wish the witness to give evidence, a supplementary witness statement should be prepared and served as soon as possible. Delay could not only be fatal to the prospects of admitting the evidence, but on occasions to the credibility of the witness.

If a witness statement is served, but the party who submitted the statement does not call the witness, then any of the other parties may call that witness to give that evidence, or put the witness statement in under the Civil Evidence Act with leave of the court (CPR, r 32.5(5)).

Witness statements require the greatest care by the Claimant's solicitor. Although the court does have discretion to vary or override the requirements of the rules, there can be no doubt that there is a real danger of relevant evidence on behalf of the client being excluded because of some slip up by the solicitor. Conversely, great care must be taken to ensure the exclusion of all unnecessary material which could provide material for adverse cross-examination. Disclosure of statements from witnesses not ultimately called to give evidence may allow them to be used by the Defendant against the Claimant.

Where a witness is called, the court will normally treat the statement as the witness's evidence-in-chief. The witness will be permitted to give evidence about matters that have arisen since the service of the statement. Unless the court grants leave, the witness will not be able to give evidence that contradicts the statement. Once the statement has been referred to in chief, the witness can be cross-examined on all its contents.

Once a witness statement has been served, any privilege attached to it disappears, although there is a provision for the court to direct, either of its own motion or upon request, that the witness statement is not open to inspection (CPR, r 32.13) and will normally do so upon application if the statement is made by or on behalf of a child or protected party.

Disclosure of witness statements

Witness statements to be relied on can be served at any point prior to the directions order on exchange. The object of the directions order is only to stop late exchange of evidence.

There may be a good reason for early service of evidence (perhaps with the statement of claim). If the evidence is compelling, an admission of liability or an urgent interim payment may result.

Disclosure of witness evidence prior to trial is in line with the overriding objections which seek:
(i)   to ensure that the parties are on an equal footing;
(ii)   to save expense;
(iii)   to deal with the case in ways which are proportionate;
(iv)   the amount of money involved;
(v)   the importance of the claim;
(vi)   the complexity of the issues involved;
(vii)   the financial position of each party;
(viii) to ensure that the matter is dealt with expeditiously and fairly; and
(ix)   to allot an appropriate share of the court's resources whilst taking into account the need to allot resources to other cases.

Fast track exchange

The fast track timetable provides for simultaneous exchange of witness statements of fact ten weeks from the date of notice of allocation. So when the solicitor receives the notice of allocation she has ten weeks in which to interview the witness, type up the statement and get the witness to sign and verify it. Since the general rule is that time is of the essence, the solicitor would be well advised to have seen and proofed witnesses well before the timetable begins. This avoids worry and any need to make an application (with risk of costs) to extend time later.

Multi track exchange

Again, the practice directions envisage simultaneous exchange on a date to be approved by the court. Time will be of the essence and it is unlikely that, without special reason, exchange will be allowed outside of a 12-week time limit after disclosure.

Witness summons

Whilst working on such a tight timescale, it is essential that at the point of service of witness statements, the solicitor diarises the preparing and service of witness summons. Witness summons are dealt with in more detail in Chapter 22 (Preparing for trial).

WITNESS SUMMARY

Where evidence has been obtained from a witness, but not in the form of a witness statement, it is possible to serve a summary of the evidence that the witness is expected to have been able to give were he to be called. Witness summaries are dealt with under CPR, r 32.9.

This procedure is appropriate where, for example, a witness has completed an accident report form but is not traceable at reasonable expense. Permission to adduce evidence by witness summary is required. It is also necessary to bear in mind that the best evidence is that given at trial by a properly proofed and strong witness. A summary of evidence without calling the witness cannot be anything other than second best evidence and is always likely to be seen as such by a trial judge.

However, the procedure may be attractive to Defendants anxious to cut costs and to avoid their witnesses being cross-examined. In such circumstances the Claimant's solicitor should consider carefully whether to oppose admission of the witness summary and/or whether to attempt to trace the witness and take a statement.

A witness summary must contain the witness's name and address unless these particulars are sensitive for some reason, in which case the court may order that they be withheld.

A witness summary must generally be served within the period that other witness evidence is served.

It must contain the evidence if known which would be included in a witness statement and if the evidence is not known, in anticipation of finding the witness to call them to trial, the matters about which the party serving the witness summary proposes to question the witness and the source of any matters of information or belief.

WITNESS DEPOSITIONS (CPR, RR 34.8–34.12)

There is provision in CPR Part 34 for a witness to be examined prior to the trial by either a judge or an examiner appointed by the court. The person examined – the deponent – can be resident either in the UK or outside. In practice, this provision is unlikely to be used in cases that are not of significant value or complexity.

Occasions on which an examination is made by deposition are likely to include claims where a crucial witness is too ill to travel or likely to die prior to trial. Deposition evidence is likely to be regarded as more powerful, for reasons set out below, than evidence given by way of a witness statement. Deposition evidence is at present relatively uncommon.

When it is clear that evidence by way of a deposition would be beneficial, then the solicitor should apply to the court for an order under rule 34.8. The application should specify the details of the deponent and, if it is desired that the deponent produce any document for the examination, a request should be made on the application. The reasons for seeking the evidence by deposition should be stated.

If the order is granted, the party who obtains the order must apply to the Foreign Process Section of the Masters' Secretary's Department at the Royal Courts of Justice for the allocation of an examiner. An examiner will normally be a barrister or solicitor advocate who has been practising for a period of not less than three years. When the examiner is appointed, she must be provided with copies of all the documents in the proceedings necessary to inform her of the issues.

The deponent must be paid the necessary travel and loss of earnings expenses to attend on the deposition hearing. These are paid on the same scale as witness summons are paid. The examiner's travel, subsistence, and fees and the costs of the hearing are paid by the party seeking the deposition. The examiner may refuse to disclose the deposition until her fees are paid.

The deposition examination will be conducted as if the witness were giving evidence at trial. A shorthand or stenographed note must be taken. The examiner may allow the proceedings to be recorded on audiotape or videotape. The deposition itself, if not recorded word for word, must contain as near as may be the statement of the deponent.

If the deponent objects to answering any questions, then the examiner must record in the deposition or a document attached to it the question, the nature of and grounds for the objection and any answer given and must record her opinion as to the validity of the objection. The deponent can be asked by the examiner to explain the meaning of any of his answers or of any matter arising in the course of the examination.

If the deponent refuses to attend on examination then a certificate of failure or refusal to attend will be signed by the examiner and, if he had to be subpoenaed to attend, the deponent will face the possibility of proceedings for contempt of court.

The deposition itself must be signed by the examiner and any amendments initialled by the examiner and the deponent, endorsed with the time taken to conduct the examination and sent by the examiner to the court where proceedings are taking place for filing on the court record.

A deposition ordered under CPR, r 34.8 may be given in evidence at trial unless the court orders otherwise. Notice of intention to put a deposition in evidence must be served on all other parties at least 21 days before the trial date (CPR, r 34.11(2)). The court may require the deponent to attend court and give evidence orally (presuming this was not a deposition taken in anticipation of the deponent's death) and the deposition, when given in evidence at trial is treated as if it were a witness statement and will become available – generally – for inspection (CPR, r 34.11(4) and (5)).

CHAPTER 11

Evidence – Non-Expert Evidence on Liability and Quantum

Evidence gathering will be at the forefront of the solicitor's mind from the first contact with the client: evidence to win the case on liability; and evidence to maximise the damages. The possible sources of such evidence are limited in a personal injury case and the stones under which to look for it become very familiar. In this chapter, those familiar sources are considered with the exception of experts. Experts are dealt with separately in Chapter 12 because of the special rules in the CPR which apply to them.

Much evidence will be from lay witnesses and the form in which this evidence must be prepared, ie by way of a disclosed witness statement, must always be borne in mind (and is dealt with in Chapter 10).

The first interview with the client may well identify potential witnesses other than the Claimant. Where their names and addresses are known, it is best to write to them straight away, while the accident remains fresh in their minds. If the client does not know the names or addresses of witnesses, he should be asked to obtain them immediately. Any delay runs the risk of losing touch by the witness moving away or the memory of the accident fading. Near contemporaneous witness evidence is very persuasive at trial. A signed and comprehensive lay witness statement taken as close as possible to the accident date will carry much more weight than one taken many months or years later. Furthermore, the speed of the fast track (and only to a slightly lesser degree, the multi track) makes it imperative to be ready for exchange of witness statements within weeks of issue of proceedings. The aim should be, in fast track, to have witness statements ready for exchange prior to issue of proceedings.

Witness evidence may be necessary to enable a proper risk management evaluation for CFA to be performed, but except in this situation or where liability is dubious there is no reason, usually, to waste time waiting for witnesses to respond to letters to be huge and investment advice and management will need to be costed.

LAY WITNESSES ON LIABILITY

The principal lay witness on liability will of course be the Claimant. His evidence will be elicited in the initial statement.

Then, there are the people who actually saw or heard the accident, or witnessed the scene soon after or just before it took place. The solicitor must determine whether there are witnesses who can testify about the circumstances prior to the accident, remedial changes (or lack of them) since the accident, previous complaints about the situation and previous similar accidents or 'near misses'. Any evidence which will help to establish that the accident was reasonably foreseeable should be sought.

In work accidents, witnesses are usually needed to describe the system of work and the usual precautions taken for the relevant operation. Safety representatives and shop stewards, in particular, should always be asked for their views and suggestions for further leads and documents. They may have access to – or knowledge about the existence of – memos, letters, reports and minutes of meetings, including health and safety committee meetings. They may be able to supply copies, or provide the basis of an application for specific disclosure. Witnesses from the maintenance section or engineer's department should be sought if equipment may have been at fault. Managerial level witnesses are worth considering since their evidence is likely to be authoritative. However, experience shows that they are often unwilling to assist those working under them.

The solicitor and Claimant should jointly decide whether the Claimant or other colleagues should warn a potential witness that s/he should expect a solicitor's letter and the reasons for it, since many people are frightened by such things. Particular tact may be required for the family of someone killed or an employee fearful of giving evidence against an employer.[1]

Occasionally, it may be worth advertising for witnesses in the local media, at the roadside or through a union or other journal.

It is usually sufficient and, indeed most productive, to obtain the evidence of lay witnesses by means of a questionnaire, at least at the initial stages of a case (see Appendix B – Specimen correspondence). Though the questionnaire can follow a standardised format, it will invariably require adaptation to the particular case. Every page of the questionnaire should bear the solicitor's reference number and the witness's name and address. The essential information to be ascertained from lay witnesses on liability is, of course, a description of the incident, the circumstances which led up to it and its aftermath, all through the witness's own eyes and ears. The witness should also be asked who in the view of the witness, was to blame for the accident and why. The witness should be asked to draw diagram(s) (which should at no stage be disclosed to the Defendant until fully and properly considered with other information as it becomes available). Such diagrams and sketches often provide useful elucidation of the witness's description which may be hampered by lack of command of good written English.

---

[1]   Prior to the rule changes, if a statement is obtained, the court can allow it to be given in evidence (even if a Civil Evidence Act (1968) notice was required and has not been served nor a counter notice received) if otherwise it would require the witness to be called to give evidence against his/her employer: RSC Ord 38, r 29; CCR Ord 20, r 20. The rule does not apply to an ex-employee: *Greenaway v Homelea Fittings (London) Ltd* [1985] 1 WLR 234. It is not yet clear what the position is with the rule changes.

If an authoritative plan or photographs are available, they might be usefully enclosed as an aid to the witness (though some people have great difficulty in comprehending maps).

If an authoritative plan or photographs are to hand, it may be useful to include copies with the letter. Enclosed should be a blank sheet of notepaper, which, like the questionnaire, should have the witness's name, address and the solicitor's reference number typed in the corner so that it is readily recognisable when it comes back. A stamped addressed envelope must be provided.

On receipt of the witness's response the solicitor will need to weigh up whether a further questionnaire to elucidate particular matters is required, or whether it is necessary to interview the witness, or whether the information received is sufficient to either reject the witness or draft a witness statement.

If an interview is thought to be necessary, the costs implications need to be assessed. A telephone interview may be the most cost effective way forward, though sometimes only a face-to-face interview will suffice to elicit whether the witness will be likely to be acceptable in court and certainly in a claim of significant value where the issue of liability is likely to be hard fought, the solicitor should interview the important witnesses of fact face to face herself.

In all claims, the witness statement for disclosure should be prepared for and signed by the witness as quickly as possible even if not disclosed until a later stage.

A witness statement should not normally be released for disclosure without the witness being interviewed even if only on the telephone. In some cases the witnesses' letters and answers to questionnaires may be so clear, and the value of the claim (particularly in fast track) so low compared to the costs that an interview for the purpose of finalising the witness statement is not warranted, but this will be rare.

If an apparently valuable witness has disappeared, enquiries should be made as soon as possible to prevent the trail going cold. Competent and sensitive private investigators are available and very effective. In a substantial case the investment can be well worth it. It is a matter of tactics as to how soon the solicitor thinks it sensible to go to the expense of interviewing the witnesses and finalising witness statements. A lot will depend on the value of the claim and the difficulty of the liability issues. Under the personal injury protocol, the Defendant has up to three months to investigate before either admitting or denying liability. This encourages a Defendant to interview witnesses early and possibly before the Claimant's solicitor. This may not be beneficial to the Claimant's case. In any event, if liability is not admitted at an early stage, and proceedings are issued, the solicitor must prepare witness statements ready for exchange.

It is worth remembering that it is possible to take a deposition from a lay witness (see Chapter 10). If, for example, a key witness is dying, and the claim is large enough to warrant the expense, then a deposition is likely to be far more powerful evidence than a statement (CPR PD 34.3).

The possibility of a witness summary pursuant to rule 32.9 (see Chapter 10) should also be borne in mind.

THE OTHER SIDE'S EVIDENCE

The other side's witness statements when received, must, of course, be copied to the Claimant and any relevant witnesses for their urgent comments. Those comments may necessitate the preparation and service of supplementary witness statements on behalf of the Claimant. They may also suggest further lines of enquiry, further witnesses and further documents to be sought.

The Defendant's witness statements should obviously be checked for admissibility, relevance and so on. Space does not permit a review of the rule of evidence, but the rules on hearsay are worth consideration here.

HEARSAY

The regime for hearsay has fundamentally altered with the Civil Evidence Act 1995 and the CPR. The hearsay rules will need to be kept in mind when drafting the witness statements of the Claimant and his witnesses. They are even more vital when considering the other side's evidence by reason of the need to serve counter notices promptly if hearsay evidence is to be challenged. This is more fully addressed in Chapter 21, Review of evidence.

The Health and Safety Executive

In all work accidents and disease cases, it is worth writing to the Health and Safety Executive ('HSE') at the outset to ask whether it has investigated the circumstances and taken statements, plans and photographs and, if not, whether it has visited the work premises prior to the accident and made any recommendations (see Appendix B – Specimen correspondence). Because of serious understaffing, investigations are unusual, reports are short and bland, prohibition and improvement notices extremely rare and prosecutions rarer still. Employers are required to report to the HSE accidents to employees and a wide variety of other persons[2] involving more than three days off work or longer than 24 hours' hospitalisation.[3]

If the HSE has become involved, it will usually provide a statement of bare factual findings and copies of any photographs it has taken. The HSE's internal policy prevents release of its formal reports containing opinions, facts and statements until served with an order for 'non-party' discovery and certainly not whilst a prosecution is pending. Documents that may be disclosed by the HSE are: Form F155 – the factory inspector's report; Form F142 – the health and safety inspector's report; correspondence between the HSE and the employer; and Form F2508.

The Environmental Health Office

Each authority has an Environmental Health Office which deal with investigations into food safety and regulatory advice, workplace health and safety, issues to do with

---

[2]   *Woking Borough Council v BHS plc* (1994) 93 LGR 396.
[3]   Reporting of Injuries, Diseases and Dangerous Occurrences Regulations 1985, reg 3.

pest and animal control and other issues of health and public safety. Where there is an accident in a shop or a restaurant, the Environmental Health Office team will investigate and should be contacted in the same way as the HSE in respect of asking for the results of their investigations.

The police

Whether the police have had any involvement always needs to be considered. If they have, their evidence is likely to be regarded as authoritative by the court and should be sought.

Usually, the police will become involved in a road accident case if a person has been injured. The police are usually called only to the most serious of industrial accidents.

The officers who attend the scene of an accident make notes of various matters, such as names and addresses of the parties to the accident and the witnesses, car and insurance details, any witness interviews and interviews with the parties themselves. An officer often draws a rough sketch of the scene in a notebook. Where the accident is particularly serious, the police will send out one of their technical officers, who will measure skid marks, note the position of blood and debris, take photographs and make a (usually accurate) sketch plan. The police often do an on the scene assessment of the vehicles involved in the accident, noting the location of dents and other damage. Sometimes, the vehicle will be taken to a police garage for examination by a technical officer, who will report on every significant aspect of the vehicle and its performance in terms of its potential contribution to the accident.

The police report including copy notebooks, technical reports, sketch plans, photographs and statements should be sought (see Appendix B – Specimen correspondence). Special note should be taken of the MIB rules (see Chapter 33) in relation to dealing with the police and uninsured drivers.

The police will not release their full report on an accident until the Crown Prosecution Service has made a decision on whether to prosecute anybody in connection with the accident.[4] This decision must usually be made within six months of the accident. If a prosecution is to take place, then the report will not be released until its conclusion. In the meantime, for a reduced fee, an abstract of the accident report may be provided by the police together with police notebooks made up at the time.

It is vital that the solicitor checks carefully the contents of the documents disclosed by the police, especially in a complex and serious incident where several police officers will have been involved and where there is likely to be a substantial accident report prepared by the police. It is not unusual for documents to be sent in a piecemeal fashion and for the solicitor to have to press for copies of photographs/videos and other related documentation to be produced.

The police normally destroy their reports three years after the accident; therefore the initial letter to them ought to request that the report is not destroyed until the conclusion of the claim.

---

[4]   *Mallet v McMonagle* [1970] AC 166 at 176 per Lord Diplock.

The fast track protocol provides for disclosure of police reports to the Defendant upon them paying half the fees (see Appendix B – Specimen correspondence). In multi track claims, the Defendant should always be offered the police report upon payment of half the fee.

If it appears that an officer might be called to give evidence on behalf of either party, the Claimant's solicitor should always seek to interview the officer. A more detailed statement than the official one supplied should be taken, in order to assess the strength of the officer's evidence. The police usually make good witnesses in civil cases. They will always require a subpoena.

The Meteorological Office

Evidence about local weather conditions at the time of the accident or in the preceding days, or confirmation of the time of sunrise or sunset, lighting up time, phases of the moon and tides may be useful. If so, the Government's Meteorological Office is the starting point. Their reports are usually accepted without question and become agreed documents. There are other weather agencies but none have the stature of the 'Met Office'. Costs may be shared with Defendants as for police reports, though there is no express provision for this in the CPR.

The degree of localisation of weather reports is surprising to those not familiar with the service and it is often possible to get an hourly picture of weather on a particular day within a very few miles of the scene of the accident.

Traffic Control Signals Unit

In road traffic accidents where the sequence of the traffic lights are in issue, the Traffic Control Signals Unit will often provide helpful information relating to the timings of the lights and their correct sequence.

DOCUMENTARY EVIDENCE

There is an infinite variety of documents which may have some relevance to liability in the client's case. There are, however, certain classes of documents that are common to most personal injury cases. The protocol identifies most of these for disclosure in fast track claims. They are:[5]

Road traffic accident cases

Section A: In all cases where liability is at issue
(i)   Documents identifying nature, extent and location of damage to the Defendant's vehicle where there is any dispute about point of impact;
(ii)   MOT certificate where relevant;

---

[5]   Annex B of Protocol Standard Disclosure Lists.

(iii) maintenance records where vehicle defect is alleged or it is alleged by the Defendant that there was an unforeseen defect which caused or contributed to the accident.

Section B: Accident involving a commercial vehicle as potential Defendant
(i) Tachograph charts or entry from individual control book;
(ii) maintenance and repair records required for operators' licence where vehicle defect is alleged or it is alleged by the Defendant that there was an unforeseen defect which caused or contributed to the accident.

Section C: Cases against local authorities where highway design defect is alleged
(i) Documents produced to comply with s 39 of the Road Traffic Act 1988 in respect of the duty designed to promote road safety to include studies into road accidents in the relevant area and documents relating to measures recommended to prevent accidents in the relevant area.

Highway tripping claims

Documents from the Highway Authority for a period of 12 months prior to the accident:
(i) records of inspection for the relevant stretch of highway;
(ii) maintenance records including records of independent contractors working in relevant area;
(iii) records of the minutes of Highway Authority meetings where maintenance or repair policy has been discussed or decided;
(iv) records of complaints about the state of highways;
(v) records of other accidents which have occurred on the relevant stretch of highway.

Workplace claims
(i) Accident book entry;
(ii) first aid report;
(iii) surgery record;
(iv) foreman/supervisor accident report;
(v) safety representatives accident report;
(vi) RIDDOR report to the HSE;
(vii) other communications between the Defendant and the HSE;
(viii) minutes of Health and Safety Committee meeting(s) where accident/matter considered;
(ix) report to the Department of Social Security;
(x) documents listed above relative to any previous accident/matter identified by the Claimant and relied upon as proof of negligence;
(xi) earnings information where the Defendant is the employer.

Documents produced to comply with requirements of the Management of Health and Safety at Work Regulations 1999 :
(i)   pre-accident risk assessment required by reg 3;
(ii)   post-accident re-assessment required by reg 3;
(iii)   accident investigation report prepared in implementing the requirements of regs 4, 6 and 9;
(iv)   health surveillance records in appropriate cases required by reg 5;
(v)   information provided to employees under reg 8;
(vi)   documents relating to the employees' health and safety training required by reg 11.

Workplace claims – disclosure where specific regulations apply

Section A: Workplace (Health Safety and Welfare) Regulations 1992
(i)   Repair and maintenance records required by reg 5;
(ii)   housekeeping records to comply with the requirements of reg 9;
(iii)   hazard warning signs or notices to comply with reg 17 (traffic routes).

Section B: Provision and Use of Work Equipment Regulations 1998
(i)   Manufacturers' specifications and instructions in respect of relevant work equipment establishing its suitability to comply with reg 5;
(ii)   maintenance log/maintenance records required to comply with reg 6;
(iii)   documents providing information and instructions to employees to comply with reg 8;
(iv)   documents provided to the employee in respect of training for use to comply with reg 9;
(v)   any notice, sign or document relied upon as a defence to alleged breaches of regs 14–18 dealing with controls and control systems;
(vi)   instruction/training documents issued to comply with the requirements of reg 22 insofar as it deals with maintenance operations where the machinery is not shut down;
(vii)   copies of markings required to comply with reg 23;
(viii) copies of warnings required to comply with reg 24.

Section C: Personal Protective Equipment at Work Regulations 1992
(i)   Documents relating to the assessment of the personal protective equipment to comply with reg 6;
(ii)   documents relating to the maintenance and replacement of personal protective equipment to comply with reg 7;
(iii)   record of maintenance procedures for personal protective equipment to comply with reg 7;
(iv)   records of tests and examinations of personal protective equipment to comply with reg 7;
(v)   documents providing information, instruction and training in relation to the personal protective equipment to comply with reg 9;

(vi)   instructions for use of personal protective equipment to include the manufacturers' instructions to comply with reg 10.

Section D: Manual Handling Operations Regulations 1992
(i)   Manual handling risk assessment carried out to comply with the requirements of reg 4(1)(b)(i);
(ii)   re-assessment carried out post-accident to comply with requirements of reg 4(1)(b)(i);
(iii)   documents showing the information provided to the employee to give general indications related to the load and precise indications on the weight of the load and the heaviest side of the load if the centre of gravity was not positioned centrally to comply with reg 4(1)(b)(iii);
(iv)   documents relating to training in respect of manual handling operations and training records.

Section E: Health and Safety (Display Screen Equipment) Regulations 1992
(i)   Analysis of work stations to assess and reduce risks carried out to comply with the requirements of reg 2;
(ii)   re-assessment of analysis of work stations to assess and reduce risks following development of symptoms by the Claimant;
(iii)   documents detailing the provision of training including training records to comply with the requirements of reg 6;
(iv)   documents providing information to employees to comply with the requirements of reg 7.

Section F: Control of Substances Hazardous to Health Regulations 1999
(i)   Risk assessment carried out to comply with the requirements of reg 6;
(ii)   reviewed risk assessment carried out to comply with the requirements of reg 6;
(iii)   copy labels from containers used for storage handling and disposal of carcinogens to comply with the requirements of reg 7(2a)(h);
(iv)   warning signs identifying designation of areas and installations which may be contaminated by carcinogens to comply with the requirements of reg 7(2a)(h);
(v)   documents relating to the assessment of the personal protective equipment to comply with reg 7(3a);
(vi)   documents relating to the maintenance and replacement of personal protective equipment to comply with reg 7(3a);
(vii)   record of maintenance procedures for personal protective equipment to comply with reg 7(3a);
(viii) records of tests and examinations of personal protective equipment to comply with reg 7(3a);
(ix)   documents providing information, instruction and training in relation to the personal protective equipment to comply with reg 7(3a);
(x)   instructions for use of personal protective equipment to include the manufacturers' instructions to comply with reg 7(3a);

(xi)   air monitoring records for substances assigned a maximum exposure limit or occupational exposure standard to comply with the requirements of reg 7;

(xii)   maintenance examination and test of control measures records to comply with reg 9;

(xiii) monitoring records to comply with the requirements of reg 10;

(xiv)   health surveillance records to comply with the requirements of reg 11;

(xv)   documents detailing information, instruction and training including training records for employees to comply with the requirements of reg 12;

(xvi)   labels and health and safety data sheets supplied to the employers to comply with the CHIP Regulations.

Section G: Construction (Design and Management) (Amendment) Regulations 2000

(i)   Notification of a project form (HSE F10) to comply with the requirements of reg 7;

(ii)   health and safety plan to comply with requirements of reg 15;

(iii)   health and safety file to comply with the requirements of regs 12 and 14;

(iv)   information and training records provided to comply with the requirements of reg 17;

(v)   records of advice from and views of persons at work to comply with the requirements of reg 18.

Section H: Pressure Systems and Transportable Gas Containers Regulations 1989

(i)   Information and specimen markings provided to comply with the requirements of reg 5;

(ii)   written statements specifying the safe operating limits of a system to comply with the requirements of reg 7;

(iii)   copy of the written scheme of examination required to comply with the requirements of reg 8;

(iv)   examination records required to comply with the requirements of reg 9;

(v)   instructions provided for the use of operator to comply with reg 11;

(vi)   records kept to comply with the requirements of reg 13;

(vii)   records kept to comply with the requirements of reg 22.

Section I: Lifting Operations and Lifting Equipment Regulations 1998

(i)   Records kept to comply with the requirements of reg 6.

Section J: Noise at Work Regulations 1989

(i)   Any risk assessment records required to comply with the requirements of regs 4 and 5;

(ii)   manufacturers' literature in respect of all ear protection made available to the Claimant to comply with the requirements of reg 8;

(iii)   all documents provided to the employee for the provision of information to comply with reg 11.

Section K: Construction (Head Protection) Regulations 1989
(i)   Pre-accident assessment of head protection required to comply with reg 3(4);
(ii) post-accident re-assessment required to comply with reg 3(5).

Section L: Construction (General Provisions) Regulations 1961
(i)   Report prepared following inspections and examinations of excavations, etc to comply with the requirements of reg 9;
(ii) report prepared following inspections and examinations of work in cofferdams and caissons to comply with the requirements of regs 17 and 18.

Section M: Gas Containers Regulations 1989
(i)   Information and specimen markings provided to comply with reg 5;
(ii) written statements specifying the safe operating limits of a system to comply with reg 7;
(iii) copy of the written scheme of examination required to comply with reg 8;
(iv) examination records required to comply with reg 9;
(v)   instructions provided for the use of operator to comply with reg 11.

NB Further standard disclosure lists will be required prior to full implementation.

The Civil Evidence Act 1995, s 8 provides that any document admissible as evidence may be proved simply by the production of that document or even by production of a copy. No witness is necessary. The copy must be authenticated as approved by the court, but if this is done, it is irrelevant how far removed from the copy is the original.

Any document forming part of the records of a business or public authority may be received in evidence without any further proof. All that is required to prove the truth of the record is a certificate signed by an officer of the business or authority (s 9) (retained by CPR, r 33.6(2)).

Evidence such as a plan, photograph or model not contained in witness statements, affidavits, expert opinion, given orally or by rule 33.2 (hearsay) may be admitted provided notice is given (CPR, r 33.6(3)).

Following the Civil Evidence Act 1995, if a witness is unavailable, a document made by that witness may still be admitted as hearsay evidence. Such evidence is no longer inadmissible in cases commenced after 31 January 1997. All the party wishing to rely on the evidence needs to do is serve notice of the intention to rely on the document and give reasons why the witness will not be called (CPR, r 33.2). The notice should be served no later than the latest date for serving witness statements. A failure to give notice does not affect the admissibility of the evidence, but may be taken into account by the court in considering costs and the weight to be given to the evidence (s 2(4)). Much evidence in the form of documents are likely to be agreed by both sides and, therefore, will not require the author to prove the document although the rules on this are greatly relaxed. A party is deemed to admit the authenticity of a document disclosed under Part 31 unless s/he serves a notice that the document must be proved at trial (CPR, r 32.19(1)). As soon as possible, witnesses must be made ready and witness statements prepared for witnesses to prove at trial all documents needed for the Claimant's case which are not agreed by the Defendant's solicitor. Refusal to agree a non-contentious document – necessitating the author's presence in court – will, of course, be penalised in costs. Service of a notice to admit should be considered, to encourage the other side to heed the costs point.

The basis of agreeing documents must be made clear. The agreement may be merely that the document is what it purports to be, or that it is written by whoever purported to write it. Agreement in these terms is insufficient if it is intended to rely on the document as proof of the truth of its contents. Take, for example, agreement about a copy of a police officer's notebook supplied by the chief constable to both sides in a road traffic accident. It may be agreed (i) that the photocopy is merely a true copy of the original; or (ii) that it represents what the officer wrote at the time; or (iii) that what is written is the truth about what happened. Both sides need to be clear what is or is not agreed, so as to have the relevant witnesses available at trial to prove whatever is not agreed.

Many documents are almost invariably agreed as the truth, for example reports from the Meteorological Office and lists of benefits paid by the Benefits Agency.

Photographs, videos, plans and models

Photographs are invaluable. Solicitors, paralegals, clerks, clients and their relatives and colleagues should all be considered as potential photographers to take pictures of scarring, equipment, defective paving stones, skid marks, or scenes of accident, as soon as possible. The date of the photograph, as already stressed, must be recorded. At a later stage, these pictures can be supplemented by more professional photographs by the expert engineer or by a photographer.

City centres are often covered by closed circuit TV/video cameras; some operated by the police, local authorities or local businesses; most public buses in major cities carry bus cameras and it is not unusual for copies of the recordings made to be acquired by the police and/or retained by the company after an accident. Most shops and factory premises are covered by cameras. Whilst these tapes may have been erased within days of the accident, where an accident may have been filmed, it is worth asking the question of whether they have been preserved.

Videos are increasingly common for quantum purposes to demonstrate disability or to challenge credibility. They are seldom used for liability but can be of benefit to illustrate industrial processes or the changing view of a driver.[6] Filmed reconstructions of accidents can be considered, but the camera distorts reality and judges are not very amenable to this form of evidence.

Where video evidence is relied upon by the Defendant, the video should be carefully scrutinised to see if footage is missing or the sequence changed.

---

6   In *Ash v Buxted Poultry Ltd* (1989) Times, 29 November, the court ordered the Defendants to permit the Claimant to make a video film of poultry processing in a repetitive strain injury case. In *Armstrong v British Coal Corpn* (1996) Times, 6 December archive film of coal mining was admitted to demonstrate the cycle of tunnelling activities and the manner in which miners held air leg rock drills (litigation establishing liability for vibration white finger in mineworkers).

Plans and maps are useful, however, and should always be considered. Models are expensive and very rarely justified on questions of liability.

Plans, maps, models, videos, films, photographs, etc may be admitted without being produced by the maker provided notice is given (Civil Evidence Act 1995, s 9). A counter notice requiring the maker to prove the evidence may be served. Notice of intention to adduce this kind of evidence must be served at least 21 days before the hearing or, if annexed to an expert's report, at the time the report is served.[7]

LAY WITNESSES ON QUANTUM

When preparing the witness statement, it must be remembered that the statement will stand as the witness's evidence-in-chief. It is therefore essential that it covers all material aspects of the claim, as the judge may refuse or limit further evidence being adduced at trial.

As with liability, the starting point for quantum evidence is the Claimant. The initial statement taken from him will describe the immediate effects of the accident or ill health and its course since onset. It will describe the effects of the injuries on domestic, working, social, sexual and leisure activities. It will outline the treatment received, by whom, when, where and the costs of it and related to it (for example, travel). It will describe the effects and side effects of treatment. The initial statement will describe the Claimant's life before the accident or ill health, the pain and horror of the accident or onset of disease and the Claimant's state of mind before, during and since. Where the injured person is dead, those nearest and dearest must do their best to supply all this information.

These matters should be investigated very closely and not simply left to doctors. Loss of amenity should be a matter for the Claimant, though it will be supported by medical evidence. For example, a cut tendon on the second finger of the dominant hand might not materially interfere with the client's work, social or domestic life. It may, however, end his career as a top amateur darts player, his sole sport and hobby. An elbow injury to the non-dominant arm may impose little limitation on most activities and no pain except when pressed. The injury may, nevertheless, severely disrupt a Claimant's sex life. A post traumatic fear of travel in cars and buses as a result of the accident could radically upset the Claimant's working and social life.

Evidence on these matters may be brought in various ways. Interference with sports and hobbies that were an important part of the Claimant's life may be graphically demonstrated by the production of medals, cups, photographs and certificates. The effects of an accident can be supported by the Claimant's spouse, parents, siblings and close friends. The need for this evidence should not be overlooked. Work colleagues, especially managers above the Claimant, friends, neighbours, fellow sportsmen and women, school teachers, scout leaders, military officers, holders of religious office and the like should all be considered as potential witnesses.

The witness statement of the Claimant must not only address general damages, but also set out the justification for the claims for special damage; all the quantification

---

[7]   CPR, r 33.6.

is a matter for the schedule of loss. Particular care should be taken with claims for personal care, domestic assistance, DIY or gardening. The statement should state why it was no longer possible to carry out those tasks, who provided them instead, for what cost and over what period of time.

Such evidence may be taken by telephone, or interview, or by questionnaire and letter. If it appears useful for trial it must be formulated, of course, as a witness statement and exchanged in the usual way.

The employer

Where there is a loss of earnings claim, details must be obtained[8] from the client's employer (or last employer). Often in work accidents, the employer will also be the Defendant. In other cases, the employer will be simply another witness. Consideration needs to be given to the most appropriate time to obtain this information. In a fast track claim, there is a duty on an employer who is also the Defendant to provide disclosure of earnings information after the letter of claim is sent (see Chapter 4). Where the employer is not the Defendant and where the claim is capable of early settlement, a full and accurate estimate of loss of earnings may well be needed to serve with the letter of claim, or certainly prior to issue of proceedings. These occasions are likely to be where the client has already returned to work and no long-term loss of earnings appears likely. In other cases, it may be sensible to wait and see how the client's recovery proceeds before seeking information which will probably need to be updated later.

The nature of the information required should be set out comprehensively and precisely in the letter (see Appendix B – Specimen correspondence). Follow-up letters to request information omitted or to clarify items is a waste of the solicitor's time and unwelcome to the employer who has to draw up the earnings schedules. The letter should explain why the information is needed and should enclose, if it is known or suspected that the employer requires it, an authority from the client to release the information. The letter will then seek the client's gross and net weekly earnings for a period (usually 13 weeks – though this should be extended if any of the weeks were untypical) before the accident. It is useful to ask for a few – say six – weeks' figures after the return to work, to ensure that a change in pay rates has not taken place while the client has been off sick. The employer should be asked for details of all changes in rates and the dates and amounts produced thereby during the period of absence.

The employer should also be asked to confirm the precise dates of absence. It is no longer necessary to quantify any monies paid out by way of statutory sick pay while the client was unwell. Overtime earnings, bonus and pension entitlements should be specifically requested. If there is anything unusual about the pay, such as bonus or commission, or where it is difficult to understand the earnings loss, the employer should be asked to explain the position. Confirmation of the client's job title should be sought, in case this is questioned later.

---

[8]   Loss of earnings, like any other item of special damage, must be particularised and proved: *Hayward v Pullinger and Partners Ltd* [1950] WN 135; *Bonham-Carter v Hyde Park Hotel Ltd* (1948) 64 TLR 177.

The employer must be asked whether the Claimant is obliged to repay any earnings received during absence and should also be asked to supply a copy of the employment contract or other agreement establishing this. Most large employers now include a contractual provision to recover payments made to an employee whilst they were off sick as a result of a third party's negligence when the employee recovers money from that party and they will readily respond to a request for details of their continuing outlay. The solicitor should establish with the client which of them will, ultimately, repay the money to the employer so as to ensure the client's sick pay entitlement is replenished. If the payment of sick pay is a conditional loan, it should not be deducted from the plaintiff's damages but will be a separate head of claim.[9] The solicitor ignores this aspect of the claim at her peril as a large and irrecoverable claim from the client's damages is likely to spur the client into a claim against the solicitor.

Where the client's earnings vary from week to week, comparative earnings figures should be sought for other employees identified by the client as those whose earnings he believes are most comparable. These comparators may need to be called as witnesses if the comparable nature of their jobs is challenged. Witness statements may therefore need to be prepared.

Where the client has had a number of short jobs, each of the employers in the period leading up the accident should be contacted for the relevant details.

Increases in earnings after the date of trial are not recoverable as part of the future loss of earnings claims where their cause is, in effect, inflation or the change in the value of money.[10] Increases in earnings which are not the product of inflation, for example promotion or merit increases, which would have occurred but for the accident, are recoverable. The solicitor should ascertain these possibilities from the Claimant and get confirmation from higher managers, colleagues and trade union officers. For potential promotions the following must be established: the likelihood, but for the accident; the position and salary of each level of likely promotion; and the likely timespan of the Claimant achieving each level. Documentary evidence in the form of academic and trade qualifications, assessments, personnel files and reports are relevant and should be sought on disclosure. They will certainly be sought by the Defendant if such a claim is made. Wage rises prior to trial are likely to be less contentious and the employers' wages department may confirm the increases without the need to seek evidence from work colleagues.

In considering loss of earnings, the possibility of other forms of employment must be taken into account.[11] Damages can be awarded for the loss of the chance of qualifying for a particular job.[12]

It is always useful to have the name, if the client can provide it, of the person in the employers from whom wages and other details should be sought. Employers who are not the Defendant are notably bad at responding to requests for wages details. Extracting information from large employers such as local authorities and government

---

[9]   *IRC v Hambrook* [1956] 2 QB 641 at 656–657.
[10]   *Mallet v McMonagle* [1970] AC 166 at 392 per Lord Diplock.
[11]   *R v Milling, ex p West Yorkshire Police Authority* [1997] 8 Med LR 217.
[12]   *Doyle v Wallace* [1998] PIQR Q146.

departments can be very time-consuming and its helps enormously to have identified the appropriate individual to correspond with.

Where the employer is a Defendant it will be for the Defendant's solicitor to prepare a witness statement. Where the employer is not the Defendant and is providing information necessary to prove part of the Claimant's claim, if the evidence is not agreed (wage details usually are, promotion prospects may not be) then a witness statement will have to be prepared in the usual way for the appropriate named person in the organisation.

For the self-employed Claimant

For the self-employed, the Claimant's accountant is a necessary witness to show actual earnings and losses. The Claimant's prospects but for the accident, may also require expert evidence from comparable or leading figures in the field of the Claimant's work. It may be necessary to instruct an employment consultant who will carry out useful research into work and earnings prospects, even in highly specialised occupations. If such evidence is required witness statements will be required and any evidence by way of expert opinion will need the leave of the court.

For the unemployed Claimant

The Claimant who was unemployed at the time of the accident, but remains so because of the injury, requires evidence from the last employer and possibly from other less recent employers. Evidence of the Claimant's records from HM Revenue & Customs may also need to be produced. The number of years to go back will depend on the size of the loss, the length of absence from work following the accident and the period of unemployment. The evidence of an employment consultant may be needed, as well as from fellow workers as comparators, to show that the Claimant would, in spite of being unemployed at the time of the accident, have obtained work but for it – unless he can prove a concrete job offer.

Pensions

Loss of pension entitlement is notoriously difficult to compute, but evidence must be sought from the pension company or trustees, often via the employer. Thereafter expert accountancy evidence may sometimes be necessary to assess the loss.

National Insurance Contributions Agency

It is possible to write to Special Section A, Longbenton, Newcastle upon Tyne NE98 1X and ask for an employment history for the Claimant. This history will detail all employers where national insurance was paid. A small fee is payable and very worthwhile when the solicitor is uncertain of the client's working history.

HM Revenue & Customs

Revenue records may be particularly needed for casual, seasonal, temporary and other 'atypical' workers. Such Claimants may well require evidence from potential employers, trade union officials, colleagues in the same line of business of other people knowledgeable in the trade who can vouch for the availability of work, and the level of earnings which the Claimant might have achieved but for the injury. An employment consultant may be required. HM Revenue & Customs, if provided with authority from the Claimant, will provide a list of his employments with dates and earnings, net and gross. The Claimant's local office should be approached if he is unaware of the office dealing with him.

Benefits

An important part of the solicitor's job is to ensure that the client receives full Department of Social Security ('DSS') benefits. Clients will then receive the regular income to which they are entitled while off work. This is especially important, as it may be a couple of years before the case is concluded. If the Claimant fails to claim state benefits, no deduction from damages is made for failure to mitigate the loss.[13]

Employees who sustain injury or disease arising out of or in the course of their employment may be entitled to industrial disablement benefit, if sufficient national insurance contributions have been paid prior to the period of absence from work. Those who are injured permanently will be entitled to industrial disablement gratuity, assessed according to the client's level of disability. This assessment is useful evidence in itself. Clients who are injured outside the course of their employment and who pay the national insurance contribution will be entitled to sickness and/or incapacity benefit. For those who do not pay the contribution to the national insurance scheme, there will be an entitlement to income support only.

The Compensation Recovery Unit ('CRU') offset benefits. The majority of personal injury Claimants are required to offset relevant state benefits that have been paid to them as a result of their injuries against like heads of loss. An exception is a personal injury claim where the claim cannot be pursued because the instructed solicitor has been negligent and the solicitor is sued instead.

The rules are complex and have changed over the years, but the basic principle is that the compensator is the person who is liable to repay the benefits, rather than the Claimant. However, the compensator (the employer, negligent driver or whoever) deducts certain repayable benefits from the damages payable to the Claimant. The compensator has a duty (under the Social Security (Recovery of Benefits) Act 1997 and regulations made under it) to register the claim with a branch of the DSS known as the CRU. Registration is on form CRU1.

DSS benefits paid during a maximum period of five years from the date of the accident, or from the date that a recoverable benefit was first claimed in disease cases are recoverable against past loss only.

---

[13]   *Eley v Bedford* [1972] 1 QB 155.

In order to register the claim the DSS will need to know the Claimant's name, address, date of birth and national insurance number. These details will always be taken from the client when the solicitor first takes instructions and is a required element of the initial letter of claim under the protocols.

The Social Security (Recovery of Benefit) Act 1997 amended the previous scheme to enable general damages to be ring-fenced from benefit recoupment. This was a considerable improvement for Claimants who had previously found that fairly meagre damages intended to compensate them for injuries were eroded in order to pay benefits. The 'new' scheme which applies to all compensation payments paid post 6 October 1997 allows benefits to be recouped on a 'like for like' basis only, as follows:[14]

Head of compensation	Benefit to be offset
Compensation for loss of earnings during the relevant period	Disablement working allowance
	Disablement pension under s 103 of the 1992 Act
	Incapacity benefit
	Income support
	Invalidity pension and allowance
	Jobseeker's allowance
	Reduced earnings allowance
	Severe disablement allowance
	Sickness benefit
	Statutory sick pay
	Unemployability supplement
	Unemployment benefits
Compensation for cost of care incurred during the relevant period	Attendance allowance
	Care component of disability living allowance
	Disablement pension increase payable under ss 104 or 105 of the 1992 Act
Compensation for loss of mobility during the relevant period	Mobility allowance
	Mobility component of disability living allowance

This can have an important impact in settlement negotiations. Where the general damages for pain, suffering and loss of amenity is relatively low but the benefits paid are large, the incentive to go to trial on a case with a realistic chance of defeating the Claimant on liability may be tempting for a Defendant who, but for the benefits

---

[14]   Per Sch 2.

element might otherwise have been prepared to pay the general damages claim to avoid the expense of trial. In such a case the Claimant is only fighting for the generals and so the equation looks very different to him.

The CRU will issue a statement of benefits paid upon request by the Defendant (it is not generally possible for the Claimant to request a statement in other than exceptional circumstances). The Defendant will seek and serve such a statement when the matter is approaching settlement or trial. This should be checked carefully for accuracy with the client. A review of the statement can be requested, but an appeal only lies after settlement of the claim. It is often possible to infer when the Defendants may make an offer to settle a claim as a CRU certificate arrives beforehand!

When an interim payment is made the compensator will be liable to repay, at once to the DSS, any recoverable benefits in the relevant period up to the date of the interim payment. As interim payments are often paid in respect of special damages, the value of benefits against which the special damages can set, needs to be considered so as to ensure that the Claimant receives a significant sum.

Certain benefits are not listed under the 1997 Act above and are therefore not caught by the statutory provisions. An example is housing benefit. However, the courts have held that such benefits should still be offset against a claim for loss of earnings.[15]

Where the Defendant wishes to make a Part 36 payment into court, the amount paid in will be net of the appropriate benefits received. If the payment in is accepted within 21 days, the Defendant must account to the CRU for the deductions made in respect of benefits within 14 days of the acceptance. Where the Claimant makes a Part 36 offer to settle a claim, then this offer must also take account of received benefits which the Defendant will be liable to repay to the CRU. Since the Claimant may not know the amount of benefits received at that moment, it is sufficient to make the offer gross but acknowledging that the Defendant will be required to pay to the Claimant the gross sum less the value of the appropriate benefits which the Defendant will have to pay the CRU.

Attention needs to be paid to the amount of benefit that a client has received and the effect that this has on the progress of the claim. Any settlement will only stop the benefit recovery 'clock' ticking at the point of formal agreement. It is important that delays are not incurred by the Defendant in requesting a final certificate.

For further information contact the CRU in Hebburn, Tyne & Wear (see Useful Addresses). The CRU staff are generally helpful in their response to queries and will also supply a copy of their useful publication 'Recovery of Benefits' to those who request it.

Private health insurers

If the client received any medical treatment funded by private health insurance then the insurers must be written to and asked whether or not there is a contractual provision within their agreement with the client that the former's outlay is included

---

[15]   *Clenshaw v Tanner* [2002] EWCA Civ 1848.

in the claim. They should be asked to provide a copy of the relevant contractual provisions, and full details of the outlay. The insurers' response will need to be checked with the client. If benefits are continuing, the information will need to be periodically updated. At the end of the claim, if the case is settled for less than full value (perhaps as a result of contributory negligence) private health insurers are often helpful in accepting a reduction pro rata on their outlay.

Local authority departments

Where the client has received home help or other care (including, sometimes, special education) provided by the local authority, the authority's appropriate department (usually social services) must be asked in writing whether or not they will rely on any statutory or other provision entitling them to recover from the client the costs of providing that service. If so the costs to be recovered must be provided and, if continuing, updated from time to time. A clear explanation must be given to the client in the event of a positive response from the authority and the costs of the services provided must be included in the special damage claim.[16]

Other losses

Small items, such as clothing and jewellery, will usually be agreed without the need for strict proof. The loss of a no-claims bonus on the insurance of a written-off car will invariably be agreed on the basis of the insurer's letter. Other costs, such as additional trousers required because of wear from a calliper, or gloves for turning the wheels of a wheelchair, will probably need no more support at trial than the Claimant's say-so often without the need for the Claimant to produce a receipt for the repairs.[17] However, the Claimant should be firmly advised to keep all possible receipts. He should also be advised to keep a log book of all expenses incurred by reason of the injury if it is thought that we may be overlooking repeated expenses. Hidden costs such as additional heating or laundry or more frequent visits to the baths for therapeutic swims should be looked out for.

The rule is that all reasonable expenses may be recovered. This is a question of fact to be proved by the Claimant in every case.

The additional costs of home decorating which would have been done by the Claimant but for the injuries, perhaps because the Claimant can no longer raise his/her arm above shoulder height nor mount a ladder, require preferably two estimates from local decorators, builders or estate agents. The estimate should state how frequently both the interior and the exterior will require redecoration, so that an annualised cost can be calculated. Only the labour cost is recoverable, because the materials would have been needed whether or not the accident had occurred. The estimates must therefore separate the labour costs from the materials cost. These estimates are usually agreed without requiring a witness statement to be prepared and the witness

---

[16] Health and Social Service and Social Security Adjudications Act 1983, s 17.
[17] *Jones v Stroud District Council* [1986] 1 WLR 1141.by the solicitor seeking evidence before taking the next steps in preparing the case.

called. If challenge is made the letter of estimate may be used as a witness summary. Maintenance of the home (ie repairs, renewals, etc) which can no longer be performed because of the injuries are dealt with in the same way by similar potential witnesses.

Inability to maintain the family car (assuming it was maintained before the accident by the Claimant's labour) requires estimates from garages, again separating labour costs from parts.

Recovery of damages can be made for post-accident inability to tend the garden, do heavy digging or prune fruit trees, on the basis of estimates by gardening firms. If the client has had to give up an allotment or vegetable patch, the solicitor must calculate the annual purchase of lost fruit and vegetables.

The cost of other handicaps may be met in similar ways, for example, additional taxi costs can be estimated on a periodic basis by local taxi firms. Additional car costs can be calculated on the basis of estimates of the cost of owning and running a particular vehicle. These estimates are provided by the AA and RAC at a reasonable charge and are accepted by the courts. They should be annexed to the Claimant's witness statement on quantum.

Estimates of the kind listed above are usually agreed, subject to liability, or to proof of causation, or to proof of medical incapacity. Every aspect of the Claimant's life should be discussed to see what additional, and possibly hidden, costs the accident or ill-health has brought or may bring – work, travel, sports, hobbies, holidays, domestic and other relationships, domestic tasks, shopping and so forth. With experience and imagination, the solicitor can investigate these matters with the Claimant. With serious disability, however, it is worth instructing an expert who will often turn up many aspects of loss of which the Claimant was barely conscious.

CATASTROPHIC INJURIES

Much of the evidence needed for quantum in such cases is in the sphere of expert evidence (see below), but one matter which should never be overlooked is the additional costs of entertainment for a Claimant whose world has been tragically limited and whose former pastimes and work are curtailed. The claim could include the cost of a raised garden at wheelchair height, a computer and associated equipment, more videos, use of a suitably adapted car for visiting the countryside, cinemas and friends, and so on. Housing costs by adaptation or purchase are almost inevitable in catastrophic cases.

ACCOUNTANTS

In addition to the Claimant's accountant in self-employed cases, accountants may provide expert evidence on the value of a claim. This is unlikely to be required in the ordinary case and the courts are most reluctant to award costs in respect of accountancy evidence in personal injury cases. However, in complex cases, the cost of an accountant (and they are expensive) may be justified. Such cases may involve complicated dependency claims in fatal cases or cases where the recovery is likely to be huge and investment advice and management will need to be costed.

CHAPTER 12

Evidence – Expert Evidence on Liability and Quantum

The intention of the CPR is to limit expert evidence to that which is 'reasonably required to resolve the proceedings' (CPR, r 35.1).

In most circumstances, joint selection, if not instruction, of experts is encouraged preferably resulting in the avoidance of need for oral evidence from the expert. The fast track personal injury protocol provides for joint instruction of experts, but the CPR also envisage the use of joint experts in multi track claims. CPR Part 35 deals with experts.

The CPR remind experts that their overriding duties are to the court rather than the person who gave the instructions. It was the intention of the CPR to attempt to abolish the practice of each party instructing favourite experts who support either Claimants or Defendants and 'who know who are paying them'. Technically, the court becomes the instructor and therefore the expert may write to the court requesting directions to help him in carrying out his function as an expert. He can do this without notifying either party although the court is likely to, when giving directions, notify the parties of the fact (CPR, r 35.14).

The expert must summarise his instructions from the parties as given within his report (CPR, r 35.10(3)). This summary must include any written or oral instructions. Thus, if the solicitor telephones the expert, the former must be careful to avoid expressing off the record doubts or insights which the expert may feel obliged to disclose in the summary of instructions in his report. Documents, letters and attendance notes detailing the instructions given to the expert are disclosable, but disclosure will not normally be ordered unless there is doubt over the accuracy of the expert's summary.[1]

It is vital to observe the warning that if a party instructs an expert without permission of the court (ie outside of the protocol procedure and prior to the giving of directions on the matter) then they do so at the peril of both not being allowed to call that particular expert, and/or not recovering the expert's fees.

---

[1] The personal injury protocol makes it clear that either side can instruct an expert first by using the terminology 'the first party' and 'the second party'.

There is provision to limit the amount of fees and expenses recoverable in respect of an expert instructed by a party. The court can order that the expert fee is paid into court prior to instruction.

This is particularly unsatisfactory for Claimants. Without legal aid, a Claimant may be not be able to pay (or risk) the difference between the fee sought by an expert and that allowable by the court. Insurance companies acting for Defendants will not be so inhibited.

In the fast track, no oral expert evidence is allowed without permission of the court and permission will not be given unless it is necessary to do so in the interests of justice. It is not clear what such circumstances may be but it is clear that a robust attitude to evidence is generally taken in cases of small value. However, it is possible to argue that such circumstances include the situation where there is a clear difference of opinion on prognosis (assuming that the Defendants have their own expert evidence) and the matter cannot be resolved by questions in writing.

In a multi track claim, at the case management conference the court is likely to insist that experts in specialities not by then instructed by either side should therefore be jointly instructed. It is essential to consider the pros and cons of joint instructions before the case management conference, and to try to get the Defendant to accept an expert from the Claimant's list. If the Defendant refuses, he will be on the defensive when asked by the court to explain the reasons why, at the case management conference, and may be forced to agree to the Claimant's list there. In some cases (and particularly in complex claims of high value) it may be best to proceed (with abundant costs risks) to instruct unilaterally a known reliable expert so as to limit the opportunity for joint court appointment.

The solicitor needs to be well prepared at the case management conference about the numbers and specialities of experts, and the identities of those she wishes appointed. It thus remains wise for the solicitor to have well-established good relations with a set of respected experts in the usual fields. Such experts should be known to provide sensible and reasonably priced medical reports within a reasonable timescale and willing – speedily – to respond to questions arising on their evidence. They must also be of such independence and stature as to make them acceptable, in the event of joint instruction, to most Defendants. The experts on the Claimant's solicitor's list should be listed by the various expert witness guides. In any event, the solicitor should take to the case management conference copies of the CVs of any experts she wishes to instruct as the District Judge or Master will almost certainly want to see them; further, the proposed expert should detail the balance of their instructions in respect of the Claimant only, Defendant only and joint instructions and, without a very good reason, no expert who does not undertake a balance of instructions between the parties should be considered.

In the event of the Defendant refusing to agree an expert prior to the case management conference, the solicitor should be prepared for court appointment of the expert at the conference and have a list of experts in the relevant speciality that she has ascertained are willing to accept instructions in the particular case. It is best practice to offer the District Judge or Master a choice of two or more experts in respect of whom the solicitor has CVs available.

If a party discloses an expert report and subsequently decides not to rely on it, another party may use that report as evidence at the trial (CPR, r 35.1) although it is almost certain that they would have to get permission to call the expert at trial. If a report is not disclosed, then it cannot be relied upon without permission from the court.

INSTRUCTING AN EXPERT

In fast track claims

There must be compliance with the personal injury protocol. Before any party instructs an expert in a fast track case, a list of the names of one or more experts under consideration in the relevant speciality must be provided.

The personal injury protocol promotes the practice of the Claimant obtaining his own medical report and disclosing it to the Defendant, who may then ask questions of that expert and/or agree the report and who does not obtain his own medical evidence. The protocol provides that the Claimant puts forward the names of 'one or more' experts – in practice, it is sensible to offer three choices of expert names. The Defendant then has 14 days in which to reply and object or accept one of the suggested instructions. If the Defendant objects, he should put forward alternative names for consideration. If no objection is received, then the Defendant is not generally entitled to rely on its own expert evidence within that speciality. If no consensus of opinion can be reached, then the parties can instruct their own experts.

There is a joint letter of instruction to the medical expert contained within the protocols (see Appendix B – Specimen correspondence).

This is merely a suggested letter and can be amended; however the court will expect that at the very least the questions suggested in the draft letter are asked of the expert.

In multi track cases and generally

First, the solicitor must ensure that either she has the permission of the court to instruct the expert, or that the client is well aware of the possible costs consequences of not having the court's permission. Any other authority to instruct the expert should be considered too, so if the client's expense insurers require their permission to be given, this should be sought or else the solicitor may not be indemnified against the cost of the report.

Once a suitable expert has been identified, a letter of instruction must be sent. The substance of the expert's instructions must be summarised in his report (see above) so that this fact must be borne very much in mind when drafting the letter of instructions. Indeed, the letter itself may be ordered to be produced if there is debate as to the instructions on which the expert opinion was based.

The letter of instruction setting out an outline of the nature of the claim should be given together with details of the type of injury. The issues on which expert opinion sought must be specified. The expert should be asked to confirm that they can offer the relevant expertise. A check should be made of any potential conflict of interest (for example, in case the expert may be already instructed by another party). An estimate of the fees involved (including disbursements for tests or investigations needed to allow the expert to express a concluded view) and confirmation that the expert can accept the instructions will, of course, already have been obtained by phone or letter. Once it is established that the expert will accept instructions, a full letter of instruction must be sent. Best practice is to bear in mind whilst drafting it that this letter may, at some point, be disclosable in the proceedings and, in any event, the substance of the expert's instructions must be set out in his report (see above). Sent with the letter should be all the relevant documents and statements. Again it must be assumed that these will be disclosable at some point in the future.

The expert's report should begin by setting out in substance the instructions, written and oral, that the expert has received prior to writing the report.

The expert must be asked to set out in the report details of their qualifications. It is good practice to get them to annex their CV to the report. The expert will then set out the assumed factual matrix, his process of reasoning and his conclusions as a matter of opinion. If a range of views is tenable then the range should be set out as well as the reasons for the expert's preference amongst the range and must give details of any literature or material relied on in making the report. If tests or other experiments have been employed the report should state whether they have been carried out under the expert's supervision, and, in any event, the qualifications of the person who carried out any such test or experiment.

There should be a summary of the expert's conclusions.

The report should conclude by stating that the expert understands and has complied with his duty to the court to the best of his knowledge and belief and end with the standard form statement of truth – 'I confirm that insofar as the facts stated in my report are within my own knowledge, I have made clear which they are and I believe them to be true, and that the opinions I have expressed represent my true and complete professional opinion' (CPR 35 PD 2.2).

INSTRUCTING A SINGLE JOINT EXPERT

When the court orders that a single joint expert is to be instructed, then one party, the Instructing party, writes a letter of instruction which should be approved by the other instructing party (see Appendix B – Specimen correspondence).

The best practice is for the joint letter of instruction to contain the questions that both parties would like the expert to address. This will both save time and costs. It is best if the Claimant's solicitor is always the instructing party; that way she can be assured that the instructions are sensible and that the expert receives all relevant materials and she has control over the timetable.

An expert's jointly instructed report must, of course, contain all the qualification, summary and verification statements as set out above.

The court may give directions in relation to any inspection, examination or experiments which the expert wishes to carry out. This might, it is thought, include access to the Defendant's or even a third party's premises. It would certainly permit invasive investigations to be carried out on the Claimant and the solicitor should be aware of this and, if necessary, obtain a medical report or letter setting out reasons against the invasive investigation which may include the dangers or unpleasantness of doing it, or the lack of persuasiveness of the likely results.

Where there is difficulty over securing agreement to instruct an expert jointly, the court may seek to exercise its power to order that the parties pay the costs of the expert's fees into court. In this case the solicitor should be quick to remind the Master or District Judge of the inherent unfairness of pitching the finances of an unfunded Claimant against the limitless wealth of insurers.

Where joint experts are instructed, the rules provide that payment of the expert's fees and expenses is shared between the instructing parties.

CLARIFYING AN EXPERT REPORT

When an expert report is served, any party can ask that expert, once and within 28 days of service of the report, questions in writing. It does not matter if the expert was instructed jointly or otherwise. The questions must be for clarification of the report (ie not a form of cross examination) unless the court orders otherwise or the other party agrees. The questions can be sent directly to the expert, but a copy should also be sent to the solicitor instructed on the other side (see Appendix B – Specimen correspondence).

The fees charged for answering these questions are to be paid by the party instructing the expert in the first instance.

When expert evidence is both obtained and exchanged, the solicitor should send copy reports received to the client and seek his comments. In many cases these may be best noted over the phone or interview rather than asking for comments in writing. In a claim large enough to involve counsel, he should be sent copies of all the reports and instructed to consider whether and, if so, what written questions need to be asked. The solicitor must read the reports carefully and in good time to ensure that if the client raises points or questions they can be dealt with.

The last date to submit written questions to the expert must be diarised and if any questions are to asked, both the client and counsel (if involved) should be sent a copy of them.

Questions should not be asked for the sake of it. Any questions asked will form part of the report. Scoring an own goal by asking for clarification of a point that is likely to prove unhelpful to the Claimant is obviously to be avoided.

If the expert fails to answer the questions either timely or at all then the court may order that the expert is not to give evidence and that the fees of that expert are not recoverable from any other party.

Amending an expert report

Where there is a single expert report obtained under the fast tract protocol, if the first party has asked the expert to amend the report prior to service, the original must also be disclosed. Otherwise the second party will be entitled to rely upon another report. This is likely to result in a costs penalty.

EXPERTS' MEETINGS

At the case management conference, the court will provide a timescale for the experts or confer to meet to attempt to resolve their differences. This meeting will normally take place, in the interests of saving costs, by telephone conference although in a large claim or where there are issues of complexity a face to face meeting is recommended. Claimants' lawyers now need to take more time with their expert prior to the meeting so as to pin him down to those issues on which he will be immoveable and those on which he accepts there is scope for compromise and what his bottom line may be on each issue capable of compromise. Such a discussion between solicitor and expert might stiffen the resolve of the expert tempted to compromise for his own convenience but it should not prevent the expert altering his position at the meeting in the light of compelling evidence or argument the significance of which he had not previously appreciated.

The purpose of the experts' meeting is to identify the issues, which issues are agreed and which remain in dispute. The experts are encouraged to reach agreement over the issues in dispute.

The court will only order that the solicitors draw up an agreed list of items for discussion by the experts in very complex matters. Normally, the experts will be expected to draw up their own list. There will be a direction that the experts file a statement showing the issues on which they agree, the issues on which they disagree and a summary of their reasons for disagreeing. Where there is an order that the parties should provide the experts with a list of questions, it is better if the Claimant is in the driving seat and submits a list to the Defendant. Counsel ought, in a large claim or where there are very complex issues upon which the success of the claim can turn, to be involved in the preparation of this list (see Appendix B – Specimen correspondence). The outcome of the meeting as to agreed or disagreed issues can be conveniently set out by the experts by reference to the questions posed. The meeting will be on a without prejudice basis unless the parties agree otherwise and where experts agree the agreement shall not bind the parties unless the parties expressly agree to be bound. In practice the court provides that a joint statement must be served by the experts and this will bind them at the date of signature. If they resile from their agreed position the expert will have to give a very good explanation for doing so.

In preparation for an experts' meeting, the expert should be written a full letter of explanation, sent so that the expert, who may never have engaged in such a meeting, is aware of significance of it. A full set of updated evidence should be sent to the expert, and this should include the witness statements and experts' reports. Any documents that are relevant (such as updated medical notes) should be sent to the expert to prepare them fully for the meeting. The solicitor should consider having the discussion with the expert (in person or on the phone) described above. A convenient occasion may be a conference with counsel on liability if there is one.

The Claimant's expert should be warned not to accept any bullying or high-handed tactics by the Defendant's expert (which is not unknown). He should be aware that the meeting will not bind the parties unless they agree that it should. Usually, this will mean that the experts will have the opportunity to reflect on the meeting (should they need to do so) before finally committing themselves to agreement on an issue by signing the joint statement

With these matters in mind, it is important that the Claimant chooses an expert to advise who is firm and confident, though not inflexible, but this is true whether in relation to experts' meetings or trial. The dogmatic and inflexible expert is likely to have his evidence rejected by the court: the diffident or pusillanimous expert may accept his opponent's theories. It is important, though to instruct an expert who is not scared of attending trial or too busy to do so conveniently. Such an expert will have, probably subconsciously, a powerful factor pointing to compromise in an experts' meeting. An expert who is known to change their views for their own personal reasons, or who is known to report positively in the first place but then, when pushed in the witness box or meeting, changes their mind, should never be instructed in the first instance.

The client must also understand the effect of experts' meetings. He should be sent an explanatory letter beforehand and a copy of the report afterwards.

Unless specifically requested, it is probably better to let the experts meet alone and prepare their own minute of the meeting. Experts will often speak more frankly to each other in the absence of solicitors.

AN ASSESSOR (CPR, R 35.15 AND 35 PD 6.1–6.4)

While the courts have long had the power to appoint assessors to help them reach an independent view on matters, it has been almost unheard of to see an assessor in personal injury trials. The rules provide that the court may appoint an assessor to deal with a matter in which the assessor has skill and experience. It is difficult to envisage when this may be. Sir Nicholas Scott has said that this is likely to be when the court has various expert views before it and is unable to make a decision on which experts to prefer. However, this begs the question of what is left for the judge, who has heard conflicting views from experts and must make his mind up on the evidence, to do. In any event, there is a currently a lack of clarity on how an expert assessor should be appointed.

ENGINEERS AND OTHER EXPERTS ON LIABILITY

The judgment of whether and when to instruct an independent engineer comes only with experience. In the past it was common to instruct an engineer in work accidents. There are a number of independent firms of consultant engineers who do nothing but write reports and give evidence in personal injury litigation. Their experience of writing reports and giving evidence has made some of them highly respected by judges. On the other hand there has been judicial hostility to the use of experts where 'common sense' is sufficient to understand the accident and the precautions which it is said should have been taken. This hostility is evident in the CPR and under the CPR caution should be exercised before instructing an engineer and risking non-recovery of his costs. The Claimant's solicitor can feel more relaxed with larger claims.

It remains usually worth having an engineer if machinery or equipment is involved, even for the simplest and most straightforward accident. The criteria applied by some Claimants' lawyers when deciding whether to instruct an expert engineer are: if the machinery, equipment or safety precautions require explanation, plans or detailed photographs; if the system of work is challenged; or if the safety of plant or materials is challenged. Stuart Smith LJ has said: where it is necessary to show that a prudent employer should have taken precautions not taken by the Defendants, there should normally be expert evidence.[2] The Association of Personal Injury Lawyers (see Useful Addresses) has a list of engineers. Alternatively, the Law Society's Expert Witness Directory the Academy of Expert Witnesses and the UK Register of Expert Witnesses[3] gives extremely helpful resumés of the listed engineers and their particular areas of interest.

While most work related cases can be dealt with by the general consulting engineer, there are cases which require a specialist expert. Engineers are often useful in slipping cases for analysing flooring materials and coefficients of friction.[4] Engineers or chemists are invaluable where dangerous substances are involved. An architect or surveyor may be called on where building design or maintenance is at fault. Aircraft, lift, mine or marine engineers may be needed in relevant cases. The bio-engineering or ergonomics expert may be useful in relation to work stations which are often the cause of chronic disability, such as repetitive strain injury. Academics may be useful in areas of esoteric knowledge, such as highly specialised processes or substances. Handwriting experts are sometimes useful in investigating authenticity of documents.[5] Experts should refer to the recommendations of the British Standards Institution ('BSI') where they are applicable. The Court of Appeal has held that BSI recommendations represent the consensus of professional opinion and practical experience on sensible safety precautions. Though not legally binding, they are strong evidence of good practice at the date of issue.

If in doubt as to whether a particular expert can help, they should be telephoned and asked whether they have the relevant expertise. A copy of their CV should be obtained together with details of their publications and specific areas of expertise and interests. The expert who wishes to help, who is likely to keep to timetables and who has a genuine interest is almost certain to respond well to such overtures.

An engineer is usually the best choice to take any necessary photographs and to prepare plans.[6] Very occasionally, a professional photographer or mapmaker is justified.

---

[2]   *Dale v British Coal Corpn (No 2)* (1992) 136 Sol Jo LB 199.
[3]   *Law Society Directory of Expert Witnesses* – FT Law & Tax. *UK Register of Expert Witnesses* – JS Publications.
[4]   See also *Watch Your Step*, Health and Safety Executive, HMSO, 1985. This contains measurements of slip resistance for different floor coverings and the relevant legislation.
[5]   In a criminal case, it has been held that a judge cannot assume the role of a handwriting expert: *R v Simbodyal* (1991) Times, 10 October. More flexibility might be allowed to a civil judge.
[6]   Notice of intention to evidence the engineers' photos and plans must be given when the expert's report is served: CPR, r 33.6(6).

In spite of judicial confidence in the court's 'common sense' in preference to expertise, the Claimant and lay witnesses should not usually be relied on except in the simplest case to explain cause and prevention convincingly to the judge where those matters are disputed by the Defendant. This is because there is usually an imbalance of expertise. The Claimant may not be very articulate; the Defendant's managers may be more astute. Often, a Defendant employer will have 'in-house' experts, who may be senior operating personnel or engineers familiar with the relevant materials, machines and equipment to give evidence. Expert senior employees often have a tendency to defend 'their' equipment and systems of work against criticism. Often, Defendants will introduce this evidence into court by describing it as factual evidence and exchanging it by way of witness statement and, indeed, the evidence may be predominantly factual rather than opinion. Nonetheless, it may put the Claimant at a disadvantage. The overriding objectives state that the parties should be as far as possible on an equal footing. This may be a good reason for the Claimant can call expert evidence to counter defence 'factual' witnesses.

Whilst it may be the usual course, it should not be the invariable rule for the Claimant's lawyer to engage an engineer. There are many accident (though few industrial disease) cases which are obviously so simple that the court will simply refuse, under the rules, to allow expert evidence to be adduced. Or, where an unnecessary expert has been introduced there will be a costs penalty.

In road traffic accidents, the use of experts is less frequent, since usually the scope of dispute about cause and prevention is often straightforward.[7] Maps of the accident scene and photographs of the same can be easily obtained. Aerial maps can be simply downloaded and used for reference purposes. However, specialist road traffic accident reconstruction experts can be useful where the circumstances of the accident need to be reconstructed, lines of sight plotted, speed of vehicles and pedestrians calculated, or the cause of the accident established by calculations from the length of skid marks, fragments of paint, dents, the location of accident debris or blood, and so on. Ergonomics experts can provide calculations of length of stride to help determine whether a pedestrian stepped, or ran, into the road. A precedent for instructing a road traffic engineer is at Appendix B – Specimen correspondence. In a significant accident, the police themselves may well have obtained an in-house reconstruction report and in such a case, the court, at the case management hearing, may be minded to disallow the use of an independent reconstruction expert in favour of the police expert report which could be submitted in writing alone. Whilst this on occasion may be sensible, it should be remembered that the police evidence is not always infallible and that the way the police look at an accident is often quite different to the way a civil practitioner approaches blame. Where there is a fatality then the solicitor should, if possible, attend the Inquest and ask questions of the police reconstruction engineer to clarify any parts in their report which remain unclear. It is not unknown for the police expert to be wrong and the wary solicitor should be alive to this fact.

Experts' reports to be relied upon must be permitted by the court and the CPR, and disclosed. In the multi track disclosure of contentious expert reports on liability

---

[7]   Expert evidence in a road traffic accident based solely on eyewitness accounts is not admissible: *Liddell v Middleton* [1996] PIQR P36.

issues almost invariably will be by mutual exchange on directions orders. Occasionally for the purposes of an interim payment, for example, an expert report may be disclosed unilaterally by the Claimant's solicitor. Great care must be given to the wisdom of unilateral disclosure of expert evidence since it allows the Defendant's expert to direct his fire. On the other hand such unilateral disclosure may force the Defendant to reveal their own hand, and provide persuasive reason for the judge to allow the evidence at the case management conference.

DOCTORS AND OTHER EXPERTS ON QUANTUM

The rules for expert evidence are the same for doctors as for other experts. However, because of the need to attach a medical report to the particulars of claim it is usual for the first (and often the only) medical report to be produced on the unilateral instructions of the Claimant.

Medical evidence is essential, of course, in a personal injury claim on the issue of quantum. Occasionally it is also necessary on issues of liability. This situation will arise not merely in clinical negligence claims but also on issues of causation as in industrial disease cases, or in relation to the effect of certain precautions (for example, on whether head injuries would have been less severe or unaffected by the wearing of a seat belt).

Though evidence relevant to the Claimant's pain, suffering and loss of amenity is principally given by doctors, such evidence may also be provided by the Claimant who should describe the injuries, their treatment and effects in his witness statement. If, at the time of taking instructions, the Claimant's injuries are visible, photographs should be taken immediately, before bruises disappear, scars fade, or plaster casts are removed. Bruising is difficult to photograph and alongside scarring often justifies a professional photographer, though for more visible injuries 'home snapshots' may be sufficient. A medical report may ultimately render these photographs unessential, but often they will remain a useful supplement.

Even for fast track claims, a medical report is always required, even where the injury appears simple and straightforward, or where all the injuries seem to have healed with no apparent after-effects.[8] A doctor's evidence is the best and most persuasive form of evidence on physical and mental injury. Furthermore, the obtaining of a medical report guards against the possibility that both client and solicitor are unaware of some underlying damage or future possibility of symptoms or treatment, which only a medical expert could identify.

When considering the list of medical experts to put forward to the other side for potential agreement, the first question is whether the medical report should be obtained from the hospital which gave the treatment (the treating hospital) or from an independent expert (see Appendix B – Specimen correspondence). The advantage of the treating hospital is that the report may be quicker and less expensive, and written with immediate access to all the hospital records, often by the doctor who treated the Claimant and who may have noted the injuries on admission. The

---

[8]   Of course, the solicitor should be cautious about the recovery of costs when dealing with a claim that may fall into the small claims track.

disadvantages of a report from the treating hospital are that it is usually written by a senior registrar rather than a consultant. Although senior registrars are immediately junior to consultants, they are unlikely to have much court experience and their evidence may be less likely to persuade a judge if disputed by a consultant instructed by the Defendant who has more experience, recognition, and more familiarity with courts.

Furthermore, a report from a treating hospital will often be short, optimistic and ill-designed to maximise the client's compensation, which requires reviewing every facet of the way in which the injury affects, has affected and will in the future affect, the client and his life. This is because most doctors, including consultants, are not greatly experienced in the process and requirements of personal injury litigation, and they will be too busy to spend much time on the process.

Where evidence is sought from the treating hospital it is useful to identify the Claimant by hospital number as well as name, address, date of birth, date and time of admission, and the department to which admitted. It is good practice to ask for the Claimant to be seen for the purposes of an up-to-date report, and by the consultant if that is necessary.

There is almost no occasion on which a report from a GP will be adequate (save perhaps where limitation is impending). They do not have the status, nor the experience, nor usually the time to write an effective report or become an authoritative witness.

All doctors will require to see the client for an up-to-date medical examination solely for the purposes of their reports, even if the client has only recently been seen for treatment.

If the case is at all serious it is likely that an expert who has not treated the client will be required. It is therefore usually preferable to go straight to a consultant who has not been involved in the treatment of the patient.

As for other experts, the personal injury solicitor will have assembled a list of familiar medical experts in the usual fields (orthopaedic and psychiatric) who are familiar with writing medical reports for court and giving evidence. They will be accessible and understand the requirements of the rules of report writing. They will understand the need for careful unbiased consideration of all aspects of the Claimant's injuries – for example, the future likelihood of returning to the particular physical demands of the Claimant's work, or the future risk of epilepsy, osteoarthritis or any loss of expectation of life. Such possibilities will be considered as a matter of course by a medical expert experienced in litigation and the solicitor can usually rely on an omission to mention them in the report as indicating that there has been no change in the Claimant's pre-accident condition. Failure to mention these details by the inexperienced doctor may simply mean that it was not realised that such matters needed consideration.

Claimants' solicitors will quickly get to know those doctors whose reports tend to be sympathetic to Claimants and those who tend to accuse Claimants of malingering in every case (often expressed in euphemisms such as 'functional overlay', 'compensationitis', etc).

Some doctors write good reports but at the joint expert discussions or door of the court tend to try and compromise towards the Defendant's doctor's position. Some tend to write reports of unattractive brevity but can be counted on to stand by their report, and more important, to persuade the Defendant's expert or judge, in court. Others, who provide both a full report and a firm performance in court, tend to be so overworked that it takes many months to get an appointment.

Building up the necessary knowledge about medical experts will be helped by membership of the Association of Personal Injury Lawyers ('APIL'). APIL provides names of medical (and other) experts, information about them and facilitates communication about them with other lawyers. This is particularly useful in relation to medical experts outside the usual, in unfamiliar specialties or in parts of the country remote from the solicitor's usual practice. The solicitor should note on the file why she chose the particular expert and whether the expert has been used in the past. This will assist the costing master when costs are assessed.

Inevitably, good independent consultants are in great demand and it can often take three or four months to obtain an appointment for the client. They also usually charge more than hospital doctors. Many of the most used medical experts rely largely on medico-legal work for their income, whereas for hospital doctors, fees for reports are a modest supplement to their NHS salaries.

The orthopaedic consultant

The expert most commonly sought is an orthopaedic consultant, because most cases involve musculo-skeletal injury to soft tissue, ligaments and broken bones. However, other injuries and diseases may require attention from different specialities. The choice of specialist is usually obvious, but it is worth mentioning three particular areas of medicine.

The neurologist

Neurologists are, of course, appropriate for lesions of the nerves and brain. In addition, there are those difficult, but all too common cases, where symptoms of pain or loss of power in the back, legs or arms, are said by the Claimant's orthopaedic doctor to be 'difficult to explain', or said by the Defendant's expert to be simply 'compensationitis'. Damage to the nerves, particularly in an injury involving the back, may cause symptoms in the extremities. A neurologist is sometimes worth considering in difficult cases because he is sometimes able to explain the mechanism by which symptoms, inexplicable by orthopaedic consultants, may have been caused by the client's injury. A neurologist is not usually the first port of call unless there is a traumatic brain injury following a blow to the head, and then the neurologist may recommend psychometric testing by a psychologist to evaluate whether or not there is ongoing brain damage.

The psychiatrist

It should be explained to the client that a psychiatrist is invariably instructed by the lawyer where there is some mental, emotional or personality disturbance as a result of the accident or because of the injuries. This will plainly be necessary where there has been a severe reaction. However, lesser symptoms may also require a psychiatric report. These include depression, difficulty in sleeping, irritability, swings of mood, headaches, loss of concentration, loss of memory, loss of libido, lethargy, unsociability, or fear of using road transport after a traffic accident. Instructing such an expert does not imply doubts as to the Claimant's sanity. Psychiatric evidence may also be indicated where there is no organic cause indicated for the symptoms and the Claimant's genuineness is called into question. It may also be appropriate where the Claimant's reaction to the injuries appears disproportionate (for example, excessive feelings of unattractiveness because of trivial scarring).

On the advice of the psychiatrist, other associated experts may also need to be instructed, such as a clinical psychologist who may need to undertake psychometric testing – especially where there is a possibility of brain damage following a head injury.

Sometimes, the psychiatrist will say that treatment such as counselling would help. If so, the costs of this can be claimed on a private patient basis and the psychiatrist must be asked to give an estimate of the likely cost per session and duration of treatment.

The plastic surgeon

Many personal injury cases involve scarring or burns. In such cases a plastic surgeon may be instructed to consider the prognosis for natural or artificial improvement. If the latter, an estimate of the cost of treatment should be given, which may be claimed as an item of future loss. Consideration can be given to having the improvement carried out prior to trial; it may then be claimed as an item of special damage.

Continuing disability

Whether or not the client may have a provisional damages claim, the medical expert should be asked to give an opinion on whether, at some definite or uncertain time in the future, the Claimant will, as a result of the injuries, develop a serious disease or suffer a serious deterioration in his physical or mental condition. The expert should be asked to predict – even if reluctant to do so – the percentage chance of such worsening and the time span during which it could occur.

REHABILITATION

The expert should consider what treatment or further assistance should be provided to assist the Claimant to a full recovery. Types of rehabilitation experts include physiotherapists, osteopaths, chiropractors, speech therapists, psychiatric counsellors, all of whom play their part in the early rehabilitation process. Further, if an expert recommends a particular course of treatment that may be not available or only of limited availability under the NHS then the Defendant should be invited to fund a course of that treatment themselves directly or make an early interim payment towards the costs of that treatment. Consideration should already have been given to early rehabilitation as part of the personal injury protocol procedure.

Further medical evidence

As the case develops, consideration must be given to whether it is necessary to obtain other medical evidence. The views of the primary medical expert instructed, counsel's views, the specialties of the experts appointed by the Defendant and the contents of their reports may well indicate the need for further experts to be instructed. Best practice is that all necessary medical experts are identified prior to the case management conference and directions order. However, there will inevitably be times when the need for further evidence is identified only later, perhaps by way of one medical expert recommending the opinion of another expert, for example the orthopaedic expert recommending a psychiatric evaluation. If directions have already been given, as soon as it becomes clear that a further expert must be instructed, an application should be made to the court for permission to adduce further expert evidence. Such an application must be served with a supporting witness statement from the solicitor giving good reasons for why the additional evidence is necessary.

JOINT INSTRUCTIONS

The protocol letter of claim only requires an indication of the injuries to be stated (personal injury protocol 3.2).[9] The personal injury pre-action protocol requires at 3.14 that a party wishing to instruct an expert should give the other party a list of proposed experts. If the other party does not object to any on the list (or fails within 14 days to object to any) or objects to some on the list, then any of the unobjectionable experts may be instructed by the first party and the other party will lose the right to instruct its own expert.[10] These provisions apply to medical experts (like all other experts) and apply from before the issue of proceedings.[11] Hence the Claimant, in fast track cases, will always need to offer experts for agreement prior to instructing the expert, or be prepared to offer to the court a good reason for failing to do so.

It will only be where the Defendant objects to all on the Claimant's list, within the time scale, and the Claimant cannot agree the Defendant's preferred expert list, that the Defendant gains the right to instruct its own expert (personal injury protocol 3.17). In such a case, the court will consider whether either party had acted unreasonably – which might result in costs orders, or perhaps even exclusion of the expert evidence.

Where the Defendant seeks its own medical report, it is not unreasonable to stipulate on behalf of Claimant that he be accompanied during the examination by a friend or other third party though probably not if the examination is by a psychiatrist,[12] if the Claimant is nervous or the Defendant's doctor has a reputation for roughness and hostility,[13] though in the latter cases doubtless objection will have been taken to the doctor by the Claimant's solicitor. The Claimant's solicitor can object on other

---

9   CPR, r 7 and Form N1 no longer require a medical report to be served with the particulars of claim.
10   Save where the first party agrees, or the court orders, or the original report is amended and the first party refuses to disclose the unamended report: personal injury protocol 3.18.
11   As personal injury protocol 3.21 makes clear.
12   See *Whitehead v Avon County Council* (1995) 29 BMLR 152.
13   *Hall v Avon Area Health Authority* [1980] 1 WLR 481.

grounds (for example, invasive,[14] unnecessary investigative techniques; pro-Defendant lack of independence[15] in many previous reports; doctor too far away – others in the speciality being more easily accessible). Where the Defendant proposes to instruct its own choice despite objection, consider making an application to object to the same. The court's decision will be an attempt to balance the parties' interests. Under the rules, the court may wish to hear from the Claimant personally about his objection.

The client should, of course, be told the circumstances in which the Defendant is entitled to have their own medical evidence. The client should be reassured that this is not only normal, but if proceedings have not already been issued it is a good sign that the Defendant is taking the case seriously! The Claimant should be told to notify the solicitor immediately of any untoward behaviour or worrying comments by the Defendant's doctor.

In appropriate circumstances the Claimant could request a medical examination of the Defendant on pain of being struck out.[16] Such an occasion might arise in a road traffic claim where an allegation is that the Defendant was unfit to drive through an infirmity which would have caused a reasonable person not to do so. Almost certainly this request will have to be made of the court for an order that the Defendant attend for examination.

Where the Defendant instructs its own expert, it must pay the Claimant's reasonable travelling expenses, subsistence and loss of earnings in attending the examination. If the Claimant is very infirm, or is asked to travel some distance, then the Defendant should be expected to fund direct taxi expenses. It is important to tell the Claimant to keep a receipt for such expenses to be sent to the Defendant. The Defendant's expert should not have previously treated or examined the Claimant. Unless the Defendant decides to rely on a medical report, there is no obligation to disclose it. Where the Defendant discloses its report but does not use it, the Claimant may rely on it.[17]

Letter of intention to instruct an expert to the proposed Defendant

The protocol envisages joint selection of medical experts with no oral evidence at fast track trials. Some time between the letter of claim, and notification of insurers, and prior to issue of proceedings, instruction of medical experts is likely to be necessary.

As indicated above, in every case a letter (see Appendix B – Specimen correspondence) must be written to the Defendant providing them with a list of experts in each relevant area of expertise. It falls to the Claimant to organise the access to

---

[14]   In *Aspinall v Sterling Mansell Ltd* [1981] 3 All ER 866, the court would not allow examinations involving the use of a hypodermic syringe, the administration of a drug, or exploratory operations, but in *Prescott v Bulldog Tools Ltd* [1981] 3 All ER 869, the court was prepared to allow examinations involving short-term injury, provided that the Claimant was compensated accordingly.

[15]   *Lacey v Harrison* [1993] PIQR P10.

[16]   *Starr v National Coal Board* [1977] 1 WLR 63.

[17]   *Harmony Shipping Co SA v Saudi-Europe Line Ltd* [1981] 1 Lloyd's Rep 377.

relevant medical records.[18] The Defendant should be so informed and also reminded that if they object to the suggested experts then they must do so within 14 days.

The letter should warn that if no reply is received within 14 days then the Defendant will not be entitled to rely on their expert evidence in most circumstances (see above).

It is likely that some insurers will counter the Claimant's solicitor's offered experts with a list of the well-known, tired and predictable Defendant-inclined doctors. The Claimant's solicitor will have to prepare a dossier and share with colleagues in her firm and through organisations like APIL,[19] information which will provide a rational basis for rejecting unsympathetic, unpleasant and biased medical experts.

Letter of instruction to the medical expert

The protocol provides a suggested standard format (see Appendix B – Specimen correspondence). The letter could be tailored to suit the firm's house style but must contain the essential ingredients of the suggested standard. If it is a joint letter of instruction, it must say so, and, of course, must be agreed before being sent. When agreed, a copy of the letter should be sent to the insurers for their records at the same time as the original is sent to the expert.

The expert will be asked to consider the injury suffered, the treatment given, any details of pre-accident illnesses that may be relevant, and the Claimant's present condition and prognosis.

It is essential to ensure that the nominated doctor has sight of all relevant medical records (including X-rays, etc) at the time of reporting. This is clearly envisaged by the protocols. In any event, it is not uncommon for an accident to exacerbate pre-existing medical problems and sometimes clients attribute pre-existing problems to the accident in question. It has always been the case that a comprehensive medical report in the early stages can save embarrassing revisions later on. Best practice in a more valuable fast track claim is to gather the Claimant's medical records copy them and send the copy to the expert.

If there is a witness statement in disclosable form, this should be sent to the expert. The letter of instruction should also point to any specific matters the solicitor thinks should be investigated, for example, an estimate of the costs of treatment likely to be needed now or in the future. It is essential to ensure that the expert is asked these questions, especially where there is a joint instruction with the Defendant who may have no interest in finding out whether the orthopaedic surgeon thinks a course of physiotherapy or osteopathy will help the client as it may involve them paying out a larger sum by way of compensation. If possible, the expert should provide details of the likely length and cost of such treatment. The issue of rehabilitation should be considered and if early treatment will improve the Claimant's prognosis then the expert should be asked to consider what therapy will help in this regard.

---

[18]   As required by personal injury protocol 3.15.
[19]   The Association of Personal Injury Lawyers, 33 Pilcher Gate, Nottingham, NG1 1QF, 0115 958 0585 for membership, 0906 553 5229 for experts.

The expert must be asked to conclude the report with a statement of truth.

The standard letter envisages the expert being able to provide a report within weeks – this seems a very optimistic expectation given that most orthopaedic surgeons (and the majority of small value claims centre around orthopaedic injury) have waiting lists of months.

The court has a power to limit the experts' fees and it will often exercise that power, especially in fast track cases. The rules provide that jointly instructed experts are paid for jointly by the parties.

It is common for solicitors to use medical agencies to obtain medical records and expert reports in both fast track and multi track claims. It is often a condition of legal expense funding that a particular agency is used. If an agency is used, the solicitor should insist on copies of the clinical notes being forwarded to her for her file, and should note that the decision in *Wollard v Fowler* has set the level of fees that such agencies may set for certain types of clinical reports.

The letter of instruction must contain an undertaking to pay the expert's fee. The cost of a first orthopaedic report is usually between £400–£600.

No letter of instruction should be sent until the funding as between Claimant and solicitor has been clarified. If the case is funded by legal expense insurance then the authority of the funders is normally required.

It is essential that the report is forwarded to the client for comment and approval when it is received. If there are material inaccuracies, then the expert should be asked to reconsider and/or amend his report.

IN MULTI TRACK

The provisions above and the personal injury pre-action protocol expressly apply to fast track claims.[20] The provisions apply equally in 'spirit, if not to the letter' in multi track claims. Consequently, the regime outlined above should only be departed from in multi track cases with good, clear (and written up) reasons.

There are almost certainly going to be times in multi track claims where an early unilaterally instructed report is needed; perhaps to establish the likely level of compensation, perhaps to establish whether or not the matter is more suited to the multi track, or perhaps as part of the risk management process before entering into a no win, no fee agreement. In these circumstances it is normal for the court to allow the costs.

If an early medical report is obtained in a multi track claim, it should be served with the proceedings on issue under the general obligation to serve evidence.

Over the years, hospitals and GPs have increased their charges considerably to provide information. Despite the Access to Medical Records Act 1988 which provides that no more than £50 ought to be payable, more is often demanded especially to copy x-rays and it is often quicker to pay the demand rather than fight the matter. Where a

---

[20]   Personal injury protocol 2.3 and 2.4.

client has several or maybe tens of x-rays there can be a prohibitive cost in copying them. The best way forward is to ask the relevant hospital to provide a schedule of x-rays; send the schedule onto the relevant expert and ask them to tick those which they must see to provide their opinion. This cuts down considerably on the costs.

Care and treatment

Where the Claimant faces the need (or possible need) for treatment and care in the future – whether an occasional prescription for pain killers or constant nursing care and physiotherapy for life – expert evidence must be produced about the need for those requirements and their cost. The provisions in relation to experts will therefore need to be borne in mind. The first step is to procure evidence to establish the Claimant's need for care and treatment. This is given by the doctors. Evidence on the costs of such care and treatment may be supplied by the doctor, or even by the Claimant (in the simple case of a claim for a monthly prescription of painkillers) but is often best given by experts in the provision of care and treatment. This is a small and well established area of expertise in which the leading medico-legal experts are very well known in the courts. They can value precisely what will be provided and at what capital and annual costs. These experts are often former nurses and occupational therapists and will always be able to value general or specialised nursing care and the costing of equipment, etc. They will usually obtain estimates of the cost of institutional care and associated costs and may often call on specialties to deal with particular aspects of the cost of the care regime. Usually where other experts are required it is better for the solicitor herself to liaise with the other experts; these may be physiotherapists, speech therapists, occupational therapists and the like. There are also architects specialising in accommodation for the disabled, who can deal with costs of new and adapted housing to cater for disabilities. In all these areas, APIL can suggest names. A precedent for instructing a care expert can be found at Appendix B – Specimen correspondence.

The medical evidence and the evidence as to the cost of care and treatment must be both comprehensive and consistent. A court will not award damages for 24-hour nursing attendance recommended by a nursing expert, if the doctor says that only an unskilled helper is necessary for three hours a day, five days a week. Care provided by a devoted spouse, relative or neighbour on a non-commercial basis may nonetheless be the subject of a claim valued at a commercial level.[21] This is the case for both past and future care.

The cost of past or future operations or treatment required, such as the replacement of an arthritic joint or counselling, should always be claimed. The appropriate medical expert must be asked (if necessary by a supplementary question – see above) to assess these costs including associated costs (overnight stay, anaesthetist's fee, etc). Though most people are treated by the NHS, the cost of private care is recoverable if reasonable. The court disregards the possibility of avoiding this expense by taking advantage of the NHS.[22] Provided that the medical treatment is reasonably incurred

21   *Donnelly v Joyce* [1974] QB 454, reaffirmed in *Hunt v Severs* [1994] 2 AC 350: but not if the care is provided by the tortfeasor.
22   Law Reform (Personal Injuries) Act 1948, s 2(4).

(a doctor's advice is usually sufficient justification even if subsequently proved to be wrong), it does not matter if the particular treatment transpires to be unnecessary or is more expensive than other alternatives.[23]

Catastrophic injuries

The same principles of collecting evidence apply as before, but more aspects of the Claimant's life are affected to a greater extent and all need consideration. Several different medical specialists may be required. Damage to the brain may require reports from a neurologist, psychiatrist, neuropsychologist or psychotherapist in addition to experts on other parts of the injured body. The nature of nursing and therapy needs and costs will require detailed investigation. Annualised costs of care must take into account the additional costs of provision while full time carers are on holiday or sick, and the likelihood of cover being required from time to time between the resignation of one carer and the appointment of another. The severely incapacitated Claimant is entitled to go on holiday and the costs of this and the accompanying care need assessment. There must be provision for additional care if the Claimant falls ill, the likelihood of which may be increased by disability.

The huge range (too great to be dealt with here) of additional costs incurred by the severely injured are admirably dealt with in *Special Damages for Disability* by Noble and others.

EMPLOYMENT CONSULTANTS

Employment consultants, who specialise in providing evidence of earnings and job availability in whatever locality and trade the Claimant may be in, are extremely useful in many situations beyond those referred to specifically above. They are especially useful where it is a child or young person who is seriously injured and there are questions over what the child or young person would have done in their working life. Their reports are the product of skilled knowledge, research in the particular case, and their courtroom experience. However, in recent years the courts have discouraged the use of employment consultants in all but the larger and more complex claims.[24] A precedent for instructing an employment expert is at Appendix B – Specimen correspondence.

An employment consultant is classified as a non-medical expert so provision must be made by a direction to allow to the employment consultant to be called.

The solicitor should note on the file why that particular employment expert has been chosen.[25]

---

[23]   *Clippens Oil Co Ltd v Edinburgh and District Water Trustees* [1907] AC 391; *Rialas v Mitchell* (1984) 128 Sol Jo 704; Kemp & Kemp, *The Quantum of Damages*, 5-019.

[24]   Though see *Larby v Thurgood* [1993] ICR 66: employment consultants' evidence valued by the court, but no need to see the Claimant personally since material so gained by the expert would be inadmissible and waste the court's time.

[25]   For example, because it was necessary to consider the realities behind the superficial facade of future employment prospects: *Ward v Newalls Insulation* [1998] 2 All ER 690.

The employment consultant can also deal with any claim for loss of earnings capacity (ie handicap on the labour market).

CHAPTER 13

Negotiations, Offers and Payments In

The CPR emphasise the spirit of co-operation that should now pervade personal injury (and other) litigation. Nonetheless tough and adversarial negotiations will, forever, be an integral part of this work.

This chapter deals with negotiations both pre and post the issue of proceedings. It also deals with the regime of offers and payments in, regulated by Part 36 of the CPR.

Only offers made in accordance with CPR, r 36.2 will benefit from the consequences specified in Part 36, although an offer which does not comply with the provisions will still be very much taken into account in the exercise of the court's discretion on costs.

Negotiations to settle a claim may start before the issue of proceedings or afterwards and, indeed, up to the door of the court. A solicitor wishing to negotiate settlement of any or all of the parts of a claim should ensure that she has the authority of the client to do so (preferably in writing), the authority of any funding body or insurer – if required – and that any offer is made either in accordance with Part 36 r 2 or on a without prejudice basis if she does not intend it to be an open offer.

This chapter deals with negotiations at any stage.

The first prerequisite to negotiating is to have a clear view of what you wish to negotiate. Generally, this will be the value of the claim. This may not be easy. There are many heads of damages and a variety of factors which must be applied to each. If an amicable settlement cannot be reached, and the case is heard at court, the matter will be left to the judge whose identity may not be known until the day before the trial and may be mean, generous, cynical or trusting, and many aspects of damages provide a range of values from which the judge may choose.

Negotiation should not be attempted and offers should be rejected (or at least asked to be kept open) until such time as the solicitor has enough information to make an informed assessment of the value of the case.

Both the Defendant and Claimant are able to make 'a Part 36 offer to settle' his or her claims prior to the issue of proceedings. Once proceedings are issued, the Defendant can no longer make a Part 36 offer; he must make a Part 36 payment into court if he wishes to have an unfettered entitlement to rely upon the provisions and consequences of the Part 36 procedure. The court has a power to make a significant costs and interest award against a party if he recovers less than the offers made provided the offers or payments into court are made within the letter of the Rules. The downside of this weapon for Claimants is that the Claimant may need to make the opening bid – a task that has customarily always been left to the Defendant, with the result that many a Claimant has accepted with alacrity an overbid by the Defendant.

It is often the case, especially with fast track work, that a Claimant may be well advised to accompany their letter of claim with an offer to settle. Provided the offer complies with the rules, it will be on a 'without prejudice' basis and will almost certainly concentrate the Defendant's mind on settlement.

DEFENDANTS AND INSURANCE COMPANIES

Insurers will be acting for most Defendants, whether the case is a road accident, an injury at work or a tripping case. If a case is to be contested, insurance companies usually appoint from their retained firms of solicitors. In recent years many insurance companies have reduced their panels of solicitors, apparently for greater control and to increase the volume to each as a basis for demanding reductions in cost. Solicitors specialising in personal injury work for Claimants will face the same solicitors for Defendants time and again.

While there are advantages in getting to know the opposition, there are also dangers. A principal benefit is that defence lawyers' tactics and style become predictable.

A bit of give-and-take with familiar opponents can be useful to both sides. Voluntary agreements to vary time are allowed in certain circumstances under the rules and opposition for the sake of it not only produces costs penalties, but also causes the Defendant to remember the solicitor's name the next time she wants a favour!

The reverse side of familiarity is that it is more difficult to hide the fact that a Claimant may have 'a difficult case' from an insurance representative or solicitor who knows the Claimant's solicitor well. It also becomes easier to surrender, perhaps subconsciously, to the temptation of settling cases that ought to be fought. Certainly the risks of this are increased with claims funded on a 'no win no fee' basis. There is a balance to be struck. On the one hand, it is undesirable to become too cosy with the insurers and their solicitors to the detriment of the client's interest.[1] On the other hand, to become so hard with insurers that they are looking for opportunities to take every point and use every stratagem against the Claimant's solicitor is also contrary to the client's interest.

Traditionally, it has often been possible to obtain an offer to settle a near-hopeless case during discussions of several cases, where a number are being dealt with by the same firm.

---

[1]   The court warned against solicitors striking up cosy relationships (in the context of vacating fixed dates) in *Boyle v Ford Motor Co Ltd* [1992] 1 WLR 476.

It should be remembered that the court will 'encourage' the use of alternative dispute resolution ('ADR') mechanisms and a less adversarial approach. In a complex multi track claim, it is often the case that the Master or District Judge will insist on the provision of a timescale for the parties to consider some form of dispute resolution, whether by way of ADR or the less formal provisions of a round table meeting. Some insurance companies retain the control of negotiations once proceedings have begun; others hand over control to their solicitors. Where the negotiations are handled by solicitors, the insurers remain behind the scenes and the Defendant's solicitor usually has to obtain instructions from them before any deal can be struck. At times, the negotiations are complicated by the presence of re-insurers. Insurance companies often arrange for the re-insurance of large risks. Where a case is to be settled at or beyond the financial level at which the re-insurers come to assume all or part of the risk, the Claimant's solicitor still deals with the first insurer's solicitors. However, the latter have to obtain authority both from their insurance clients and the re-insurers.

Some large Defendants carry their own risks without insurance. The government, health authorities and some public transport undertakings are examples. Such organisations have such a huge financial base that they can cover all potential liabilities, without fear of being unable to meet damages claims. These bodies usually have their own in-house solicitors as well. They separate the solicitor from the rest of the organisation so that the formal relationship of solicitor and client within the organisation is preserved. The drawback for the Claimant may be that decisions in settlement negotiations often have to be decided by a committee within the organisation which meets infrequently, thus causing delay. Historically, the only way to deal with this has been to keep pressing the case forward towards trial. Thus the organisation's solicitor will be able to tell the decision-making body that delay in giving sufficient authority to settle is costing the organisation more money.

In general terms, the Claimant's solicitor should avoid becoming involved in the bureaucratic procedures of the Defendant's financial backers. This is best done by refusing the Defendant unreasonable extensions of time to seek authority to make settlement offers, and by issuing proceedings. The Claimant should also seriously consider making a well-pitched Part 36 offer (see below).

Unless the Claimant's solicitor is convinced that there is a clear and unambiguous intention to settle the case speedily shown by the Defendant's insurers, proceedings should be issued as soon as the Claimant's solicitor is ready. An advantage of this in fast track road traffic accident cases is that issuing proceedings takes the case out of the fixed costs regime. A tardy insurer who fails to make a reasonable offer to settle then has to meet the costs consequences associated with their delay. Readiness involves (as discussed in earlier chapters) the following:
(i) funding has been secured or a CFA entered into;
(ii) the case has a reasonable prospect of success;
(iii) pre-issue protocols have been fully complied with;
(iv) the case is fully prepared for issue of proceedings and the time limits which will follow.

Negotiations can, of course, proceed as the court action proceeds. As costs mount, the prospect of the case getting quickly to court is by far the most powerful inducement to bring about an early and satisfactory settlement. The solicitor who pursues a negotiated settlement without getting on with the case is doing the client a grave disservice.

The Defendant's insurers often say that it is not their policy to admit liability but they are prepared to negotiate on a 'without prejudice' basis. This attitude has to be considered carefully. It is an unwise solicitor who allows a client's claim to be delayed by attempting to negotiate settlement when it is clear that the insurers are only stalling progress.

It cannot be overstressed that delay for the Defendant is often an economic imperative. The passage of time allows a significant number of Claimants to die or become dispirited and give up their claim. Unpaid compensation damages remain part of the insurer's investments earning interest daily, and this forms a significant proportion of the insurer's profits. While it is true that, if the Claimant receives compensation, interest is payable on special damages at (usually) half the 'special account' rate, this is a future cost, which is significantly less than the actual rate of return received by the insurers while that money is invested. General damages attract interest only at the meagre rate of 2% per annum and then only from the date of service of the writ or summons. This rate even after the general fall in interest rates, remains less than the investment value to the insurer of retaining that money. Delay means profit and is, therefore, a proper business objective for the insurer.

TACTICS

There is an obvious exception to the general rule that negotiations should not hold up litigation. That is where the solicitor forms the view that the claim is unlikely to succeed. Before abandoning such a case, no matter when that view is formed, it is almost certainly worthwhile for the solicitor to apply some pressure on the Defendant, if only to seek to achieve a 'nuisance value' settlement. This means a nominal payment by the Defendant to settle, in preference to taking the case all the way through to trial to defeat the Claimant, with the risk of not recovering all actual costs. Of course, the solicitor's doubts should not be communicated to the other side, nor should the solicitor be seen to be looking for a nuisance value offer. On the other hand the solicitor must not intentionally mislead the Defendant. Now there is no legal aid for the majority of personal injury claims, the Defendant will have a clear idea as a result of early disclosure of this information, that a claim is funded with a 'no win no fee' agreement and after the event insurance. In such a case the Defendant will know the funding exists to pay their own costs if they win.

When negotiating with Defendants, the cardinal rule was historically *never* to put forward the first figure. Since the advent of CPR the Claimant is able to make an offer to settle the case,and this rule has had to be revised.

It is clear that the Claimant or Defendant who puts forward the initial figure is, in effect, setting, respectively, the upper or lower limit for the negotiation. Only significant changes in the Claimant's prognosis – or developments in the claim as it progresses that makes one or both of the Parties reconsider the liability/causation issue are likely to alter this limit.

It is almost a truism that Defendants' first offers are below the figures at which they are prepared to settle. So, a second general rule of negotiating is that the opening offer should not be accepted, or at least not immediately. An exception to this is where it is absolutely clear not only that the offer is an extremely good one, but also that the continuation of negotiations may jeopardise the offer, which might be withdrawn. This, however, is almost unheard of – see below. The Claimant's response should almost always be to make a higher counter-offer, even if the original offer seems to be above the real value of the case. However, the implications and 21-day period for Part 36 offers by Defendants (see below) must be borne in mind. This truism works both ways and a Defendant may well regard a Claimant's Part 36 offer as an opening bid. The solicitor's duty is to obtain the best settlement for the client. Furthermore, if one party sees the claim as being more valuable than the other, it is foolish to assume that the former is wrong and the latter right. There is nothing improper in seeking a higher settlement than that which it is thought a court might award. While there is a duty not to put forward untruthful or misleading matters in negotiating, there is no duty to draw Defendants' attention to errors or misunderstandings in their assessments. In contrast, there is, of course, a duty to ensure that the court is not led into error or misunderstanding.

It almost never happens that an insurer will withdraw an offer if it is not accepted. The occasions on when this may happen is when new information comes to light, for example, a video of the Claimant doing tasks that he has told his experts he cannot do or perhaps where a prognosis alters in the Claimant's favour. However, neither solicitor nor client should feel harassed or panicked by the imposition of a (sometimes quite unreasonable) deadline for acceptance of an offer, though the 21-day period (and its costs implications) for Defendants' Part 36 offers and payments in must be treated with respect, especially when a Part 36 offer is made within 21 days of the trial (see below). The insurer will not usually refuse to renew an offer where acceptance is late, unless some previously hidden weakness in the Claimant's (or strength in the Defendant's) case has been discovered between the expiry of the deadline and the acceptance by the Claimant. In every other instance, the insurer will be delighted to be rid of the case, at the offer figure, without incurring extra costs.

A deadline for acceptance of an offer (or payment in) needs to be taken more seriously, however, if further significant expenditure will be incurred by the Defendant after the deadline and thus has some reason beyond pressurising the Claimant. Often, the Defendant makes an offer before the trial brief is sent to counsel, but even if the brief has been delivered, costs are unlikely to be so large in proportion to the settlement figure that the Defendant will prefer to fight rather than reinstate an offer which it knows the Claimant will now accept. Further, in fast track cases, trial costs are fixed.

On the other hand, it is bad practice to let a (sensible) deadline expire so as to attempt to pressure the Defendant to increase the offer. It is not always obvious what the reasons are for the imposition of a deadline – it may not be simply to add to the psychological pressure on the Claimant, and ignoring the 21-day deadline for Defendants' Part 36 offers or payments in puts costs at risk. However, it is not the practice of Defendants to substitute a lower offer for no other reason than that the deadline for an offer has expired. This would be a high risk strategy for the Defendant.

Less experienced defence negotiators will sometimes make a ridiculously low first offer or, at a later stage, an unacceptably low payment into court. This should be treated with contempt and it is unwise to be lured into going back with an alternative figure unless it is a Part 36 offer to settle. By refusing to respond to unrealistic offers, the pressure is on the Defendant to put forward an improved offer without the Claimant's side giving away anything.

The Part 36 power to make offers on behalf of Claimants is a tool that requires finesse in its use. Such an offer may be usefully made at a stage of the negotiations where it is clear the Defendant is seriously interested in settlement, but its without prejudice offer(s) is considered to be low and additional pressure is required to increase it. It is never sensible for a Claimant's solicitor to develop a habit of asking for a 'high' offer by way of Part 36 and then reduce the offer two or three times as the case progresses. This is an inexperienced and weak method of litigating and negotiating on behalf of the Claimant.

Solicitor and client

Every Defendant's offer and every Part 36 payment into court, even if it is absurdly low, must, of course, be conveyed to the client, always in writing or confirmed in writing, with clear advice on its acceptability. An example can be found in Appendix B – Specimen correspondence.

Likewise, every Part 36 offer by the Claimant's solicitor must be the product of explanation, discussion with and authority by the client.

In advance of negotiations, the valuation of each element in the claim and the upper and lower bracket for each, as well as the risks of winning and losing on liability, contributory negligence and each aspect of each head of damages need to be explained to the client. Where the Claimant decides to reject a Part 36 offer or payment in with the cost implications, the client may need a degree of support as he faces the prospect of giving evidence and risking costs.

Where the client is being advised under a 'no win no fee' policy, with after the event insurance, or with the benefit of legal expense insurance, then a payment in or offer may trigger the need to report the offer to the insurers. Careful notice of the policy provisions and diarisation of the position is necessary if the policy conditions are not to be invalidated.

Some solicitors like to agree with the client a 'bottom line' which is the lowest acceptable figure. It is wise not to be too dogmatic, however, since factors can arise in preparation of the case, and indeed in the course of negotiation, which were previously unforeseen or perhaps overlooked. Furthermore, fixing a bottom line may induce, subconsciously, an inertia about extracting a higher amount, once the Defendant has made an offer at, or above, the minimum.

Of course, at all stages of the procedure the client must be kept informed. This is particularly essential in relation to negotiations, offers and payments in.

Negotiating technique

The techniques of negotiation are beyond the scope of this book. It is foolish to imagine that the books and courses available for the business skills of negotiation are of no value to the personal injury lawyer. American personal injury practitioners have given much study to these techniques.[2]

It is wise to develop more than one approach and to bear in mind not only that every negotiator has his/her own style(s) but that every case requires a style appropriate to it. In one case, it may be appropriate to take an unwavering stand on a particular figure, making it clear from the start that the client will accept only that figure, or fight. In another case, it may be wiser to demonstrate flexibility and exchange offer for counter-offer time and again, until compromise is reached.

Sometimes, it may be best to make it clear that the solicitor is running the negotiation and that the client will accept whatever is advised. At other times, it may be useful to convey – as long as it is not untrue or misleading – that, though the solicitor sees the reasonableness of the Defendant's proposal, the client is determined and will not budge.

Solicitors will sometimes feel that it is most productive to argue the minutiae of the issues, heads of claim and calculations, but in other cases, it may be useful to deal only in global figures and not to condescend to detail at all.

One technique of negotiation is to establish such a relationship that the opponent feels embarrassed to put forward an offer too far away from that proposed by the other. The Claimant's solicitor may try this technique and seek to impose such a relationship on the Defendant's representative. The Claimant's solicitor should always be careful that the technique is not imposed in reverse so inhibiting a high claim.

Negotiations may take place by letter, but this is not very effective for either side in 'getting the feel' of the opponent and the opponent's case. Such letters should be marked 'without prejudice'.[3] Negotiations can take place by telephone, and this has its attractions. A telephone discussion can be broken off easily to get time to consider the situation and think out the next tactic, and then resumed easily. A telephone discussion removes all eye contact and body language. This may be advantageous or

---

[2]   See the many articles and reviews of other material in the magazine Trial Lawyer published monthly by the Association of Trial Lawyers of America (see Useful addresses).

[3]   Documents marked 'without prejudice' which form part of negotiations are prima facie privileged from disclosure at the trial, even if they do not contain an offer. Discussions and/or documents passing between the parties with the purpose of resolving a dispute are privileged, even if the express words 'without privilege' are not used: *Chocoladefabriken Lindt and Sprungli AG v Nestlé Co Ltd* [1978] RPC 287. Conversely, the words 'without prejudice' do not by themselves render privileged a document so marked: *South Shropshire District Council v Amos* [1986] 1 WLR 1271. 'Without prejudice' in a letter means without prejudice to the position of the writer of it, if the terms proposed therein are not accepted. If the terms (or some of them, if severable) are accepted, an enforceable contract may be established. The court can look at the correspondence to decide if this is so: *Tomlin v Standard Telephones and Cables Ltd* [1969] 1 WLR 1378. The parties can use a form of words that enables the 'without prejudice' correspondence to be referred to, even though no concluded agreement is reached. Conversely, the parties may exclude reference to such correspondence, even where an agreement is reached. The privilege does not depend on the existence of proceedings: *Rush and Tompkins v GLC* [1989] AC 1280. If one party switches from 'without prejudice' to open negotiations, s/he must make the change clear to the other side. It might not be enough to use the word 'open': *Cheddar Valley Engineering Ltd v Chaddlewood Homes Ltd* [1992] 1 WLR 820.

disadvantageous, according to the personality and skill of the solicitor and the opponent. The Claimant's solicitor must consider in each case the comparative advantages of each method.

Insurers often suggest meeting to discuss cases. This can be useful, but it is obviously necessary for the solicitor to be on top of every aspect of the case and its calculations. A convention which should always be insisted on is that such a meeting should take place in the Claimant's solicitor's own office. This has the benefit that she is on home territory and can control the layout, environment and timing so as to have maximum psychological advantage.

At whatever stage negotiations occur, the solicitor should try not to be caught off guard by the Defendant's representative. If the latter telephones unexpectedly to talk about a settlement, the Claimant's solicitor should call back later, after the file has been re-read, or should simply listen to the proposal and refuse to react in any way, saying that instructions need to be taken before any response is made. Time can thus be taken for a considered response. If the Defendant's insurers arrive at a meeting with a video unseen by the Claimant's solicitor, the meeting should be aborted to give the solicitor time to see and consider the video, and take instructions.

The Claimant's solicitor should not be harassed into putting forward a figure before she has fully valued the case. An unprepared valuation might be regretted later. No agreements must be reached without the client's confirmation of the same. A clear note of any meeting must be kept on the file to record what was said.

It goes without saying that the solicitor must resist any temptation to advise settlement of a case either to reduce workloads or to ensure that costs are paid more quickly. There are particular ethical difficulties when advising clients under a 'no win no fee' agreement (see Chapter 6).

Solicitor and counsel

Generally, it is the solicitor's job to conduct the negotiations up to delivery of the brief. An exception to this is where there is to be a joint round table meeting between solicitors, insurers and Counsel with an attempt to settle the claim before trial. If counsel has been involved and is to conduct the trial, Counsel should be kept abreast of events, especially in the months leading up to the trial. On the eve of trial, counsel will usually take over negotiating with the other side's counsel, but the team work developed prior to the hearing should continue (see Chapter 22 on Preparing for trial).

In some cases, it is an effective technique to hand over negotiations to counsel, perhaps in the fortnight or so before trial or on an appropriate interlocutory hearing, to deal with the opposing barrister. If counsel is delegated to negotiate, it is, of course, vital that the solicitor refuses to discuss anything with the Defendant's solicitor which may affect those negotiations. There can only ever be one negotiator at any time, otherwise one may undermine the other.

It should be unnecessary to remind counsel of the need to obtain instructions from the client before agreeing any settlement. This is counsel's duty, but it has happened that inexperienced counsel has assumed authority to reach a settlement within a certain bracket although such authority has not in fact been given. A cautious solicitor may therefore wish to remind counsel unknown to her of this duty. Counsel should always seek the views of the instructing solicitor and the client whilst negotiating. Three heads are better than one, both as to the advisability of settlement at a particular figure and on the tactics to adopt.

Counsel's advice is often required on Part 36 offers, particularly those made by the Claimant. The possibility of seeking such advice should be borne in mind by every Claimant's solicitor.

Part 36 offers by Claimants

Historically, the development of personal injury practice positively discouraged the Claimant from making the first offer to settle a claim whether by way of compromise of a part of the liability issue in a case, or in terms of its full value. The ability of the Claimant to make a Part 36 offer (which did not exist pre-CPR)[4] has changed the landscape. Whilst Part 36 offers may be made by either side, this chapter focuses particularly on their use by Claimants. A Part 36 offer can only be made once the claim has been valued by the solicitor. It is therefore particularly apt for use in fast track cases, since such cases have to be fully prepared before issue in order to be able to comply with the very strict time limits. Part 36 procedure enables one party, at any time during the conduct of the claim, to offer to accept a certain sum to settle the whole, or any identifiable part of a claim. The benefit of a Part 36 offer is that it puts the opponent on risk as to costs if the offer is rejected and the damages awarded are lower than the offer. On the other hand, if the damages award is higher than the rejected offer, the party making the offer is exposed to the usual risk of an order for costs against him (see rule 36.10).

Proceedings do not have to be issued for a Part 36 offer to be made. Part 36 offers can be made both in the run up to and during the course of trial, subject to special rules (see below). A Part 36 offer is treated as 'without prejudice save as to costs'. The offer can be made on behalf of a child or patient, but the solicitor must ensure (as in all cases) that the appropriate consents are obtained prior to making an offer. It would be unwise (verging on negligent) to offer to attempt to settle a child or patient's claim, if it is a substantial one, without counsel's opinion on the matter and where there is a proposed settlement on behalf of a child or patient the court's approval of the settlement must generally be obtained.

Where there is likely to be a finding of contributory negligence by the Claimant, this should be considered when making a Part 36 offer, especially where there is a subrogated clause for recovery of benefits such as payments made by a private health insurer. Often, these institutions will agree to accept a reduction in their outlay in such circumstances, and they should be approached and requested to accept a reduction prior to the offer being made.

---

[4] The Part 36 offer supersedes the use by Claimants of the *Calderbank* offer (from *Calderbank v Calderbank* [1976] Fam 93), which curiously was rarely used by Claimants.

A Part 36 offer cannot be made in a small track claim (CPR, r 27.2(g)). It can be made on a counterclaim and in an appeal proceeding. Recoverable benefits under the recovery of benefits provisions must be considered (see Chapter 11).

The Part 36 offer must be in writing, state on its face that it is intended to have the consequences of Part 36 and state whether it relates to the whole of the claim or identify to which part it relates (CPR, r 36.2(2)). It may be made using Form N242A. It must express whether it includes interest (the presumption will be that it does). Provided it is made not less than 21 days before the start of the trial it must remain open for 21 days and the offer must so state (CPR, r 36.2). The other party can require clarification of an unclear Part 36 offer within seven days of service and apply to the court if it remains unclear (CPR, r 36.8).

The offer is made when it is served on the other party (CPR, r 36.7). The offer may be accepted at any time (whether or not the party making the offer has subsequently made a different offer) unless the offeror has served a notice of withdrawal (CPR, 36.9(2)). The court's permission is not required to accept a Part 36 offer unless there are multiple Defendants, deductible benefits have been paid to the Claimant since the date of the offer and more than 21 days have elapsed, an apportionment is required or the trial has started (CPR, r 36.9(3)). If accepted within the 21-day period, the Claimant will be entitled to the costs of proceedings up to the date of the Defendant serving its notice of acceptance (CPR, r 36.10). If the offer is accepted after the expiration of the 21-day period or the offer that was accepted was made less than 21 days before the start of the trial, then the parties must agree the liability for costs. If not, the court will decide who should bear the costs (CPR, r 36.10(4)).

Once the offer is accepted, the claim is stayed. Obviously, if the offer relates to part only of the claim, it is only that part of the claim that is stayed. If approval of the court is required before a settlement can be binding (ie the case of a child or protected person), the stay takes effect only when the approval has been given (CPR, r 36.11).

If the Defendant rejects the Claimant's offer to settle and is awarded more than the offer by the court, then the Claimant will, unless the court considers it unjust to do so (CPR, r 36.14(3)), be awarded interest on the whole or any part of the award at a rate not exceeding 10% above base rate for some or all of the period starting with the latest date on which the Defendant could have accepted the offer without the court's permission. The court also has the power to award indemnity costs and interest on those costs at a rate not exceeding 10% above base rate. The court's award of costs where the Claimant beats the Defendant's offer takes into account a variety of factors (CPR, r 36.14(4)) including the terms of the offer, the stage at which it was made and the conduct of the parties in relation to the provision of information relevant to the offer. It is possible to make an offer when there are less than 21 days before the trial. If costs are agreed then the sum can be accepted. If costs are not agreed, or if the trial has actually begun then the court must give permission to accept the offer and will decide where liability for costs falls.

A Part 36 offer remains open indefinitely, though the automatic costs consequences apply only to acceptance within 21 days. If the intention is that the offer is to lapse after the 21-day time period then the period after which it is to lapse must be specified, either within the offer letter or in writing at a later time. It is wise to consider withdrawing the offer after a certain time period in case of developments within the case that alter the value of the same.

A Part 36 offer can be 'improved on' – the sum proposed may be increased or decreased. Notice of this must be served on the other side for it to be effective.

Special provisions apply where the Claimant wishes to accept a Part 36 offer made by one or more, but not all, of a number of Defendants if the Defendants are sued jointly or, in the alternative, an offer accepted by one will necessitate the Claimant's discontinuance against the other Defendants together with consideration of provision for their costs (CPR, r 36.12).This should be carefully considered by the Claimant as success against one Defendant may be interpreted as 'loss' against another; this could provoke serious costs problems where there is a 'no win no fee' agreement (see Chapter 5 on Funding). If the Defendants are alleged to have several liability, then the offer will be pitched accordingly so that if one Defendant accepts, the action may continue against the others (CPR, r 36.12(3)).

Part 36 offers by Defendants

Defendants too can make use of the Part 36 offer procedure.

Prior to 6 April 2007, the rules provided that, post issue of proceedings, a Defendant who wanted to make an offer under Part 36 should pay into court any sum offered by way of a Part 36 notice to settle the claim. On that date, the rules were amended and there is no longer the requirement that money is actually paid into court.

A Part 36 offer by the Defendant must also be made in writing. It must state whether it relates to the whole of the claim or to part of it, or to an issue that arises in it and, if so, to which part or issue. It must state whether it takes into account any counterclaim (CPR, r.36.2(2)). It must clearly state the amount of the offer, and may offer a lump sum, or periodical payments, or both a lump sum and periodical payments (CPR, r.36.5). If it makes an offer for future pecuniary loss, it must state the amount offered by a lump sum, and may state what part of the lump sum relates to damages for future pecuniary loss. If there is an offer for periodical payments, it must state the amount and duration of the payments, and the amount of substantial capital purchases and give details of the funding of the payments. It will be treated as offering a sum inclusive of interest – unless it expresses otherwise – to the last date upon which the offer can be accepted. It must state whether or not the offer is made without regard to liability for recoverable benefits under the Social Security (Recovery of Benefits) Act 1997 or whether it is intended to include deductible benefits. If it includes deductible benefits, it must state the gross amount of compensation[5] and the name and amount of any benefit by which that gross amount is reduced in accordance with the Social Security (Recovery of Benefits) Act 1997. It must also state the net amount of such deductions which have been made.

If a Defendant has applied for (but not received) a recoupable benefits certificate, a Part 36 offer may be made and, as long as a Part 36 payment is made within seven days of receiving the certificate, the Part 36 costs consequences apply (CPR, r 36.15).

---

[5]   In a road traffic accident, if the Defendant pays hospital expenses direct under s 157 of the Road Traffic Act 1988, it must notify the court and the parties: 36 PD, para 11.2.

Where further deductible benefits have accrued since the Part 36 offer was made and the court's permission to accept the Part 36 offer is requested, the court may direct that the amount of the offer payable to the Claimant shall be reduced by a sum equivalent to the deductible benefits paid to the Claimant since the date of the offer.

Practitioners need to take particular care when assessing an offer to settle where there are recoupable benefits. Rule 36.14(1) provides that a Claimant fails to better a Part 36 payment if he fails to obtain judgment for more than the gross sum specified in the Part 36 notice. However, in a recent case, the Court of Appeal said that the Defendant cannot rely upon that provision to circumvent the Claimant's entitlement to recover his general damages in full.

If the Claimant rejects a Defendant's offer (wins the case, but receives an award less than the offer and payment to settle by the court), then the court will order the Claimant to pay any costs incurred by the Defendant after the latest date on which the payment or offer could have been accepted without the court's approval (CPR, r 36.14(2)). Generally, this will mean from the expiration of 21 days after notice of the offer was given.

It is also important to note that just because a Claimant beats the Defendant's Part 36 offer, it does not necessarily result in an automatic entitlement to costs as used to be the case. CPR 36.14(1)(a) refers to whether a Claimant 'fails to obtain a judgment more *advantageous* than a defendant's Part 36 offer'. In deciding whether a judgment is in fact more advantageous, the judge is entitled to look at the broader picture and not purely the financial success. Accordingly, where a Claimant only narrowly beats a Part 36 offer and that gain is more than offset by the irrecoverable cost of pressing on to trial, a judge at first instance was upheld on appeal in ordering the Claimant to pay the Defendant's costs from the time when the offer should have been accepted.[6]

If the Defendant's offer is accepted[7] within the time limit, then the claim will be stayed. If the offer relates to the whole claim, the stay will be upon the terms of the offer. If it relates only to part of the claim (perhaps an apportionment of liability), then the claim is stayed upon the terms of the offer and unless the parties have agreed costs (ie the offer is accepted within the time limit and so includes costs) then the court must decide, upon application, the issue of costs. This is particularly so if an offer is accepted outside the time limit specified.

The approval of the court is, of course, necessary for acceptance of an offer and payment in respect of a patient or child.

PART 36 PAYMENTS INTO COURT

Prior to April 2007, if the Defendant wished to make a Part 36 offer to settle a claim, then they had to lodge the amount on offer in court and serve a notice of a Part 36 offer and lodgement of money in court. There are still a significant number of cases where money has been lodged in court and PD 36B brings into line how payments made prior to that date should be treated/accepted. Essentially, the same

---

6   *Carver v BAA plc* [2008] EWCA Civ 412.
7   By notice (CPR, r 36.11).

provisions apply as for offers made under the new rules. If a Claimant had the right to accept the money prior to April 2007, then that right still exists subject to any restriction on that right. So if the Claimant wishes to accept the offer out of time, then he or she must lodge the appropriate request with the court who will then, on notice to the Defendant, make a decision on the issues of costs.

More than one Defendant (CPR, r 36.12)

Where Defendants are sued jointly or in the alternative and if one Defendant makes a Part 36 payment into court then the Claimant can accept provided he discontinues against the other Defendants who have not made the payment in and those Defendants consent in writing.

In practice, the sensible Claimant will attempt to negotiate (before discontinuance) for the Defendant which made the payment in to pay the costs of the other Defendants or alternatively for them to bear their own costs if such a result is not achieved. If they do not, then the Claimant will be responsible for the other Defendants' costs. This could have a significant costs effect on after the event insurers where there is a 'no win no fee' in existence and lead to the solicitor not recovering her costs if the claim against the other Defendants is deemed 'lost' by virtue of discontinuance.

Where Defendants have several liability the Claimant may accept the offer in respect of the relevant Defendant and continue against the others.

More than one Claimant

If there are two or more Claimants, then any payment in must be apportioned. If not agreed, the court will determine the appointment.[8]

Appeals

Unless a fresh CPR Part 36 offer is made during the appeal proceedings, the machinery of Part 36 is not open to the Court of Appeal to consider a Part 36 offer made in the primary proceedings.[9]

Costs

If a Claimant wins at court but fails to better a Part 36 payment by failing to obtain judgment for more then the gross sum specified in the Part 36 payment notice (ie the total sum inclusive of recoverable benefits) then, unless it considers it unjust to do so[10] the court will order the Claimant to pay any costs incurred by the Defendant after the latest date on which the payment could have been accepted without needing the permission of the court (CPR, r 36.14). The offer will specify the time limit in

---

[8]   *Walker v Turpin* [1994] 1 WLR 196.
[9]   *Various Claimants v Bryn Alyn Community (Holdings) Ltd* (LTL, 24 March 2003).
[10]   The factors will doubtless be those under rule 36.21(5).

which the offer can be accepted, but it cannot be less then 21 days after the expiration of notice of the Part 36 offer.

If the Claimant does not accept an offer and goes on to beat it at court, the Defendant will be ordered to pay the Claimant's costs in the usual way.

PART II

Issue to Trial

CHAPTER 14

Alternative Dispute Resolution ('ADR')

Personal injury practitioners were first required to consider the possibility of alternative means of resolving disputes by ADR by a practice direction in 1995.[1] It required the Claimant's solicitor to complete a pre-trial checklist which included the following questions:

> '10. Have you or your Counsel discussed with your client(s) the possibility of attempting to resolve this dispute (or particular issues) by alternative dispute resolutions?
> 11. Might some form of alternative dispute resolution procedure resolve or narrow the issues in this case?
> 12. Have you or your client(s) explored with the other parties the possibility of resolving this dispute (or particular issues) by alternative dispute resolutions?'

CPR Part 1.4(2) now directs that when actively managing cases, the court should encourage the parties to use an ADR procedure if the court considers that appropriate and facilitate the use of such procedure. The pre-action protocol for personal injury claims directs that the parties should consider whether some form of ADR would be more suitable than litigation and the parties may be required by the court to provide evidence that alternative means of resolving the dispute were considered (para 2.16).

WHAT IS MEANT BY ADR?

ADR has been described as:

> 'Any method of resolving an issue susceptible to normal legal process without resorting to that process. It includes mediation and other non-binding procedures. It excludes litigation and arbitration.'

In the context of personal injury litigation, ADR is best likely to describe either mediation or a round table settlement negotiation.

---

[1] *Practice Note – Civil Litigation: Case Management* [1995] 1 All ER 508. This Practice Note extended the financial court practice to the Queen's Bench and Chancery Divisions of the High Court.

Mediation

This is most likely to apply to personal injury and clinical negligence disputes, although Scott LJ (in charge of the implementation of the CPR) has stated that he did not believe that personal injury litigation was suitable for ADR. Senior Master Turner has written:

> 'I see the future of the courts in these terms:
> 1.   A Master and the other judges in the High Court must assess those actions which will now come before them at a very early stage to identify candidates for mediation and then actively encourage its use.
> 2.   At the same time they must learn to spot from the papers in the case what it is that the respective parties want out of the dispute – so often different targets – and then to educate the parties as to why mediation can achieve these ends in a way that litigation cannot do.
>
> The lawyers involved on either side must actively seek both these aims and regard trial in court as a failure.'

This does not exclude personal injury cases.

Mediation is the process whereby the parties appoint a neutral person to mediate between the parties to the dispute in order to assist them to reach a solution which is in their best interests. The mediator seeks to help the parties to reach a conclusion which they can live with. The mediator should not impose or even suggest terms of compromise. It is a 'facilitative' procedure if the mediator does not advise the parties of his or her own opinion on the merits of the dispute. It is 'evaluative' if the mediator is expected to express his own opinion.

The elements of the more common 'facilitative procedure' are as follows:

(i)   a mediator is appointed.[2] The date and venue should be fixed and all parties should agree that the proceedings are to be without prejudice;

(ii)   the procedure should be agreed. In a typical case each side prepares a written summary of not more than five pages long, exhibiting two documents which should not exceed about 20 pages;

(iii)   at the mediation each party makes a short presentation of the key elements of its case to the mediator and the other side. It is important that this is carefully prepared so that it is compelling for both the other party and the mediator. It should also be presented with the spirit of mediation in mind;

(iv)   thereafter the parties retire to separate rooms and the mediator visits each party in turn to explore their position, needs, assessment of risks, assessment of offers whilst keeping each side's concessions or admissions and background information confidential, as directed;

(v)   as the mediator passes to and fro, the two sides will hopefully move to a common position. If reached, this is then incorporated into a written agreement or Tomlin Order. The agreement can incorporate issues that would be unenforceable in a court of law such as an apology.

---

[2]   A list of mediators appropriate to the case can be obtained from either of two organisations – CEDR at Prince's House, 95 Gresham St, London EC2 7NA (Tel 020 7600 0500) or ADR Group at Grove House, Grove Rd, Bristol BS6 6UN (Tel 020 7946 7180).

Mediation negotiations are largely about debating and valuing the litigation risk confronted by each party. The neutral mediator with no interest in the outcome facilitates and enhances the debates on litigation risk privately with each party and then between the parties. In quantum cases, the mediator will ask the parties to prepare properly calculated and estimated heads of claim in detailed schedules and counter-schedules in advance of the mediation.

Round table settlement negotiation

Increasingly, parties recognise that an independent mediator is not necessary to facilitate settlement negotiations between them and that the same effect can be achieved more efficiently by the parties agreeing to meet at either side's offices. As in a mediation, each party tends to have its own room and a third room is often available if Counsel are involved to enable them to negotiate on a without prejudice basis, reverting back to their clients in their holding rooms. More often than not, once the parties have expressed an agreement to attend a round table settlement negotiation, compromise is achieved. However, from a Claimant's perspective, it is nearly always imperative to ensure that the Defendant's insurer is present at the settlement meeting or, at the very least, has assurances that the insurer client will be readily contactable to be able to give instructions. Otherwise, the negotiation can often merely serve as a fishing expedition by the Defendant to see what extent the Claimant is prepared to move.

WHEN IS ADR APPROPRIATE?

ADR is non-mandatory. However, there has been a marked growth in the use of ADR, largely as a result of the Court of Appeal decision in *Dunnett v Railtrack*.[3] In that case, the Court of Appeal had given permission to the Claimant against the decision at first instance in a low value claim but strongly recommended that ADR should be explored. The Defendant refused because it was confident of success on appeal. Although it was successful on appeal, the Court of Appeal awarded no order as to costs. They held that it was the lawyer's duty under CPR, r 1.1 to further the overriding objective. If the parties turned down ADR out of hand they would suffer the consequences when costs came to be decided. In *Neal v Jones Motors*,[4] the Court of Appeal deducted £5,000 off the costs of an insured respondent to a personal injury appeal who won on the law but failed to respond to a suggestion to try mediation made by the court. However, in *Halsey v Milton Keynes General NHS Trust*,[5] the Court of Appeal stated that the fundamental principle that the unsuccessful party should pay the costs of the successful party should not be departed from unless it is shown (the burden being on the unsuccessful party) that the successful party acted unreasonably in refusing to agree to ADR. The court gave guidance as to the factors to be considered by the court in deciding whether the refusal was reasonable or not. Factors that could be relevant include the nature of the dispute, the merits of the

3   [2002] 2 All ER 850.
4   [2002] EWCA Civ 1731.
5   [2004] 1 WLR 3002.

case, the extent to which other settlement methods had been attempted, whether the costs of ADR would be disproportionately high, whether the delay in setting it up would be prejudicial and whether there was a reasonable prospect of success.

The most significant increase has related to clinical negligence rather than personal injury, largely due to the large costs of those proceedings, the difficulty in obtaining legal services funding for low value claims and the complexities of the issues involved. Both the Legal Services Commission and the NHSLA are encouraging its use through funding. Importantly, in a new model practice direction published by the Queen's Bench Masters assigned to clinical negligence cases, parties are required to mediate during the six weeks before the trial window opens and if they do not do so, to file with the court sealed written reasons for declining, to be considered by the court on the issue of costs. The Chief Medical Officer in his consultation document 'Making Amends' also recommends greater use of mediation in clinical negligence cases.

Nowadays, personal injury litigation is conducted by expert lawyers in the field and it will often be the case that direct negotiation can achieve all that mediation is intended to facilitate. However, there may be cases where mediation could fulfil a particular need (for example, a published apology) or get the negotiations under way earlier than court process. Further, it is particularly useful in cases where the Claimant and Defendant may continue in a relationship, such as employee/employer claims or motor claims between family members.

As for any negotiation, before entering the process of mediation, and therefore before taking a decision as to whether mediation is preferable to trial, the solicitor acting for the Claimant must have knowledge of at least the following: the real prospects of succeeding in court; the real value of the claim; the needs of the clients and the extent to which they could be satisfied by mediation or court; and the result desired beyond which would be in the best interests of the client. After all, it will generally only be after negotiations have failed that mediation should be tried.

As a result of the CPR, this information should be available quite early in the case, as should an assessment which can be made of the valuation of the case by the other party. Whilst not all information or expert reports may be to hand by then, most experienced lawyers will have sufficient material to enable them to assess prospects and advise whether settlement is feasible or attractive at an early stage or later.

There is no doubt that a Claimant with a good personal injury case should not delay. Speedy prosecution of court proceedings is likely to increase the chances of a satisfactory settlement or judgment. Parties are suspicious of ADR because, to some extent, it is possible to gauge the strengths and weaknesses of the other side's case or at least the other side's perception of those strengths and weaknesses. It would certainly be an abuse of the ADR procedure if a party entered into it with only the motive of obtaining this information in mind. If the mediator felt that this was the motive s/he should immediately terminate the mediation.

CHAPTER 15

Issue and Service

Before the issue of proceedings, the solicitor must be in a position to comply with the relevant pre-action protocols. By this time, she should have a clear idea of the likely level of value of the claim, she will know whether or not it is going to be a claim allocated to the fast track or multi track and she has considered if, when and what Part 36 offer to settle the claim the Claimant should be advised to make. Whilst it is advisable that a fast track claim is fully prepared and capable of settlement prior to the issue of proceedings, it is certain that a proportion of cases will not fulfil this ideal. There will be clients whose apparently small injuries deteriorate or have unforeseen consequences. There may be difficulties in establishing prognosis. Urgency may be required in order to obtain a desperately needed interim payment (in a strong case). There will be the client who turns up just as the three year time limit is about to expire.

Unless protective proceedings are being issued to protect time from expiring, proceedings should only be issued if the solicitor is satisfied that there is a reasonable prospect of success, a settlement is not imminent, funding is secure, a medical report is to hand (or at least that the injuries can be fully and properly identified) and that there is sufficient information to draft a schedule of damages.

The client must authorise issue of proceedings (see Appendix B – Specimen correspondence). In some cases, the client, person or organisation funding the claim must authorise the issue of proceedings. In some cases, the client will insist on the issue of proceedings, even if the solicitor advises against it. In such circumstances, the solicitor should record her advice and the client's instructions in a letter to the client. Unless the client is funding the case privately, the solicitor must check with the funder to ensure that the latter will fund the case further in the light of the solicitor's negative advice. Where the case has the benefit of legal services funding, is funded by a trade union or by an insurance policy, the appropriate body must immediately be notified of the disagreement, before issue. There is nothing unethical about the solicitor continuing to act in such cases if the funder agrees to fund the case. If funds are no longer forthcoming (and the solicitor's negative advice will normally form a reason for terminating a conditional fee agreement), then the client must be advised that the solicitor cannot continue to act.

The letter to the client requires careful drafting to record the client's instructions, the solicitor's advice and the reasons for it, the funding implications, the consequences of continuing the case in the face of negative advice, and the time applicable if the client drops the case but may think of pursuing it again later. The client must be asked to write, acknowledging receipt of the letter and confirming his instructions to proceed (or not). These steps are an essential protection against any subsequent allegation of negligence. The client who insists on proceedings being issued against advice will normally become a private fee paying client and it is wise for the solicitor, at this point, to ask for a substantial sum to be lodged in the firm's client account to put her in funds to continue working.

A lot of the work involved in investigating and forming a view on the case, may already have been done for risk assessment purposes when entering into a conditional fee agreement and will certainly have been done (if an early CFA was entered into and protective proceedings were not issued) to get to the point of issue of proceedings. However, the essence of good risk management is continuing assessment and immediately prior to issue is a critical moment to carry out a further full assessment of the case.

The issue of proceedings transfers control of the procedural timetable from the solicitor to the court. If the solicitor cannot comply with the court timetable then she is going to find herself under great time pressure, she may have the claim struck out or face potential personal costs orders against her if she cannot keep within time limits. It is not appropriate to issue proceedings and then prepare the case as the matter proceeds. Most if not all of the preparatory work (often then in some large or complex personal injury claims) must, in the light of the CPR, be done before the case is issued. This is called 'front loading'.

NUMBER OF ACTIONS

It is not necessarily an abuse of process to institute two actions arising from the same cause of action provided that the two actions do not proceed separately to judgment. There is no rule that a second action be struck out where there is one action in existence based upon one cause of action and the second action is commenced on the same cause of action; the second action is commenced on a different cause of action but with the same origin in an accident causing personal injury. So long as there is no risk of the two proceeding to judgment, there is no strike out available.[1] Inevitably, the two actions will be consolidated.

DEFENDANTS

It is crucial to ensure that the Defendant will be able to meet a judgment debt, or that there are insurers or an institution behind the Defendant who will do so. In the unusual case where there is no response from the Defendant or the insurers within the recommended protocol timetable – and usually within a few days of the initial letter

---

[1]   *Kahl v Holderness Borough Council* [1995] PIQR P401.

being sent, or where the response gives rise to suspicion, then the Defendant's position should be investigated.

In the even more unusual situation where there is evidence that the Defendant is likely to dissipate assets out of the jurisdiction, an application for freezing injunction may have to be made (whether or not proceedings have been started) to prevent this happening (see rule 25.1(1)(f) and PD Interim Injunctions, 25 PD 6). The court (either High or County) must be convinced that the remedy is just.

If the case is a road traffic accident, where the Defendant was driving a vehicle and where no insurers have confirmed that they will cover the Defendant's liability, the Motor Insurers Bureau must be notified formally (see Chapter 33 on Motor drivers and owners). There are strict timetables and procedures to this notification and it is imperative, if the MIB is to accept liability, that these are adhered to.

Identity/choice of Defendant

It is important to select the right Defendant. Usually, this presents no problem, but where there are several potential Defendants, it is generally wisest to sue those against whom liability is clearest. In an employer's liability claim, this will generally be the employer owing the non-delegable duties owed by an employer to its employee. If there is sufficient time before primary limitation expires, it is often sensible to commence the proceedings against such a party well before the expiry of the three-year time period. This then places the onus on them, as primary Defendants, to decide whether others should be brought in as third parties to the action and at the very least, to put forward a positive case in its defence. A decision can then be made as to whether to join the third party as another Defendant or not. The advantage in adopting such an approach is that it usually provides the Claimant protection on costs should the claim ultimately fail against the third party at trial. Furthermore, it is inevitably more difficult to negotiate settlement in a multi party action than where there is only one Defendant. It may also cause problems in obtaining an interim payment.

The court has to be satisfied that the Claimant was reasonable in joining more than one Defendant. A reasonable doubt concerning which Defendant may be liable has been sufficient for the court to make an order for payment of the Claimant's costs, ordering the unsuccessful Defendant to pay the costs of the successful Defendant either directly[2] or indirectly.[3] However, the Claimant cannot presume that because two or more Defendants blame each other, he will automatically recover costs of pursuing the successful Defendants. It must be a genuine either/or case.[4]

Where the primary Defendant adds third parties to the action by way of Part 20 proceedings, the Claimant's lawyers may add those parties as further Defendants if the allegations made against them by the primary Defendant are sufficiently strong. As noted above, the Claimant may avoid that burden if he joined that person as a Defendant only because the primary Defendant had first brought in the innocent

---

[2]   *Sanderson v Blyth Theatre Co* [1903] 2 KB 533.
[3]   *Bullock v London General Omnibus Co* [1907] 1 KB 264. For the principles of applying these orders, see *Mayer v Harte* [1960] 1 WLR 770.
[4]   *Irvine v Commissioner for Police* [2005] EWCA Civ 129.

Defendant as a third party. The risk to avoid, in taking this course of action, is that the statutory limitation period expires before the potential third party is joined as a Defendant, assuming that the latter's identity is known to the plaintiff. A Defendant who is found at trial to have no liability is entitled to costs.

Where the Claimant knows that the injuries were caused by one or other of two (or more) potential Defendants, but only one, and does not know which Defendant is responsible the Claimant should sue both in the alternative.[5]

If the Defendant is an individual and dies intestate before the commencement of the proceedings, the Claimant's solicitor should obtain a copy of the letters of administration and commence the proceedings against the named administrator. Alternatively the solicitor should apply for an order that a person be appointed to represent the Defendant's estate and thereafter commence proceedings against that person.[6]

If proceedings to avoid limitation problems are issued, it is wisest to issue proceedings against *all* potential Defendants, irrespective of probable blame, so as to protect the Claimant's position. Within the four-month validity of the claim form, proceedings could be served first on one or two of the Defendants and subject to the contents of their Defence, a decision could be made as to whether or not proceedings should be served on the remaining Defendants.

In road accident cases caused by drivers of commercial vehicles, it is usually sufficient to sue the employer or vehicle operator on the basis of their vicarious liability. If, however, there is any doubt about whether the driver was acting in the course of his/her employment so as to establish vicarious liability, the best policy is to sue both. In the rare event of a dispute over vicarious liability, the court will look at the reality of the relationship between the driver and vehicle operator as found in express or implied terms of the contract.[7]

In 'tripping' cases the local authority should be sued first unless the tripping hazard clearly belongs to an independent statutory undertaker, such as a Water Board and would not form part of a highway inspector's responsibilities. If it is absolutely clear which contractors are responsible and the hazard is likely to have arisen between inspections, they should also be joined. If not, it should be left to the local authority to identify the appropriate Defendants. The disclosure requirements under the protocols should help with the old and time consuming problems of getting the local authority to identify which contractor was where at the time of the accident.

In work cases, the usual practice is to sue the employer as well as any other party obviously at fault. So, for example, where an accident has happened while the client is on another contractor's premises, both the employer and other contractor should be sued.[8] The employer's responsibility to ensure that the employee has a safe place

---

[5] *Halford v Brookes* [1991] 3 All ER 559, per Lord Donaldson MR at 574.
[6] The effect of RSC Ord 15, r 6A(4)(a) is preserved in the new rules and continues to apply, see *Foster v Turnbull* (1990) Times, 22 May.
[7] *Ferguson v John Dawson & Partners (Contractors) Ltd* [1976] 1 WLR 1213; *Lee Ting Sang v Chung Chi-Keung* [1990] 2 AC 374; and *Lane v Shire Roofing (Oxford) Ltd* [1995] PIQR P417.
[8] *Dexter v Tenby Electrical Accessories Ltd* [1991] COD 288, [1991] Crim LR 839; see also *Alcock v Wraith* (1991) 59 BLR 20, [1991] NPC 135.

of work and a safe system of work does not end at the factory gates.[9] This is so even if the Claimant is working under the direction of a supervisor employed by another.[10]

The Consumer Protection Act 1987 established liability for defective products from 1 March 1988. The producer (or anybody that can be identified from the product or its wrapping to be the producer) or the importer may be sued. Suppliers may be sued if they fail to identify the producer within reasonable time of being so requested (see Chapter 32 on Liability for products and premises).

It is important to use the correct address for service on the Defendant (see below, re service). This may be vital if limitation is about to expire. It is good practice to do a company search on a corporate Defendant to establish the address of the registered office although the new provisions for service are more relaxed. Where the Defendant is not domiciled in England and Wales, application must be made for service out of the jurisdiction.[11]

In cases where there is uncertainty as to the correct title of the Defendant to be named in the proceedings, care should be taken to illicit this information from the Defendant prior to issue. If the Defendant is obstructive in providing the information, it should be emphasised that you will draw their conduct to the attention of the court should there subsequently be a need to apply to amend the name of the Defendant. This is particularly important in cases where primary limitation is due to expire and a subsequent amendment may need to be made after limitation has expired.

Insolvency of an insured Defendant

Where a Defendant was insured but becomes insolvent, the Claimant's ability to enforce a successful claim against the insurers is protected by the Third Parties (Rights Against Insurers) Act 1930.[12] This statute enables the injured person to stand in the shoes of the insured and claim against the insurer.[13] In these circumstances, the solicitor should write to the insured party and ask for copies of the contract of insurance, receipts and other relevant documents. These may also be obtained from the insured's insurance company, if known. The plaintiff has a right to demand, and the liquidator of a company has a duty to provide, details of a company's employers' liability insurance.[14] The solicitor should notify the insurance company, by recorded delivery letter, of proceedings to be brought against the insured, if this is an express

---

[9]   *Smith v Cammell Laird* [1940] AC 242; *McDermid v Nash Dredging and Reclamation Co Ltd* [1987] AC 906; *Morris v Breaveglen Ltd* [1993] PIQR P294, but see *Cook v Square D Ltd* [1992] PIQR P33. For the application of statutory duties to different parties, see *Redgrave's Health and Safety* (4th edn, 2002) LexisNexis UK.

[10] *Nelhams v Sandell Maintenance Ltd* [1996] PIQR P52.

[11] The effect of RSC Ord 11 is preserved under the CPR.

[12] Where the Defendant is not insured there may be no liability on the part of the company directors for this failure: see *Richardson v Pitt-Stanley* [1994] PIQR P496, but note the Employer's Liability (Compulsory Insurance) Act 1969 (below) in relation to employee cases.

[13] Section 3 of the Act operates to avoid evasive dealing between the insured and insurer. Injunctive relief may be appropriate: *Woolwich Building Society v Taylor* [1995] 1 BCLC 132.

[14] Third Parties (Rights against Insurers) Act 1930, s 2(1). The liability of the insurer to the insurer arises from the moment when the accident occurred or the damage suffered: *Post Office v Norwich Union Fire Insurance Society Ltd* [1967] 2 QB 363.

stipulation in the policy.[15] It would seem that judgment should then be obtained against the insured in the usual way.[16] Subsequently, if necessary, proceedings can be commenced directly against the insurance company for the judgment order.

The Act is not confined to but is particularly useful in relation to persons injured at work since then employers are obliged to be insured by virtue of the Employer's Liability (Compulsory Insurance) Act 1969.[17]

Bankruptcy, liquidation and dissolution of a Defendant

A body must exist as a legal entity if it is to be sued. Corporations in compulsory liquidation have a winding-up order issued by the Companies Court. After the winding-up order is made, but before the Defendant company is dissolved, proceedings are commenced or continued by an application to the Companies Court for permission to claim against it.[18] This is usually a formality. If a company has already been dissolved it ceases to exist as a legal entity and an application to the Companies Court is necessary to restore the company to the register[19] in order to sue it. This is an expensive procedure and normally only used where the claim is going to be large. A company is dissolved automatically three months after the date of the final return lodged by the liquidator with the registrar of companies. Companies in voluntary liquidation have no order from the Companies Court and leave to commence proceedings is not required.

The effect of a declaration restoring the company to the register is to avoid the dissolution with retrospective effect as far as the existence (but not the activities) of the company is concerned. Therefore, by virtue of the restoration, a Claimant's cause of action against a company accrues on the date on which it would have accrued but for the dissolution and the provisions cannot be used to argue that time does not run.[20] An order should not normally be made unless notice has been given to those parties who could be expected to oppose the direction, such as the company's insurers. Further, when making the order, the judge should not direct that the period from dissolution to restoration should not count for limitation purposes unless the court was satisfied that an application under s 33 of the Limitation Act 1980 was bound to succeed. Instead, it should order limitation to be tried as a preliminary issue.[21] If a company has gone into liquidation and the details of the employers' liability or other insurance are not known, consideration ought to be given to joining the directors of the company personally, if it can be shown that one or more of them might personally be liable in tort.[22]

[15]   *Pioneer Concrete (UK) Ltd v National Employers Mutual General Insurance Association Ltd* [1985] 1 All ER 395.
[16]   *Bradley v Eagle Star Insurance Co Ltd* [1989] AC 957.
[17]   See *Munkman on Employer's Liability* (12th edn, 1995) pp 541–542.
[18]   Insolvency Act 1986, s 130(3).
[19]   Companies Act 1985, s 651.
[20]   *Smith v White Knight Laundry Ltd* [2002] 1 WLR 616.
[21]   *Smith v White Knight Laundry Ltd* [2002] 1 WLR 616.
[22]   See *Ambler v Hepworth* PMILL, vol 9, no 1, p 4.

After a bankruptcy order has been made against an individual debtor, no action may be commenced without the leave of the court having bankruptcy jurisdiction.[23] Any action commenced without such leave will be stayed.

LIABILITY

It is not within the scope of this book to consider the law on liability.

INJURY, LOSS AND DAMAGE

In fast track cases full details of financial losses are likely to be complete at the stage of issuing proceedings. Prior to issue, the protocol is unhelpful on when a schedule must be served – it simply states a schedule of special damages with supporting documents shall be submitted as soon as possible (personal injury protocol at 3.13). However, by the time of issue the position is clearer. PD 16 states that the Claimant must attach to his particulars of claim a schedule of details of any past and future expenses and losses which he claims. In respect of medical evidence, PD 16 provides that where the Claimant is relying on the evidence of a medical practitioner the Claimant must attach to or serve with his particulars of claim a report from a medical practitioner about the personal injuries which he alleges in his claim (16 PD 15.1(3)).

WHICH TRACK?

Prior to issue, the solicitor will have decided the appropriate track. Most claims for personal injuries will be litigated by a solicitor through the fast track, fewer through the multi track. It will only be in very low value claims where general damages are below £1,000 that a case will be litigated in the small claims track by a solicitor.

ISSUING

Apart from Part 8 claims

Before issuing a claim form, it is necessary to follow the relevant pre-action protocols for personal injury claims, as the CPR enables the court to take into account compliance or non-compliance with the protocols which is particularly pertinent to the court's general powers of case management (rule 3.1(4) and (5), on issues relating to relief from sanctions (Part 3.9(1)(e)) and issues of costs (Part 44.3(5)(a)).

The process of starting a claim is greatly simplified under the CPR. There is no longer a writ in the High Court with its county court equivalent – 'the summons'. The new rules simply state 'proceedings are started when the court issues a claim form at the request of the Claimant' (CPR, r 7.2).

---

23   Insolvency Act 1986, s 285(3).

Unless the value of the claim exceeds £50,000, proceedings for personal injury must be commenced in the county court.[24]

Rule 7.4 provides three possible ways of providing the particulars of claim. First, the Claimant may include the particulars of claim on the claim form itself (CPR, r 7.4(1)(a)). Secondly, on a separate document served with the claim form (CPR, r 7.4(1)(a)) and thirdly, as a separate document and serve them within 14 days after service of the claim form, and no later then the latest time for service of the claim form (CPR, rr 7.4(1)(b) and (3)). This means that if the solicitor issues a claim form which must be served by a certain date, then she cannot leave it to the expiration of that date to serve and rely on a further 14 days' extra time to serve particulars of claim. It is options 2 and 3 which are most typically adopted. After issue, the court will complete and serve a notice of issue form.

Unlike a failure to serve the claim form in time, the court has a general discretion to extend the time for serving the particulars of claim even when it is served outside the relevant time period.[25] However, where there is a concern that this might arise and no agreement can be reached with the Defendant to extend time, it is advisable to serve the claim form and issue an application to extend time for the service of the particulars before the time limit expires. That will avoid having to satisfy the court under the more stringent CPR, r 3.9 checklist.[26]

The Claimant must serve with the claim form a schedule of special damages and a medical report if medical evidence is to be relied on (as it invariably will be in a personal injury claim).

To issue a claim, complete and forward the claim form with the appropriate fee to the relevant court. The claim form is a simple document and provides for the likely bracket of value to be inserted to assist the court in making a decision on allocating the matter to the relevant track. Both for lodging with the court and for service, the documentation must consist, at least, of:

(i)   the claim form and a certificate of service if the document is to be served separately from the particulars of claim;

(ii)   particulars of claim;

(iii) a 'response pack' containing:

      (a)   admission form N9C;

      (b)   acknowledgment of service form;

      (c)   form of defence and counterclaim N9D;

(iv) notice of issue of legal aid certificate (if any);

(v)   solicitors' certificate/consents of next friend (if any);

(vi) schedule of special damage and financial loss;

(vii) medical report;

(viii) any other evidence which the Claimant intends to rely on, such as witness statements disclosed early.

---

[24]   Part 7 PD para 2.2.
[25]   *Totty v Snowden* [2002] 1 WLR 1384.
[26]   *Sabrina Robert v Momentum Services Ltd* [2003] 1 WLR 1577.

Part 8 procedure

The circumstances in which the CPR Part 8 procedure is required is set out at the end of Chapter 29. In the context of personal injury litigation, the procedure will be used where a claim by or against a child or patient has been settled before the commencement of proceedings and the sole purpose of the claim is to obtain the approval of the court to the settlement. Secondly, in a claim for provisional damages which has been settled before the commencement of proceedings and the sole purpose of the claim is to obtain a consent judgment. The documents required to commence a Part 8 claim are:

(i)   claim form N208 and any statement of claim appended;
(ii)   acknowledgement of service N208;
(iii) schedule of loss;
(iv)   medical evidence;
(v)   Legal Services Funding certificate (if any).

The court will issue and complete a notice of issue of Part 8 process.

Service

Practitioners must be very careful to adhere to the strict requirements governing service of proceedings. Failure to comply with the provisions is liable to result in a professional negligence claim. Particular aspects of service which must be borne in mind are:

(i)   the time limits for service (taking into account the deemed date of service provisions);
(ii)   the limited circumstances in which the court will extend the time for service of the claim form; and
(iii) the importance of ensuring that proceedings are served in the correct manner.

The general rule is that the claim form must be served within four months (and a month is defined at rule 2.10 as a calendar month) after the date of issue or within six months if service is outside the jurisdiction (rules 7.5(2) and (3)).

Care should be taken to comply with the deemed date of service requirements and to ensure that the claim form is served before its four-month validity expires. The modes of service are set out in CPR, r 6.2. Where a document is served (see CPR, r 6.7):

(i)   by first class post – service is deemed the second day after it was posted;
(ii)   through the document exchange – service is deemed the second day after it was left at the DX (and see PD service 2);
(iii) by leaving it at a permitted address for service – service is deemed the day after it was delivered to or left at the permitted address;
(iv)   by FAX – service is deemed if it is transmitted on a business day before 4pm on that day, or in any other case on the business day after the day on which it was transmitted (and see PD service 3.1 and 3.2);
(v)   by other means of electronic communication (email) – the second day after the day on which it was transmitted (and see PD service 3.3 and 3.4).

A business day means any day except Saturday, Sunday or bank holiday, and a bank holiday includes Christmas Day and Good Friday (rule 6.7(3)).

Failure to comply with the above has led to extensive satellite litigation and provides pitfalls for the unwary.[27] The deemed date of service provisions are not rebuttable by evidence of prior actual receipt.[28]

Agreement by the parties to extend the time for service

The parties can agree to extend the time for service of the claim form between themselves, but if they do so, the agreement must be in writing in a document or exchange of documents by the parties which confirm the agreement. A letter from one party only or internal file notes is insufficient to comply.[29] Accordingly, if this approach is adopted, it is imperative that confirmation is obtained in writing from the other side.

Application to the court to extend the time for service

The Claimant can apply for an order to extend the period of time for service under Part 7.6. He must do this within the period of validity of the claim form or within the period of time specified by any order on service of the documentation. The application is deemed to be made when it is issued, not when it is heard or decided.[30]

However, the court is limited in its power to grant an extension of time in cases where the Claimant applies outside that time frame. In those circumstances, the judge can only extend time where the court has been unable to serve the claim form or the Claimant has taken all reasonable steps to serve the claim form, but has been unable to do so and, in either case, the Claimant has acted promptly (CPR, r 7.6(3)). The latter are relevant factors to be taken into account even when the application is made within the four-month validity of the claim form, but is not determinative of the outcome. The court is required to consider how good a reason there was for the failure to serve in time. This is subtly different from the court's discretion when the application is made after four months have elapsed, as in those circumstances the court cannot extend time unless all reasonable steps had been taken.[31]

This has very important ramifications. The court has repeatedly held that there is no discretion to cure defective service either by extending time for cases falling outside of the CPR, r 7.6 criteria or under its powers to rectify errors of procedure under CPR, r 3.10.[32] A solicitor who delays service until the end of the four months may find, for whatever reason, that service was ineffective. An application to extend will almost certainly then fall outside the period of validity and potentially outside the court's jurisdiction to grant an extension of time. It follows that rather than risking applications to extend time, a Claimant is much better placed to serve proceedings well in advance of the expiry of the issued claim form and then to agree an extension

---

[27]   *Anderton v Clwyd CC* [2002] 3 All ER 813; *Wilkey & DAS v BBC & Moyles* (22 October 2002, unreported).
[28]   *Godwin v Swindon Borough Council* [2001] EWCA Civ 1478.
[29]   *Thomas v Home Office* [2007] 1 WLR 230.
[30]   *Collier v Williams* [2006] EWCA Civ 20.
[31]   *Collier v Williams* [2006] EWCA Civ 20.
[32]   *Vinos v Marks & Spencer* (2000) Independent, 17 July; *Elmes v Hygrade Food Products Ltd* [2001] All ER 158.

of time with the Defendant for complying with any further steps. The court has power under CPR, r 3.10 to remedy a failure to serve the particulars of claim, but not a failure to serve the claim form.[33]

Any application to extend time must be supported by evidence. The statement should set out all the circumstances relied on, the date of issue, the expiry date of any extension and a full explanation as to why the claim has not been served (PD 8.1). This application may be made 'without notice' (CPR, r 7.6(4)).

Dispensing with service

The Court of Appeal had been prepared to order in exceptional circumstances that service be dispensed with under CPR, r 6.9. It distinguished between cases where the Claimant did not even attempt to serve in time by the permitted methods under CPR, r 6.2 (where the discretion would not be exercised) and those cases where the Claimant had made an ineffective attempt to serve in time (where the discretion remained unless the Defendant could prove prejudice or there was some other good reason)[34] or had served in time in a manner which involved a minor departure from one of the permitted methods of service. The failure to comply with the requirement to obtain written consent to service by fax in para 3.1(1) of the CPR Part 6 PD could not fairly be characterised as no more than a minor departure from the provisions of CPR, r 6.2(1)(e).[35]

Defendant applying for service of the claim form

CPR, r 7.7 provides that if a claim form has been issued but not served, the Defendant can serve notice requiring service or discontinuance within 'a period specified in the notice' – this must be at least 14 days. If the solicitor does not comply with the notice the court may, upon application by the Defendant, dismiss the claim or make any other order it thinks just. The solicitor should therefore not tell the Defendant that she has issued unless she wishes them to compel service!

Mode of service

The modes of service are set out in CPR, r 6.2. The claim form may be served by personal service in accordance with rule 6.4, by first class past, by leaving it at a place specified within rule 6.5, through a document exchange or by fax or other electronic means. However, the Part 6 PD at 2.1 and 3.1 sets out additional requirements in respect of service of the claim form by document exchange or by electronic means. The latter, in particular, can only be adopted where the Defendant or his legal representative has expressly indicated in writing that he is willing to accept service by electronic means and the number/address to which it is to be sent.

33 *Totty v Snowden* (2001) Times, 10 August.
34 *Anderton v Clwyd CC* [2002] 3 All ER 813.
35 *Kuenyehia International Hospital Group* [2006] EWCA Civ 21.

A decision must be made on whether the court or the solicitor is to serve the claim form. Where it is served by the court (which will usually be by first class post), the court will send the Claimant a notice of the date on which the claim form is deemed served (CPR, r 6.14). If the court fails to serve it will give notice of non-service to the party seeking service whose responsibility service thereafter becomes (CPR, rr 6.11 and PD Service 8.2).

If the solicitor serves he must, after service, complete and forward a certificate of service (form N215) within seven days of service of the claim form if the claim form is served separately from the other documentation. Without this judgment in default cannot be obtained (CPR, r 6.14(2)(b)). There is a separate form N218 for service on a partner.

If the claim form is to be served by the court it must include the Defendant's address for service (rule 6.13) which must be within the jurisdiction (England, Wales and any part of the territorial waters of the UK adjoining England and Wales). The Defendant's address may be its solicitor's address if the solicitor is authorised to accept service on the Defendant's behalf but not otherwise (CPR, r 6.13(2)). Apart from the above – and some particular provisions where there is a contractual agreement as to method of service (CPR, r 6.15) – the well established service rules apply. That is to say service may be effected personally (CPR, r 6.4(1)) or on a solicitor (CPR, r 6.4(2)) authorised to accept service, an authorisation for which must be confirmed in writing (CPR, r 6.4(2) and (6)). However, it is essential that the Claimant adopts the nominated mode of service. Service of the claim form on the Defendant personally when solicitors have been nominated to accept service will invalidate the service (CPR, r 6.4(2)(b)).[36] By the same token, service on a solicitor who has not provided written confirmation will also be invalid.[37] To avoid any risk of error where the court is to serve the claim form, the Claimant should be careful to put the Defendant's solicitor's address for service on the claim form if he is authorised to accept service rather than merely relying upon an accompanying letter.

A document is served personally on an individual by 'leaving it with that individual' (CPR, r 6.4(3)). A document is served personally on a company or corporation by 'leaving it with a person holding a senior position within the company or corporation' (CPR, r 6.4(4), 6 PD service 6.2). A document is served personally on a partnership where partners are being sued by leaving it with a partner or a person who has control or management of the partnership business at its principal place of business (CPR, r 6.4(5), PD service 4).

If a party does not give a solicitor's address for service and fails to give either his resident or business address for service (as required by CPR, r 6.5(2) and (3)) and has no solicitor instructed to accept service (CPR, r 6.4(2)), then unless the court orders an alternative (CPR, r 6.8), the following table applies:

[36]   *Nanlegan v Royal Free Hampstead NHS* (2001) Times, 14 February.
[37]   *Smith v Probyn* (2000) Times, 29 March.

Nature of party to be served	Place of service
Individual	• Usual or last known residence.
Proprietor of a business	• Usual or last known residence; or
	• Place of business or last known place of business.
Individual who is suing or being sued in the name of a firm	• Usual or last known residence; or
	• Principal or last known place of business of the firm.
Corporation incorporated in England and Wales other than a company	• Principal office of the corporation; or
	• Any place within the jurisdiction where the corporation carries on its activities and which has a real connection with the claim.
Company registered in England and Wales	• Principal office of the company; or
	• Any place of business of the company within the jurisdiction which has a real connection with the claim.
Any other company or corporation	• Any place within the jurisdiction where the corporation carries on its activities; or
	• Any place of business of the company within the jurisdiction.

A litigation friend must be appointed for a child or patient (see Chapter 29 on Claimants under a legal disability). Service effected on a child or patient is in accordance with the following table (CPR, r 6.6(1)):

Type of document	Nature of party	Person to be served
Claim form	Child who is not also a protected party	One of the child's parents or guardians;
		or
		if there is no parent or guardian, an adult with whom the child resides or in whose care the child is.
Claim form	Protected party	One of the following persons with authority in relation to the protected party as:

Type of document	Nature of party	Person to be served
		(ii) the attorney under a registered enduring power of attorney,
		(iv) the donee of a lasting power of attorney,
		(vi) the deputy appointed by the Court of Protection;
		or
		if there is no such person, an adult with whom the protected party resides or in whose care the protected party is.
Application for an order appointing a litigation friend, where the child or protected party has no litigation friend	Child or protected party	See rule 21.8.
Any other document	Child or protected party	The litigation friend who is conducting the proceedings on behalf of the child or protected party.

It is possible to make an application to the court to permit an alternative form of service (CPR, r 6.8(1)). The court will consider the application on its merit, and such application must be supported by evidence and may be made without notice (CPR, r 6.8(2)). However, the rule cannot be applied retrospectively.[38]

The court has the power to dispense with service of a document and such an application may be made without notice (CPR, r 6.9). As noted above, the Court of Appeal has restricted the circumstances in which this provision can be used to cure defective service.

Special provisions apply for service of the claim form out of the jurisdiction. These are set out in CPR, rr 6.17 to 6.31.

---

[38]   *Elmes v Hygrade Food Products Ltd* [2001] All ER 158.

Transfer between courts

The court has the power to transfer a case between the High Court and the county courts and within district registries of the High Court (CPR, r 30.1).

Transfer can be ordered either upon application or by the court of its own motion (CPR, r 30.2). Although CPR, r 30.2(c) gives the court power to strike out an action commenced in the wrong court, in view of the overriding objective, the power is only likely to be exercised in extreme cases.

The criteria governing transfer is set out in CPR, r 30.3(2) and in particular, includes the financial value of the claim, whether it would be more convenient or fair for the hearing to be held in another court, the issues and the general importance of the case.

The norm is for county court cases which are allocated to the multi track to be transferred to the nearest trial centre for case management.

CHAPTER 16

Claimant's Statement of Case

INTRODUCTION

Lord Woolf identified[1] a range of critical points concerning the current process of pleadings. In particular, he noted a failure clearly to specify the issues in a case, insufficient concentration on the facts, and generally being too long winded. Emphasis was also attached to the lack of judicial scrutiny and the reluctance to penalise the late delivery and amendment of pleadings. Thus delay and inconvenience was commonly incurred by the parties.

The CPR has abolished the distinction between county court and High Court pleadings. No longer does the Claimant choose between a statement of claim or particulars of claim. The pleadings are now referred to as the 'statement of case'.

The statement of case is the generic name given to all pleadings (ie particulars, defence, reply, etc). It specifies a party's contentions in the case. The name covers both the Claimant's and the Defendant's cases. The Claimant's case is initially set out in the claim form with the particulars of claim and the additional documents which are required (see below) and the Defendant's case is contained in the defence.

The effect of the reform is to ensure, as far as possible, that the issues in dispute can be identified as early as possible and the evidence relevant to them. Although the possibility remains for the Defendant to neither admit nor deny an allegation but to simply require proof, the rules strongly encourage the Defendant to make a positive case. If a Defendant intends to put forward a contrasting version of events, it must specify and justify this in the defence. Further, reasons must be stated for disputing a statement of value, medical report or schedule of losses and, where possible, the Defendant is required to provide alternatives.

Proceedings begin when a court issues a claim form at the request of the Claimant (CPR, r 7.2) and the rules relating to the use of this claim form are contained in Chapter 15. However, these rules do not apply to proceedings brought by the alternative procedure under CPR Part 8, ie where the Claimant seeks the court's decision on a question which is unlikely to involve substantial dispute of fact or

---

[1]   Interim Report, section V, Chapter 20.

where a practice direction specifies Part 8 may apply. This procedure will be rare in personal injury cases, but it does have some application. It is dealt with at the end of this chapter.

INSTRUCTIONS TO COUNSEL

Whether counsel is instructed to settle the statement of case initially, or is brought in at a later stage, it is important for the solicitor to ensure that the instructions to the barrister are appropriate. What counsel is required to do should be made explicit and precise. The right balance should be sought between ensuring that counsel has all the relevant documents and not sending down the solicitor's entire file on the case.

Both in London and elsewhere, there are a substantial number of good, efficient and effective barristers, sympathetic to Claimants, who specialise in personal injury work. Most are members of the Association of Personal Injury Lawyers (APIL) and, with experience, the solicitor will build up a list of barristers who can be relied on.

Expertise is not enough. One of the qualities a solicitor is entitled to demand – the lack of which should result in a barrister being taken off the solicitor's list – is speed in returning drafting and advice. A statement of case in a straightforward case with competent instructions, without any computation of special damage, should take an experienced counsel no more than 30 or 45 minutes to draft. Solicitors are entitled to expect that a statement of case will be returned (unless marked 'urgent') within three to four weeks of delivery, excluding holidays. If the papers are likely to take longer than this, the barrister should make sure that the solicitor is given the reason for the delay. The solicitor (upon whom the responsibility for time limits ultimately rests) should not have to worry that the barrister's delay in dealing with straightforward papers will jeopardise the case.

It is a general principle of giving instructions not to repeat what is in the documents, but to give an overview, so that counsel knows what to look for when reading the documents. Thus, the brief should, after listing the documents contained in it, begin with a short summary of the facts of the case. In publicly funded cases, the documents must include a copy of the legal services funding certificate and in a conditional fee case, a copy of the agreement and written confirmation that after the event insurance is in place or not as the case may be. A rambling repetition of the Claimant's proof of evidence is a waste of time, since the barrister must read the original. The solicitor's own ideas on the case are valued and should be set out and any particular aspects that need consideration at that stage should be identified. The purpose of the instructions is to obtain the benefits of the barrister's skill and experience, but these benefits will be enriched by the sharing of the solicitor's skill and experience.

Caveats

The term 'pleadings' has gone, but for the sake of convenience the term 'pleader' will be used to identify the maker of a statement of case.

The purpose of the statement of case is to put the client's case as succinctly as possible. All reasonably plausible allegations should be stated, bearing in mind that the case may have been only partly investigated by the time the statement of case is drafted. It is, of course, not permissible to put forward a case for which there is no supporting evidence. The statement of case may be prepared on the basis of the Claimant's statement ready for exchange. More likely however is that it is prepared on the basis of a proof of evidence of the Claimant. Commonly the task of preparing the Claimant's statement for disclosure and the statement of case will be undertaken simultaneously on the basis of the same material.

If working from a proof of evidence, the pleader must allow for the possibility that it has not been prepared as well as it might have been. It is common for failures of communication or errors to creep into the proof of evidence so that it does not, in some vital respect, reflect the reality of the client's experience. For example, the solicitor may not have fully understood the situation described by the Claimant, the latter may have been still in shock or confused, or there may be uncorrected typographical errors. If the statement of case perpetuates an error, at trial there will be a danger of perceptive cross-examination exploiting some discrepancy between the statement of case based on the proof of evidence and the Claimant's own testimony in the witness box.

With this in mind, though bearing in mind Lord Woolf's plea for 'cards on the table', the pleader should be cautious about revealing any unnecessary detail in the Claimant's proof of evidence. The pleader should opt for broad, rather than detailed, assertions. Sketch plans drawn by a client – no matter how skillfully – should not be relied on. Nor should the accuracy of any measurements taken by the Claimant be assumed, except in the broadest way. Further detail may be insisted on later by the Defendant in a request for further and better particulars. If so, very specific information may have to be sought from the Claimant and experts.

STANDARD PROCEEDINGS

In the vast majority of cases, the claim form will be used to start proceedings as governed by CPR Part 16. The claim form must (CPR, r 16.2(1)):

(i)   contain a concise statement of the nature of the claim (see below);
(ii)   specify the claimed remedy;
(iii) contain a statement of value (if appropriate, see below);
(iv)   contain any such other matters as set out in a practice direction.

Particulars of claim

The claim form must either contain or be served with the particulars of claim or the parties of claim must be served within 14 days of the claim form or within the time allowed for service of the claim form, if less (CPR, r 7.4).[2] The particulars of claim are the substance of the Claimant's case. They *must* include (CPR, r 16.4(1)):

(i)   a concise statement of the facts on which the Claimant relies;
(ii)   a statement as to interest sought (see below);

---

[2]   If this is not the case, the Claimant must state on the claim form that the particulars of claim will follow (CPR, r 16.2(2)). The court has power to remedy an error of procedure in serving the particulars of claim under CPR Part 3.10 (*Totty v Snowden* [2002] 1 WLR 1384).

(iii) if aggravated, exemplary or provisional damages are sought, then a statement to this effect and the grounds for such;
(iv) any matters as set out in a practice direction.

The practice direction (16 PD) supplemental to CPR Part 16 specifies matters that must be included in specific claims.

If the particulars of claim are not included in the claim form:
(i) they must be verified by a statement of truth as follows:

> '[I believe] [The Claimant believes] that the facts stated in these particulars of claim are true' (16 PD, para 3.4);[3]

(ii) they must contain (16 PD, para 3.8):
   (a) the name of the court in which the claim is proceeding;
   (b) the claim number;
   (c) the title of the proceedings; and
   (d) the Claimant's address for service.[4]

The particulars of claim *must* include (16 PD, paras 4.1–4.4):
(i) the Claimant's date of birth;
(ii) a brief description of the circumstances of the personal injury;
(iii) details of any provisional damages claimed;[5]

(CPR Part 41 deals with the application of provisional damages)
(iv) in a fatal accident claim (16 PD, paras 5.1–5.3):
   (a) that the matter is brought under the Fatal Accidents Act 1976;
   (b) details of the dependents;[6]
   (c) a claim for bereavement (where appropriate); and
   (d) that a claim is brought on behalf of the deceased's estate under the Law Reform (Miscellaneous Provisions) Act 1934 (where appropriate) (16 PD, para 5);
(v) where a claim is based upon a written contract a copy of the contract should be attached and any general conditions incorporated should be included (16 PD, para 9.3);
(vi) where a claim is based upon an oral agreement, the contractual words used and when and who made them (16 PD, para 9.4);
(vii) where a claim is based upon an agreement by conduct, the conduct and when and who acted (16 PD, para 9.5);

---

3   PD 3.4.
4   PD 3.8.
5
   '4.4 In a provisional damages claim the Claimant must state in his particulars of claim:
   (1) that he is seeking an award of provisional damages under either s 32A of the Supreme Court 1981 or s 51 of the County Court Act 1984;
   (2) that there is a chance that at some future time the Claimant will develop some serious disease or suffer some serious deterioration in his physical or mental condition; and
   (3) specify the disease or type of deterioration in respect of which an application may be made at a future date' (Pt 15 PD(F)).
6   Such details shall include the name, date of birth and nature of dependency.

(viii) any relevant conviction under s 11 of the Civil Evidence Act 1968[7] (16 PD, para 11.1). The Claimant must specifically set out (inter alia):
  (a) any allegation of fraud;
  (b) notice of knowledge of a fact;
  (c) details of unsoundness of mind;
  (d) details of wilful default;
  (e) any facts relating to mitigation of loss or damage (16 PD, para 10.2).

Further, the Claimant must attach a schedule of past and future expenses (16 PD, para 4.2) along with a medical report if such evidence is to be relied upon (16 PD, para 4.3). If it is a conditional fee case, a valid notice of funding (Form N251), but filed when the claim form is issued and served with the claim form.

Although not specified by Part 16 or the practice direction, if the claim is outside the primary limitation period, the Claimant has to specify the date of knowledge.[8]

A subsequent statement of case must not contradict or be inconsistent with an earlier one. Where new matters come to light the appropriate course may be to seek permission to amend the statement of claim (16 PD, para 11.2).

Interest

If a Claimant is seeking interest, then this must be stated in the particulars (CPR, r 16.4(2)). He must state on what basis the interest is claimed and if a specific amount of money is claimed, the particulars must include the percentage rate claimed, the dates from or between which it is claimed, the total amount claimed to date and the daily rate accruing after the calculation date.

The typical claim for interest is as follows:

'The Claimant claims interest pursuant to section 69 of the County Courts Act 1984 [or 35A of the Supreme Court Act 1981 for High Court actions] upon such sums as may be found to be due to him for such periods as the court deems just, at the rates:
  (a) on general damages, at 2% per annum from the date of service of the proceedings until the date of judgment or sooner payment;
  (b) on special damages at the full rate in respect of those items of loss which have fully crystallised and which he will be unable to recover from the Defendant until the trial of the action. Alternatively, at half the appropriate rate.'

Statement of value

As a claim in respect of personal injuries will always be one in which a claim for money is made, the claim form must always include a statement of value (CPR,

---

[7] The particulars must include:
  (i) the type of conviction and the date;
  (ii) the court which made the finding; and
  (iii) the issue in the claim to which it relates.
[8] See *Nash v Eli-Lilly* [1993] 1 WLR 782.

r 16.3(1)). This must state, as precisely as possible, the amount claimed (CPR, r 16.3(2)). This means one of three possibilities:

(i)   the specific amount, if known;
(ii)   the bracket within which the claim is thought to lie;[9] or
(iii)   that the Claimant cannot evaluate the claim.

Further the Claimant must include the amount anticipated as general damages for pain, suffering and loss of amenity. This must be specified as either above or below £1,000 (CPR, r 16.3(3)).

A typical example in a fast track case is:

> 'AND the Claimant claims:
> Damages in excess of £5,000 but limited to £15,000 where damages for pain, suffering and loss of amenity are more than £1,000;
> Interest pursuant to section 69 of the Courts Act 1984.'

If the claim form is issued by the High Court, then the claim form must specify that the Claimant anticipates recovery of £50,000 or more (CPR, r 16.3(5)(c)). In calculating anticipated recovery for this purpose, the Claimant must disregard interest, costs, contributory negligence, any counterclaim or set-off or any money to be paid to the Secretary of State for Social Security under the Social Security (Recovery of Benefits) Act 1997 (CPR, r 16.3(6)).

Essential information for pleading

In order to begin drafting a claim, certain minimum essential facts are required. Here are checklists of the necessary information in three common situations.

Road traffic accidents

(i)   The identity of the parties;
(ii)   the make and registration number (and any other means of identification, such as colour, bicycle, moped, motorcycle, car, van or lorry) of any vehicle involved in the collision;
(iii)   the location of the accident;
(iv)   the directions in which the Claimant and the Defendant were travelling, defined in any appropriate way: by compass bearing, destination, road name, carriageway, etc;
(v)   the date and, preferably, the time of the accident;
(vi)   a description of how the accident happened;
(vii)   whether any prosecution ensued and, if so, for what offences, in which court, when and the result;
(viii) the Claimant's date of birth;
(ix)   a medical report;
(x)   a description of loss of amenities;
(xi)   a statement of damages.

---

[9]   (i) not more than £5,000; (ii) £5,000 to £15,000; or (iii) over £15,000.

Accidents at work
(i)   The identity of the parties and their work relationships;
(ii)   the Claimant's job description;
(iii) the Claimant's place of work;
(iv)   the nature of the work or processes carried out at the place of work, so as to determine which regulations or statutory provisions (if any) apply;
(v)   the location of the accident;
(vi)   the date and, preferably, the time of the accident;
(vii) a description of how the accident happened;
(viii) the Claimant's date of birth;
(ix)   a medical report;
(x)   a description of loss of amenities;
(xi)   a statement of damages.

Fatal accidents

In addition to the above, the following facts are also needed:
(i)   the date when letters of administration were taken out, or grant of probate made, and where;
(ii)   brief details of any claim for loss of dependency and its basis;
(iii) particulars of the Claimant and of the deceased. It is all too early to confuse the details of the two.

Format of the pleading

So long as the statement of case contains the information essential to make out the Claimant's claim and that which is demanded by the practice direction, there is no requirement to lay out the statement in any particular way. However, such documents have traditionally adopted a familiar form which is, because of its familiarity and succinctness easy and quick to read and assimilate. The format in the principal kinds of personal injury claims is described below.

Road traffic accidents

The first paragraph of the standard traffic injury claim describes the accident. It usually starts 'On or about the [date], the Claimant was [walking, cycling, driving] along [name of road] at or near [some identifiable point: junction, bus stop, public house, etc] when the Defendant drove a [car, van, etc]'. This last phrase should describe in a few words how the accident happened. It may be that the Defendant drove his car 'around a bend and collided head on with the Claimant' or 'crossed the central white line and drove into the Claimant's carriageway so forcing the Claimant to swerve and collide with a lamp post'. Or it may be simply that the Defendant drove his lorry 'into the Claimant'. All that is necessary is to give sufficient words to identify the place and date of the accident and how it occurred. The second paragraph begins: 'The said accident was caused by the Defendant's negligence'.

Under the heading 'Particulars of negligence', there are then set out the allegations of negligence which are levelled at the Defendant. The full range of the allegations possible in road accident cases is so limited that they are set out here, and will cover all but the most exceptional case.

'The Defendant:
(a) drove [or cycled or walked] when it was unsafe to do so (this is appropriate when the activity which caused the accident was lawful and proper but for the fact that the Defendant did it in circumstances where it caused the accident);
(b) drove [or cycled or walked] . . . (this is the appropriate place to make the allegation that simply doing what the Defendant did was negligent because it was unlawful or inherently dangerous, for example, driving on the wrong side of the road, driving without lights, driving through a red traffic light);
(c) failed to accord precedence to the Claimant;
(d) drove into [the path of] the Claimant;
(e) drove too fast;
(f) failed to keep any or any proper lookout and/or failed to observe or heed in time, adequately or at all:
    (i)   the presence, position and direction of travel of the Claimant and his [vehicle]; and/or
    (ii) [stop, warning or other signs or signals, or the presence of a road junction, bus coming the other way, black ice on the road, or whatever other visible or audible things there were which should have caused the Defendant to do things differently];
(g) failed to warn the Claimant in time, adequately or at all of the movement of the Defendant's [vehicle];
(h) drove into the Claimant and/or failed to stop, slow down, [accelerate], swerve, or so to control or manage the Defendant's [vehicle] as to avoid the accident;
(i) failed to steer a safe course;
(j) failed to maintain proper control of the [motor vehicle] that s/he was driving [or lost control of the Defendant's vehicle];
(k) the Claimant will further rely on the conviction of the Defendant for the offence of . . . at the . . . Magistrates' Court on [date] as evidence of the negligence of the Defendant, the said conviction having arisen out of the matters referred to in paragraph 1 herein and being relevant to the issues in this action;
(l) the Claimant will further rely on the happening of the said accident as evidence in itself of the negligence of the Defendant (*res ipsa loquitur*).'

The claim then goes on to deal with injury, loss and damage, which is dealt with later in this chapter.

Pedestrian tripping cases

The usual pattern in this frequent source of litigation is as follows. The first paragraph gives the date and place[10] of the accident and describes what the Claimant was doing

---

[10]   Some precision is required: *James v Preseli Pembrokeshire District Council* [1993] PIQR P114.

when he tripped or fell on the highway or pavement. Either as part of the first paragraph or in a separate second paragraph, the link with the Defendant must be made, stating in what capacity the Defendant caused the hole or obstruction. If the Defendant is being sued as the highway authority, then this paragraph should say so.

The allegations of liability will primarily be made on the ground of negligence. Consideration should be given to the Occupier's Liability Acts 1957 and 1984.[11] However, where a highway authority is being sued, there will be an allegation of breach of statutory duty, for example:

'In breach of section 41 of the Highways Act 1980 and/or negligently, the Defendants failed to repair and/or maintain the said highway properly or at all in that . . . [for example, a paving stone had been removed leaving a hole approximately three inches deep].'

There is also the possibility of suing in nuisance in such cases, for example:

'Further or in the alternative, by reason of the matters aforesaid, the Defendants their servants or agents were guilty of nuisance in that they rendered the use of the said highway dangerous.'

The principal allegations of negligence are obvious: creating the hazard; failing to remove it (in whatever ways are appropriate); failing to inspect and/or heed it; failing to fence, light or mark it; failing to ensure that the road was safe. So, for example, in a hole-in-the-pavement case, the following pleading would be typical:

'The Defendant:
(a) caused or permitted the hole in the pavement;
(b) failed to fill, level, or cover the hole so as to ensure that the same was even and level with the surrounding pavement surface;
(c) failed to inspect regularly, sufficiently often or at all and/or heed the presence of the hole in the pavement;
(d) failed to fence or guard the hole and/or pavement;
(e) failed adequately or at all to light, mark or warn of the presence of the hole in the pavement;
(f) failed to ensure that the pavement was safe for pedestrians.'

Animal injuries

Injuries caused by animals to humans are not a common source of litigation but are sufficiently frequent to merit brief mention here.[12] The Animals Act 1971, s 2(2) provides that where an animal does not belong to a dangerous species, the keeper of

---

[11] The obligation to make grounds open to the public, reasonably safe does not include an obligation to protect against dangers that are themselves obvious. See *Cotton v Derbyshire Dales District Council* (1994) Times, 20 June. If the land is a public right of way, then the landowner is not liable for injuries caused by negligence non-feasance. See *McGeown v Northern Ireland Housing Executive* [1995] 1 AC 233.

[12] Liability under the Animals Act 1971, s 2(2) has been discussed in the Court of Appeal in: *Cummings v Granger* [1977] QB 397; *Curtis v Betts* [1990] 1 WLR 459; *Smith v Ainger* [1990] CLY 3297; *Hunt v Wallis* [1994] PIQR P128. A claim to the Criminal Injuries Compensation Authority should also be considered.

the animal is liable for the injury if s/he knew that (i) the injury was of a kind which the animal, unless restrained, was likely to cause, or which, if caused, was likely to be severe; and (ii) the likelihood of the injury was due to the animal's particular characteristics, not normally found in animals of the same species.

The claim should identify the Defendant as the keeper of the animal. The incident (including date, time and place) should be described in a separate paragraph. As knowledge on the part of the keeper of the animal's propensity to attack or bite is a prerequisite for liability under the Act (s 2(2)(c)), this will typically be followed by a paragraph along the following lines:

> 'Those characteristics were well known to the Defendant. In particular, his dog was known regularly to run up and bark at horses as they proceeded through the premises and on a number of occasions had caused horses to bolt until brought under control by the Defendant.'

Police stations keep a dog register containing complaints about particular dogs. Such complaints and any relevant conviction should also be pleaded.

Accidents at work

The particulars of claim in an accident at work case are usually very formalised.

The first paragraph describes the relationship between the Claimant and the Defendant and brings in any statutory provisions which relate to the place of work, though the latter are sometimes put in a separate paragraph. Thus, a typical example would be:

> '1. At the time of the matters described below, the Claimant was employed as a lathe operator by the Defendants at their premises at The Works, Railway Cuttings, East Cheam, Surrey.
> 2. At all material times, the provisions of the Workplace (Health, Safety and Welfare) Regulations 1992 and the Provision and Use of Work Equipment Regulations 1998 applied to his work.'

Second or third Defendants, having some relationship with the Claimant other than a contract of employment, usually have a separate paragraph each.

With only one Defendant, the second paragraph gives the date and place of the accident and a short description of how it happened. The description should be prefixed by the words *'in the course of employment'* so as to put beyond doubt the allegation that the Claimant's accident was sustained while working for the employer.[13] The description of the accident should be short and in broad terms. The pleader's duty is to plead material facts and not evidence. As has been mentioned earlier, the pleader must bear in mind that the explanation of the accident which s/he reads in the instructions and Claimant's statement may not be wholly accurate, for a whole range of reasons. Where significant discrepancies are apparent, the pleader should, of course, contact the solicitor to try to ascertain the true position before drafting.

---

[13]   For a case on employees travelling to and from work, see *Smith v Stages* [1989] AC 928, HL. The court is prepared to look at the reality of the relationship: *Ferguson v John Dawson and Partners (Contractors) Ltd* [1976] 1 WLR 1213; *Lee Ting Sang v Chung Chi-Keung* [1990] 2 AC 374; and *Lane v Shire Roofing Co (Oxford) Ltd* [1995] PIQR P417.

Two typical examples of a concise but clear second paragraph in a work accident case are as follows:

> 'On or about 18 August 1999, the Claimant in the course of his said employment took a pace into the battery room in order to get cleaning materials when he slipped on liquid detergent on the floor which had leaked from a plastic container. The slip caused the Claimant to fall to the ground striking his knee on a battery.'

> 'On or about 27 March 1999, the Claimant in the course of his said employment had switched off the robot machine and lifted the guard in order to remove a broken robot within the said machine when the machine operated and the blade amputated the Claimant's left index finger.'

Often the accident will have been caused by a fellow employee. The second paragraph should name the employee (where the name is known), make clear that s/he, too, was an employee of the Defendant and that s/he was acting 'in the course of his/her employment'.

The third paragraph of the particulars of claim sets out the breach of duty to which the accident is attributed. In every case, allegations of negligence will be made, and in almost every case breach of regulation, but it is worth remembering that the duty in tort reflects a parallel duty arising under the contract of employment, so the action may occasionally be brought in contract as well as tort.[14]

Pleading breach of statutory duty

The breadth of application of the 1992 and subsequent Regulations mean there will usually be breaches of statutory duty. These may be stated in a separate paragraph or as part of the same paragraph as the allegations of negligence. The statutory breach may depend on the nature of the workplace, the nature of the process, the nature of the work of the Claimant, or the place[15] in the premises where the incident occurred.

The relevant facts giving rise to the application of the relevant regulation or statute must be pleaded as well as the breaches alleged.

Pleading should be approached creatively and it is necessary to keep up to date with developments in the regulations and case law.[16]

---

[14]   See *Munkman on Employers' Liability* (12th edn, 1995) pp 75–76. Where the Defendant's liability in contract is the same as its liability in tort or negligence, the court may reduce or apportion the damages claimed in contract, in accordance with the Law Reform (Contributory Negligence) Act 1945: *Forsikrings-aktieselskapet Vesta v Butcher* [1988] 3 WLR 565.

[15]   *Gunion v Roche Products Ltd* 1995 SLT 38; a fork lift truck can be a 'place' within the meaning of the Factories Act 1961, s 29.

[16]   The six regulations are: Management of Health and Safety at Work Regulations 1992, SI 1992/2051 (which do not give rise to civil liability); Workplace (Health, Safety and Welfare) Regulations 1992, SI 1992/3004; Provision and Use of Work Equipment Regulations 1992, SI 1992/2932; Personal Protective Equipment at Work Regulations 1992, SI 1992/2966; Manual Handling Operations Regulations 1992, SI 1992/2793; Health and Safety (Display Screen Equipment) Regulations 1992, SI 1992/2792. For detail see *Redgrave's Health and Safety* (4th edn, 2002) Parts 3–6; and *Munkman on Employers' Liability* (12th edn, 1995) chapters 10–14.

There is some debate about the extent to which the 1992 Regulations fulfil the obligations under the European Directives from which they were derived,[17] so that consideration must also be given by the pleader to whether the Directive should be relied on directly (against a state employer) or indirectly for the purposes of construction of the relevant regulation. It is suggested that the former would need to be claimed, the latter would be for argument. It is also worth bearing in mind that statutory requirements may, in appropriate cases, affect the duty in negligence. In *Butt v Inner London Education Authority*,[18] it was held that a machine which injured a printing apprentice in a college of further education should have been fenced, under a duty in negligence which was analogous to the Factories Act 1961, s 14. The Management of Health and Safety at Work Regulations 1992 now imposes civil as well as criminal liability and is particularly relevant where a failure to carry out an adequate risk assessment is alleged.

As well as the principal statutes relating to workplace safety, there are the more general statutory duties under the Occupier's Liability Act 1957 and the Defective Premises Act 1972. The Consumer Protection Act 1987 also needs to be considered, but it is probably wisest to plead it explicitly.

A large number of statutory duties are qualified by the phrase 'so far as is reasonably practicable'. The Claimant should never plead this qualification to the duty. It is for Defendants to establish on the evidence not only that they could not do whatever was necessary 'so far as was reasonably practicable', but also to state that defence and the essential facts required to establish it if they intend to rely on it.[19]

In the past the Defendant has been entitled to meet an allegation that it failed to provide a safe system of work with a denial: there was no obligation to plead the basis on which it was alleged the system provided was safe.[20] This is no longer permissible since a Defendant denying an allegation must state its reasons for so doing and must state its own version of events if they differ from the Claimant's version (CPR, r 16.5(2)).

As a general rule, the Claimant should avoid referring to the Employer's Liability (Defective Equipment) Act 1969 in the statement or particulars of claim. The facts giving rise to liability under this Act, of course, have to be stated, but referring to the Act specifically may alert an unskilled Defendant's pleader to the danger of making admissions in the defence which would allow the Claimant to enter judgment. Instead the defence pleader is likely to make denials or non-admissions simply in order to keep the case alive on liability. The Act must be specified eventually and the time to do it is by way of a reply or by an amendment to the statement of case after the defence has been received.

Some lawyers tend to claim the breaches of statutory duty separately from the negligence. Specialist pleaders are divided on this issue. The advantage of dealing

---

[17]   On the impact of the European legislation, see Redgrave's *Health and Safety* (4th edn, 2002) pp 3–7, 12–22; and *Munkman on Employers' Liability* (12th edn, 1995) chapters 9–14.
[18]   (1968) 66 LGR 379.
[19]   *Nimmo v Alexander Cowan and Sons Ltd* [1968] AC 107, HL; *Larner v British Steel plc* [1993] ICR 551, CA. The practice described does not appear to be changed by the advent of the CPR.
[20]   *Buchan v Hutchinson & Co Ltd* 1953 SLT 306.

with breaches of statutory duty and negligence separately is that it makes clear that an allegation of negligence is not intended to be coterminous with the parallel allegation of breach of statutory duty. The advantage of claiming parallel duties together is that it is much shorter and less repetitious to do so. That practice, however, requires that any allegation of negligence which the pleader considers goes beyond the scope of a parallel breach of statutory duty must be pleaded separately.

Pleading negligence

The principal allegations of negligence in an accident at work are usually obvious. A checklist is needed to ensure that all appropriate allegations have been made. The starting point of such a checklist is *Wilsons Clyde Coal Co Ltd v English*,[21] where the House of Lords laid down the principal health and safety duties in negligence owed by an employer to an employee. This list can be expanded to a series of allegations which seem to cover all the usual cases. The list below has been adapted to cover the basic principles of the 1992 Regulations.[22] A form of words has been used below that will require greater or lesser adaptation to the circumstances of the particular case. Some will be completely inappropriate for some cases. The personal injury pleader will be familiar with the substantive law which is reflected in the following checklist. The list is intended merely to provide lawyers with an aide-memoire, to ensure that all lines of attack in relation to accident or ill health at work have been covered.

> 'The Defendant:
> (a) failed to provide and/or maintain safe, appropriate and adequate equipment, appliances, machinery, plant, or works;
> (b) caused, permitted or failed to prevent [the event, escape, spillage, hole, explosion, etc] happening;
> (c) failed to provide and/or maintain [the means of containing the danger: extractor hoods, guards, marked alleys for forklifts, etc];
> (d) failed to provide to and/or maintain for the Claimant any or any adequate safe personal protective equipment, in particular [helmet, goggles, toetector boots, etc];
> (e) caused or permitted the Claimant to take the avoidable risk of Y;
> (f) failed to combat the risk of Y at source;
> (g) failed to make any or any sufficient suitable provision to avoid the risk of Y;
> (h) failed to adapt the work and/or the workplace to the Claimant;
> (i) failed to make any or any suitable and sufficient assessment or evaluation of the risk of Y and/or keep the same under review;
> (j) failed to develop and/or implement a coherent and overall risk prevention policy.'

---

21   [1938] AC 57.
22   The allegations need modification to suit disease claims.

Allegations (h) to (j) are derived from the 1992 Regulations, but it is submitted that notwithstanding their statutory force, they now set a strongly arguable standard for negligence.[23]

'(k) failed to provide and/or maintain a competent staff.'

This is a difficult allegation to prove, since it is necessary to show that the employer knew or ought to have known that the relevant member(s) of staff were incompetent.

'(l) failed to provide and/or maintain effective training and instruction; failed to provide and/or maintain effective supervision.'

This allegation is particularly relevant for new starters, young people and those with some physical or mental disability.

'(m) failed to provide and/or maintain a safe place of work and/or access thereto and egress therefrom.'

Failure to maintain a safe place of work should invariably be pleaded unless the engineer's report excludes the possibility that something about the place of the accident (transient or permanent) causes or contributed to the accident.

'(n) failed to provide and/or maintain a safe system of work.'

Pleaded in this general form, this applies both to the particular means of performing the task delegated to the employee and to the broader means by which the employer carried out the operations which involved the Claimant in performing that task. It is an allegation which should always be pleaded.

'(o) failed to inspect adequately, regularly, sufficiently often or at all; failed to heed the report of inspections carried out by [name] on [date]; failed to institute and/or maintain a system of inspection.'

This is a useful line of attack when there have been previous occurrences of some failure of equipment or structure.[24]

'(p) failed to warn and/or inform the Claimant of the risk of Y;
(q) failed to face, cover, mark off, illuminate, place hazard warning signs upon;
(r) failed to heed the previous similar accident to [name] on [date];
(s) failed to heed previous oral/written complaints of [name] on [date] to the effect that Y was dangerous and might cause an accident;
(t) failed to institute and maintain a system of recording and investigating previous accidents and/or complaints.'

Previous accidents and complaints should be particularised as far as possible, though it is often useful to say that 'further particulars will be given after disclosure and inspection'.

'(u) the Claimant will further rely on the happening of the accident in itself as evidence of the breach of statutory duty and/or negligence of the Defendants, their servants or agents.'

---

[23]   See Redgrave's *Health and Safety* (4th edn, 2002) p 14, para 2.16; p 21, para 2.40.
[24]   This line of attack derives from *Barkway v South Wales Transport* [1950] AC 185, supported by *Northwestern Utilities Ltd v London Guarantee and Accident Co* [1936] AC 108.

This is the allegation of *res ipsa loquitur*.[25] Some prefer to plead it in a separate paragraph. Alternatively, it is often convenient to put the point towards the end of the allegations of negligence and breach of statutory duty.

> '(v) the Claimant will further rely on the conviction of the Defendants for the offence of Y contrary to section Y of the Health and Safety at Work Act 1974 at the Y magistrates' court on [date], as evidence of the breach of statutory duty and/or negligence of the Defendants, their servants or agents; the said conviction having arisen out of and being relevant to the matters referred to in paragraph 2 herein.'

Reliance on previous convictions may also be put in a separate paragraph but it is most conveniently added at the end of the allegations of breach of statutory duty and negligence. Previous convictions are rare in accidents at work, but the Health and Safety Executive does prosecute and such convictions are relevant.

Applying the allegations

By way of example, this checklist can now be applied to a hypothetical lifting case, where the Claimant's back has been injured by carrying a heavy box. Such an accident is now specifically covered by the Manual Handling Operations Regulations 1992, breach of which will need to be specifically pleaded. Against a state employer consideration will have to be given also to the Manual Handling Directive (90/269/EEC) to see whether there are additional breaches of the Directive which may not be breaches of the Regulations.[26]

In this example, the pleader will wish to consider adopting the above formulae to allege the following. The employer failed to avoid the need to lift or handle the boxes manually. There was no or inadequate assessment of the risk if there was no alternative to manual handling. The contents of the box were not made easier and safer to handle (by, for example, being split between several containers or being put on a container of more convenient shape or size, or by the provision of handles on the box). The employer caused or permitted the Claimant to do the job when there were stronger workers available, or when the employer knew or ought to have known through proper health surveillance that the Claimant was weak or had a bad back. No lifting equipment was provided. The Claimant and his/her workmate were not properly trained or instructed how to lift and carry the weight. The weight of the box and its heaviest side were not marked. The Claimant and/or workmate were not properly supervised. The workmate might be said to be incompetent. The system of work was at fault in general and in particular in the layout of the work, which required the Claimant to lift these boxes from ground level, rather than their being stored on benches at waist level. The place of work was not kept safe (even though there were no new facts contained in this allegation). The Defendant employers failed to inspect and heed the system of work being employed. They failed to devise a safe system of work. They failed to warn the Claimant of the dangers of lifting heavy weights at all, or of lifting heavy weights in the manner utilised by the Claimant.

---

[25] Though it is not necessary to claim *res ipsa loquitur* expressly: *Bennett v Chemical Construction (GB) Ltd* [1971] 1 WLR 1571.

[26] See above.

There were previous accidents and complaints. *Res ipsa loquitur* would be claimed as a matter of course, as would any conviction of the Defendants for this accident.

As a final check, the lawyer should consider the underlying essentials of health and safety at work cases, to see whether every allegation deriving from them has been made. Did the employer:

(i)   assess the risk;
(ii) use the safest means possible to achieve the employer's objective (not just the safest means of performing the allotted task);
(iii) adapt the work to the worker;
(iv) provide medical surveillance, information and training for the worker;
(v)   contain the danger;
(vi) protect the worker from the danger?

These last two principles can be applied to any accident or industrial disease case. For example, if the Claimant has slipped on some oil, application of the first principle provides the initial allegation, viz, that the machine from which it leaked should have been properly maintained so that it did not leak.[27] Another allegation would be that there was a failure to provide a trough or barrier to prevent foreseeable accidental leaks. Yet another allegation would be that the oil, having got onto the floor, should have been cleaned away, covered over (by duckboards or the like), or had sand, sawdust or fuller's earth applied to it. Application of the last principle gives rise to the allegation that the spillage, floor or gangway should have been fenced off or properly illuminated, or that warning of the danger should have been given or, perhaps, that non-slip boots should have been provided.

In a noxious fumes case, the penultimate principle gives rise to the allegation that the process should have been carried out with substances which did not give off noxious fumes or by a technology which prevented noxious fumes being given off. It gives rise also to the allegation that exhaust equipment should have been provided to extract the noxious fumes before they got into breathable atmosphere. The last principle gives rise to the allegation that the Claimant should have been provided with a respirator.

Often allegations will be made against a fellow employee. The fellow employee should be identified in the second paragraph of the claim. That paragraph should also set out the facts giving rise to the vicarious liability relied on. The allegations against the fellow employee will always be in addition to broad allegations against the employer for failing to provide a safe system and place of work, safe equipment, risk assessment, safest means of achieving the objective, and the like. The allegations against the fellow employee will usually be far more limited and specific. For example, 'John Smith lowered the fork lift forks when it was unsafe to do so', etc.

Finally, it is worth emphasising that allegations should almost invariably be made in the negative, as failures by Defendants to carry out their duties. Occasionally, a positive allegation that the Defendant did something is appropriate, but the Claimant should never plead that the Defendant should have done something. It is not the Claimant's obligation to plead what the Defendant should or could have done, although many of

---

[27]   So the duty under the Factories Act 1961, s 28(1) was not only to clean the floor but to prevent substances from getting there: *Johnston v Caddies Wainwright* [1983] ICR 407.

the allegations will contain implicit charges to this effect, and at trial the Claimant may rely on evidence of what a reasonable employer would have done. That is a matter of evidence usually provided by experts and not a matter of fact to be stated. The duty is to claim negative only.[28] Furthermore, a Claimant who claims positively may be asked for further information. If Defendants deny negative allegations, they may be asserting a positive case for which the Claimant is entitled to details.[29]

Occupational diseases

Disease cases follow the same format as accidents at work. The only significant difference is that disease is often contracted over a period of time rather than in a single incident. The second paragraph of the claim should attempt to specify the beginning and the end of the period during which the disease was caught. When alleging breach of statutory duty, it must be considered whether this period is covered by statutory provisions different from those currently in force. Some diseases, like asbestosis, may take decades to manifest themselves. It is often necessary to plead breaches of long-superseded statutory provisions, such as the Asbestos Regulations 1931 and the Factories Act 1937, if they were in force at the time of the exposure.

Where the client has been suffering from an industrial disease for some time there could be difficulties in establishing when, for the purposes of the Limitation Act 1980, the date of knowledge arose. In these circumstances it is better to let the Defendant take the point on whether an action is time barred. For this reason it is better not to refer to the Limitation Act in the initial claim but to deal with it by way of reply or to amend the statement of case subsequently if the limitation point is raised.

International carriage by air

The Warsaw Convention, arts 17, 18 and 19 contain an exhaustive list of liabilities. The Convention was intended to provide a uniform set of rules eliminating conflict of laws issues and jurisdictional questions, prescribing a limitation period and including elaborate provisions so as to achieve uniform documentation. Article 17 provides the only remedy open to a passenger who suffers injuries arising out of, or from, or in relation to an international flight on which s/he has been carried.[30]

Provisional damages cases and periodical payments

The courts have the power to award provisional damages.[31] Provisional damages apply where there is a chance that at some time in the future the Claimant will, as a result of the Defendant's breach of duty, develop some serious disease or suffer some serious deterioration in his physical or mental condition.[32] It is commonly claimed

---

[28]   *Manchester Corpn v Markland* [1936] AC 360; *Harnett v Associated Octel* [1987] CLY 3072.
[29]   *Pinson v Lloyds and National Provincial Foreign Bank Ltd* [1941] 2 All ER 636 at 644 per Stable J.
[30]   *Sidhu v British Airways plc* [1995] PIQR P427.
[31]   CPR Part 41.
[32]   *Wilson v MOD* [1991] 1 All ER 638.

in cases where there is a risk of developing epilepsy as a result of a head injury or a risk of developing mesothelioma in an asbestos claim. There must be a serious deterioration. Accordingly, the provisions have been held not to apply where there is a risk of deterioration due to degenerative change.

If provisional damages are claimed, the facts on which the claim is based must be pleaded.[33] An example of the wording to be used is annexed to the PD to Part 41.

Some personal injury practitioners are against making claims for provisional damages, though the authors consider it a useful addition to the Claimant's armoury. It is argued that, except in unusual cases, the Claimant is generally better off receiving damages immediately, not only for his/her present condition, but also for the foreseeable risk of deterioration, in spite of the fact that provisional damages, plus a further award if and when the deterioration occurs, appear to reflect better the justice of the case. Deterioration may be a long time coming and the Claimant may have lost touch with his/her solicitors or may forget or be too ill to recall that such provision had been made. The future condition may be overlaid by some other medical condition and sometimes the Claimant may not want the possibility of further litigation. Defendants tend not to like provisional damages claims either. Although a claim for provisional damages must specify the type of future claim and a cut off date, the file remains uncertain. Defendants may therefore be prepared to buy off a provisional award by paying considerably more than they otherwise would.

As well as provisional damages awards, since 1 April 2005, the courts have had the power to make periodical payments awards in respect of damages for future pecuniary loss. This is largely the preserve of very high value claims where particular concerns are raised as to the life expectancy of the Claimant or there is some other good reason to consider that a lump sum would not be appropriate. It is considered more fully in Chapter XXX. The rules state at Part 41.5 that each party may in its statement of case state whether it considers periodical payments or a lump sum is the more appropriate form for all or part of the award of damages and provide relevant particulars of the circumstances relied upon. The court may order that such statement be given if it has not been (Part 41.5(2)) or require more detailed particulars to be given.

Particulars of injury

The third paragraph in a road accident case and the fourth paragraph in an accident or disease at work case should begin:

> 'By reason of the facts and matters set out above, the Claimant has suffered personal injury, loss and damage.'

Then follows the heading 'Particulars of injury'. First of all, the Claimant's date of birth must be stated.[34] Stating the Claimant's age is only likely to cause confusion. Then, the nature of the injury, the medical treatment received, the continuing effect

---

[33]   See CPR Part 41.
[34]   *Practice Direction (Personal Injuries: Pleading)* [1974] 1 WLR 1427.

of the injury, and any disability for work or handicap on the labour market, may be addressed.

Although the Claimant's solicitor must serve any medical report relied upon with the statement of case[35] it is nevertheless occasionally useful to summarise these four aspects of the injury in the statement/particulars of claim. The medical report may not, for example, cover the indirect effects of the injury or indirect disability for parts of the work or handicap on a particular labour market. So, for example, a short summary medical report may simply say that the Claimant has a fractured tibia and remains in plaster and on crutches but can carry out sedentary work. The particulars of injury may elaborate that terse statement by pointing out that the Claimant, though attending work daily, can perform only part of his/her normal tasks and can no longer work overtime because of the injury. It may also point out that the Claimant has lost a season playing semi-professional rugby league and is unable to have sexual intercourse in the position preferred by himself and his wife to such an extent that the marriage has been adversely affected. The effect of the injury on the Claimant's pastimes, domestic, social, sexual and sporting life can be set out.

It is not, in theory, necessary to claim handicap on the labour market (or loss of earning capacity, as it is perhaps better described), since it is an item of general damages. However, it is good practice to do so[36] and the appropriate place is under the heading 'Particulars of injury'. The failure to plead it invites arguments about whether it should be permitted as a head of recoverable damages at trial. The same applies to a claim for loss of congenial employment.

The following standard sentence or a variant is usually inserted at the end of the particulars of injury. This is useful to ensure that the immediate suffering of the Claimant is not overlooked in the pleading:

> 'The Claimant experienced pain, shock and suffering and continues to suffer in his domestic, social and working lives.'

Or:

> 'The Claimant is and will remain at a permanent handicap on the open labour market.'

Fatal accidents

The format for a fatal accident claim is as stylised as the previous examples. The description of the Claimant is as given in the claim form and includes, if appropriate, after the Claimant's name that s/he is the widow/widower and administratrix/ administrator or executrix/executor of the estate of the named deceased person. Letters of administration are taken out when the person dies intestate; the Claimant is referred to as the administrator/administratrix of:

> 'Mary Smith, daughter of the deceased born on [date]
> (b) The nature of the claim in respect of which damages are sought is that, at the time of his death, the deceased was a healthy and happy man, aged 42,

---

[35]   16 PD, para 4.3.
[36]   *Chan Wai Tong v Li Ping Sum* [1985] AC 446, PC.

earning, at the date of his death, £200 per week net and the said dependants were wholly dependent for support on the deceased's said earnings and on the services provided by him. By his death the dependants have lost the said means of support and services and have thereby suffered loss and damage.

(c) The Claimant has suffered bereavement.

Further by reason of the facts and matters aforesaid the deceased's estate has suffered loss and damage.

PARTICULARS OF DAMAGE

Funeral expenses

Loss of earnings between 15 August and 12 October 1998 at £200 per week = £1600,

Damages in respect of pain, suffering and loss of amenity between 15 August and 12 October 1998,

Travel and accommodation expenses for the Claimant in attendance at hospital on the deceased at £150 per week between 16 August and 12 October 1998 = £1200.'

Amending a statement of case

A party may amend his statement of case without permission at any time before it is served on any other party (CPR, r 17.1(1)). However, once the statement of case has been served, it may only be amended with the written consent of all other parties or with the permission of the court (CPR, r 17.1(2)). The court's permission is always required after service if the amendment involves adding, removing or substituting a party (CPR, r 19.4). Even if the permission of the court is not required, the court may disallow any resultant amendment (CPR, r 17.2). The rules do not state what principles the court should apply in exercising its discretion, although it will always seek to give effect to the overriding objective. In principle, permission is likely to be granted unless the proposed amendment has no prospects of success or the amendment is very late and the trial date would be jeopardised.

If the party wishes to amend the statement of case after the end of the relevant limitation period then s/he may only do so in specific circumstances (CPR, r 17.4). Regard must be had to the provisions of CPR, r 19.5, together with s 35 of the Limitation Act 1980.

In relation to an amendment outside the limitation period involving a new cause of action, CPR, r 17.4(2) follows the requirements of s 35(5)(a): namely, if the new cause of action arises out of the same facts or substantially the same facts as are already in issue, the court may allow the amendment. The courts will generally interpret this provision in favour of the party applying as it would be inconsistent with the overriding objective to force the party to start a new claim out of time.[37]

---

[37]   *Goode v Martin* [2002] 1 WLR 1828.

In relation to an amendment outside the limitation period involving a new party in personal injury actions, CPR, r 19.5(4) gives the court the power either to determine whether the Limitation Act provisions apply or should be disapplied at the time of the application to amend or to direct that the amendment be allowed but for issues of limitation to be determined at trial. Further, the courts may allow an amendment to correct a genuine mistake as to the name of a party if it was not one which would cause reasonable doubt as to the identity of the party in question or to alter the capacity in which a party claims.[38]

The typical costs order following an amendment is that the costs of and occasioned by the amendment are borne by the party making the amendment. This can be of particular importance in the context of a late amendment. If the late amendment substantially alters the case that the Defendant has to meet and without which the claim will fail, the Defendant is entitled to the costs of the action down to the date of the amendment.[39] However, at the opposite extreme, if a party refuses to consent to an amendment that it had no reasonable prospect of opposing, it will be ordered to pay the costs of the hearing.[40]

Statement of truth

Statements of cases (including both claim and defence) must be verified by a statement of truth. Indeed a statement of truth must verify (16 PD, para 3.4):[41]
(i)   a statement of case;[42]
(ii)   any further information;
(iii)   a witness statement;[43]
(iv)   amended statement of case;
(v)   application notice.

The form of the statement of truth depends on the document in question. If the statement of truth is contained within the document then it should be in the following form:

Claimant

'[I believe]/[The Claimant believes] that the facts stated in this statement of case are true' (16 PD, para 3.4).

Defendant

'[I believe]/[The Defendant believes] that the facts stated in this defence are true' (16 PD, para 14.2).

---

[38]   CPR Part 19 deals further and generally with adding and subtracting parties.
[39]   *Beoco Ltd v Alfa Laval Co Ltd* [1995] QB 137.
[40]   *La Chemise Lacoste SA v Sketchers USA Ltd* (unreported, 24 May 2006); *Newman v Adlem* (unreported, 16 November 2004).
[41]   CPR, rr 22.1(1)–(3).
[42]   Otherwise the statement of case can be struck out (CPR, r 22.2(1)(a)).
[43]   Failure to do so may make it inadmissible; CPR, r 22.3.

If the statement of truth is contained in a separate document, then it must be headed with the title of proceedings and the claim number, and the document being verified should be clearly identified (CPR, r 22.1(7)).

The statement of truth for a witness statement must be signed by the person making it. A statement of truth for other documents may be signed by the party on whose behalf it is made or by his legal representative (CPR, r 22.1(6)). If the statement of case is not verified by a statement of truth, it remains effective unless struck out, but the party may not rely on the statement of case as evidence of any matters set out in it (CPR, r 22.2(1)).

The court orders by its own motion or any party may apply for a verification of truth. The consequences of a false statement of truth are set out in CPR, r 32.14.

Part 8 procedure

Part 8 of the CPR sets out an 'alternative procedure' for bringing a claim. This is restricted to claims in which the Claimant seeks a court decision on a question or issue which is unlikely to involve substantial dispute of fact or where a practice direction indicates that Part 8 is appropriate (CPR, r 8.1(2)).[44] In the context of personal injury claims, this is most commonly encountered when the court's approval is sought for the settlement of a claim involving a child or protected party prior to the issue of proceedings (CPR, r 21.10(2)).

The general rules concerning the statement of case do not apply (CPR, r 8.9). The Claimant need only lodge and serve the claim form (CPR, r 8.2) and any supporting written evidence (CPR, r 8.5). All the Defendant has to serve and lodge is an acknowledgment of service and any written evidence, within 14 days of the service of the claim form.

---

[44]   For example, CPR Pt 8 PD(F) para 1.4 specifies that a claim for provisional damages which have been settled before commencement should be dealt with by Part 8 where the sole purpose of the claim is to obtain consent judgment.

CHAPTER 17

The Defence

The defence is also referred to as a statement of case. It is the Defendant's opportunity to put its version of the claim. The rules that apply generally to a Claimant's statement of case, equally apply to that of the Defendant.

RESPONDING TO THE CLAIM

Upon receipt of the particulars of claim, the Defendant may respond in three ways:
(i)   file or serve an admission (in accordance with Part 14);
(ii)   file a defence (in accordance with Part 15); or
(iii)   file an acknowledgment of service (in accordance with Part 10).

A Defendant wishing to admit only part of the claim may respond in the form of both (i) and (ii) above, together.

THE DEFENCE

The defence remains the forum by which the Defendant presents his/her 'statement of case'. However, unlike the Claimant, the defence is primarily in the form of rebuttal not assertion. Rule 16.5 specifies how the Defendant must deal with the particulars of claim.

The defence must state whether, in relation to each allegation, the Defendant denies, admits or is unable to do either and requires proof regarding each allegation in the particulars of claim (rule 16.5(1)). When an allegation is denied, the defence must put forward a positive case and state the reasons for the denial and, if it is intended that the Defendant will put forward a contrasting version of events, the Defendant's version must be stated (rule 16.5(2)). Thus defences put in the alternative are unlikely to be justifiable in future.

Unless the defence expressly states that it is admitted, any amount of money claimed requires proof (rule 16.5(4)). If the defence fails to deal with any other allegation, it is taken to be admitted (rule 16.5(5)). Though, if a Defendant fails specifically to deal with an allegation, but has set out the nature of the defence case, and this deals with the issue in the allegation, then it is taken that the allegation is required to be proved (rule 16.5(3)).

If the Defendant disputes the Claimant's statement of value (see earlier), then the reasons must be stated and the Defendant's own statement of value of the claim must be asserted (rule 16.5(6)).

The defence must be verified by a statement of truth (rules 14.1, 22.1(1)(a) and 16 PD, para 14) as follows:

> '[I believe] [The Defendant believes] that the facts stated in the defence are true.'[1]

As with the Claimant's declaration in the particulars of claim, the Defendant is verifying the facts in the statement of case rather than propositions of law. It requires the party to have an honest belief in what is being put forward and to discourage the pleading of cases unsupported by evidence which are put forward in the hope that something might turn up on disclosure or at trial.[2]

The absence of a statement of truth is that the statement of case may be struck out (rule 22.2) The consequence of a false statement of case is that contempt proceedings may ensue (rules 14.3, 32.14).

Under the Statements of Case practice direction, specific contents of a defence are specified for personal injury claims (16 PD, para 15). Where the Claimant has attached a medical report, then the defence must state whether this report is admitted, disputed (with reasons) or neither. If the Defendant intends to rely on a medical report, this must be attached (16 PD, para 15.1).

If the Claimant has included a schedule of past and future expenses and losses, again the defence should state which items are agreed, disputed or neither and when disputed an alternative figure should be supplied where appropriate in a counter-schedule (16 PD, para 15.2).

The defence must also give details of the expiry of any limitation period relied upon (16 PD, para 17.1).

Both parties may refer in his statement of case to any point of law, give the name of any witness he proposes to call or attach to the statement of case any document which he considers is necessary to his claim or defence (Part 16 PD, para 13.3).

REPLY TO DEFENCE (CPR, R 16.7)

The Claimant may reply to the defence. If so, the reply must be filed with the allocation questionnaire and served on all the other parties (rule 15.8) at the time of filing together with a statement of truth (Part 22). A Claimant who does not file a reply is *not* taken to have admitted matters raised in the defence (rule 16.7(1)). If a reply is filed, any matters not dealt with shall be taken to be required to be proved (rule

---

[1]   Part 22.
[2]   *Clarke v Marlborough Fine Art (London) Ltd* (2001) Times, 4 December.

16.7(2)). Once the reply has been served, no party can file or serve any further statement of case without the permission of the court (rule 15.9).

It is unusual for a reply to be necessary in personal injury litigation. A reply is usually only required when an issue raised in the defence needs specific response. For example, if the defence raises a limitation issue or a counterclaim is included.

FURTHER INFORMATION (CPR PART 18)

Requests for further and better particulars and interrogatories are a thing of the past. They have been re-named 'further information'. This is dealt with in Part 18, but does not apply to claims proceeding on the small claims track unless the court of its own initiative orders a party to provide further information (rule 27(2)(3)). In all other cases, the court may now at any time order a party to clarify or give additional information on a matter in dispute, irrespective of whether or not it is in the statement of case (rule 18(1)). Therefore, the requirement for additional material and information is entirely controlled by the court.

Most of the procedural requirements are contained in the Further Information practice direction which supplements Part 18.

Preliminary requests for further information or clarification (18 PD, para 1)

A party seeking clarification or information ('the first party') must serve on the party from whom the information is sought ('the second party') a written request ('a request') stating a date by which the response to the request should be served. The date must allow the second party a reasonable time to respond. The emphasis is on strictly what is necessary and proportionate and the avoidance of disproportionate expense.[3]

The request should:
(i)   be concise;
(ii)   be strictly confined to matters which are reasonably necessary;
(iii) be proportionate to enable the first party to prepare his or her own case or understand the case that s/he has to meet;
(iv)   be contained so far as possible in a single comprehensive document (which may take the form of a letter if the request and/or reply are brief, otherwise in a separate document;
(v)   if made in a letter – in order to distinguish it from routine correspondence:
    (a)   state that it contains a request made under Part 18; and
    (b)   deal with no matters other than the request;
(vi)   the request must (whether in letter or document form):
    (a)   be headed with the name of the court and title and the number of the claim;
    (b)   in the heading state that it is a request made under Part 18, identify the first party and the second party and state the date on which it is made;

---

3   *King v Telegraph Group Ltd* [2005] 1 WLR 2282.

     (c)   set out in separate numbered paragraphs each request for information or clarification;

     (d)   where a request relates to a document, identify that document and (if relevant) the paragraph or words to which it relates;

     (e)   the date by which the first party expects a response to the request;

(vii) a request (if not in letter form) may, if convenient, be prepared so that the response can be given in the same document. If so:

     (a)   to do this the numbered paragraphs of the request should appear on the left-hand half of each sheet so that the paragraphs of the response may appear on the right;

     (b)   where a request is prepared in this form an extra copy should be served for the use of the second party.

Responding to a request (18 PD, para 2)

A response to a request must be in writing, dated and signed by the second party or his or her legal representative. Where the request is made in a letter:

(i)   the second party may give response in a letter or in a formal reply;

(ii)   if in letter form it should identify itself as a response to the request and deal with no other matters than the response.

Unless the request is intended to incorporate the reply in the same document (see above) and the second party uses the document supplied for that purpose the response must:

(i)   be headed with the name of the court and the title and number of the claim;

(ii)   in its heading identify itself as a response to that request;

(iii) repeat the text at each separate paragraph of the request and set out under each paragraph the response to it;

(iv) refer to and have attached to it a copy of any document not already in the possession of the first party which forms part of the response.

A second or supplementary response to a request (whether in letter or document form) must identify itself as such in its heading.

Every response must be verified by a statement of truth.

Second party objections (18 PD, para 4)

If the second party objects to complying with the request or part of it or is unable to do so at all or within the time stated in the request s/he must inform the first party promptly and in any event within that time. This may be done in a letter or in a separate document (a formal response), but in either case reasons must be given and, where relevant, a date expecting compliance should be given. If the request can only be complied with at a disproportionate expense the second party should give that reason in response and explain briefly why that view is taken. There is no need for the second party to reply to the court provided s/he has responded as stated above.

Application for orders under Part 18 (18 PD, para 5)

(See also Part 23 (Applications) and the Applications practice direction.)

An application notice for an order under Part 18 should set out or have attached to it the text of the order sought and in particular should specify the matter in respect of which the clarification or information is sought.

If a prior request for information or clarification has not been made the application notice should, in addition, explain why not. If a request has been made, the application notice or the evidence in support should describe the response, if any. Consideration should be given to whether evidence in support or in opposition to the application is required.

If the second party has made no response to the request properly served, the first party need not serve the application notice on the second party, and the court may deal with the application without a hearing. The second party must have been given at least 14 days and/or the time stated for the response must have expired. Otherwise the application notice must be served on the second party and on all other parties to the claim.

An order made under Part 18 must be served on all parties to the claim.

The court has the power to make a summary assessment of costs at the hearing of such an application (16 PD, para 5.8).

CONNECTED PLEADINGS

Counterclaims and other additional claims (Part 20)

Part 20 of the rules covers any claim other than a claim by a Claimant against a Defendant (rule 20.2(1)). It expressly includes a counterclaim by a Defendant and an additional claim by a Defendant against any person for contribution or indemnity or some other remedy whether or not that person is already a party. Claims under this Part were formerly known as Part 20 claims, but as a result of amendments to the rules, they are now known as 'additional claims'. Any additional party brought into the proceedings is now known in the first instance as 'Third Party', or if there are two, 'Fourth Party' and so on and the document claiming against them is entitled, 'Defendant's Additional Claim against Third Party' or 'Fourth Party' as the case may be.

A counterclaim by the Defendant against the Claimant should normally form one document with the counterclaim following on from the defence. If it is filed with the defence, the Defendant does not need the court's permission. However, even if it is not filed with the defence, it may be made at any other time with the court's permission (rule 20.4(2)). Such an application must be supported by evidence stating the stage which the proceedings have reached, the nature of the additional claim to be made, a summary of the facts on which the additional claim is based and the name and address of any proposed additional party (PD 20 para 2.1). An explanation for any delay in making the claim should be given.

A Defendant may, further, make a counterclaim against any person other than the Claimant by applying to the court for that person to be added as as an additional person (rule 20.5(1)). If such an order is made, the court will give further directions as to the management of the case (rule 20.5(3)).

A Defendant having filed an acknowledgment of service or a defence may then make an additional claim for contribution or indemnity against another Defendant by filing a notice[4] and serving this on that other Defendant (rule 20.6). Again, the court's permission is not required if it is filed and served with his defence or, if that additional party is added to the claim later, within 28 days of after that party files his defence. Otherwise, the court's permission is required (20.6(2)).

All other additional claims (ie not involving a counterclaim or a claim for contribution or indemnity from another party) are made when the court issues the appropriate claim form (rule 20.7). As before, the court's permission will be required unless it is issued at the same that the defence is filed.

When the additional claim requires the permission or order of the court, the following matters *may* be considered (rule 20.9(2)):
(i)   the connection between the additional claim and that of the Claimant against the Defendant;
(ii)   whether the additional Claimant is seeking substantially the same remedy which some other party is claiming from him; and
(iii)   the connection of the questions of fact/law raised in the additional claim to issues and parties already involved (or not involved).

In addition, the courts *must* continue to have regard to the overriding objective of the rules (Part 1).

Where the additional claim form is served on a person who is not already a party, it must be accompanied by forms for defending the claim and admitting the claim, a form for acknowledging service and a copy of every statement of case which has already been served, together with such further documents as the court may direct. The additional claim form must also be served on all existing parties (rule 20.12). As soon as a defence is served, the court will arrange a case management hearing. The defence will be entitled, 'Third Party's Defence to Defendant's Additional Claim' and so on, depending upon what number additional party they are.

Default judgment (Part 12)

Default judgment can be claimed by the Claimant only if the Defendant has failed to serve either a defence or an acknowledgment of service with the requisite time limit (rules 12.3(1)). Once entered, no point can be taken on an assessment of damages which is inconsistent with any issue settled by the judgment on liability.[5]

A Defendant may now serve an acknowledgment of service before having to serve an actual defence. The period for filing such an acknowledgment is 14 days after the

---

4   This notice must contain a statement of the nature and grounds for the claim.
5   *Pugh v Cantor Fitzgerald International* (2001) Times, 20 March.

claim form is served (or 14 days after the particulars of claim if later) (rule 10.3). Therefore, the Claimant may obtain judgment in default if there has been no acknowledgment of service or defence to the claim within this period (rule 12.3(1)).

If an acknowledgment is served, then the defence must be additionally given 28 days after the service of the particulars of claim (irrespective of when the acknowledgment was, in fact, served) (rule 15.4). So, even if an acknowledgment has been served, the Claimant may obtain a default judgment if no defence is served within 28 days of the service of the particulars of claim (rule 12.3(2)).

A default judgment is expressly excluded in certain circumstances. A claim under the Part 8 procedure (rule 12.2) may not be judged in default. Similarly, if a Defendant has applied for summary judgment, satisfied the whole claim (including costs) or has admitted liability and requested time to pay, then a default judgment cannot be obtained (rule 12.3(3)).

The Claimant may obtain a default judgment simply by filing a request in the relevant practice form (rule 12.4(1)). However, if the claim is against a child or a protected person, in tort by one spouse against the other or against the Crown, then the Claimant must make an application for a court order (rule 12.10).

The default judgment must be set aside if the judgment was wrongly entered (rule 13.2). In any other case, the court may still set the judgment aside (or vary it) if the Defendant has a real prospect of successfully defending the claim or it appears to the court there is some other good reason to do so (rule 13.3(1)). The court must have specific regard to whether the Defendant has made the application to set aside promptly (rule 13.3(2)).

The phrase 'real prospect of success' is a re-statement of the test for summary judgment in Part 24, the only material difference being that under Part 24, the onus is on the party Claimant to establish that there are grounds for his belief that the respondent has no real prospect of success whereas under Part 13, it is on the Defendant to satisfy the court that there is good reason why a judgment regularly obtained should be sent aside. It is not enough to show an 'arguable defence'. The Defendant must show that he has a real prospect of successfully defending the claim, although a judge should not conduct a mini-trial.[6]

Summary judgment (Part 24)

The court may give summary judgment against a Claimant or Defendant on a particular issue or on the whole claim if it considers that either the Claimant or the Defendant has no real prospect of succeeding and there is no other reason why the case or issue should be disposed of by a trial (rule 24.2). As noted above, in order to defeat the application, it is sufficient for the respondent to show some real prospect of succeeding on the claim or issue. The prospect must be 'real' as opposed to false, fanciful or imaginary. It is not a summary trial and ordinarily, if the respondent to the application can demonstrate that there is any factual issue that needs to be resolved by the court, the application will tend to fail. It is an extremely difficult application

---

[6] *Swain v Hillman* [2001] 1 All ER 91.

to succeed upon, particularly in the context of personal injury litigation which is so factually dependent or where some form of positive case is advanced. An example of where it might succeed is where the Defendant in its defence admits that there was a fault in work equipment that caused the injury and the equipment was governed by a strict liability provision under, for instance, the Provision and Use of Work Equipment Regulations 1998.

In view of the Draconian nature of the application, a party bringing an application for summary judgment must rigorously comply with the procedural requirements. A Claimant may not apply for summary judgment until the Defendant has failed an acknowledgment of service or a defence unless the court gives permission or a practice direction applies otherwise (rule 24.4).

The application notice must include a statement that it is an application for summary judgment made under Part 24 (24 PD 2(2)). Further, the notice or evidence must identify concisely any point of law or provision in a document on which it intends to rely and/or state that it is made because the applicant believes that on the evidence the respondent has no real prospect of succeeding on the claim or issue as the case may and in either case, that the applicant knows of no other reason why the disposal of the claim or issue should await trial (Part 24 PD 2(3)).

The respondent must file any witness statement in reply seven days before the hearing (CPR, r 24.5). If the court determines the application in the respondent's favour, the court is likely to then give directions for further case management of the case (CPR, r 24.6).

The costs of such an application will generally follow the event. Obviously, if the application is brought by the Defendant the claim is dismissed, the Claimant will be liable to pay the costs of the action and not just the application.

Strike out

Further, rule 3.4(2) makes provision for the court to strike out any statement of case (or part of) if it discloses no reasonable grounds for bringing or defending the claim (rule 3.4(2)(b)), or is an abuse of process or likely to obstruct just disposal of two proceedings (rule 3.4(2)(a)), or where there has been a failure to comply with a rule, practice direction or order (rule 3.4(2)(c)). This should be done at the earliest possible opportunity.[7] The grounds for such strike outs are developed in the Striking Out Statement of Case practice direction. These include a failure to set out facts to support the claim, statements which are incoherent or make no sense, or which simply discloses no cause of action (or defence), or a claim which is vexatious, scurrilous or obviously ill-founded, or a defence statement which is above denial (see 3 PD, paras 1.4–1.6). These provisions are considered more fully in Chapter 19.

An application that a claim is bound to succeed or bound to fail is made under rule 3.4 or Part 24 (or both).

---

[7]   *Halliday v Shoesmith* [1993] 1 WLR 1.

Admissions (Part 14)

A party may admit the truth of the whole or any part of another's case (rule 14.1(1)). This is done by giving notice in writing (rule 14.1(2)) which can be in a statement of case or simply by letter. In such circumstances, the other party may apply for judgment on the admission (rule 14.3).

There are four possible admissions a Defendant may make in a claim (rule 14.1(3)):

(i)   an admission of the whole of a claim for a specified amount of money;
(ii) an admission of part of a claim for a specified amount of money;
(iii) an admission of liability in a claim for an unspecified amount of money without a specified offer; or
(iv) an admission of liability in a claim for an unspecified amount of money and make an offer to pay a specified sum.

The time for making an admission is within 14 days of the service of the claim form or particulars of claim (if later) (rule 14.2(1)). However, an admission may still be made after this period if no default judgment has been obtained (rule 14.2(3)). Furthermore, the rules now importantly cover the position of pre-action admissions made after 6 April 2007. If the admission is made after the party has received a letter of claim or before such letter is received, but expressly stated to be made under Part 14, the party may only withdraw that admission at a later stage if the other party agrees or gives his consent (rule 14.1A(3) or on application to the court (rule 14.1A(5)). When considering any such application to withdraw the admission, the court must have regard to the following non-exhaustive list of matters (PD 14 para 7.2):

(i)   the grounds on which the applicant seeks to withdraw the admission including whether or not new evidence has come to light that was not available at the time of the admission;
(ii) the conduct of the parties including any conduct which led to the party making the admission to do so;
(iii) the prejudice that may be caused to any person if the admission is withdrawn or refused as the case be;
(iv) the stage in the proceedings at which the application to withdraw is made;
(v)   the prospects of success of the claim or part of the claim in relation to the which the offer was made; and
(vi) the interests of the administration of justice.

For admissions made prior to 6 April 2007, the principles set out in *Sowerby v Charlton*[8] will apply and in the case of multi track claims, it will be difficult to oppose the withdrawal.

Specified claims

The Defendant should use practice form N9A for admissions where there is a specified amount of money.

[8]   [2005] EWCA 1610.

If the Defendant admits the whole of the claim (rule 14.4) the Claimant may simply apply for judgment. If no request for time (see below) is made, the request for judgment should specify the date of payment or the date and rate of instalments.

If the Defendant admits only part of the specified claim (rule 14.5) the court serves notice of this on the Claimant and he is required to state that he either accepts the amount admitted in full satisfaction, does not admit the amount (in which case the claim will proceed) or accepts the offer, but disputes any payment method suggested by the Defendant.

The Claimant must file the notice within 14 days of service on him, if this is not done, the proceedings will be stayed until it is (rule 14.5(5)).[9]

If the Claimant accepts the amount, judgment may be obtained for the amount admitted (rule 14.5(6)).

Unspecified claims

In a claim which is for an unspecified amount of money (the more usual in a personal injury case), the Defendant should make any admission on the practice form N9C.

If the admission is made without any offer to pay a specified sum (rule 14.6) the Claimant simply obtains judgment and this is entered for a sum to be decided by the court. If judgment is not sought within 14 days of the admission notification, the proceedings are stayed until this is done (rule 14.6(5)).

The most significant type of admission is that as to liability in an unspecified claim where the Defendant offers a specified amount of money (rule 14.7). The court serves notice on the Claimant requiring him to state whether he accepts it or not. Again the notice must be returned within 14 days or the proceedings are stayed (rule 14.7(4)).

If the amount is accepted, the Claimant may simply obtain judgment for the amount offered (rule 14.7(5)). However, if the Claimant does not accept the offer, he may still obtain judgment (rule 14.7(9)) for an amount to be decided by the court. Therefore, a Defendant must be wary of making such admissions. The system is not in the form of a payment into court, it is an unequivocal admission as to liability. The Defendant loses any power of negotiation if an admission is made.

Where it is left for the court to decide the amount, it shall give such directions as it considers appropriate (rule 14.8).

Request for time to pay

When a specified amount is due, a Defendant may make a request for time to pay (rule 14.9). If the Claimant accepts the request, then judgment is entered on the terms in the request.

However, if the request is rejected by the Claimant, judgment is entered nevertheless, but it is left for the courts to decide the time and rate of payment (rule 14.11).

---

[9]   Although rule 14.5(4) requires the Claimant to file and serve the notice, rule 14.5(5) refers to staying proceedings only if the notice is not filed within 14 days of being served on the Claimant.

CHAPTER 18

Applications

This chapter deals with applications that may need to be made (or revisited) from time to time. In a straightforward personal injury case, no applications may be necessary because of the extensive automatic provisions and the court's case management powers. The general rules about applications for court orders can be found in Part 23 and the Applications practice direction.

For fast track and multi track cases, there are special provisions for seeking the alteration of the case management timetable (CPR, rr 28.4 and 29.5). Agreement between the parties is not normally sufficient, a court order must be sought. Accordingly, an agreement to extend time or postpone a date may be ineffective (though it may help on costs).

Part 23 and the Applications practice direction provides a code which must be applied in the light of the overriding objectives. Every application should be made as soon as it becomes apparent that it is necessary or desirable to make it (PD 2.7). Delay may be penalised.

Applications remain a significant weapon of the personal injury lawyer. They continue to be the tool to force the reluctant Defendant to act. Applications may also be required to protect the Claimant and his solicitor from court sanction if a case management timetable cannot be fulfilled.

The procedures for making an application are simple. There are only slight variations between taking out an application in the High Court, county court or District Registry. The basic form of an application should be kept on disc and altered as necessary.

Applications can be heard before a Master (in London), Registrar in a District Registry, District Judge or judge. Appeals against a Master or District Judge's decision will go to a judge in chambers.

The Summary Assessment of Costs[1] practice direction states that if an application contains a request for the other party to pay the costs of the application, and neither party is publicly funded, then the general rule is that the court should make a summary

---

[1]   Costs practice direction, 1 February 1999.

assessment of the costs unless there is a good reason not to do so, and that the costs should be paid within 14 days of the date of the order. Not later than 24 hours prior to the hearing date each party who intends to seek a costs in any event order must supply every other party with a brief summary statement of the amount of costs sought on the application.

GENERAL RULES ON CONTENT OF THE APPLICATION

If the need arises to make an application the solicitor should consider whether the application should be made separately or may be left to the next fixed procedural hearing (PD 2.8). The court has the power to consider the case as a whole at any hearing (PD 2.9), so the person who attends the application must be ready to deal with the case as a whole and the judge may give case management directions unrelated to the application. The solicitor who sends a representative unfamiliar with the case may find themselves ordered to appear before the court to explain why its time has been wasted. At each point in the case management process the representative appearing before the court must have knowledge of the case with the authority to make decisions.

The application must be issued in the court in which the case is proceeding. It is issued by filing an 'application notice' (practice form N244) and the applicant must serve a copy of this on each respondent, together with any written evidence relied on, and a draft of the order sought. The notice must comply with any relevant time limits (for example, those imposed under the Civil Evidence Act 1995). The notice must state (rule 23.6) what order the applicant is seeking and briefly why the order is sought. It is possible for the applicant to rely on matters set out in the notice as evidence (but this cannot be at trial) and if so, the application must be verified with a statement of truth (Statements of Truth practice direction 1.2). The notice must also state whether or not the party wishes the matter to be dealt with at a hearing or without a hearing. If written evidence has already been filed in the proceedings, and/ or served on the parties, then it does not have to be refiled or reserved. This does away with the old nonsense of serving a whole set of reports appended to an affidavit when they have already been served.

SERVICE

A copy of the notice must be served 'as soon as practicable after it is filed' (PD 4.1) – this indicates that the familiar practice of serving at the last permissible moment will be considered unacceptable by the court. In any event, unless there is a specific rule that states otherwise, it must be served with at least three clear days before the court is to hear the matter, unless the court directs otherwise (rule 23.7(1)(b), PD 4.1). Where there is insufficient time for service informal notice must be given (presumably, as early as possible) when secrecy is required (PD 4.2).

Service of an application notice is not required where there is exceptional urgency, by consent of all parties, with permission of the court, where the application is to be made out an already fixed hearing orally and the other parties have been notified informally and where a court order, rule or practice direction permits (PD 3).

If the solicitor relies on the court to serve the notice, she must file with the notice any written evidence she wishes to rely on in support.

The court can vary the time to serve the notice, and can deal with orders by consent. If the parties agree to the court dealing with the matter without hearing, then they can do so and the court will decide the application on the evidence filed with it in the parties' absence.

Where a party fails to attend the hearing of an application and the court makes an order in that party's absence, it has the power on application or of its own initiative to re-list the application.

When the court receives the application form it will notify the applicant of the date and time of the hearing (if there is to be one) (PD 2.2). If no hearing is requested then the application form will be sent directly to the master or district judge who will consider whether it is suitable to deal with in the absence of a hearing, PD 2.3). The court will consider whether or not any directions as to the filing of further evidence should be made (PD 2.5), whether or not a hearing is ordered.

CONSENT APPLICATIONS

Where both parties agree to the court making an order – for example that a voluntary interim payment be made – then, in most cases, the application may be by consent. In such a case, the relevant fee for the application must have been paid, and both parties must signify their consent to the order being made. The words 'we consent to an order being made in the above terms' will suffice. In addition, the parties must submit to the court any relevant material that it may need to be satisfied that it is appropriate to made the order (PD 10.4). A letter will do.

A consent order may be made by a court officer (rule 40.6(2)) without a hearing or judicial intervention where no party is acting in person, in the following circumstances:

(i) a judgment or order for:
    (a) the payment of an amount of money (including a judgment or order for damages or the value of goods to be decided by the court); or
    (b) the delivery up of goods with or without the option of paying the value of the goods or the agreed value;

(ii) an order for:
    (a) the dismissal of any proceedings, wholly or in part;
    (b) the stay of proceedings on agreed terms, disposing of the proceedings, whether those terms are recorded in a schedule to the order or elsewhere;
    (c) the stay of enforcement of a judgment, either unconditionally or on condition that the money due under the judgment is paid by instalments specified in the order;
    (d) the setting aside under Part 13 of a default judgment which has not been satisfied;
    (e) the payment out of money which has been paid into court;
    (f) the discharge from liability of any party;

(g) the payment, assessment or waiver of costs, or such other provision for costs as may be agreed.

TELEPHONE HEARINGS

There is a specific power to deal with applications by way of telephone hearings (PD 6). By virtue of PD 6.2, in all those courts where telephone conferencing facilities are available, allocation hearings, listing hearings, interim applications, case management conferences and pre-trial reviews with time estimates of less than one hour will be conducted by telephone unless the court orders otherwise. The exception to that provision relates to cases where the application is made without notice to the other party, all the parties are unrepresented or more than four parties wish to make representations at the hearing.

If a party does not wish the hearing to be by telephone, such request must be made at least seven days before the hearing or such shorter time as the court permits and may be made by letter. The court will then determine such request.

The practice direction provides that the applicant's legal representative must arrange the conference with one of the approved panel of service providers (see www.hmcourts-service.gov.uk) for precisely the time fixed by the court. The operator must be told the telephone numbers of all those participating and the sequence in which they are to be called. If counsel are to be used it is the responsibility of the applicants legal representative to ascertain from all the other parties whether they have instructed counsel and, if so, the identity of counsel, and whether the legal representative and counsel will be the same or different telephone numbers. The call sequence will be; the applicant's legal representative (and his counsel if on a different number), legal representative and counsel for all other parties, then the judge. Essentially, the rules provide that the parties must be ready and waiting for the judge.

Speaker-phones cannot be used if they cause the judge or any other parties difficulties in hearing.

The telephone charges fall within the cost of the application.

The legal representative charged with the carriage of the telephone hearing must file and serve a case summary and draft order by no later than 4pm on the last working day before the hearing if the case is a multi track case and in any other case, if the court so directs. Similar provisions apply to any party wishing to rely upon a document at the hearing.

VIDEO-CONFERENCING

There is a provision within the practice direction for the court to deal with an application by way of video-conference if such facilities exist (the Bar Council in London provide these facilities at £180 per hour plus VAT at the time of writing).

ATTENDANCE

Rights of audience before a master or district judge are not restricted. In many straightforward applications it has, in the past, been sufficient for a clerk to represent the Claimant. However, the solicitor must remember that the court under its case management powers can and will look at the case as a whole on any application (PD 2.9). There must be a balance to strike between being cost conscious of hourly rates, and affording the court the opportunity to review the whole matter with the solicitor in charge of the case.

TACTICAL APPLICATIONS

A number of procedural applications remain available to both sides and should be kept in mind from the time of service of the proceedings. These can be very useful weapons in the Claimant's solicitor's hands, but some can be equally useful if used at the right moment by the Defendant's lawyers.

The applications to consider here are for judgment in default, to strike out the whole or part of a pleading, to obtain summary judgment, to consolidate actions, to dispose of a case on a point of law, for a split trial and for an interim payment. Some are more common than others.

Notices of intention to proceed (after delay) are included though there will remain little place for such notices in the new case management system under the new rules. Withdrawal and discontinuance are also dealt with here.

JUDGMENT IN DEFAULT

When the Defendant has failed to file an acknowledgment of service or has failed to file a defence within the relevant time limit, judgment in default may be obtained. The boxes at the bottom of form N205B should be filled in. The procedure for obtaining judgment in default are set out in Part 12 and is more fully discussed in Chapter 17.

Defendants can apply to have such judgment set aside, but will need to show good reason and do so promptly. The penalty, even if successful in getting the judgment set aside, is, however, threefold. First, the Defendant will normally have to pay the costs. Secondly, the Claimant's lawyers will have exercised decisive control and so will have won a psychological advantage. Thirdly, the Defendant's lawyers will be embarrassed at having to explain to their client how judgment came to be entered against them.

STRIKING OUT STATEMENT OF CASE

The court has the power to strike out all or part of a statement of case under rule 3.4(1) if it discloses no reasonable grounds for bringing or defending the claim, that it is an abuse of the court's process or is otherwise likely to obstruct the just disposal of the proceedings or that there has been a failure to comply with a rule, practice direction or court order.

The court may strike out of its own motion, or upon application by any party. If the court has struck the matter out of its own initiative the order must state that the affected party may apply to have it set aside, varied or stayed. If the court does not specify a time limit in which to apply to set aside, it must be done within seven days after service of the order. Delay is almost certain to defeat an application to reinstate.

On an order to strike out a statement of case the court 'may make any consequential order it considers appropriate'. These provisions are considered more fully in Chapter 19.

STRIKING OUT FOR NON-PAYMENT OF FEES

The court may automatically strike out a case (under rule 3.7) if a Claimant does not pay the allocation questionnaire or pre-trial check list fees by the date specified by the court, where no application for exemption from or remission of the fee has been made before the specified date. The court will then automatically allow the Defendant his costs of the proceedings to the date of strike out.

If this happens the Claimant may apply to have the claim reinstated – if the court allows this it will be conditional on the Claimant paying the fee or filing notice of exemption or remission from paying the fee within two days of the order.

SUMMARY JUDGMENT

The provisions for summary judgment can be found in Part 24 and the associated practice direction on the Summary Disposal of Claims. There are various provisions for obtaining summary judgment. An application for summary judgment will commonly be made when the Defendant has made a full admission in the Defence and before the case management questionnaire has been filed. However, the court on reviewing the case at any point, but especially on first review when it allocates the matter to the relevant track can exercise its power to give summary judgment.

Either the Claimant or the Defendant may apply for summary judgment in the matter in hand. The court, of its own motion, can also fix a hearing for summary judgment.

The grounds for summary judgment are that the Claimant/Defendant has no reasonable prospect of successfully succeeding or defending in the claim or issue, and there is no other compelling reason why the case or issue should be disposed of at a trial (rule 24.2(a)). This provision is in addition to the strike out powers above and may be based (PD 1.3) on a point of law or evidence which can reasonably be expected at trial (or lack of it), or both.

Summary judgment may be given in most types of proceedings, including personal injury proceedings.

Consideration should be given to applying for summary judgment at the time of issue; the rules provide that the application can be made either after filing of the acknowledgment of service or a defence (rule 24.4(1)).

Applications for summary judgment by the Claimant are rarely used in personal injury cases but there are opportunities, for example where the insurers simply will not make an admission in a claim where they are obviously going to have to concede. It may also be considered in a claim where there is an element of risk and the Claimant would like to force early evidence out of the Defendant, though there will be a cost penalty on failure. It is akin to the procedure used for an application for an interim payment – and might, occasionally, be combined with an interim payment application in a very strong case.

If an application for summary judgment is made after filing of the acknowledgment of service it will stay the filing of the defence. It may well be better since the Defendant must file a positive defence to see what it may say before applying for summary judgment.

Summary judgment is ideally sought when the Claimant files his allocation questionnaire after service of defence and before the claim is allocated to the relevant track. The application is made on notice; this must include a statement that it is an application for summary judgment and made under Part 24 (PD 2(2)). The notice, or evidence served with it, must identify concisely any point of law or provision in a document on which the application relies,[2] and it must state that the application is made because the applicant believes that on the evidence the respondent has no real prospect of succeeding on the claim or issue or as the case may be successfully defending the claim or issue to which the application relates (PD 2(3)). The applicant must state that he knows of no reason why the matter should not proceed to trial (PD 2(3)).

For the above reason, when making the application, the solicitor must be quite clear that she has researched all the relevant avenues of evidence. So, for example, in a road traffic accident case, summary judgment should not be applied for until the police report has been disclosed.

The application should identify the written evidence on which the applicant relies (PD 2(4)), but the applicant may file further evidence if necessary (rule 24.5(2)). The application must draw the respondent's attention to his rights to serve his own evidence and the time limits within which he must do this (PD 2(5)).

The respondent (or parties if the application is on the court's own motion) must be given 14 days' notice of the date fixed for the hearing and the issues it is proposed the court will deal with on the application (rule 24.5(3)). The respondent, if he wishes to rely on evidence, must file it and serve copies on all other parties at least seven days before the return date for the hearing (rule 24.5(1)). If the applicant wishes to rely on written evidence in reply he must file it and serve a copy on the respondent at least three days before the summary judgment hearing (rule 24.5(2)).

If the court fixes a summary judgment hearing of its own motion, then any party who wishes to rely on written evidence must file it and serve copies on every other party to the proceedings at least seven days before the hearing and replies to that evidence must be filed and served at least three days before the hearing date (rule 24.5(3)). Evidence that has already been filed does not need filing again (rule 24.5(4)). All written evidence must be verified with a statement of truth.

---

[2] Under the old rules, more than one application could be made provided the new application was made in relation to a new issue: *Bristol and West Building Society v Brandon* (1995) Times, 9 March. There seems no reason why this principle should not apply under the CPR.

A summary judgment hearing will take place before a master or district judge. Either may direct that the matter be referred to a judge for hearing.

Where it appears that it is possible that a claim or defence may succeed but improbable that it will do so, the court may make a conditional order against that party (PD 5.2). A conditional order may require a party to pay a sum of money into court or to take a specified step in relation to his claim or defence as the case may be and provides that the case may be struck out if the party does not comply. Conditional orders to pay money into court will not be unusual, it is assumed against personal injury Claimants: this measure is surely intended for Defendants, but the CPR and practice direction do not expressly say so and this rule may be used to put pressure on a Claimant with a weak case. How it will be used where the Claimant is legally aided or under a CFA with after the event insurance, is not yet clear.

If the application does not specify that costs are required no order on costs will be made. Otherwise, the court will usually make an order for assessment of costs, to be paid forthwith to the date of the hearing.

If the Claimant is successful in obtaining summary judgment or liability, provision will need to be made to assess damages. The matter will go to a case management hearing for directions for this purpose.

The advantage of making or obtaining summary judgment for the Claimant is to remove the risks of litigation on liability, and to do so speedily. Such an order will have a profound effect on negotiations. It also enables a speedy application for an interim payment.

DISPOSAL OF CASE ON POINT OF LAW

The practice direction provides that an application for summary judgment under rule 24.2 may be on a point of law, which includes a question of construction of a document (rule 1.3). The mechanics of an application for disposal of a case on a point of law are as for the other forms of summary judgment.

JUDGMENT ON ADMISSIONS

If the Defendant admits the whole of the claim (ie liability subject to assessment of damages), whether in writing or by way of pleadings, the Claimant may proceed to obtain judgment (CPR, r 14.6(4)).The request found on the bottom of the notice of issue (unspecified amount) form N205(b) may be adapted for this purpose if the court does not supply an appropriate 'practice form' (as required by CPR, r 14.6(4) – form N205B is not appropriate as it stands since it is directed to judgment in default of defence *or admission*). Under rule 14.6(5) the claim is stayed if the Claimant does not file a request for judgment within 14 days after service of the admission on him.

If the Defendant admits liability he may do so by filing a notice on form N9C which provides for admission of liability with application for the court to determine the amount or with an offer to pay a specified amount. This form is primarily designed for an individual Defendant, requiring him to set out his income and expenditure and family circumstances. It is hardly appropriate for an insurance company! The Claimant again, must respond to the court within 14 days. If the notice is not returned within 14 days after service, the claim is stayed until the notice is filed (CPR, r 14.6(4)). The Claimant's response will state whether he accepts any offer made on the notice.

If the Defendant's offer is not accepted or no offer is made then the Claimant files a request by adapting form N205B seeking judgment, assessment of damages and costs. Directions will then be given for a hearing.

The court may allow a party to amend or withdraw an admission, subject to conditions (CPR, r 14.1(5)). The rules have now been extended to cover pre-action admissions made after 4 April 2007 to avoid the effects of *Sowerby v Charlton*.[3] That case had held that pre-action admissions in multi track claims could be withdrawn as of right. This inevitably caused consternation to Claimants who had proceeded with the claim pre-issue on the assumption that the Defendant would not resile from its admission, only to find a full denial of liability served with the defence. Under the new provisions, if the admission is made after the party making it has received a letter of claim or is stated to have been made under Part 14, the withdrawal can only be made before commencement of proceedings if the other party agrees or after the commencement of proceedings if the other party agrees or the court gives permission (CPR, r 14.1A(3)). The non-exhaustive criteria which the court will apply in considering such application are set out at PD 14.7.2. Namely:

(i)   the grounds upon which the applicant seeks to withdraw the admission including whether or not new evidence has come to light which was not available at the time the admission was made;
(ii) the conduct of the parties, including any conduct which led to the party making the admission;
(iii) the prejudice which may be caused to any person if the admission is withdrawn;
(iv) the prejudice that may be caused to any person if the application is refused;
(v)   the stage in the proceedings at which the application to withdraw is made; in particular in relation to the date or period fixed for trial;
(vi) the prospects of success (if the admission is withdrawn) of the claim or part of the claim in relation to which the offer was made and
(vii) the interests of the administration of justice.

CONSOLIDATING ACTIONS

Consolidation[4] of actions to enable two or more actions to be heard simultaneously by the same judge may be ordered where there is 'some common question of law or fact bearing sufficient importance in proportion to the rest of the subject matter of the actions to render it desirable that the whole should be disposed of at the same time'.[5]

---

3   [2005] EWCA Civ 1610.
4   The old RSC Order 4, rule 9 and CCR Order 13, rule 9 are not preserved. Details on consolidation are to be found in Part 3 under the court's case management powers.
5   *Payne v British Time Recorder Co Ltd* [1921] 2 KB 1.

In personal injury cases, the question of consolidation usually occurs where separate actions have been commenced by separate Claimants against the same Defendant arising out of the same occurrence. It is possible to consolidate the actions up to the point of a decision (or admission) on liability, giving conduct to one Claimant's solicitor to save costs. The actions may then be separated for determination of quantum.[6] Where there are several cases it may be appropriate or preferable to stay some actions and determine liability first in a selected 'lead' case.[7] If the lead case fails or is settled, another can be substituted if the generic issue has not been resolved by the failure or settlement of the lead case.[8] Actions cannot be consolidated if there are different Defendants in each action, even if the claims relate to the same incident. The procedure for consolidation is overshadowed now by the well-established procedures for multi party litigation.

The court's power to consolidate and join are contained in Part 3 under its general case management powers. See rule 3.1(2)(g) and (h). The application should be made as soon as possible. The nearer any of the cases are to trial, however, the greater the likely objections and the more likely that the court will refuse to consolidate because of the difficulties it would cause the Defendants. An application for consolidation should be made to the master in the High Court or to the District Judge in the county court. The courts usually favour consolidation because of the saving of time and expense, unless one party will clearly be prejudiced. A judge, at a case management conference, may order consolidation of several claims arising out of the same incident as the court's own motion. The solicitor should be prepared to deal with such a proposal.

Where different issues may arise on the pleadings in cases arising out of the same incident, it may be preferable to ask the court to order that the cases be heard consecutively by the same judge.

SPLIT TRIALS

Trials can be split (pursuant to CPR, r 3.1(2)(i)), so that liability is determined at the first hearing and the issue of quantum, if liability is established, is dealt with at a later hearing. Split trials are encouraged by the court for obvious economic reasons. Rightly, it is supposed that once liability is determined, quantum is likely to be subsequently negotiated to agreement. Often split trials are beneficial to Claimants. Once liability is dealt with, any argument for a discount of damages for the risk is for the solicitor (and counsel if instructed) under a CFA. Where prognosis is uncertain an early trial on liability will save further delay when prognosis becomes sufficiently certain to have a trial on quantum. In such a case interim payments may be more easily obtained after a successful trial on liability.

Where the issue of quantum is complex and will be expensive to try, it may be in both parties' interest to determine liability first to see whether it is necessary to run to the costs of investigation of, and trial on quantum.

---

6   *Healey v A Waddington & Sons Ltd* [1954] 1 WLR 688.
7   *Amos v Chadwick* (1877) 4 Ch D 869.
8   *Bennett v Lord Bury* (1880) 5 CPD 339.

Judicial case management favours split trials. It is available for both fast track and multi track cases and must be considered at the case management allocation point. In fast track cases, a split trial may be the only way of fixing a trial date within the 30-week period (see Chapter 4), because of the lack of availability of experts. It may also be a way of keeping the trial length within the one day required of fast track cases. Furthermore, a reduction in the number of experts by trying liability alone may permit the case to be maintained as fast track (one expert per party per field with a limit of two fields).

On the other hand, a split trial is rarely appropriate if there is not a clear demarcation between issues of liability and quantum. For instance, if the medical expert will not only be called to give evidence on the quantum of damages but also whether the Defendant's breach of duty caused the Claimant to suffer injury in the first place. In those circumstances, where the issues are inextricably linked, the judge may well consider that there is little cost saving in having the medical expert potentially attend two separate trials.

STAYING PROCEEDINGS

An application to stay proceedings continues to be a tool of the Defendant commonly used when the Claimant has failed to comply with a procedural requirement, such as failing to attend a medical examination by the Defendant's expert or to give authority to the Defendant to obtain the Claimant's medical records or produce a detailed Schedule of Damages. For the stay to be granted, the failure must be in relation to something that the Claimant is obliged to do.

The court has under its general case management powers (rule 3.1(2)(f)) the power to stay a case of its own initiative, and this tool will be used as a means of compelling a party to comply with a particular direction.

A stay may be sought by one party (after issue of proceedings) for 28 days to allow attempts to settle the claim or resolve it through ADR (CPR, r 26.4, PD – Case Management – Preliminary Stage: Allocation and Re-Allocation 3). The court may extend the stay for such period as it considers appropriate, conditional upon the Claimant telling the court if the case has settled (CPR, r 26.4(4)).

There are situations in the CPR for an automatic stay to be applied, for example (under rule 14.6(5)), if the Defendant makes an admission pursuant to Part 14 the case will be stayed if the Claimant does not make an application for judgment within 14 days.

DISMISSAL FOR WANT OF PROSECUTION AND FAILURE TO SET DOWN

Before the advent of the CPR, the courts took measures to speed up cases by rigorous application of CCR Order 17, rule 11(9) in the county court,[9] to automatically strike out claims which had not been set down for trial within 15 months after close of pleadings (or nine months after an order to set down). With the new rules, these

---

9   As to which see *Rastin v British Steel* [1994] 1 WLR 732, CA.

provisions are no longer required since the strict timetables imposed by the CPR and the courts under the case management functions have so many sanctions at every stage.

NON-COMPLIANCE WITH THE RULES

Where there has been a failure by the other side to comply with a rule, practice direction or court order, consideration should always be given to issuing an application; otherwise the court might consider that there has been an implied consent or waiver of the breach. Although CPR, r 3.4(2)(c) gives the court power to strike the claim out in such circumstances, the court will almost invariably consider alternative sanctions, such as imposing sanctions and costs orders. This is more fully set out in Chapter 19.

NOTICE OF INTENTION TO PROCEED

It used to be the case that where a year or more had elapsed since the last proceeding in a cause or matter, a notice (by letter), usually of intention to proceed had to be served. The effect of this was that the Defendant then had four weeks in which to issue an application to strike out the action. Again, with the new rules and court's case management role this procedure is now defunct.

DISCONTINUANCE

The procedure for discontinuing all or part of the claim is governed by CPR Part 38. The desirability of discontinuance may arise for a variety of reasons and at any stage of the case. It may be that what was a promising claim turns out on investigation to be hopeless. It is preferable to discontinue or withdraw as soon as the decision is made, since any delay may cause the Defendants to incur further, unnecessary costs, eg, commissioning experts' reports. The pre-action protocols should lessen the likelihood of discontinuance of an action immediately after issue of proceedings. If the Defendants have complied properly with the requirements upon them, then the Claimant should have a good idea of what the defence will contain.

If discontinuance becomes necessary, agreement (so that, for example, costs lie as they fall) should always be explored. Otherwise, costs are usually awarded against the withdrawing or discontinuing party.

Under rule 38.2(1), the right to discontinue exists at any time. However, if the Claimant has had an interim payment, he can only discontinue if the Defendant who has made the payment consents in writing or the court gives its permission (and almost certainly orders the payment to be returned) (CPR, r 38.2(2)(b)). If there is more then one Claimant, all must confirm consent to the discontinuance or the court must give its permission (CPR, r 28.2(2)(c)).

To discontinue all or part of a claim, the Claimant must (CPR, r 38.3) file with the court and serve a notice of discontinuance on every party. Appended to the notice must be any consents – if relevant. If there is more then one Defendant, the notice must clearly state which Defendant the Claimant is discontinuing against. The

Defendant has the right to have the notice set aside in certain circumstances, but this application must be made within 28 days of service of the notice of discontinuance (CPR, r 38.4).

Unless the court's permission is required to discontinue, discontinuance takes effect on the date when the notice is served on the Defendant and proceedings are at an end against him on that date (rule 38.5). The Defendant will be entitled (by CPR, r 38.6) to his costs to the date of service of notice; if the discontinuance relates only to part of the action he will be entitled to costs of that part of the action. This rule does not apply to small claims where the cost provisions are either fixed or at the court's discretion. A Claimant who for good reason wishes to avoid the costs penalty must apply for an order under rule 38.6(1). This will be comparatively rare, but may apply, for instance, in cases where a Defendant had failed to comply with any of the pre-action protocol, forcing the Claimant to issue proceedings which it transpires have little prospects of success.

The court's permission will be needed to institute a fresh action where the Claimant discontinues the old action after service of the defence and wishes to bring another claim against the Defendant on substantially the same facts (CPR, r 38.7). Again, this is likely to be granted where the Claimant was misled, important new evidence has come to light or there has been a change in the law. However, it would have to be an exceptional case and issues of limitation may arise.

The court will not normally order the Claimant to pay the costs of a partially discontinued case until the end of the claim. However, pursuant to CPR, r 38.8, it is open to the court to order that the costs on an issue should be paid at the time of discontinuance and in the event of failure to pay, for the proceedings to be stayed.

INTERIM PAYMENTS

An interim payment[10] is a payment on account of damages to be made to the Claimant prior to the full trial of the action. Interim payments are dealt with in Part 25 (CPR, r 25.1(1)(k)) and the associated Interim Payments practice direction.

In order to obtain an interim payment in a personal injury case, it is necessary to show that the Defendant has admitted liability, or judgment has been obtained with damages to be assessed, or the court is satisfied that if the case went to trial the Defendant would be held liable for a substantial sum of money (CPR, r 25.7(1)). If the case involves two more Defendants and the order is sought against any one or more of those Defendants, an additional requirement is that all the Defendants are either insured in respect of the claim or the MIB in a road traffic accident or a public body (CPR, r 25.7(1)(e)). An interim payment ordered by the court must not be more than a reasonable proportion of the likely amount of the final judgment and must take into account any contributory negligence, set-off or counterclaim (CPR, r 25.7(4) and (5)). Obviously, the court will be cautious and keen to ensure that there is no real risk of there having to be an order at the conclusion of trial for repayment of sums which may well have been dissipated. Further, judges are conscious that large interim payments can result in disappointment when judgment is eventually entered and there is little money left to be paid.

---

[10]   CPR, para 25.1(1)(k) and rules 25.6–25.9.

It is implicit from the practice direction (PD 2.1(2)) which requires an application to specify the items in respect of which the interim payment is sought, that these items must be reasonable. The Claimant does not have to demonstrate that a certain sum is required to cover any particular need over and above the general need that a Claimant has to be paid his damages as soon as reasonably may be done.[11] Furthermore, the court is not concerned with what the Claimant proposes to do with the money received.[12] When the Court of Protection is involved, it is for that court to decide when and how the money is to be spent.

In many cases, it may be more convenient to pursue or obtain payment at a case management hearing than to seek by a separate hearing. An application for an interim payment can be made in a fast track claim, but because of the speedy progress of the case to trial, an interim payment may well be of marginal benefit unless there is a split trial.

An application can be made at any stage for an interim payment after the Defendant's acknowledgment of service has been lodged, or should have been lodged (CPR, r 25.6(1)). However, it will usually be worth waiting to see the defence, which, even if it does not admit liability, may, because of the requirement to serve a positive defence, make it easier to prove that the Claimant is likely to succeed at trial.

Interim payment are obtained more easily by consent nowadays, particularly upon proof of need where the payment may diminish a source of continuing loss which the Defendant may ultimately bear.

The Claimant's solicitor should always write to the Defendant's solicitor asking for a voluntary interim payment before issuing an application, otherwise costs are risked. A voluntary interim payment will not require a court order, although such an order by consent may be preferred by some Defendants. In the absence of an order an exchange of correspondence can set out the conditions for payment.

An interim payment cannot be accepted on behalf of a child or patient without a court order.

The application is made, at first instance, to the master or district judge, and is usually a private room appointment, and, where it is foreseen that difficult questions may arise on liability, most probably attended by counsel.

The application must be supported by evidence (rule 25.3(2), PD 2.1) setting out the sum of money sought by way of interim payment and the items or matters in respect of which the interim payment is sought. Details of special damages and past and future losses must be provided. The medical reports and other documents must be attached. An interim payment is no longer exempt from the first charge to the Legal Aid Fund and it must be declared to the Board when the client's eligibility for legal aid may be reassessed. Further it falls within the definition of a compensation payment and is now subject to deduction of benefits paid under the Social Security (Recovery of Benefits) Act 1997, so that the Defendant making the interim payment will be liable to repay an amount equal to the total certified recoverable benefits if an order is made. These considerations will affect the amount which the solicitor will advise

11   *Stringman v McArdle* [1994] 1 WLR 1653.
12   *Campbell v Mylchrest* [1998] PIQR 20.

should be sought. The court must be told the sum of money for which final judgment is likely to be given. Caution should be exercised in this respect, especially when it is difficult to value a claim because of an inability to fully quantify due to the lack of a proper prognosis. There seems no reason why a bracket should not be given. The court must be given reasons for the necessary assertion that the Claimant is likely to win. Details of any relevant other matters must be stated. In a Fatal Accidents Act claim, the details of the dependants on whose behalf the claim is made and the nature of the claim must be given. The evidence required need not be an affidavit as in the past but best practice suggests that there should be a lead statement, usually by the solicitor handling the case containing a statement of truth and setting out the background to the case, the stage it has reached and its expected course. This statement should exhibit the evidence (wage slips, estimates, expert reports, etc) necessary for the application.

It is evident from the above that substantial disclosure of the Claimant's case is required in an interim payment application. With the cards-on-the-table regime of the CPR, this may not be any disadvantage. Indeed the application may provoke earlier disclosure of the Defendants' case. However, there are cases where early disclosure of the Claimant's case may be thought to be so disadvantageous as to militate against an application for an interim payment.

The application notice and evidence must be served at least 14 days before the hearing (CPR, r 25.6(3)). If the respondent to the application wishes to rely on written evidence he must file it and serve copies on all other parties at least seven days before the application (CPR, r 25.6(4)). The applicant can reply to that evidence, but must do so at least three days before the hearing of the application (CPR, r 25.6(5)).

The rules provide that if any evidence has already been filed, or served, it need not be filed or served again (25.6(6)). The application should mention such evidence and state that it has been filed or served.

Though subsequent applications for interim payments may be made (CPR, r 25.6(2)), it may be preferable (for Defendant insurers as well) for the court to make an order that an interim payment be paid in instalments (CPR, r 25.6(7)). So if there is a continuing loss of earnings, the court may consider a monthly instalment payment to be appropriate. If an order that payments are made by way of instalments is required, the order should set out the total amount of payment, the amount and number of each instalment and the date on which it should be paid and to whom it should be paid (PD 3).

If the application is opposed, then the Defendant should obtain a CRU certificate and file it with the court. Any order will take such payments into account.

The application may be combined, in suitable cases with an application for summary judgment.

An interim payment once made can be ordered to be adjusted or even repaid (CPR, r 25.8).[13]

---

[13]   RSC Order 29, rule 17(a).

The Claimant can request more than one interim payment (CPR, r 25.6(2)) and the competent practitioner should always be alive to the possibility of requesting further interim payments.

Whether or not an interim payment has been made must not be disclosed to the trial judge until questions of liability and the amount of money to be awarded have been decided, unless the Defendant agrees (CPR, r 25.9). It is sometimes the case in a quantum trial that the Defendant seeks to show reasonableness by consenting to reveal the extent of interim payments made.

AFFIDAVIT EVIDENCE IN APPLICATIONS GENERALLY

Under the old rules, many applications had to be made with affidavits in support; usually served with the application and certainly within time limits – even if they were more honoured in the breach. The new rules discourage affidavit evidence; further, there is often (but not always) no requirement to serve evidence with the application. The wording is usually 'written evidence may be served'; and timescales set for the response to this written evidence. Certainly, all written evidence is required to be endorsed with a statement of truth. Rule 32.15 provides that nothing will prevent the use of affidavit evidence. However, affidavit evidence is a rarity, certainly in personal injury litigation. The rules specifically provide that if an affidavit is filed, the extra costs associated with filing an affidavit rather than a written statement may not be recoverable.

Non-Compliance with Court Orders

STRIKING OUT OF A STATEMENT OF CASE

CPR, r 3.4(2)(c) gives the court a discretion to strike out a statement of case if it appears to the court that there has been a failure to comply with a rule, practice direction or court order. The court's approach to this provision was first clarified in *Bigguzi v Rank Leisure plc.*[1] Having emphasised the importance of keeping the time limits and the court's unqualified discretion to strike out a claim, the Court of Appeal held that under the CPR, the court had a broad range of powers and in many cases, there would be alternatives to the draconian step of striking out the claim. For instance, it may order the party to pay a sum of money into court (rule 3.1(5)) or repeat the order, but impose conditions (unless orders), (rule 3.1(3)). The court must exercise its wide discretion fairly and justly in accordance with overriding objective under Part 1, while recognising their responsibilities to litigants in general not to allow the same defaults to occur as had occurred in the past.

Recognition of the broad range of powers was subsequently adopted further in other cases, although they inevitably depend on the facts of the case: for instance, the length of and explanation for the delay; whether the other party has suffered prejudice as a result and if it can be compensated for by some order relating to costs or interest[2] and the degree of prejudice which one or other party will suffer as a result of the default. In reality, it will usually only be in those cases where a fair trial would no longer be possible that the judge could properly strike the claim out.

Accordingly, the courts have recognised a difference between cases where liability is in dispute and one where it is not. Under the old rules, it tended to make little difference. The choice was a stark one, either to strike out or not. Where liability is not in dispute, the court is more ready to protect the other party by making an order for costs: in a case of unacceptable delay by a Claimant, it can also disallow interest. If a payment into court had been made a long time ago which would have been realistic, but is no longer effective as a result of the delay, consideration can be given to that on the issue of costs: the court can decide not to strike out on condition that the

1   [1999] 1 WLR 1926.
2   *Walsh v Misseldine* (2000) Times, 29 February.

judge at trial should consider whether or not the payment in was one that should have been accepted at the time.[3]

Where the breach of an order has led to an inability to provide a fair trial, a court will have little option but to strike out a claim. On the other hand, failure to comply with a rule, practice direction or court order that has not rendered a fair trial impossible may amount to a breach of art 6 of the ECHR.[4]

Further, the Court of Appeal has stated that where there has been a breach of an order, a party seeking to strike out should make its application as soon as it becomes apparent rather than waiting to exacerbate the delay.[5] It is no longer acceptable to let sleeping dogs lie, as such an approach is inconsistent with the ethos of the CPR and Part 23, PD para 2.7.

UNLESS ORDERS

CPR, r 3.1(3) gives the court power to make an order subject to conditions and to specify the consequence of failure to comply with a rule, practice direction or relevant pre-action protocol. An example of such an order would be, for instance, that unless the Defendant files a counter-schedule by 4.00pm on 5 April 2008, it shall be debarred from contesting the Claimant's schedule of loss. The conditions must be expressed clearly and precisely and be capable of compliance.

In cases where judgment has not been entered, the sanction imposed by the court for failure to comply with the unless order will have effect unless the party in default applies for and obtains relief (rule 3.8). Where the sanction is the payment of costs, the party in default may only obtain relief by appealing against the order for costs (rule 3.8(2)).

When the court considers whether or not to grant relief from sanctions, it is expressly required to consider all the circumstances, and in particular, each of the criteria set out in CPR, r 3.9:[6] These are:
(i)   the administration of justice;
(ii)   whether the application for relief was made promptly;
(iii)   whether the failure to comply was intentional;
(iv)   whether there is a good explanation for the failure;
(v)   the extent to which the party in default has complied with other rules, practice directions, court orders and any relevant pre-action protocol;
(vi)   whether the failure to comply was caused by the party or his legal representative;
(vii)   whether the trial date or the likely date can still be met if relief is granted;
(viii) the effect which the failure to comply had on each party; and
(ix)   the effect which the granting of relief would have on each party.

The application for relief must be supported by evidence in a witness statement. Each item of written evidence must contain a statement of truth.

---

3   *Walsh v Misseldine* (2000) Times, 1 March.
4   *Annodeus Entertainment Ltd v Gibson* (2000) Times, 3 March.
5   *Asiansky Television v Bayer Rosin (a firm)* (2001) Times, 19 November.
6   *Bansal v Cheema* (13 September 2001, unreported); *Woodhouse v Consignia plc* [2002] 1 WLR 2558; *R C Residuals Ltd v Linton Fuel Oils Ltd* [2002] 1 WLR 2782.

POWER OF THE COURT TO RECTIFY AN ERROR OF PROCEDURE

Where there has been an error of procedure, such as a failure to comply with a rule or practice direction, the error does not invalidate any step taken in the proceedings unless the court so orders and the court may make an order to remedy the error (rule 3.10).

The rationale behind the provision is that non-compliance does not nullify the proceedings or any step taken unless the court so orders. The court can remedy the error, for instance, instead of striking out the claim. It will commonly be applied where the default is of small consequence and has been complied with by the time of the hearing. For instance, the court has held that a failure to serve the particulars of claim in compliance with the rules (as opposed to the claim form) was an error that could be remedied under rule 3.10.[7] Failure to serve the claim form could not be remedied because the power is only available 'except where the rules provide otherwise'.[8]

EXTENDING TIME LIMITS

An application to extend the time made before an order or rule has been breached will circumvent the need for the court to apply the criteria for relief from sanctions set out in rule 3.9.[9]

Under CPR, r 3.1(2), the court may extend or shorten the time for compliance with any rule, practice direction or court order. The order may be made retrospectively. The Court of Appeal set out guidelines in *Sayers v Clarke Walker*,[10] where the Defendant failed to file a notice of appeal in time in accordance with CPR, r 54.4(2). In deciding how to exercise the power, the court must take into account the overriding objective in rule 1.1. In cases of any complexity, the court should also have regard to the matters set out in rule 3.9 which provides a checklist. As noted above, the court has no power to extend the time limit for service of a claim form except in accordance with the provisions in rule 7.6.

---

7   *Totty v Snowden* [2002] 1 WLR 1384.
8   *Vinos v Marks & Spencer plc* [2001] 3 All ER 784.
9   *Sabrina Robert v Momentum Services Ltd* [2003] 2 All ER 74.
10 [2002] 3 All ER 490.

CHAPTER 20

Disclosure and Inspection

THE MISCHIEF

Lord Woolf in his interim report[1] identified the cost of and delays associated with 'discovery' of documents as one of the major problems associated with the system. This was a particular problem in the larger cases (para 28). He also noted that the requirement in England and Wales obliging a party to disclose documents which are damaging to his or her own case was a distinguishing feature from other non-common law jurisdictions (including Scotland).

THE SOLUTION

Lord Woolf accepted the desirability of retaining discovery because of its contribution to the just resolution of disputes, but recognised that the benefits only outweigh the disadvantages if substantially greater control over the scale of discovery is exercised. He proposed that the solution lies in finding a satisfactory form of control and then ensuring that it is enforced.

He distinguished between the following categories of documents:

(i)   the parties' own documents: these are documents upon which a party relies in support of his contentions in the proceedings;

(ii)   adverse documents: these are documents of which a party is aware and which to a material extent adversely affect his own case or support other parties;

(iii) the relevant documents: these are documents which are relevant to the issues in the proceedings, but which do not fall into categories (i) or (ii) because they do not obviously support or undermine either side's case. They are partly the 'story' or background. This category of documents, though relevant, may not be necessary for the fair disposal of the case. It is fair to say that this category produces disproportionately the greatest number of documents disclosed and to least effect;

(iv)   train of inquiry documents: these are the documents referred to by Brett LJ in the *Peruvian Guano* case[2] where Brett LJ stated:

---

[1]   Access to Justice, June 1995, Chapter 21.
[2]   (1882) 11 QBD 55.

'It seems to me that every document relates to the matters in question in the action, which not only would be evidence upon any issue, but also which, it is reasonable to suppose, contains information which *may* – not which *must* – either directly or indirectly enable the party requiring the affidavit either to advance his own case or to damage the case of his adversary. I have put in the words 'either directly or indirectly', because, as it seems to me, a document can properly be said to contain information which may enable the party requiring the affidavit either to advance his own case or to damage the case of his adversary, if it is a document *which may fairly lead him to a train of inquiry which may have either of these two consequences* [italics added] ... In order to determine whether certain documents are within that description, it is necessary to consider what are the questions in the action: the court must look, not only at the statement of claim and the Plaintiff's case, but also at the statement of defence and the Defendant's case.'

Categories (i) and (ii) comprise what Lord Woolf referred to as 'standard discovery' and now form part of the requirements for 'standard disclosure'. Categories (iii) and (iv) are 'extra discovery'. He then went on to consider the types of proceedings to which the categories should apply and the time at which the obligation to give discovery should arise. He did not consider small claims. He proposed that standard discovery only should apply to the fast track. However he accepted that 'very strong grounds indeed' would have to be shown for extra discovery in categories (iii) and (iv) in fast track cases (para 28).

He accepted that in multi track cases the general approach will be more difficult. It will have to be varied according to the individual circumstances of the particular case. In such cases he felt the procedural judge, if he thought this was necessary, could direct relevant (category (iii)) or even *Peruvian Guano* (category (iv)) documents to be disclosed although he envisaged that it would be 'extremely rare', perhaps only in cases involving allegations of dishonesty for category (iv) discovery to be required.

As part of the safeguards he proposed that a party will be required to certify that his solicitor has explained to him his obligation to disclose documents and that he has made disclosure in accordance with that obligation (para 37). The obligation to give discovery should be a continuing one (para 40).

By his Final Report, Lord Woolf proposed to restrict the basic duty of disclosure to categories (i) and (ii) ('standard disclosure'). The court may allow 'extra disclosure' categories (iii) and (iv) in an exceptional case.

Initial disclosure, he held, should only apply to relevant documents of which a party is aware at the time when the obligation to disclose arises. Lord Woolf recognised the difficulty with the test of awareness.[3]

---

[3]   Paragraph 41, '...the test of awareness is particularly problematic where the disclosing party is not an individual; in a company, firm or other organisation, it is likely that a number of people will have known about relevant documents. My proposal here is that there should be an obligation for the organisation to nominate a supervising officer whose task would be to identify individuals within the organisation who were likely to recollect relevant documents'.

He considered that practical objections to his proposals such that they would make it easier to evade the obligation for discovery. However, he stated:

'My proposal has the effect of preventing a party, if he acts reasonably honestly, from putting forward a case which he knows to be inconsistent with his own documents. It thus offers not a perfect, but a realistic, balance between keeping disclosure in check while enabling it still to contribute to the achievement of justice' (para 45).

Part 31 of the CPR and the associated Disclosure and Inspection practice direction, deal with disclosure of documents. The term 'discovery' has no longer any relevance. Part 31 only applies to fast track and multi track claims. Small track claims are exempt (rule 31.1(2)).

MEANING OF DISCLOSURE

A party discloses a document by stating that the document exists or has existed (rule 31.2).

A document that contains a modification, obliteration or other marking or feature is treated as a separate document if that modification, etc is to be relied upon (rule 31.9). This can include documents relating to a matter not at issue between the parties, such as third party disclosure.[4]

MEANING OF THE DOCUMENT

'Document' means anything in which information of any description is recorded; and 'copy' in relation to a document means anything onto which information recorded in the document has been copied, by whatever means and whether directly or indirectly (rule 31.4). It follows that the definition is not limited to paper writings, but extends to anything upon which evidence or information is recorded, including tape recordings, videos[5] and even a computer database which forms part of a business's records insofar as it can be converted into a readable form.

STANDARD DISCLOSURE

It should be recalled that a Claimant and Defendant are required to disclose certain documents with their statements of case.

The court will normally order standard disclosure unless it dispenses or limits such disclosure or unless the parties agree in writing to dispense with or limit such disclosure (rule 31.5).

Standard disclosure requires a party to disclose only (rule 31.6):
(i)   the documents on which he relies;

---

4   *Rall v Hume* [2001] 3 All ER 248.
5   *Manatee Towing Co and Coastal Tug and Barge Co v Oceanbulk Maritime SA and Laura Maritime Inc* [1999] 1 Lloyd's Rep 876.

(ii)   the documents which:
    (a)   adversely affect his own case;
    (b)   adversely affect another party's case; or
    (c)   support another party's case; and
(iii)   the documents which he is required to disclose by a relevant practice direction.

When giving standard disclosure, a party is required to make a reasonable search for the documents listed above (rule 31.7).

The factors relevant to deciding the reasonableness of a search include:
(i)   the number of documents involved;
(ii)   the nature and complexity of the proceedings;
(iii)   the ease and expense of retrieval of any particular document; and
(iv)   the significance of any document which is likely to be located during the search (CPR, r 31.7(2)).

The extent of the search which must be made will depend upon the circumstances of the case. The parties should bear in mind the overriding principle of proportionality (CPR, r 1.1(2)(c)).[6] It may be reasonable to decide not to search for documents coming into existence before some particular date, or to limit the search to documents in some particular place or places, or to documents falling into particular categories. If a party considers it unreasonable to search for such document he must state this in the disclosure statement and identify the category or class of document (CPR, r 31.7(3)).

Disclosure is limited to documents which are or have been in a party's control. Control includes those in his physical possession or previous possession. The right to such possession or the right to inspect or take copies of it (CPR, r 31.8).

DISCLOSURE BEFORE PROCEEDINGS START[7]

The application

(See generally Part 23.)

An application (see Part 23) for pre-action disclosure is provided for by the CPR (rule 31.16) and must be supported by evidence. There is no need to provide an affidavit. A witness statement supported by a statement of truth will suffice (CPR, r 31.16(2)).

The requirements for pre-action disclosure are:
(i)   the respondent is likely[8] to be a party to the subsequent proceedings;[9]

---

6   *Forrester v British Railways Board* (1996) Times, 8 April (decided under the old law): in a case involving a fatal fall from a train, the BRB were not required to disclose all accident reports regarding door locking. Disclosure would still probably be withheld under Part 31 due to the proportionality principle.

7   The Claimant can apply under s 33 of the Supreme Court Act 1981 or s 52 of the County Court Act 1984.

8   'Likely to' means 'may well' be a party and is not a high threshold test, *Black Sumitomo Corpn* [2002] 1 WLR 1562.

9   Thus Lord Woolf's proposal that pre-action discovery against non-parties be introduced in personal injury cases has not been implemented.

(ii)   the applicant is also likely to be party to proceedings;
(iii)   only disclosure to the extent of 'standard disclosure' (see rule 31.6) will be ordered; and
(iv)   such disclosure has to be desirable in order to:
    (a)   dispose fairly of the anticipated proceedings;
    (b)   assist the dispute to be resolved without proceedings; or
    (c)   save costs.

The order for pre-action discovery will specify the documents or classes of documents which the respondent must disclose, and require the respondent to specify any documents – which are no longer in his control or in respect of which he claims a right or duty to withhold inspection. The order may also require the respondent to indicate what has happened to any documents which are no longer in his control and specify the time and place for disclosure and inspection. The court should not embark upon any determination of substantive issues on the application. It is normally sufficient to found an application if the substantive claim pursued is properly arguable and would have a real prospect of success.[10]

Procedure for standard disclosure

List of documents

Each party has to make and serve on the other parties a list of documents in practice form N265. The list must identify the documents in a convenient order and manner and as concisely as possible (31 PD, para 3.2). It will normally be necessary to list the documents in date order, to number them consecutively and to give each a concise description (for example, 'letter, Claimant to Defendant'). Where there is a large number of documents all falling into a particular category, they may be listed as a category rather than individually, for example, '50 bank statements relating to Account No ... at ... Bank, to and from'; or '35 letters passing between ... and ... between 1995 and 1998' (31 PD, para 3.2).

The list must indicate those documents withheld from inspection due to a claim of right or duty; and the party must state in writing (which should normally be included in the disclosure statement and must identify the document or part thereof to which a claim relates) that he or she has such a right or duty and the grounds on which s/he claims that right or duty. The party must also identify those documents no longer in the party's control with a short explanation of what has happened to those documents (31 PD, paras 4.5 and 4.6).

Disclosure statement (31 PD, para 4)

Unless the parties agree in writing a list of documents must contain a disclosure statement.

A disclosure statement should be made by the party disclosing the documents. It should:

[10]   *Rose v Lynx Express* [2004] EWCA Civ 447.

(i)   set out the extent of the search made;

(ii)   certify that the maker understands the duty to disclose documents; and

(iii) certify that to the best of his or her knowledge s/he has carried out that duty (see Appendix B – Specimen correspondence).

It should expressly state that the disclosing party believes the extent of the search to have been reasonable in all the circumstances and draw attention to any particular limitations on the extent of the search which were adopted for proportionality reasons and give the reasons why the limitations were adopted, for example, the difficulty or expense that a search not subject to those limitations would have entailed or the margin of relevance of categories of documents omitted from the search (31 PD, para 4.2).

If a party deliberately suppresses a document, this constitutes contumacious conduct which might justify the striking out of the whole of an action or defence even if a fair trial is still possible.[11]

When a party making the disclosure statement is a company, firm, association or other organisation the statement must also identify the person making the statement (including name and address and office or position held), and explain why s/he is considered an appropriate person to make the statement (31 PD, para 31.10(7)).

A disclosure statement may be made by a non-party when this is permitted by a relevant practice direction.

Duty of disclosure continues during proceedings

If the disclosing party is legally represented, that representative is under a duty to ensure that the person making the disclosure statement understands the duty of disclosure under rule 31 (31 PD, para 4.4).[12] The obligations imposed continue until the proceedings come to an end (CPR, r 31.11). If further documents come to the attention of the disclosing party, s/he must immediately notify every other party and prepare and serve a supplemental list.[13]

Disclosure in stages

The parties may agree in writing or the court may direct that disclosure or inspection or both shall take place in stages (CPR, r 31.13).

Disclosure in specific tracks

Small claims

After a case has been allocated to the small claims track (to which Part 31 does not apply), directions should be given by the court (CPR, r 27.4).[14] If 'standard directions'

---

[11]   *Landauer Ltd v Comins & Co* (1991) Times, 7 August.

[12]   See also *Rockwell Machine Tool Co Ltd v EP Barrus (Concessionaires) Ltd* [1968] 1 WLR 693; also the importance of preserving documents are unfavourable to the party's case.

[13]   See *Vernon v Bosley (No 2)* [1999] QB 18. It is the duty of the party's advocate to advise disclosure and if refused the advocate should withdraw from the case.

[14]   Unless a preliminary hearing is fixed or the court intends to deal with the case without a hearing.

are given the parties must serve on the other parties and the court, at least 14 days before the date fixed for the hearing, copies of all the documents on which he intends to rely. This should include any expert reports (CPR, r 27.4(3)(a)).

At the appendix to practice direction 27, form B is an example of this standard direction. Further, Form A lists the documents which may be relevant in a case involving a road accident.[15]

A court may also make any special directions in order to best deal with the case. Form F gives an example of some of these.

Fast track

Directions should be given on the allocation of a case to the fast track (CPR, r 28.2(1)). These should include provision for the disclosure of documents (CPR, r 28.3). Disclosure will usually be specified as 'standard', but if the court considers this not to be appropriate, it may direct that no disclosure should take place or specify the documents or classes of document that should be disclosed (CPR, r 28.3(2)). The Fast Track practice direction (28 PD, para 3.12) proposes that the timetable for disclosure should generally be four weeks after the notice of allocation. The appendix to the practice direction gives the standard directions and lists the options relating to disclosure.

Multi track

The court must give directions and/or fix a case management conference or pre-trial review when a case is allocated to the multi track (CPR, r 29.2). Again, the directions must include an order as to disclosure and the Multi Track practice direction (29 PD) states that the court may limit the disclosure to standard disclosure or less (para 4.7(3)(a)). The court may further direct that disclosure can take place by the supplying of copies of all documents, but the parties must either serve a disclosure statement with the copies or agree to disclose without such a statement.

Right of inspection of a disclosed document

A party to whom a document has been disclosed has a right to inspect the document except where:
(i)   the document is no longer in the control of the party who disclosed it (CPR, r 31.3(1)(a));
(ii)   the party disclosing the document has a right or a duty[16] to withhold inspection of it and has so stated in the disclosure statement (CPR, rr 31.3(1)(b) and 31.19(3)); or

---

15   Namely expert reports, witness statements, invoices or estimates, documents regarding other special damage and any sketch plans or photographs.
16   The rights and duties to withhold are beyond the scope of this book. However, mention should be made of legal professional privilege. A document qualifies as privileged if the sole, or at least, the dominant purpose for which the document was prepared was submission to a legal advisor for legal advice in view of anticipated litigation: *Waugh v British Railways Board* [1980] AC 521. This privilege is not attached until a decision is taken to defend a claim: *Alfred Crompton Amusement Machines Ltd*

(iii)   a party considers that it would be disproportionate to the issues in the case to permit inspection of standard disclosure documents and has so stated in the disclosure statement (CPR, r 31.3(2)).

A party may also inspect (CPR, r 31.14) any document mentioned in:
(i)   a statement of case;
(ii)   a witness statement;
(iii)   a witness summary;
(iv)   an affidavit; or
(v)   subject to rule 35.10(4), an expert's report (CPR, r 31.14).

Where a party has a right to inspect a document (CPR, r 31.15):
(i)   that party must give the party who disclosed the document written notice that s/he wishes to inspect it;
(ii)   the party who discloses the document must permit inspection not more than seven days after the date on which he received the notice; and
(iii)   that party may request a copy of the document and, if he also undertakes to pay reasonable copying costs, the party who disclosed the document must supply him or her with a copy not more than seven days after the date on which s/he received the request.

Specific disclosure or inspection (CPR, r 31.12)

If the disclosure of documents given by a disclosing party is thought to be inadequate (31 PD, para 5.1) an application may be made for an order for specific disclosure (see rule 31.12). The application notice must specify the order that the applicant intends to ask the court to make and must be supported by evidence (not affidavit evidence) (31 PD, para 5.2). The grounds on which the order is sought may be set out in the application notice itself or alternatively in the evidence filed in support of the application. It will be necessary to set out the reasoning and suspicions that lead to the belief that a certain class of document is in the Defendant's possession (31 PD, para 5.3).

The court will take into account all the circumstances of the case and in particular the overriding objective described in Part 1. It may order the party to disclose documents or classes of documents specified in the order, or carry out a search to the extent stated in the order and disclose documents located as a result of that search (CPR, r 31.12(2) and 31 PD, para 5.4).

The court may also order specific inspection of a document where the other party has stated in his or her disclosure statement that s/he will not permit inspection of

---

v Customs and Excise Commissioners (No 2) [1974] AC 405, HL. If a privileged document is accidentally allowed for inspection, the contents may only be used by the inspecting party with the permission of the court (CPR, r 31.20). Cf *Pizzey v Ford Motor Co Ltd* [1994] PIQR P15; *Derby & Co Ltd v Weldon (No 8)* [1991] 1 WLR 73 (in which it was for the party who had accidentally disclosed the privileged document to seek an injunction to prevent the use of that document). A party has the right to blank out ('redact') part of a document on the grounds of irrelevance: *GE Capital Corporate Finance Group v Bankers Trust Co* [1994] 1 WLR 172. A further ground for non-disclosure is public interest immunity. This is dealt with in rule 31.19(1) and is beyond the scope of this book.

the document on the grounds that it would be disproportionate to do so (CPR, r 31.12(3)).

A typical disclosure statement

'I, the above named Claimant [or Defendant] [if party making disclosure is a company, firm or other organisation identify here who the person making the disclosure statement is and why he is the appropriate person to make it] state that I have carried out a reasonable and proportionate search to locate all the documents which I am required to disclose under the Order made by the court on [*number*] day of [*month*]. I did not search:

(1) for documents pre-dating [*date*],

(2) for documents located elsewhere than [*location*],

(3) for documents in categories other than [*category*].

I certify that I understand the duty of disclosure and to the best of my knowledge I have carried out that duty. I certify that the list above is a complete list of all documents which are or have been in my control and which I am obliged under the said Order to disclose.'

(See PD Pt 31, Annex A.)

Orders for disclosure against a person not a party

For some time there has been a general principle that an innocent party who becomes involved in tortious acts of others so as to facilitate their wrongdoing is under a duty to assist any injured party by giving full information and disclosing the identity of the wrongdoer.[17] This principle is not affected by the CPR.

See Part 23 for the general rules about applications for court orders. An application for disclosure against a person who is not a party to proceedings is permitted under s 34 of the Supreme Court Act 1981 or s 53 of the County Court Act 1984. It does not include pre-action disclosure.

The application must be supported by evidence. This does not include affidavit evidence (CPR, r 31.17(2)).

The court may make an order under this rule only where:

(i) the documents are likely to support the case of the applicant or adversely affect the case of one of the other parties to the proceedings; and

(ii) disclosure is necessary in order to dispose fairly of the claim or to save costs (CPR, r 31.17(3)).

The order must specify the documents or the classes of documents which the respondent must disclose and require the respondent to specify any documents no longer in his or her control, or in respect of which he claims a right or duty to withhold inspection (CPR, r 31.17(4)). The order may also require the respondent

---

[17] *Norwich Pharmacal Co v Customs and Excise Comrs* [1974] AC 133, see particularly at 175 per Lord Reid.

to indicate what has happened to any documents, if appropriate, and specify the time and place for disclosure and inspection (CPR, r 31.17(5)).

The following are the most common non-parties who are asked for disclosure:
(i)   Health and Safety Executive: this body sends inspectors to the most serious work place accidents. An outline of the findings will normally be available, but a Claimant will only get a full report if a court order is obtained;
(ii)   Department of Social Security: the benefit details of the Claimant will be obtained through the working of the CRU, but, occasionally, an application may be necessary for the discovery of the DSS medical board notes and findings.[18]

Consequence of failure to disclose documents or permit inspection

A party may not rely on any document which he fails to disclose or in respect of which he fails to permit inspection unless the court gives permission (CPR, r 31.21). It is anticipated that the court will have powers to award cost sanctions in cases where documents come to light that should have been disclosed as part of standard discovery.

Inadvertent disclosure – restriction on the use of privileged documents

These can only be used with the permission of the court (CPR, r 31.20). The established principles applicable to cases of inadvertent disclosure of privileged documents have not been affected by the CPR.[19] The relevant principles are as follows:

There is a two-stage test:
(i)   was it evident to the solicitor receiving privileged documents that a mistake had been made? If so, the solicitor should return the documents;
(ii)   if it was not obvious, would it have been obvious to the hypothetical reasonable solicitor that disclosure had occurred as the result of a mistake? If so, privilege is retained. In a case close to the line as to whether a mistake has been made, the solicitor receiving the documents should pick up the telephone and ascertain whether an error had occurred;
(iii) if it would not have been obvious to a reasonable solicitor, privilege is lost.[20]

Subsequent use of disclosed documents

This is outside the scope of this book (see further rule 31.22).

---

18   *O'Sullivan v Herdmans Ltd* [1987] 1 WLR 1047.
19   *Breeze v John Stacey and Sons Ltd* (1999) Times, 8 July.
20   *Guinness Peat Properties Ltd v Fitzroy Robinson Partnership* [1987] 1 WLR 1027 at 1045–6; *Pizzey v Ford Motor Co Ltd* [1994] PIQR P15; *IBM Corpn v Phoenix International (Computers) Ltd* [1995] 1 All ER 413 at 421; and *Breeze v John Stacey & Sons Ltd* (1999) Times, 8 July.

Document guidance

As a useful guide, the following are documents that should normally be expected to be disclosed by a Defendant in various personal injury cases. Practitioners are referred also to the specific pre-action protocols for personal injury claims. If they are not disclosed, specific disclosure should be sought:

Work accidents

(i)   The employer's risk assessment required to be performed in every work situation since 1 January 1993 under Management of Health and Safety at Work Regulations 1992, reg 3, and in specified situations under Health and Safety (Display Screen Equipment) Regulations 1992, reg 2, Personal Protective Equipment Regulations 1992, reg 6, and Manual Handling Operations Regulations 1992, reg 2;

(ii)   the employer's safety policy statement required under the Health and Safety at Work Act 1974, s 2(3);

(iii)   any accident investigation report which is not privileged (see above);

(iv)   if the accident involves a machine: all written instructions regarding its use and maintenance; if the machine may have malfunctioned: all maintenance records;

(v)   receipts, orders, invoices or other correspondence relating to the machine or spare parts for it, or materials used with it (including cleaning where appropriate);

(vi)   receipts for purchase of and records of maintenance of safety equipment;

(vii)   the records of this and all other accidents involving the specific or a similar machine or piece of equipment, or occurring in the specific area, or in the same or a similar manner, whether these are recorded in the accident book, daily log, memorandum or wherever else the Claimant and his witnesses think they may have been written down;

(viii) employers used to be obliged to write to the DSS on a B176 form, giving certain details of the accident, where their employee subsequently had time off to recover. With the introduction of the statutory sick pay scheme, this document is more rarely available now, but should be sought in case it has been used;

(ix)   the safety committee's[21] minutes and agendas (if any);

(x)   any note, report or memorandum from the safety officer and/or safety representative;

(xi)   the accident report form (F2508). Under the Reporting of Injuries Regulations 1985, a report must be made if the injured employee is off work for more than three days or kept in hospital for 24 hours or more;

(xii)   correspondence with the Health and Safety Executive, if any;

(xiii) all statements made to the employer by the Claimant and witnesses after the accident;

(xiv)   first aid report;

---

[21]   Which may exist pursuant to the Safety Representative and Safety Committee Regulations 1977 made under s 15 of the Health and Safety at Work Act 1974.

(xv)   the Claimant's medical records held in the Defendant's medical centre;
(xvi) records of the Claimant's earnings, both gross and net;
(xvii) if there is a continuing loss and there is doubt as to how much the Claimant
       would have continued to earn: wage details in respect of two of the Claimant's
       work colleagues in comparable positions, by whom authority has been given
       to obtain such wage details.

Tripping accidents

(i)   The highway inspector's report for 12 months prior to the accident;
(ii)   all details of accidents that have occurred on that stretch of road over the
       previous 12-month period;
(iii) all contracts for work done by contractors in the vicinity within the previous
       three-year period.

Public transport accidents

(i)   The highway inspector's report;
(ii)   the internal investigation report.

Road accidents

For the great majority of road accidents, the only relevant documents are in relation
to the Claimant's special damage claim. That is why the automatic directions specify
that the Defendant does not have to supply a list. That is not, however, always the
case. For example, if the defence is that the vehicle went out of the Defendant's
control, perhaps because of a mechanical defect after repair, then discovery will be
needed of all instructions, invoices, bills, receipts and correspondence with the
repairer, MOT certificates, service records, etc.

CHAPTER 21

Review of Evidence

The solicitor should regularly review the strengths and weaknesses of the case at each stage of progression. However, more formal reviews are necessary at certain times – dependent upon various factors particular to the case in question. It used to be the practice that a full review of every case was carried out, usually by counsel, at the stage when the pleadings had closed, disclosure was complete or nearly so, witness proofs and reports, or the bulk of them, were to hand and the time limit for setting down was approaching. With the advent of fast track litigation, it is not usually necessary to instruct counsel in simple claims; however, a formal review by counsel may be demanded by the person or organisation funding the claim, of the firms in-house procedure upon a certain trigger; issue of proceedings, exchange of expert and witness evidence, a certain period prior to trial. Certainly it is good practice to engage in at least three formal reviews irrespective of any external demands and the writers suggest these are:

(i)   prior to exchange of witness statements;
(ii)   after exchange of witness statements but before exchange of experts' reports; and
(iii) after exchange of experts' reports.

Whether or not counsel is engaged in these reviews must be dependant upon the value and complexity of the claim; whether or not counsel is retained under a 'no win no fee agreement' and the Bar Council provisions appertain. Certainly, if the claim is of significant value then counsel should be involved in at least one review and this should be either before exchange of the Claimant's expert reports where these are likely to be controversial or after expert evidence has been exchanged.

ADJOURNMENT PENDING DECISION IN SIMILAR CASE IN HIGHER COURT

If it is known that the instant case involves a question of law that is the subject of appeal in another case, consideration should be given to applying to adjourn the instant case pending the outcome of that decision. The court will look at the balance of prejudice and does not necessarily have to apply the law as there laid down.[1]

---

[1]   *Kingscastle Ltd v Owen-Owen* (1999) Times, 18 March and *Re Yates' Settlement Trusts* [1954] 1 WLR 564.

COUNSEL'S ADVICE

The decision as to when the thorough analysis of the whole case is to be undertaken is a matter for the solicitor to judge, unless there is a prior agreement with counsel (for example, as part of a CFA agreement). The matter should remain with the barrister who has drafted the pleadings and who will conduct the case at court. Nothing in the CPR affects the client's choice of lawyer, including a QC if necessary.[2]

For the purpose of this book, it is assumed that the review is done by counsel in writing in the form of advice on evidence, merits and quantum. However, it is possible to substitute the word 'solicitor' for the word 'counsel' throughout this chapter as the same rules in relation to reviewing the file apply to the solicitor should she carry out the review as they do to counsel.

In any event, rather than asking for a paper review, the solicitor should not be shy of organising a face-to-face conference with counsel, the client and if necessary relevant experts. This is often highly effective in organising or clarifying difficult evidential issues and the costs can often be reduced by bringing in the expert by way of telephone conference. A careful note should be taken of the conference which can stand in the stead of a written advice. So far as a written advice on evidence, merits and quantum is concerned, a fairly standard format may be used to ensure that all aspects are covered. These are reflected in the sub-headings below. A solicitor carrying out a review at any of the three stages should use the same sub-headings. It is of immense value if a fresh brain is brought to overview the case, especially where unpalatable advice needs to be given to the client.

Assuming counsel is instructed to advise on evidence, merits and quantum, the instructions (preceded by an enquiry to counsel's clerk) should state on the outside that the advice is required by a certain date, especially if the case is a fast track claim, since at this stage time will be very short indeed in consequence of the tight timetable imposed by the CPR. It is very unlikely that the court would extend time to provide specifically for counsel providing any advice and the solicitor should be wary of instructing any counsel who cannot return paperwork within a reasonable period of time. If counsel is instructed, he or she should be sent a complete set of the relevant papers, properly indexed into separate sections. It there is any doubt over the relevance of a particular document then it should be sent to counsel to consider.

Facts

The initial paragraph of the advice sets out the facts of the case concisely, in no more than half a dozen sentences and usually only two or three.

Statement of case

The statement of case should be reviewed, including commentary on any further pleadings steps identified which should (if possible) be drafted. This includes any

---

[2]   *Maltez v Lewis* [1999] 21 LS Gaz R 39.

amendments to the particulars of claim or any reply. The statement of case should be amended to include any allegations or claim for damages that might take the Defendant by surprise at trial. Simply telling the Defendant may not be enough to justify a late application. It is in the court's discretion and is effectively unappealable.[3] It may be necessary to seek further information of the defence case. There should then follow a review of remaining major aspects of the case as revealed by the defence.

Lay witnesses on liability

The next heading of an advice should be 'Evidence on liability and contributory negligence'. The gathering of this evidence has been considered in Chapters 9–11. The usual practice at this stage is to consider the Claimant's evidence, noting in particular any weak areas or areas where further instructions or amendment of witness statements are required. Successive paragraphs will deal with each of the potential lay witnesses. Consideration is given as to whether they have dealt with all aspects within their knowledge, whether amendment of the statement is needed, and what the particular dangers or advantages in calling each of them are. If witness statements have been exchanged, consideration must be given as to how the Claimant and his witnesses will deal with the Defendant's statements and whether further evidence is needed in the light of the Defendant's statements. The Defendant's statements will be analysed and any that can be agreed should be indicated (though the possibility that the witness will not come up to proof because the statement is exaggerated should be kept in mind).

If witness statements have not been exchanged, then advice is required on the draft statements prepared from the proofs, on the statements yet to be prepared and, if necessary, counsel should draft the statements from the proofs provided (funding permitting). Providing that the solicitor has obtained a signed witness statement from a witness, there is no reason why counsel cannot see that witness in conference if she considers it necessary to clarify issues arising.

Advice should always be given as to any other potential lay witnesses, or categories of witness, who might be contacted and proofed. Thought should also be given to whether any matters disclosed on discovery or any allegations made in the defence or the Defendant's witness statements have been or need to be put to witnesses. If the Claimant's character appears likely to be attacked, consideration needs to be given to potential character witnesses.

Sometimes, those giving evidence about the system of work, previous accidents and previous complaints (and complainants) have not been adequately investigated. Safety representatives, shop stewards and workers in the maintenance department responsible for the relevant equipment should not be overlooked. Pedestrians/bystanders to road traffic accidents should similarly be contacted for their version of events.

A witness statement is not proved until spoken to by the maker in the witness box.[4] In cases where the witness is unable to attend trial because they are overseas, ill, cannot

---

[3]   *McLaughlin v Metropolitan Police Comr* [1994] PIQR P294.
[4]   CPR, r 32.2(1)(a).

be traced, have forgotten or are deceased, the party must have served the witness statement on the other side and given them notice that the witness is not being called and the reasons why (rule 33.2).

If the Claimant or witnesses have commented on the Defendant's witness statements and documents, the possibility of amending witness statements needs consideration.

Where negligence is alleged against a Defendant's employee and a helpful witness statement is obtained from that employee, the court has a discretion to admit that statement as evidence if, otherwise, the Claimant would be obliged to call that employee at trial.[5] Usually, such witnesses should if possible be available at trial.

A witness can give evidence to an English court via television linkage, under rule 32.3, this is of particular use if the witness is overseas. A protocol for the use of video links in court proceedings has been prepared by the Bar Council, and the court will order evidence to be given by video link in appropriate cases.[6] A statement recorded on video can be admitted in pre-1997 cases under the Civil Evidence Act 1968, s 2, if proved by a person who heard it.

Late witness statements

If witness statements are likely to be served late, an application should be made under CPR, rr 3.1(2)(a) or 32.10 to extend the time for service. Provided the application for an extension is made before the expiry of the time limit, the court has a general discretion to extend and does not need to apply the criteria set out in CPR, r 3.9.[7] By way of contrast, if a time limit imposed by the court has been missed and the other side will not consent to the extension, in principle the party seeking to rely upon the extension must apply for relief from sanctions under CPR, r 3.9. In such circumstances, the court must consider each of the matters listed systematically. Where there has been a history of repeated breaches of timetables and court orders, or something in the conduct that gave rise to a suspicion that it was not bona fide, and the court thinks that the other side should have protection, the court may:

(i)   order a defaulting Defendant to pay a substantial sum of money into court (as a penalty under rule 3.1(5)); or

(ii)   in very extreme circumstances, exclude that party from adducing the evidence at trial.[8]

In practice, the court is usually tolerant of delay and is reluctant to impose the sanction of prohibiting evidence that may help achieve a fair result at trial. However, late disclosure of expert evidence due to a genuine mistake which is not prejudicial to the other party will be permitted, although the costs of doing so are likely to be paid by the defaulting party.[9]

---

[5]   *Champion v London Fire and Civil Defence Authority* (1990) Times, 5 July.
[6]   The court's jurisdiction to order evidence to be received by video link appears in *R v Horseferry Road Magistrates' Court, ex p Bennett (No 3)* (1994) Times, 14 January.
[7]   *Robert v Momentum Services Ltd* [2003] 1 WLR 1577.
[8]   *Mealey Horgan plc v Horgan* (1999) Times, 6 July.
[9]   *Scott Kenkins v Anthony Groscott* (23 September 1999, unreported).

Experts on liability

After the lay witnesses, it is usual for counsel to consider next the expert witnesses and, in particular, the engineer or road traffic accident specialist. The nature of their evidence has been considered in Chapter 12. The solicitor will have sent copies of the expert evidence exchanged by the Defendant to the Claimant's counterpart and at this stage counsel should ensure the Claimant's experts have dealt with all matters raised by the Defendant's experts in their evidence. Counsel should advise whether their reports need to be supplemented by further ones, or whether any other experts need to be called in, such as a meteorologist or a chemist. Sometimes a conference is required to deal with a problem which is apparent from a report. Counsel is not entitled to suggest to an expert how a report should be written,[10] but it is proper to suggest that irrelevant material is excluded or that certain wording is ambiguous and should be clarified.

Plans, photographs and video evidence

The illustrative value of any available plans and photographs should be considered. If they are helpful, the solicitor should be advised to make sufficient copies for the trial and to attempt to agree them with the other side. If the plans or photographs are inadequate or there are none, counsel should consider whether they should be obtained. The precise nature of the plans and photographs desired should be specified and whether these should be done by a professional. Film or video evidence is common nowadays, as many major roads in cities have cameras and it is common for security cameras to cover shops/factories/workplace situations. Consideration should always be given to asking for such evidence to be preserved and produced.

As the onus is on the Claimant to prove the case, clarity is important, so good photographers must be used. Good and accurate aerial photographs are readily available from internet map references. Any photographs or a sketch plan should be given to the Defendant to give them a reasonable opportunity to agree them. If they are not agreed, the maker must be called. If no specific objection is taken, then they are still admissible in evidence at trial.[11]

Evidence (as plans, photographs or models) which is not contained in a witness statement, affidavit or expert's report, given orally at trial or hearsay (notice given) is not to be received at court unless either the court so orders or notice of such evidence has been given (rule 33.6). This rule includes documents received in evidence without further proof under s 9 of the Civil Evidence Act 1995.[12]

Defendant's video

Under rule 33.6, unless the court orders otherwise, a particular plan, photograph or model shall only be receivable at trial if the party intending to produce it has given

10   *White v London Transport Executive* [1982] QB 489.
11   CPR, r 32.19; *McSorley v Woodall* [1995] PIQR P187. If unreasonable objection is taken, the court may make a specific order as to costs.
12   Ie documents that form part of the records of a business or public authority verified by an officer of that business or authority.

notice to the other parties.[13] This rule is not concerned with discovery in the technical sense. So if the Defendant obtains a video of the Claimant's conduct and behaviour, the former has to serve notice so as to rely upon it as evidence at trial. The notice must be given at least 21 days before the trial. On receipt of the notice every party must be given the opportunity to inspect (rule 33.6(8)). This should end ambush by video at trial.[14] Further, the solicitor should challenge the admissibility of a video obtained prior to the exchange of evidence but not disclosed until after exchange – thus rendering the Claimant unable to deal in their evidence with the effects of the video.

Recent cases[15] have shown that very special reasons are required before a court should refuse inspection by the Claimant. The mere fact that the Claimant is charged with malingering will not normally of itself provide such special grounds.[16] Accordingly, if the Defendant unexpectedly produces video evidence at trial the best advice may be not to consent to the court viewing the video but apply immediately for an adjournment with costs.[17] This is particularly so, as recent case law suggests that the Defendant will rarely be excluded from relying upon the evidence, even in cases where the evidence was obtained by gaining access to the Claimant's home by deception.[18]

All Claimants should be warned early on in the case by their solicitors that there is a possibility of clandestine filming of the Claimant by the Defendant.

Documentary evidence

Counsel should next review the process of disclosure and inspection, ensuring that all the expected documents have been listed and disclosed by both sides and consider whether any further documents which have not been listed might be in existence. Disclosure is discussed in more length in Chapter 20. Counsel should have particular regard to the possibility of documents relating to alterations made after the accident, and documents relating to the purchase and maintenance of equipment where it was the cause of the accident. In work accidents, consideration should be given particularly to the risk assessments and health and safety policy statements required by statute. The absence of these will be an embarrassment for the Defendant.

Where it is suspected certain documents or classes of document have been withheld, consideration should be given to an application for specific disclosure.

If there has been a refusal to allow inspection of relevant documents, consideration should be given to the merits of an appropriate application and a challenge to any claim of right or duty.

---

[13]   CPR, r 33.6(8).
[14]   See also *Birch v Hales Containers Ltd* [1996] PIQR P307.
[15]   *Khan v Armaguard Ltd* [1994] 1 WLR 1204. If a court gives leave to adduce undisclosed video evidence, it must identify any special features that distinguish the case from *Khan*: *Libby-Mills v Metropolitan Police Comr* [1995] PIQR P324.
[16]   See *McGuiness v Kellogg Co* [1988] 1 WLR 913; *Digby v Essex County Council* [1994] PIQR P53.
[17]   *Birch v Hales Containers* [1996] PIQR P307.
[18]   *Jones v University of Warwick* [2003] 1 WLR 954.

In cases covered by the CEA 1995, a document is proved simply by the production of it (s 8). A document includes any copy no matter how far removed (CEEA 1995, s 8). Any document forming part of the records of a business or public authority may be received in evidence without further proof. All that is required is a certificate signed by an officer of the business or authority (s 9).

A party is deemed to admit the authenticity of any document disclosed under Part 31 unless he serves notice that he wishes the document to be proved at trial.[19] A notice to prove must be served either at the latest date for serving witness statements or within seven days of disclosure (whichever is later). Therefore, a decision to dispute a document's authenticity must be made at the earliest opportunity.

Documents referred to in the pleadings become part of the pleadings and can be looked at by the court without their being put in evidence.[20]

Hearsay

The Civil Evidence Act 1995 greatly reduced the need for consideration to be given to whether evidence is inadmissible due to it being hearsay. In effect the Act abolished the former principle excluding evidence of the grounds of hearsay (s 1), with the implementation of provisions to govern how such evidence should be included, and it is this that requires discussion.[21]

Section 2 of the 1995 Act specifies that as a safeguard, notice is required of hearsay evidence. However, where notice is not served, this affects the *weight* of such evidence, not its admissibility (Civil Evidence Act 1995, s 2(4)).

CPR, r 33.2 implements this safeguard. If a person intends to rely on hearsay evidence and this is either given by a witness or contained in a witness statement, the party intending to rely on this must serve a witness statement on the other parties. If the wish is not to give oral evidence, the party must state this fact and give reasons for it.

In all other cases of hearsay, evidence notice must be served which identifies the hearsay, states that it is to be relied upon and give any reason why the witness is not being called. This notice must be served no later than the last date for serving witness statements.

A failure to give such notice does not affect the admissibility of the evidence but may be taken into account by the court in considering the exercise of its powers with respect to the course of proceedings and costs and in particular, the weight to be given to the evidence in accordance with s 4.

By virtue of CPR, r 32.5, the general rule is that if a party has served a witness statement and he wishes to rely at trial on the evidence of the witness who made the statement, he must call the witness to give oral evidence unless the court orders otherwise or he must comply with the provisions for hearsay evidence.

---

[19]   CPR, r 32.19.
[20]   *Day v William Hill (Park Lane) Ltd* [1949] 1 KB 632.
[21]   Hearsay is not permitted where the evidence would have been inadmissible even if it was in an original form (for example, incompetence of a witness).

Where a party intends to rely on hearsay evidence yet does not propose to call the original maker of the statement, any other party may apply to the court to call that original maker (rule 33.4). If the court permits, that witness may then be cross-examined with the witness statement being the basis of the examination in chief.[22] The court must estimate the weight to be attached to any hearsay evidence presented at court which is not given in oral testimony (s 4). The court should consider the circumstances from which any inference of reliability could be drawn, in particular:

(i)   whether it was reasonable to produce the witness of the original statement;
(ii)   whether the evidence was contemporaneously made;
(iii)   whether multiple hearsay is involved;
(iv)   the motives of any maker to conceal or misrepresent the information;
(v)   whether the original was edited or made in collaboration; and
(vi)   whether the circumstances are such that the attachment of its proper weight is prevented.

If a party intends to attack the credibility of another party's hearsay witness who is not to attend, he must give notice of this intention (rule 35.5).

NOTICE TO ADMIT FACTS

Notices to admit facts[23] also require consideration. The question here is whether there are any facts which the Defendant should be compelled to agree or disagree. A notice to admit facts is rarely useful, but situations do arise where a notice may force a Defendant to reveal their true position on some concealed matter, or simply save the Claimant the expense and trouble of proving some difficult point. A Defendant's witness statement should always be read with the possibility of a notice to admit in mind. There may be support for propositions helpful to the Claimant and a risk of the Defendant not calling the maker of a helpful statement.

Convictions

Any criminal convictions of the Defendant which are to be relied on, must be proved by obtaining a certificate of conviction[24] from the appropriate court, if the conviction has not been admitted. This is particulary relevant in road traffic claims where the Defendant was convicted of a relevant offence. Counsel should check that there is a certificate or an admission or remind the solicitor. If necessary, notes of evidence given in the criminal proceedings may be admitted under Civil Evidence Act 1968, ss 2 and 4 and consideration should be given to obtaining them.

Merits

Unless there are major gaps in the evidence so far collected, it should be possible to express a view about the chances of overall success. First, it is necessary to identify the major issues in the case, and their strengths and weaknesses so far as the Claimant

---

22   The application must be made within 14 days of receiving the notice (CPR, r 33.4(2)).
23   CPR, r 32.18.
24   See Prevention of Crimes Act 1871, s 18 for the certificate generally and Civil Evidence Act 1968, s 11(c) for its admissibility; s 8 of the 1995 Act.

is concerned. While this may be a relatively straightforward task, the second task of giving an overall percentage chance of success on liability is difficult because it relies on experience and intuition. It is this evaluation that the Claimant's legal expense insurers or other funding body will be particularly concerned about as, of course, will be the Claimant.

The Bar Council has published Guidelines about the manner in which advice is to be given for the purposes of legal services funding. Public funding has been retained for clinical negligence claims, but the same analysis can be used for personal injury claims. The Guidelines may be obtained from the Bar Council and are set out in full in the Legal Aid Handbook. The test is two stage. First, the merits must be considered and are classified in percentage terms. 'Very good' means an estimated 80% or greater likelihood of success; 'good' is 60–80%; 'reasonable' is 50–60%; 'less than evens' is below 50%. On that assessment the second stage is to express a view as to the reasonableness of pursuing the case further. Here a cost-benefit analysis is necessary. The Guidelines should be referred to for their full terms for those advising for legal aid purposes, but the principles summarised above are sufficient for and should be applied to all cases whether funded by a third party, or by the Claimant himself, or by means of a CFA.

Contributory negligence

After an assessment of the overall prospects of success has been made, it is necessary to evaluate the chances of a finding of contributory negligence and the extent of that contribution. This two-stage evaluation is difficult and based on experience and intuition. If contributory negligence is found, experience shows that the most common finding is 25%. Findings of 33% and 50% are less common; 10%, 66% or 75% less common still. Other percentages than these are really quite rare in the authors' experience. In driving cases, the usual figure is 25% for failure to wear a seat belt, if using one would have made all the difference. Where it would have made a 'considerable difference', the figure is 15% but, if there is good reason why a seat belt was not being worn, for example if the Claimant was pregnant or unusually obese, there may be no reduction.[25]

The burden of proof to establish contributory negligence is on the Defendants. There are powerful legal authorities available for use against common allegations of contributory negligence in work accident cases.[26] Lord Wright in *Caswell v Powell Duffryn*[27] is authority for a more lenient[28] standard of care by Claimants in work cases than others:

[25] *Froom v Butcher* [1976] QB 286. For passengers not sitting in the front seat, see *Eastman v South West Thames Regional Health Authority* [1992] PIQR P42, CA (a case pre-dating the back seat belt law). For motorcyclists who have failed to fasten their chin strap (10% reduction), see *Capps v Miller* [1989] 1 WLR 839. Rear seat belts were made compulsory in Great Britain and Northern Ireland from 1 July 1991: Motor Vehicle (Wearing of Seat Belts in Rear Seats by Adults) Regulations 1991, SI 1991/1255; Road Traffic Act 1988, s 14(1) and (2).

[26] See, for example, those reviewed in Hendy and Ford, *Munkman on Employers' Liability* (13th edn, 2001) pp 521–537.

[27] [1940] AC 152, HL.

[28] Though where there is contributory negligence, it can sometimes be high where the injured employee was skilled, mature, familiar with the equipment and there were no extenuating distractions: *Gunter v John Nicholas & Sons* [1993] PIQR 67, a case where 'contributory negligence' was increased by the Court of Appeal from 25% to 66%.

'What is all important is to adapt the standard of what is negligence to the facts, and to give due regard to the actual conditions under which men work in a factory or mine, to the long hours and the fatigue, to the slackening of attention which naturally comes from constant repetition of the same operation, to the noise and confusion in which the man works, to his pre-occupation in what he is actually doing at the cost perhaps of some inattention to his own safety.'

Defendants and judges sometimes raise the possibility of 100% contributory negligence, following *Jayes v IMI (Kynoch) Ltd.*[29] This contradicts the purpose of the Law Reform (Contributory Negligence) Act 1945, which pre-supposes a share of responsibility, and the case may be wrongly decided.[30] No breach of statutory duty can be caused 'solely' through the Claimant's conduct, without any failure on the part of the Defendants.[31] Alternatively, the court might find no liability for an injury caused by a one-off task requiring common sense and for which no instructions could appropriately have been given.[32]

Lay witnesses on general damages

The next heading should be 'Evidence on damages'. As before, the first task is to review the evidence of the Claimant, to consider whether all aspects of pre-accident earnings, working, domestic, social, and sporting life and hobbies have been covered. A full picture before the accident and a full picture of the position after the accident is required. The Claimant's statement should also describe the impact of the accident, the treatment, the pain and suffering, and reaction throughout. It is becoming increasingly common in serious cases for Defendants to commission a secret video of the Claimant, see above.

The lay witnesses on damages should be assessed. The Claimant's spouse, parents, relatives, and friends should, between them, provide one or, in a very serious case, two good witnesses about the change in the Claimant since the accident. Any particular activities of the Claimant, which are no longer possible, should be amplified by these witnesses and they or the Claimant should bring to court any cups, medals, certificates or other prestigious proof of pre-accident prowess.

Where care has been, is being or will be given by family or friends, counsel should check that witness statements deal with this in sufficient detail: shopping, cooking, washing clothes and sheets, toilet care, cleaning, gardening, DIY, car repair, just spending time talking to an immobile Claimant, etc. This evidence is necessary to sustain a financial claim and a check should be made to see that there is evidence from a care expert, car repairer, gardening firm, decorators, etc to put a price on the care given by lay people, together with medical evidence to support the level and kind of care given.

---

[29]   [1985] ICR 155.
[30]   *Pitts v Hunt* [1991] 1 QB 24 per Beldam J.
[31]   *Ross v Associated Portland Cement Manufacturers Ltd* [1964] 1 WLR 768; *Boyle v Kodak Ltd* [1969] 1 WLR 661, but see *Walsh v Crown Decorative Products Ltd* [1993] PIQR P194 for a case going the other way. See the discussion in Hendy and Ford, *Munkman on Employers' Liability* (13th edn, 2001) pp 535–537.
[32]   *Devizes Reclamation Co Ltd v Chalk* (1999) Times, 2 April.

Medical evidence

The medical evidence should be reviewed, to ensure that every aspect of the Claimant's injuries – both physical and mental – have been covered adequately and every aspect of the Defendant's medical evidence has been either accepted or adequately rebutted. It is necessary to review fully the medical evidence, to ensure that the prognosis, including the risk of relapses, epilepsy, diminished life expectancy and so forth, has been fully dealt with. The medical evidence should be compared with the lay witnesses' evidence, to ensure that there is nothing missing from the medical evidence which the lay witnesses have noted, for example, depression, irritability, or a physical incapacity to do some activity important to the Claimant, but which may have been overlooked by the doctor. The medical reports should be no more than a year old, preferably less than six months unless the Claimant's condition has resolved.[33]

Reports from the different specialists should be assessed to ensure that there is no inconsistency. If any such inconsistency appears, the medical experts should be invited to speak to each other and if necessary, a joint conference should be held. A particular area where overlap is common is that of future care or treatment. For example, a nursing expert may have been instructed to report on the costs of care and it is absolutely vital that this estimated level of care tallies precisely with the level which the medical experts have prescribed for the Claimant. By the same token, the medical evidence should support any claim for care since the accident, even if given by family and friends (see above).

The estimated costs of rehabilitation and care should be reviewed carefully. Whilst most care experts are familiar with the legal process, in a substantial claim it is always worthwhile considering carefully their estimates against the lay evidence to ensure that sufficient care is being claimed. It may well be necessary to see the care expert in conference with the main medical expert to ensure that nothing is being overlooked and that there is no underestimation of the level and costs of services for the future. Where continuous care is being provided to a Claimant, it is important to ensure that provision is made for relief staff, recruitment, holidays for the carers and the Claimant and so on.

The medical evidence should also be considered to the extent that it is relevant to liability, for example, in a seat belt case if the lack of a belt might have made no difference to the injuries. In addition, it may be necessary to ask the medical expert to make explicit any implicit finding that the Claimant will be handicapped on the labour market, ie suffer a loss of earning capacity.

Since the rules requiring disclosure of the Claimant's medical report at the outset of proceedings, some of the old battles about mutual disclosure[34] may be over. However, the authorities giving grounds for a stay of proceedings where a party refuses a medical examination remain relevant.[35] Counsel should consider the extent to which there has been disclosure of the medical evidence and which reports are to be relied on and disclosed. Defendants often seek the Claimant's medical records to see whether there is some underlying condition to which they can attribute part of the

33   See *Kaiser v Carlswood Glassworks Ltd* (1965) 109 Sol Jo 537.
34   *Kirkup v British Rail Engineering Ltd* [1983] 1 WLR 1165.
35   *Megarity v DJ Ryan & Sons Ltd* [1980] 1 WLR 1237.

responsibility for the Claimant's continuing injuries. The Defendant's medical and legal advisers are entitled to see all the medical records, not just those related to the relevant injury, if a claim for future loss of earnings or loss of earnings capacity,[36] or exacerbation of pre-existing condition is claimed. Sometimes a letter from the Claimant's doctor confirming no prior relevant injury or symptoms will avoid the need to disclose the Claimant's medical records. These records are often used by Defendants for other purposes such as cross-examination as to credibility. It is at this point that it is sensible to ensure that updated clinical notes have been obtained and if not, steps taken to obtain them.

In a work accident, it is quite possible that the Defendant has medical records of the Claimant kept at a first aid centre or Occupational Health Department. This possibility should be considered and the solicitor advised to obtain them if they are likely to exist.

The Claimant's medical records, whether from the receiving hospital, the treating hospital, the general practitioner, or the Defendant's occupational health department, should be examined and commented on by counsel. As a matter of competence, solicitor and counsel specialising in personal injury law must train themselves to read and understand basic GP and hospital clinical notes; they should be familiar with the standard format of these records in order to both properly sort them in chronological order (essential where there are issues of pre-existing difficulties) and interpret them in the light of expert evidence. It is important to ensure that the Claimant's medico-legal experts have both seen a complete set of the clinical notes and has assessed them in his/her report or a separate letter, especially if they are possibly adverse.

Counsel should be alert to any mental condition emanating from the accident. The limits of compensatable 'nervous shock'[37] were extended in 1983 by *McLoughlin v O'Brian*[38] and in 1995 by *Page v Smith*[39] to pure psychiatric damage. Sometimes it may have emerged that the Claimant has suffered mentally in some way not yet reported on, for example, a fear of travel in a car or some other neurosis. In such cases, a psychiatric report should be recommended. Counsel will be alert to the fact that if the Claimant was not physically injured but suffers a nervous reaction short of an identifiable psychological illness, no damages are recoverable[40] – so no damages for mental suffering, fear, anxiety and the like. Once the Claimant has shown that he has suffered from an identifiable psychological illness he must show that it was a foreseeable consequence of the Defendant's act.[41] Post-traumatic stress disorder

---

[36]   *Dunn v British Coal Corpn* [1993] PIQR P275. If objection is taken due to the relevance of a particular document, then order should be sought from the court. See *Hipwood v Gloucester Health Authority* [1995] PIQR P447.

[37]   Medical evidence is not always needed of nervous shock or psychological disorder: *Whitmore v Euroways Express Coaches Ltd*; *Kemp*, vol II, C4-023. It would, however, be a foolhardy lawyer that failed to obtain medical evidence on such an issue.

[38]   [1983] 1 AC 410. Further refined in *Ravenscroft v Rederiaktiebolaget Transatlantic* [1992] 2 All ER 470; *Alcock v Chief Constable of South Yorkshire Police* [1992] 1 AC 310; *Taylor v Somerset Health Authority* [1993] PIQR P262; *McFarlane v EE Caledonia Ltd* [1994] PIQR P154.

[39]   [1995] PIQR P329.

[40]   *Nicholls v Rushton* (1992) Times, 19 June.

[41]   Ie that it would have caused such a reaction in a person of ordinary fortitude. See *Page v Smith* [1995] PIQR P329.

has been recognised and compensated in a large number of recent cases.[42] Chronic fatigue syndrome, also known as ME or PVFS, has been accepted as an illness which can be triggered by trauma.[43] A psychiatric report should also be recommended if there is any hint of an allegation of 'compensationitis', 'malingering' or 'functional overlay'. If Defendants wish to allege malingering, they must specifically plead it, and if they wish to make general allegations of exaggeration or compensationitis, they should call their doctor(s) to face cross-examination.[44]

Usually, the Claimant's medical evidence on the physical injuries give an adequate explanation of the mechanics of the injury, but this is not always possible. In cases where it is not, it is important to have the protection of a psychiatric report to support the Claimant's claim that he is really suffering.

Counsel's next task is to consider the extent to which the Defendant's medical evidence[45] can be agreed. If there is any significant discrepancy between the Claimant and the Defendant on their medical evidence, the Defendant's medical evidence should be agreed only on the proviso that the Claimant's evidence is to be accepted on the points of difference. The court will always order that like experts discuss areas of dispute between their evidence and prepare joint statements for the trial judge indicating their areas of agreement/disagreement.

If there is a conflict of medical opinion, the Claimant's solicitor should consider asking the Claimant's experts to fortify their opinions by providing copies of relevant parts of current textbooks and articles in journals. These can form useful material in cross-examination of the Defendant's expert. Consideration must be given to the extent to which it will be necessary to call the Claimant's medical experts to give evidence if the Defendant agrees the Claimant's medical reports. There are cases where, even though the medical evidence is agreed, it is still important to have a medical expert to give evidence so as to bring home to the judge a particular aspect of the case especially in respect of quantum issues. In an appropriate case this will not be a significant costs risk.[46] No party can adduce evidence without leave of the court. In circumstances where the Defendant is in default of exchange dates and it is feared they might seek leave to serve their evidence late, consideration should be given to seeking an order debarring them from adducing medical evidence.

The directions hearing is the appropriate occasion at which to review whether a split trial should be sought, especially if it now appears that the medical evidence is so complex and unsettled as to warrant a separate trial on liability first.

Evidence of financial loss

Having considered the medical evidence, financial losses should be reviewed. Loss of the Claimant's earnings up to date are probably capable of agreement between the

---

42 See the discussion of them in *PMILL*, vol 5, nos 4 and 5.
43 *Page v Smith* [1993] PIQR Q55.
44 *Stojalowski v Imperial Smelting Corpn (NSC) Ltd* (1976) 121 Sol Jo 118.
45 If a medical report is disclosed accidentally it can be used by the receiving party at trial: *Pizzey v Ford Motor Co Ltd* [1994] PIQR P15.
46 *Jones v Griffith* [1969] 1 WLR 795.

two sides on the basis of a letter from the employer. There should be consideration of whether or not the Claimant is required to repay earnings paid during his period of absence from work if he recovers compensation from a negligent third party and his employers are written to for details of the relevant amounts and contractual or other provisions which require him to recoup their outlay. The Claimant is entitled to rely on his medical advisers in deciding if the treatment is necessary and whether he is fit to go back to work.[47] Loss of earnings from other sources must not be overlooked (for example, part-time work). Loss of earnings by carers who have given up time to look after the Claimant are recoverable[48] and should be claimed.

In some cases, the loss of wages is in dispute and evidence from 'comparators', ie comparable earners – perhaps workmates of the Claimant, or employees in the same category as the Claimant nominated by him – is necessary. In some occupations, evidence is required from HM Revenue & Customs, the Claimant's accountants or leading members of the 'trade, profession or occupation' as to the earnings (which may include profit as well as income)[49] the Claimant in business on his own account would have enjoyed but for the accident.

All aspects of remuneration should be claimed and supported by evidence, including loss of use of company car, bonuses, tips, free or discounted goods, subsidised meals, pension and holiday pay.

Similar evidence is required about future losses. The evidence for the future should, in addition, deal with the Claimant's job security and with any prospects for promotion that would have enhanced wages. Both these questions may be dealt with by superior managers (who rarely agree to assist), by trade union officials or leading representatives of professional associations, in appropriate cases.

The disablement employment advisers (formerly resettlement officers) and a growing number of employment consultants are extremely good at giving evidence of the prospects for obtaining employment in any particular skill and geographical area and as to the wage rates payable.

Employment consultants are particularly useful in providing evidence for a claim for loss of earning capacity. Even though such specific evidence is not essential as a matter of law,[50] damages for loss of earning capacity cannot be maximised without it. Counsel should ensure that a reminder is put in the advice that the Claimant should continue to make and save copies of as many job applications (and refusals) as possible and retain any documents relating to redundancy or other similar payments. These documents must be disclosed in a supplementary list or a letter.

It is particularly important to review losses which do not flow from inability to earn. These are often overlooked. For example, a valuation is necessary to assess the annual loss caused to the Claimant who can no longer tend his allotment, orchard, or keep hens, pigs, or breed dogs, etc. The additional costs of labour to keep the garden as it was, maintain the house inside and out and service the car should be obtained. This

---

[47]   *Edward William Southgate v Port of London Authority* (14 February 1975, unreported), CA.
[48]   *Hunt v Severs* [1994] 2 AC 350 but not if the carer was the tortfeasor.
[49]   *Bellingham v Dhillon* [1973] 1 All ER 20.
[50]   *Patel v Edwards* [1970] RTR 425; *Watson v Mitcham Cardboard Ltd* [1982] CLY 78, CA; *Kemp and Kemp*, vol 2, para 9-745.

can be in the form of a letter in the first place, from reputable agencies providing such services commercially, such as gardening firms, building and decorating firms, estate managers, and garages.[51] Generally speaking, the bigger and more prestigious the agency selected, the greater will be its estimate of the labour costs, so maximising the damages claim. It is also more likely that the Defendant will accept the valuation of a large and prestigious agency without challenge. Only the labour element is recoverable, of course.

Mention has already been made of the need to have evidence of care by relatives and friends, to have that evidence costed by appropriate agencies and to have that level of care supported by medical evidence.

Valuations should also be sought of the additional costs of taxis, medical prescriptions and other forms of treatment.

The starting point for calculation of future losses is the multiplicand, ie the annual rate of loss as at the date of trial. Counsel should check to ensure that the necessary evidence to calculate this, reflecting all aspects of continuing loss comprising both loss of income and increase of expenditure, is available.

In the light of the above, the schedule of loss must be reviewed and (probably) reconstructed before being re-served. If the Defendant has complied with any directions order in respect of service of their counter-schedule, this too must be considered. If they have not, consideration should be given to seeking an order requiring them to do so. A very basic checklist on evidence of past losses follows. This may also serve as a checklist on the items of special damage for the schedule of loss:

(i)   net loss of earnings;

(ii)   care costs, including gratuitous care;[52]

(iii)   damage to property, for example, clothing, personal possessions, contents of car, watch, rings, etc – evidence by receipts, Claimant, relatives, jeweller, etc;

(iv)   damage to vehicle and associated expenditure, such as:

     (a)   loss of insurance excess;

     (b)   loss of no claims bonus;

     (c)   cost of repairs or replacement (less salvage);

     (d)   replacement car hire and insurance, or alternative means of transport such as bus, train, taxi, etc;

     (e)   car recovery costs such as towage and storage;

     (f)   pro rata period of the Claimant's insurance and or AA/RAC subscriptions whilst the car is being repaired/off the road (insurers/AA/RAC should surrender unexpired period if car is a write-off);

     (g)   engineer's fee for valuation purposes;

     (h)   loss of petrol if vehicle a write-off;

     (i)   interest on money borrowed to buy or repair vehicle;

     (j)   loss of use of the vehicle, if no hire of replacement. This must be pleaded. The value of the loss may be calculated from estimating the weekly value of having such a vehicle based on the standing and running costs

[51]   *Daly v General Steamship Navigation Co Ltd* [1981] 1 WLR 120.

[52]   *Cunningham v Harrison* [1973] QB 942.

ascertained from the AA or RAC updated running cost figures, and Glass's or Parker's updated capital value figures.[53] Alternatively, the court 'must do the best it can' to come to a reasonable estimate of the damage suffered.[54] Credit must be given for any refund of the standing charges against any award for loss of use;

(v)   travelling expenses for medical advice or treatment (but not for legal advice) including taxi, tube and bus fares and use of the Claimant's car on the same basis as above. It is not always easy to obtain receipts for such expenditure but the Claimant's reasonably contemporaneous note is usually sufficient;

(vi) medical expenses. The fact that facilities were available under the NHS is no bar to the Claimant recovering the costs of private treatment.[55] All reasonable medical expenses can be recovered such as:

   (a)   operations;
   (b)   emergency treatment in hospital;
   (c)   prescription charges;
   (d)   bandages, aids, prosthetics;
   (e)   painkillers;
   (f)   physiotherapy;
   (g)   osteopathy;
   (h)   dentistry;
   (i)   psychotherapy;
   (j)   nursing care;
   (k)   self-conducted therapy such as swimming regularly and thereby incurring admission charges or membership fees for a fitness club.

If the medical expenses have been reasonably incurred, it does not matter if they prove not to have been necessary.[56] Medical expenses may be reasonably incurred even if cheaper treatment is available.[57] Treatment based on medical advice will be reasonable in most cases. Medical evidence that the items claimed were reasonable is necessary. This is sometimes more difficult for 'alternative medicine' although with the court's emphasis on rehabilitation, the Claimant should be able to argue the necessity of such treatments on the basis that they maximise his potential to make a full recovery: acupuncture, chiropractors, homeopaths, etc. Evidence in the form of receipts are needed to confirm the actual expenditure, or at least a reasonably contemporaneous note by the Claimant. The medical expenses need not have been incurred in relation to professionally qualified medical staff. Payment to unqualified persons for elementary care or mere attendance is also recoverable if reasonable. As noted above, medical evidence is required to show that the care and attendance was reasonable; evidence from a professional agency is necessary to cost it. No claim can be made for treatment on the NHS if no expense has been incurred.[58] Recovery of outlay by healthcare providers under their subrogated rights should always be included;

---

[53]   *Birmingham Corpn v Sowsbery* [1970] RTR 84.
[54]   *Dixon's (Scholar Green) Ltd v Cooper* [1970] RTR 222.
[55]   Law Reform (Personal Injuries) Act 1948, s 2(4).
[56]   *Rubens v Walker* 1946 SC 215 at 216; *SS Baron Vernon v SS Metagama* 1928 SC (HL) 21 at 28.
[57]   *Rialas v Mitchell* (1984) 128 Sol Jo 704.
[58]   Administration of Justice Act 1982, s 5.

(vii) general expenses/losses. These could include increases in the normal expenses such as heating and lighting costs incurred through being at home more often, extra cleaning, extra telephone calls/postage, entertaining a Claimant who formerly entertained him/herself, for example, purchase of computer, video, etc and increased costs of holidays. Correspondingly, loss of use of subscriptions to a sports club or football season ticket and an irrecoverable deposit on a booked holiday. Labour costs of DIY, gardening, an allotment and car maintenance previously carried out by the Claimant will require estimates from appropriate commercial firms;

(viii) fees associated with the Office of the Public Guardian (the old Court of Protection). These are fees associated with guardianship orders and are recoverable if the Claimant's injuries have rendered him or her incapable of managing his or her affairs;

(ix) loss of earnings including any provision to recoup outlay on behalf of the Claimant's employers (dealt with above);

(x) computation of the annual value of continuing loss as at date of trial for purposes of calculating future loss.

Quantum of damages

The final heading in the advice is 'quantum of damages'. Often, after a thorough review of the case, so many steps need to be undertaken that it is not possible to evaluate fully the damages likely to be recoverable in the case. Nevertheless, where possible, an estimate of quantum should be given.

Pain, suffering and loss of amenity

The first task is to attempt to evaluate damages for pain, suffering and loss of amenity. A useful starting point is the Judicial Studies Board's *Guidelines for the Assessment of General Damages in Personal Injury Cases*, published at the beginning of each chapter of *Kemp and Kemp*, vols 3 and 4. The most up-to-date sources are Current Law, Halsbury's monthly updaters, Personal Injury Quantum Reports (PIQR), Lawtel and the *Personal and Medical Injuries Law Letter*. These should supplement the more extensive material in *Kemp and Kemp*. Having found a number of cases which are roughly similar to that of the Claimant on pain, suffering and loss of amenity, each award should be brought up to current value by use of the inflation table in *Kemp and Kemp*, vols 3 and 4. Most of the above are now available on CD-ROM or on download (for a price) through the internet. The inflation multiplier must be increased by the current annual rate of inflation for the period between the date of printing of the page and the date of computation. Practitioners should be careful to identify those cases decided before and after the Court of Appeal's decision in *Heil v Rankin*.[59] In that case, the range of awards for general damages were reconsidered and a sliding scale increase was applied to cases where general damages were in excess of £10,000. In real terms, it has resulted in only marginal increases in general damages for cases worth less than £40,000, but care should be taken to ensure that

---

[59]   [2000] PIQR Q187.

all cases decided before 21 March 2000 take into account the *Heil* uplift which increased general damages by up to one third in the most serious category of cases.[60] Whilst the JSB Guidelines have been adjusted to take into account that decision, the individual awards in *Kemp* or elsewhere will not.

Where there are multiple injuries, the overall award is usually lower than the sum of awards if each injury were inflicted on a separate Claimant. There are aspects of general damages awards which should not be overlooked, such as the loss of job enjoyment;[61] loss of a good education;[62] loss of status through inability to complete apprenticeship;[63] or loss of the chance to enhance reputation.[64]

Interest in general damages

Next, the interest on the general damages for pain, suffering and loss of amenity should be assessed. The interest rate is at 2% flat per annum from the date of service of the claim form.[65] The computation should be made to the nearest week, ie 1/52nd of 2%; for example, if there has been a two-and-a-half-year delay between issue of the claim form and trial, general damages should be increased by 5%.

Past loss

The next computation is that of special damage. The general principle is, of course, that the Claimant should, as nearly as possible, be put in the same position as he would have been had he not sustained the injury. Therefore, loss of earnings is recoverable net of tax,[66] and national insurance.[67] Then, all recoverable benefits must be deducted under the clawback of benefits rules.

Sick pay is usually paid under an agreement that it is to be set off against damages, as are payments received by an employee under a permanent health insurance scheme following incapacity resulting from an accident at work.[68] It should be ensured that sick pay is not deducted twice, ie from damages and as a result of the clawback provisions. Also, it should be confirmed whether gross or net earnings have been paid. A redundancy payment is deductible from loss of post-receipt earnings, if the redundancy is attributable to some extent to the injury.[69] If it is not attributable, then a redundancy payment is not set off against damages.[70]

---

[60]   A useful graph can be found on the personal injury calculator at www.achilles.org.
[61]   *Morris v Johnson Matthey & Co Ltd* (1968) 112 Sol Jo 32; *Hearnshaw v English Steel Corpn Ltd* (1971) 11 KIR 306; *Champion v London Fire and Civil Defence Authority* (1990) Times, 5 July. See the table in *Kemp and Kemp*, vol 1 at para 5-251.
[62]   *Jones v Lawrence* [1969] 3 All ER 267.
[63]   *Dunk v George Waller and Son Ltd* [1970] 2 QB 163.
[64]   *Marbé v Daly's Theatre* [1928] 1 KB 269.
[65]   *Lawrence v Chief Constable* [2000] PIQR Q349.
[66]   *British Transport Commission v Gourley* [1956] AC 185.
[67]   *Cooper v Firth Brown Ltd* [1963] 1 WLR 418.
[68]   *Hussain v New Taplow Paper Mills Ltd* [1988] AC 514.
[69]   *Colledge v Bass Mitchells and Butlers Ltd* [1988] 1 All ER 536, CA.
[70]   *Mills v Hassall* [1983] ICR 330.

There are a number of exceptions to these principles. These exceptions allow the Claimant to keep the money without giving credit for it against damages received from the Defendant. These are: proceeds of private insurance taken out by the Claimant (though a check should be made to ensure that the insurance company itself will not demand recoupment from any damages received);[71] charitable and benevolent receipts from third parties;[72] pension entitlement, even where the Defendant contributed to the pension scheme;[73] and assistance from friends and relatives.[74]

Generally, interest on special damages is calculated at half the 'special account rate' on each of those items which is a continuing loss. In respect of those items where the loss has ceased to accrue prior to the date of trial, there is a powerful argument that the full special account rate should be taken from the midway point of the period of accrual.[75]

Future loss

Similar principles apply to the assessment of a future loss as apply to past loss. However, for future loss, a lump sum has to be calculated to represent the present value (at date of trial or settlement) of losses which will accrue in the future. First, the annual net rate of loss as at date of trial or settlement is calculated. This is called the 'multiplicand'. It is calculated on much the same basis as past loss and includes annual rate of earnings loss, annual cost of additional transport expenses, annualised DIY labour costs, annualised loss of allotment produce, and so on. Loss of income is relatively easy to calculate.

Increased costs are sometimes more difficult to annualise but is simply done by evidence showing the period over which the expenditure is referable from which can be calculated the costs attributable to one year. For example, suppose the labour cost of redecorating a house is £500. It needs painting every five years. The annual cost is £100.

Capital expenditure is more complex. Adaptations which could add nothing to the value of the object adapted (for example, house, car) are recoverable in full, less a discount if the purchase is yet to be made. Adaptations which enhance value will only be recoverable to the marginal extent that the Claimant would not otherwise have

71 *Bradburn v Great Western Rly Co* (1874) LR 10 Exch 1.
72 *Redpath v Belfast & County Down Rly Co* [1947] NI 167.
73 *Parry v Cleaver* [1970] AC 1; *Smoker v London Fire and Civil Defence Authority* [1991] 2 AC 502.
74 *Liffen v Watson* [1940] 1 KB 556.
75 Interest on special damages is usually calculated at either the whole or half the 'special account rate', a rate which fluctuates. There are two situations here. The first is where the special damages continue to accrue to the date of trial. In this case, half the interest rate is appropriate (or half the sum at the full rate, or half the period at full rate: *Jefford v Gee* [1970] 2 QB 130). The second situation is where the special damages cease to accrue at a date prior to trial. In this case, it is mathematically more advantageous and logically correct to argue that the full rate should be taken from a date halfway through the period of accrual: *Prokop v Department of Health and Social Security* [1985] CLY 1037, CA, but note *Dexter v Courtaulds Ltd* [1984] 1 All ER 70, CA, a judgment which suggests that the proposition is applicable only in 'special circumstances' (which are ill-defined and somewhat illogical). *Prokop* followed High Court decisions in *Ichard v Frangoulis* [1977] 1 WLR 556 and *Dodd v Rediffusion* [1980] CLY 635, which were cited in *Dexter.* Since then, in *Mendha Singh v Smith Foundries Ltd* (17 July 1985, unreported), Mars-Jones J, preferred and applied *Prokop*, rather than *Dexter*, after full argument on the point.

made the purchase. There are special rules where purchase of a home is necessitated.[76] These annual costs are taken at their value at the date of trial or settlement. Counsel must ensure, as mentioned above, that no element in the multiplicand is overlooked.

A 'multiplier' is then applied to the multiplicand, a figure less than the Claimant's remaining years of life expectancy because it takes into account future contingencies (though not the possibility of future inflation). These contingencies include mortality, sickness, the advantage of accelerated payment and, in respect of earnings in particular, the chances of unemployment, promotion and retirement.

Though in most cases there will be a single multiplicand and a single multiplier, in some cases there are several multiplicands, some of which require separate multipliers.[77] Thus, a 30-year-old male Claimant, whose normal age of retirement would be at 50, and whose injury causes him to lose his job and his allotment, may have a short multiplier for his loss of earnings but a longer one in respect of loss of produce (to eat or sell) from his allotment if, for instance, it could be said that he had a reasonable expectation of cultivating it until age 70. Such a Claimant's loss of job, and with it entitlement to a pension which would have been enhanced by years of earnings and higher rates of pay, is likely to involve a loss equalling the difference between the pension he will actually receive when he reaches 50 and that which he would have received had he worked to age 50. Again, the computation is of multiplicand and multiplier, but in this case there then needs to be applied an additional discount for accelerated payment of the loss[78] since he will receive compensation for it today, aged 30, rather than in the years following his 50th birthday. A further separate calculation may be required to evaluate the cost of this Claimant's future medical care, on which the level of expenditure may be expected to escalate over the years.

In some cases, the rate of loss will differ in different periods during the Claimant's expected working life. In this situation the overall multiplier should be ascertained and apportioned in proportion to the different loss periods of the Claimant's total working life.[79]

In a straightforward case where the future loss runs from date of trial to the end of the Claimant's life expectancy, a rule of thumb for the multiplier used to be half the Claimant's life expectancy plus one. This has now gone with the advent of the Ogden Tables (currently on its 6th edn) under the authority of the House of Lords (see below).Tables of average life expectancy can be found in *Kemp and Kemp*.[80] The

---

[76]   *Roberts v Johnstone* [1989] QB 878 uprated to 3% as a result of *Wells v Wells*.

[77]   In general, the approach of averaging the losses over the period and dividing by the number of periods is not in the Claimant's interest. Note *Brightman v Johnson* (1985) Times, 17 December; *Housecroft v Burnett* [1986] 1 All ER 332.

[78]   Where an additional discount for accelerated payment has to be made beyond that which is taken into account by fixing the multiplier (ie where the plaintiff would not, but for the accident and litigation, have received any payment under the particular head of damages until some years after the actual date of trial), the discount is calculated by deducting 3% compound interest per annum: *Mallet v McMonagle* [1970] AC 166 per Lord Diplock at 176D and *Wells v Wells* [1999] 1 AC 345.

[79]   *Winwood v Bird* (1986) Butterworths Persoanl Injury Service, vol 3; *Malone v Rowan* [1984] 3 All ER 402; *Brittain v Gardner*, *Kemp and Kemp*, paras A-2002, A2-104, *Burke v Tower Hamlets London Borough Council* [1989] CLY 1201; *Kemp and Kemp*, para A4-103. This is advantageous if the rate of loss increases over the years.

[80]   *Kemp and Kemp*, vol 1, para 6-340.

special problem of multipliers and multiplicands in relation to fatal accidents is dealt with in Chapter 28.

The calculation of multipliers are derived from a discount rate for accelerated payment of 2.5%. The Claimant is receiving now earnings and other moneys that he would not have received (but for the injury) until years in the future. The 'discount rate' is the equivalent of the real rate of return (ie net of tax and after allowing for inflation) estimated over the desired number of years into the future.

The 2.5% discount rate is the basis of the multiplier which have been set out in the Ogden Tables[81] which are reprinted in *Kemp and Kemp*, vol 1. The Ogden Tables should be used as the basis of the multiplier and specific reference should be made to the explanatory notes which accompany the Tables to apply the relevant formulae. Discount can be made for contingencies only in future loss of earnings cases.

These actuarial tables are based on averages; hence if the Claimant has particular characteristics which might be thought to take her/him out of the average, an actuary may need to be instructed. If the Claimant is more at risk from the vagaries of life than the average, this option should be forgotten. If the Claimant appears less at risk, an actuary should be considered, but the courts are reluctant to entertain actuarial evidence.[82] Actuarial multipliers need to be discounted for contingencies other than mortality and accelerated payment. Ten per cent is the usual rate.[83]

Pensions pose particular problems in calculating future loss and a variety of methods have been used in the past. A good explanation of the calculations is to be found in the relevant chapters in *Kemp and Kemp*.

Handicap on the labour market

Also known as loss of earning capacity or damages for *Smith v Manchester Corpn*, the basic principles for such an award are set out in *Moeliker v A Reyrolle & Co Ltd*.[84] As a matter of law, no specific evidence is required to be directed to this head of damage. However no competent lawyer would fail to prepare evidence focused on loss of earning capacity where such a claim is appropriate. The evidence required for maximum recovery under this head is the Claimant's current net wage rate (or that which could reasonably be expected if he was in employment), his prospects for the future and, particularly, evidence of the particular difficulties in seeking and retaining employment by reason of his disabilities. This evidence can be given by the Claimant and work colleagues, especially managers. It is usual, however, to centre

[81]   The Joint Working Party of Actuaries and Lawyers, chaired by Michael Ogden, HMSO, 1984, approved in *Wells v Wells*.

[82]   *Kemp and Kemp*, vol 1, para 6-320. The status of actuarial evidence is not clear. In *Mitchell v Mulholland (No 2)* [1972] 1 QB 65 at 76, Edmund Davies LJ stated that it should not be used as the 'primary basis of assessment but as a means of cross-checking the calculations'; see also Lord Pearson in *Taylor v O'Connor* [1971] AC 115 at 140. However, in recent large medical negligence cases, the use of actuaries has been invaluable: for example, *Almond v Leeds Western Health Authority* [1990] 1 Med LR; and see *O'Brien's Curator Bonis v British Steel plc* 1991 SLT 447.

[83]   A Judicial Studies Board Paper in June 1991 described 10% as a 'very good guide', though Kemp, *Damages for Personal Injury and Death* (5th edn, 1993) p 110 suggests it is excessive.

[84]   [1977] 1 WLR 132, [1976] ICR 253. A more recent case is *Robson v Liverpool City Council* (1993) PIQR Q78.

the evidence on that of an employment consultant. Evidence should also be given by the Claimant of any reasons why he or she might be more likely to be on the labour market than the usual, for example, anticipated move out of big city to area of high unemployment for family reasons; anticipated breaks in employment for child rearing; particular insecurity of job, employer or trade.

In considering the evidence on this head of damage, a check should be made to ensure that disclosure of all the Claimant's medical records, not just those relating to the accident in question, has been made.[85]

Periodical payments

Whilst the issue of periodical payments is beyond the scope of this book, in substantial claims, consideration must be given to whether or not the court should be asked to make an award by way of periodical payments.

CONCLUSION

At each stage a review is conducted, it is an extensive task, to be approached methodically and intensively. It is not suited to a busy day at the office between phone calls and meetings.

---

[85]   *Dunn v British Coal Corpn* [1993] PIQR P275. Unless objection can be taken due to relevance: see *Hipwood v Gloucester Health Authority* [1995] PIQR P447.

CHAPTER 22

Preparing for Trial

This chapter assumes that the Claimant's solicitor has complied with the case management directions and timetable set on allocation in fast track (rule 28.2) and, in multi track, at a case management conference (rule 29.3(1)(a)) or by agreement approved by the court (rule 29.4), or, later in the process by pre-trial review (rule 29.3(1)(b)). Any variation to the timetable will have been sought (rule 28.4 in fast track, rule 29.5 in multi track) and the solicitor will now be gearing up for trial though perhaps in the hope of settlement, a prospect which may be encouraged in multi track cases by the court, of its own motion, calling a pre-trial review (rule 29.7) one purpose of which is said to be the encouragement of settlement.

One of the overriding objectives of the rules is that cases should be run in a cost proportionate way. Active case management has reduced the number of claims that go to trial by not only restricting the use of expert evidence, but by encouraging and promoting a climate of settlement. Nonetheless, even though under the old rules only a tiny proportion of issued claims ever reached the doors of the court, and still less entered it, claims will still be fought at trial and the prudent and pro-active solicitor runs each case towards a trial date whilst considering compromise along the way.

This chapter assumes that the Claimant's solicitor will already have filed the listing questionnaire and any pre-trial review in a multi track claim will have taken place (see Chapter 5 in respect of Multi track, and Chapter 4 in relation to Fast track, trials). What follows is applicable in part to fast track trials, but is generally prepared with multi track work in mind. Solicitors must bear in mind that at present costs are fixed in fast track trials, evidence is generally far more limited, the case is generally presented by the advocate with no allowance made for an accompanying solicitor and that an important goal is to ensure that the court does not form the view that the costs outweigh the benefit of bringing proceedings. This can be a somewhat difficult constraint for an injured and aggrieved client to cope with – especially in the run up to trial.

A timetable for trial is set by the court (rule 28.6 for fast track, rule 29.8 for multi track) in consultation with the parties (rule 39.4). The trial date or window, once fixed is almost unmoveable save where very powerful reasons are shown, the rule being that an order to vacate a trial hearing is an order of the last resort. The trial date or window (not exceeding three weeks for fast track: rule 28.2(2)(b); not exceeding one week for multi track: rule 29.8(c)(ii)) is fixed on the hearing for case management directions in fast track cases (rule 28.2(2)) and after receipt of the parties listing questionnaires in multi track (rule 29.8). In multi track cases, the court may hold a pre-trial review (and usually will do so if the trial estimate is 10 days or more), but the decision whether to do so is entirely the court's (rule 29.7).

As soon as the trial date (or window) is known the client, all experts, witnesses and counsel's clerk should be notified of the time, date (or window) and place of the trial.

It is good practice for the solicitor to prepare a trial plan which details all of the witnesses, both lay and expert to be called and the identity of counsel. Telephone and fax numbers postal and e-mail addresses and DX numbers should be included on the plan for easy reference purposes. The plan should provide boxes to tick and date to show that each person has been notified of the trial date. Provision should be made for the date upon which any summonses to attend the trial should be obtained and served upon lay witnesses and experts. In a large trial, where a lot of evidence is to be called, the trial days should be noted and as the matter proceeds to trial and a running order of witnesses decided, the names of each witness for each day should be inserted. The court may have fixed a trial agenda, allocating various days to various stages of the trial (see rule 29.7(1)).

Even with front loading by advance disclosure, early exchange of evidence and a 'cards on the table' approach, in every case the solicitor will spend more and more time on the case as it comes towards trial.

All elements should be kept under constant review to ensure that the various loose ends are tied up. The solicitor should not regard fulfilment of the requirements of any review of evidence, merits and quantum (see Chapter 21) as the last word and assume that no more thinking or checking needs to be done. New loopholes may emerge which need to be closed and new factors can arise which may require further steps to be taken in the final preparation for trial. The logistics of getting the right people to court on the right day is its own nightmare.

LAST MINUTE MATTERS

Experts

Expert evidence cannot be relied on unless it has been disclosed, and the expert cannot be called to give oral evidence unless the court has given leave. In a fast track trial, leave will not normally be given to adduce oral expert evidence, but if it is clear that the case cannot be heard without serious prejudice to the client, the solicitor should seek, by application, leave to bring in oral evidence.

If, for some previously unforeseen reason, a further expert needs to be brought in at a late stage, an application must be made to the court at once to ask for leave to call the expert. It should be remembered that under the CPR the court will regard a trial date as virtually unmoveable. This, however, should not deter the solicitor from making any application where it is essential to do so to achieve justice.

If further expert evidence is sought to be admitted, but consists of a report which should have been obtained earlier, then if the evidence is let in so as not to prejudice the Claimant, the solicitor may face a personal costs order for her failure to produce it earlier. The court will consider at the time of the application what prejudice there is to the Defendant and whether the expert could or should be instructed jointly. Therefore, prior to the application the solicitor should give careful consideration to these issues. The Defendant should be given early notice of further evidence and asked to agree its admission. In a case where they may want to 'match' the evidence, full access to the client for medical examination on the usual terms should be given to do so.

In a fast track claim, there may only be one joint expert. If there are opposing experts (as will be usual in a multi track case), the Claimant's experts should have been sent the reports of the Defendant's experts as they came in, with a request for comments. Where, after joint expert discussion, there is clear disagreement between the reports of the two sides, and oral expert evidence is to be given, the Claimant's experts should be asked whether they are still confident that they can support their written evidence by oral evidence and asked to comment on the strength of their opponent's views.

Where little remains in dispute perhaps after an expert's meeting or by reason of exchanges of comments on each other's reports, it may be wise to agree reports rather than run up the costs of trial attendance. If so, the scope of the agreement must be made explicit in correspondence. Nowadays courts will be prepared to resolve outstanding disputes between experts on paper alone without requiring attendance so long as these points are minor and are capable of resolution on paper (ie there is sufficient material to make a decision on the conflict). No agreement should be made however without the client's consent.

If an expert fails to comply with the provisions of the CPR (CPR, PD 35, para 1.2) the court may debar him or her from giving evidence and this discretion cannot be overridden by the parties.[1]

Photographs, plans, videos and films

Sets of any photographs, formal plans, videos and films to be used for illustrative purposes should be sent to the Defendant's solicitors earlier rather than later, to be agreed. They are usually uncontentious. If for some reason these things are not agreed, the maker will have to be called to prove them.

Sufficient sets of the photographs, plans and videos should be made to be placed in the trial bundle. This means a set for the judge, witness and the advocate of each party plus at least one spare set. If the photographs or plans are too large they should be annexed by index to the bundle. In putting together a set of photographs, if they

---

[1] *Stevens v Gullis* (1999) Times, 6 October, CA; Lawtel doc no C840050.

are loose, it is advisable to mount them on cards, have the cards numbered and then bind them in order to ensure that they are easy to handle. Photocopies of photos are usually useless. Laser copies should be made, in colour if the originals were in colour.

If video evidence is to be given live by link a check must be made to ensure that an equipped court is provided (as some few are). If recorded video evidence is to be given, the party who wishes to give the video evidence must inform the court at the time of filing the listing questionnaire, and most likely will have to hire and provide the equipment (as many courts still do not have available a CD/DVD player and associated equipment).

Witness summonses

There are occasions when it is necessary to summons a witness to attend the trial (or perhaps attend before the court on an interlocutory hearing). Some witnesses are willing, but need a formal authority to attend, for example, police officers always need to be summonsed. Some expert witnesses need to be summonsed to ensure that this particular trial (if there is a double booking) gets precedence. In the past, the decision to obtain a witness summons for an expert witness has been a matter of style. Since nowadays putting off the trial is an order of last resort and may be subject to the solicitor paying personal costs, it should be the rule to summons all experts to trial.

Lay witnesses should always be served with a witness summons. When taking a statement from them it should generally be explained that they will need to attend court, that it is the solicitor's practice to issue a summons and that they should not fear its delivery.

The witness summons will require the witness either to attend court to give evidence, or to produce documents that are under their control to the court, or to do both. This is dealt with by Part 34 and the associated Depositions and Court Attendance by Witnesses practice direction. A single witness summons form must be completed – form N20. A separate summons must be issued for each witness it is intended to summons. Two copies must be filed with the court for sealing; the court will retain one on the court file; the other is the service copy (31 PD, para 1.2). The solicitor must ensure that a copy of the sealed summons is kept for her file. If there is a mistake in the name or address of the person named in a witness summons it can be corrected before service, but it must be resealed by the court and marked 'amended and resealed' (31 PD, paras 1.3 and 1.4).

There is a provision for the witness to apply to the court to have the summons set aside. An expert already summonsed to another court may make and succeed in an application to have the summons set aside.

When issuing the summons, the solicitor is given the choice of serving it herself or having the court serve the document (rule 34.5). If there is any chance that the witness will prove difficult to serve, it should be served by the solicitor through a process server. If it is to be served by the court or by post, then the solicitor should write to the witness asking whether they are happy to accept this type of service first. Over the years solicitors tend to develop a good relationship with one or two particular process servers who are usually private detectives who specialise in finding and serving witnesses. A good process server is essential for a busy litigator. The reverse side of the witness summons contains a certificate of service to be completed by the court after service, if the court serves.

Sufficient money must be paid or offered to the witness to attend court (CPR, r 34.7, 34 PD, para 3). The solicitor must investigate carefully the costs of this as the witness has the right to be offered or paid sufficient money to travel and loss of time, ie travel from home or work to court and back, plus loss of benefit or earnings involved in the time required for travel and attendance at court – this latter is based on Crown Court rates (34 PD, para 3.3). These are not quite the generous amounts that witnesses may think; the rates are fixed pursuant to the Prosecution of Offences Act 1985 and the Costs in Criminal Cases (General) Regulations 1986. This means that if it is intended to call a witness whose loss of earnings is likely to be extensive, then the amount paid will almost certainly be inadequate and either allowed at the end in costs from the Defendant assuming the case is won, or it will have to be met by the Claimant.

Practically, this requirement to offer money to cover loss of earnings can pose difficulties; some lay witnesses will state that they are going to lose money by way of earnings without being in a position to quantify their loss formally.

The summons must generally be issued and served at least seven days prior to the start of the trial (CPR, r 34.5(1)) – it can be issued nearer the trial, but only with the court's permission (rule 34.5(2)). It must be issued in the court where the case is proceeding (rule 34.3(3)). The summons is binding until the end of the trial.

The trial bundle

Rule 39.5 deals with the trial bundle if directions have not been given on the same. It is the sole responsibility of the solicitor for the Claimant to produce the trial bundle not more than seven and not less than three days before the start of the trial (CPR, r 39.5(2)). What is contained in it is dependant, of course, on both the evidence to be produced and what has been allowed in the directions. For this reason, prior to preparing the bundle, the solicitor should take the time to re-read the directions order carefully to ensure that she neither misses anything and to ensure that she has the authority to adduce the evidence she wishes to bring in.

The solicitor should be careful, when drawing up the index, to include not only her evidence, but that of the Defendant too. The bundle will certainly contain the claim form, particulars of claim and defence, any requests for further and better particulars, and all interlocutory orders that do not deal with interim payments. All witness statements and notices of intention to rely on evidence must be included unless the evidence is contained in a witness statement or expert report and becomes admissible in that way. All of the expert evidence must be included, together with the joint expert statements. Any written responses to medical evidence, or results of expert meetings (again where admissible) must be included. Other necessary evidence, such as police reports, HSE reports, medical records where relevant, must also be included. Although there is no obligation under the rules, the Defendant(s) should be invited to agree the index. Failure to do so and time wasted by consequential late amendments to the bundle look bad and, in extreme cases, may result in a wasted costs order.

Presentation of the bundle is to some extent a matter of style; however, it must be laid out in a logical order (not necessarily strictly chronologically), paginated and indexed with a description of each document and the page number where it can be found. It is usual to present pleadings in an early section, followed by witness statements, expert evidence and then supporting documentation. If the bundle consists of more than 100 pages, then numbered dividers must be inserted, at appropriate places between groups of documents. Where dividers within a file are used, it is simplest to paginate each division separately.

The bundles should normally be contained in a lever arch or ring binder file. If there is a lot of documentation, then it should be presented in several files; and these should be colour coded for simplicity. Witnesses giving evidence in court often find themselves under great stress and it is attractive to guide them to evidence found in, say, 'the red file'.

Where files are numbered, each file should be given a separate number or letter rather than having, say, sub files of the same number, for example, 5A, 5B and 5C. A separate number for each file makes note taking and document finding significantly easier.

Ease of handling is important as is presentation. The judge's bundle should be in perfect order because some judges are quite finicky and are easily upset by papers that are out of order or badly copied.

A core bundle of essential documents is mandatory in the Court of Appeal. In a large case with substantial documentation, this may be a helpful tool as well. The core bundle should contain the key documents, and only the key documents, which will be in constant use in the trial. It should be agreed with the other side.

A typed fair copy must be made of any key documents that are illegible. The transcript will be inserted behind the transcribed document in the bundle. Proportionality is the key as to whether a document is important enough to warrant transcription. So in medical records it is normal to transcribe only the critical entries unless the records are very short. The job of transcription is sometimes voluntarily undertaken by an energetic consultant expert. If GP notes are in issue, the GP can be asked to transcribe his/her own notes. There are experts who will transcribe hospital records, if necessary. It may be sufficient for both sides' solicitors to attempt an agreed transcription by one or other of them.

Unless there is any direction to the contrary, the Claimant must file the trial bundle not more than seven days and no less than three days before the start of the trial (rule 39.5(2)). Sufficient copies of the bundle must be made. It is normal to ask the Defendant to confirm, in good time, how many copies they want and to ask them to pay for the copying costs and, where expensive binders and suchlike are used, to pay for those also. A copy must be prepared for the judge, and a copy to place in the witness box for use of the witnesses. A copy must be prepared for counsel (leader and junior if both are used) and for the solicitor to use herself in court. It is often useful, in a claim of size where expert witnesses are sitting in court, to prepare a copy for them so that they can follow the proceedings especially if they are attending to comment on the defence witness evidence. In most cases at least five bundles will be needed and the solicitor must ensure that sufficient time is allowed to get this work done. Nothing is more trying then preparing bundles under pressure!

The solicitor must ensure that the originals of the documents in the trial bundle are available at trial. If there is any question on legibility or suchlike then the court will have the opportunity to scrutinise the original document. Sometimes this is impossible. So for example, there is often a difficulty in getting a hospital to release original notes. Nonetheless all efforts should be made to ensure originals are available. This means that when originals are received by the solicitor they should be copied and the original stored in a separate part of the file and only the copy used. Certainly originals should never be sent to counsel who hate them since they cannot mark them up.

Pre-trial negotiations

The weeks leading up to the trial are often the time when the most serious negotiations (see Chapter 13 on Negotiations) take place. The Claimant's solicitor must be in full command of every aspect of the case during this period, the Defendant will be seriously considering the case and will often combine negotiations with a realistic Part 36 payment into court at least 21 days before the hearing. The judge may stimulate negotiations with a pre-trial review in multi party cases.

The Claimant's solicitor will be assisted by close liaison with counsel during these negotiations in the run-up to the trial. It is necessary to be aware of, on the one hand, the natural instinct to welcome settlement rather than face the hard work and tension of going to trial, and, on the other, the countervailing desire to be seen as a tough negotiator, bluffing it out to the last to get the highest possible award and delighted with the opportunity to perform in the court room. Awareness of these competing instincts is all the more important in a conditional fee arrangement where settlement will secure the solicitor's fees, but fighting the case in court risks them. The solicitor must remain alive to the requirements of any after the event insurers who are underwriting the CFA agreement; any offers unaccepted – and possibility the increased costs/risk of running to trial – will need to be reported to them. If not, the solicitor runs the risk of the insurers voiding the policy for non-compliance.

If settlement is reached the solicitor must ensure that the court is notified at once and the appropriate consent order drawn up. If the matter relates to an infant or Claimant under an incapacity, then the solicitor should notify the court since approval by the court may be considerably shorter than the time allocated for the trial, and if the trial is some time away, it may be possible to get a nearer date for an approval hearing.

Trial brief

It is usual in personal injury cases for the solicitor to instruct a barrister. This is, of course, not mandatory and approved solicitors may now conduct litigation.[2]

---

[2]   Courts and Legal Services Act 1990, ss 27–33.

Briefing counsel has two advantages. The first is that the costs of a solicitor's time preparing for and conducting the trial advocacy may be much greater than for a barrister. The second is that there are a significant number of highly experienced personal injury barristers whose skilled advocacy and up-to-date knowledge are of the greatest value to the client.

It is obviously desirable (unless adding the skills of a QC) to instruct at trial the same barrister as has been involved earlier perhaps having advised or drafted statements. This is not essential, nor is it always possible because counsel may have other commitments. The problem is, however, unavoidable, especially with the best barristers who are in much demand. The solicitor will naturally remove from her list any barrister who is not giving her cases the priority she believes they should have. It makes it important to form a close working relationship with the barristers on the list and points to the deniability of selecting a few from the list from the same chambers to make it easier should it be necessary to swap at the last minute. The role of counsel's clerk is also vital and there should be no tolerance of anything other than total frankness about counsels' availability and efficiency in keeping the solicitor informed.

The problem of availability is exacerbated by conditional fee arrangements. The courts are reasonably sympathetic to ensuring continuity of counsel at trial especially when they are advising by way of a CFA.

However, if the counsel who has advised throughout on a CFA is available at trial, the advantage of an established relationship with a set of chambers will come into its own. In any event, the CFA between counsel and the solicitor should deal with what happens when this occurs. Unless the new barrister offered the brief trusts the judgment of the unavailable barrister, there will have to be a hiatus whilst the new barrister conducts his or her own risk assessment and decides whether or not to accept the case.

Leading counsel are usually instructed in catastrophic injuries cases where the potential value of the claim is very substantial, where some new questions of law may be in issue, where there are a large number of Claimants, where the facts are complex, or where the case is in the public eye. When leading counsel is instructed, it is usual to retain the junior who conducted the pleadings and advised during the litigation leading up to trial. It is not essential for leading counsel to be accompanied by junior counsel and consideration should always be given to instructing leading counsel alone to reduce costs and, in particular, the risk of not recovering them. In complex cases and cases involving many plaintiffs, two (or more) counsel may well be justified by the workload. In delicate cases, retention of the junior may also be desirable. Leading counsel are usually (but not necessarily) brought in only at the trial stage and the problem of double booking is hence much less likely (silks also have far fewer cases).

The trial brief is of great importance. Sufficient time should be allocated to ensuring that its contents are both comprehensive and correct. The authors have assumed that it is counsel who presents the case at court. Where it is to be another member of the same firm of solicitors, the same exercise of constructing a trial brief should ensue. If the person handling the case is to present it, the process of preparing the brief obviously need not be carried out, but in note form or, at the very least, mentally, the same considerations should be undertaken, step by step.

The object of the brief is to provide counsel presenting the case for the Claimant with a complete but concise picture of the case. The following points, dealt with more fully below, should be covered in the instructions: identification of the party for whom the barrister is instructed; a summary of the accident and its causes; a précis of the evidence which will be available at court; the solicitor's insights into the case – its strengths and weaknesses; the likely attendance and performance of witnesses; those calculations in the schedule of damages that need emphasis (ie not the obvious ones); the arguments on damages which the solicitor feels counsel should be particularly aware of; the course and 'feel' of negotiations to date; and the solicitor's valuation of each element and the totality of the case.

Subheadings in the instructions may be useful.

The accident

A brief outline should be given as to how the accident occurred, what the principal issues will be and where the dispute(s) on liability lie.

The evidence

The evidence on each issue should be described, setting out what witnesses, documents, photographs, plans and videos are relevant and will be available at court. Counsel should be told of the strengths and weaknesses of each aspect of the evidence. The solicitor's views should be set out on liability and contributory negligence, damages, strong or weak points and any particular arguments or aspects that counsel should especially have in mind.

The brief should list all the documents included with it. These will be all those which the solicitor considers are relevant and which counsel needs to be aware of. This will be more than the court bundle. On the one hand, counsel should not be burdened with every discoverable document on both sides; on the other, there may be documents outside the court bundle which shed light on certain points to be stressed or avoided in the course of the trial. In the end, it is probably better to err on the side of providing too much, rather than too little. The primary documents to enclose begins with the trial bundle. If, for some reason, there is no trial bundle, or it has not yet been formulated then the essentials are the documents which make up the pleadings, a copy of all applications and orders, a copy of the allocation questionnaire and case management directions, and a copy of the listing questionnaire and any further directions given for the matter pre-trial. The listing questionnaire should be supplemented with details of any agreements that have been reached between the parties on evidence or any restrictions that the court has imposed in relation to evidence. In a very large or complex claim, it is likely that counsel will have already been involved prior to return of the listing questionnaire, probably by way of advising in writing or conference. Counsel should be reminded of this and, if the advice was in conference, the solicitor's notes should be included (typed up) or, at the least, the conference should be summarised in the instructions. Inclusion of counsel's earlier advices is essential whether or not the same counsel is instructed at the trial. If a case summary and chronology has been prepared and served, a copy of this should be included. If the trial bundle has been prepared or finalised, the index for this should also be included. Both parties' lists of documents must be included and, very importantly, all party and party correspondence (it is surprising how few solicitors pass onto counsel a copy of this vital insight into relations with the other side). All counsel's advices must be included, as must notices of any Part 36 payments or other offers.

Counsel must be instructed formally of the basis on which the case is being funded; although specific funding arrangements between the barrister and the solicitor and client have been discussed and finalised prior to preparation of the brief. If the court have ordered that counsel prepare a skeleton argument prior to trial, then counsel must be given notice of this together with the deadline date which should be diarised by the solicitor.

The brief should be written on the basis that counsel has no acquaintance with the case, regardless of whether the barrister has dealt with it before. This is to guard against the possibility of counsel unexpectedly becoming unavailable at trial, perhaps because a case has unexpectedly gone part heard.

The instructions start by stating for which party counsel is acting. Though unnecessary for counsel who has been on the case from the start, it ensures that a barrister who takes over the case at the last minute does not start off on the wrong foot. In all but the smallest cases, counsel's papers are best put into a ring binder file, indexed and with numbered dividers to assist in handling the information. This may accompany the trial bundle (if there is one at the time the brief is prepared).

The injuries

A description should be given of the injuries, including a very brief outline of the current position and the prognosis. Counsel should be told of any joint expert evidence and an explanation given of which experts each side is using, the position regarding any agreements on evidence, the areas of difference between the parties, their weaknesses and strengths and any special points counsel should bear in mind. If there are any difficulties regarding the timing of the appearance of any witness, counsel should be told. If there has been an expert meeting, the agreed note of the meeting should be included.

Financial loss

Unless the figures are obvious, the method of calculation should be explained. Where agreement has been reached on any of the figures, that should be stated. It is important to indicate where the financial loss claim is strong and where it is weak. Any aspects of the claim that are not obvious should be fully explained. Details should be given on how each piece of evidence that is not agreed is to be proved.

Future loss

Where there is a claim for future loss, counsel should be taken through the proposed figures with suggested multipliers and the reasons for each proposed by the solicitor.

Generals

The valuation of each head of the claim and of the case as a whole should be given. This is important and gives counsel an additional perspective on the case. If counsel disagrees, the solicitor will soon be told.

The law

If there are any points of law in the case or case-law beyond the usual, the solicitor should not hesitate to put them in the brief. Two heads are better than one.

Negotiations

Counsel should be told of any negotiations, and any Part 36 offers or payments in made by either side. Unless new evidence has arisen, these may set a bottom line for counsels' negotiations if any take place. A description should be given of the style of negotiation the solicitor has adopted in this case, the 'feel' of the other side, and the client's position regarding settlement.

Other matters

Counsel should be told of all relevant orders and applications made, and in particular any directions as to the conduct of trial (such as allocation of certain hours or certain days to specific issues, or limitation of the trial to so many days). He or she should be told of any orders to be sought at trial and any issues on costs. Counsel should be warned of any points to bear in mind for the conference with the client before the hearing.

Delivery of the brief

When the brief is delivered it is dependant upon the size of the claim and the work that counsel may have to do prior to the matter actually being heard. So if counsel is needed to be involved in deciding what should be included in the bundles, or in the preparation of skeleton arguments, then counsel should be briefed in good time prior to the deadline for those tasks. In any event, in a case of complexity and value, as a generality counsel ought to receive their brief within 14–21 days before trial.

Delivery of the brief means liability to pay the brief fee. Some solicitors hold the brief back as a tool to pressure the other side in negotiations since delivery of the brief will increase the costs. This tactic is unfair to counsel who will have held open the window of time for the trial period. It should not be used therefore later than a week before trial. Counsel who form the view that a particular solicitor delivers the brief at the last possible moment will not give that solicitor the priority which she may well need in another case. Conditional fee arrangements may well (and ought to) specify the time scale within which the brief must be delivered.

PRE-TRIAL CONFERENCE

A pre-trial conference with the client is of the greatest value and should be arranged in every case which is likely to be fought. It is generally neither advisable nor desirable to leave the pre-trial conference to the morning of the trial. Last minute problems or negotiations often arise on the morning of trial or a train may be late. The client should know his barrister in advance and have a feeling of reassurance on meeting him again. There may be occasions where the barrister will want to see a key expert again on the trial morning.

The pre-trial conference should usually be between one and two weeks before the trial; its timing is dictated by the size of the claim, work to be done in relation to agreeing evidence and negotiations between solicitors, payments into court, availability of counsel, solicitor and client, and a multitude of other factors. In general terms, the earlier the conference is, the better. The more complex the case is, the more time may be required to carry out work identified by the conference. In catastrophic cases, fatal accident cases and other highly complex cases, the pre-trial conference is the last in a series of conferences throughout the litigation. In a more straightforward case, it may be the only opportunity the client has to meet counsel before the trial. Such meetings are essential for clients to have confidence in their legal representatives and to feel more comfortable about the daunting ordeal of the trial.

A note should be made of the conference (of course) and, if there is time, a typed copy of it should be supplied to counsel and client. If the client has an unrealistic expectation, then seeing the advice in writing will often help him to take on board counsel's assessment of the case.

One of the tasks of the pre-trial conference is to inform the client what he will experience in court. Claimants should be reminded that the action is a civil case, which is conducted in what may appear to be a surprisingly informal, if not friendly, manner. Defendants are not treated as if they were arraigned in a criminal court. Clients must be told that, though the questions will be put by counsel, the answers must be addressed to the judge. Answers should be kept short and clients are entitled to take their time and need not fear saying 'I don't know' or 'I cannot remember' where that is the case. Under cross-examination, clients must not argue with counsel, but, on the other hand, they should not accept hidden assumptions or words defined in a way not used or understood by them. At all times clients must keep calm.

Experience has shown that certain stereotypes of Claimant appeal to judges, whereas others do not find favour. Undoubtedly, judges' subconscious reactions to the characteristics of Claimant's influence their view of liability and quantum. The straightforward, deferential, honest working man and the demure, long-suffering and uncomplaining widow are particular examples to which much judicial sympathy is given. Without necessarily discussing these matters in conference, it is useful to consider how such qualities may be projected. The respectful demeanour, the suit and tie, the use of dark-coloured clothing, the wearing of service uniform (and not just the armed services, but police, fire fighters, ambulance staff and so on) should be considered. Periods in the services, work for the community, for the old, the sick, the young and so on and high level sporting achievements, are all particularly useful to emphasise and should have been included in the witness statement.

The converse of this presentational problem should also be considered and explained to the client. The use of enquiry agents and secret filming is frequent and a Claimant who claims that the consequences of an indisputable back injury are that he cannot climb ladders may well fail on liability, or receive minimal damages if the Defendant shows a video of the Claimant competently painting the upper storey of his house from an extending ladder. The Defendant may seek to diminish the standing of the Claimant in other ways as well. A bad sickness or attendance record, previous accidents, disciplinary warnings and the like will not only be relevant to arguments that a Claimant had pre-existing disabilities, or that his earnings would have been diminished in the future for reasons other than disability due to the accident, or that his job tenure was insecure, or that there are reasons other than disability which will make him/her unattractive to future employers; such matters will be used, perhaps implicitly, to present the Claimant as a character to whom sympathy should not be extended.

In work accidents, consideration should be given to any trade union activities of the Claimant and of any potential witnesses. The object for the Claimant's representatives is to portray the respectable and responsible face of trade unionism, whereas the Defendant will be out to show politically motivated, unreliable trouble makers.

It is tempting, especially for barristers, to assume that the Claimant is familiar with his witness statement(s) and will give testimony in accordance with it. When advising the client of the date of the conference, the solicitor should enclose a copy of the witness statement as served and ask the client to re-read the same prior to the conference date.

At the pre-trial conference, therefore, the Claimant should be taken through the statement and any discrepancies should be explored. By now, the defence, the Defendant's witness statements, the expert evidence, the Defendant's documents and the medical evidence and records will all be available and the lines of cross-examination by the Defendant will be apparent. These should be put to the Claimant.

Despite tight timetables, the witness statement may need to be updated up to the last moment in relation to the client's latest attempts to find work, continuing pain and disability, and so on.

The solicitor handling the case should be reminded by counsel to ensure that the Claimant's witnesses have refreshed their memory by reading or having read to them their witness statements and that their comments are noted. In most cases it is sufficient to do this on the morning of the trial.

For the pre-trial conference, it is essential to check whether all the witnesses required are ready and available and have been notified and that any requiring subpoenas/witness summonses have been served. Even at this late stage, consideration should again be given to any further witness (though there will be significant problems in getting the evidence admitted). The availability and order of calling witnesses should be determined.

The reports of engineers or other experts will have been exchanged and if experts have met, they will probably have done so by now. The reports should have been received and supplied to the Claimant's experts and, in turn, their comments should be to hand. Final decisions must be taken on whether each of the Claimant's experts should be called to give evidence in accordance with their reports (assuming that reports are not joint reports, or have not been agreed).

Any conferences with experts for the Claimant, either separately or with others, so as to elucidate any difficult points, explore any apparent inconsistencies, or to provide the advocate with the fullest understanding of difficult matters should have taken place before the pre-trial conference with the client. Nonetheless the need for a further conference with an expert(s) can be reviewed again.

Attention should be given at the pre-trial conference to documents. The earliest review of evidence (see Chapter 21 on Review of Evidence) will have considered documents, but this is a last chance to ensure that matters are in order. Have all the documents requiring agreement been agreed? It is important to check the nature of any agreement: this could be that the document is what it purports to be, that it is a document made by the purported author, that it is evidence of the truth of the content of it, or that the content of it is true. If the court bundle has not been prepared, its contents should be discussed. If the bundle is ready, it should be checked. Notices (and counter-notices) to admit facts, documents and notices under the Civil Evidence Act from both sides should be reviewed.

The evidence on quantum must be considered. Medical evidence will have been exchanged and comments obtained from the Claimant's medical advisers. Sometimes, although less likely under the new rules where last minute evidence is positively discouraged, there is a flurry of last-minute medical examinations and further experts' comments. It will be necessary to ensure that the directions for exchanging medical evidence have been complied with. Further evidence may necessitate a last minute application for an order to admit it. If so the Defendant must be notified and asked to agree as soon as possible.

As at the review of evidence, merits and quantum (see Chapter 21) a further check should be made to ensure that the medical evidence ties in with evidence from therapists, nurses, architects and those giving evidence of the costs of care, treatment or other services. It is important that the losses being claimed as damages for care, therapy, services and alteration or changes to housing have a solid foundation in the medical evidence about those needs. The necessity of this linkage cannot be overstressed.

Quantum must be re-evaluated. Every element of the calculation of damages must be reconsidered and explained to the Claimant. The arguments for and against each element in the latest schedule of damages and the counter-schedule, and any arguments which may appear in correspondence should be clearly explained. The best estimate of the band of likely damages in respect of each and every element should be given to the Claimant. Some bands will clearly be wider than others. The likely award in each band (which is not necessarily the median figure) should be given. The principle of contributory negligence, if it is alleged, should be explained to the Claimant and the arguments considered. The likely bracket of percentage reduction for contributory negligence, together with an estimate of the likelihood of such reduction, should be given.

Having explained the way in which judges approach personal injury cases and their differing personalities, a total valuation of the case can be given. It is easiest to express this as a bracket between upper and lower likely figures. It is then necessary both to consider the chances of winning or losing completely and to discuss the general risks of litigation.

Only at this stage can possible settlement figures be considered. Any offers which have been received or any payments in and the principles of the latter should be explained in detail. It may be that consideration of an offer or payment in is the principal purpose of the conference. The Claimant will expect clear advice and almost certainly the CFA agreement will set out if, on rejecting or accepting this advice, what happens in the event of the payment in not being beaten. This must be given, and backed up in letter form to ensure that there is no ambiguity in what has actually been recommended.

In the light of all the information currently available, the advice on an offer or payment in will almost invariably be one of the following:
(i)   that the offer is too low, should be rejected and the case passed to trial;
(ii) that although low, it would not be foolish to accept the offer, but a further attempt should be made to seek more, but if no increase is forthcoming, it would be reasonable to go to trial;
(iii) that the offer is a reasonable one, though it would neither be foolish to press for more, nor to reject it and go to trial;
(iv) that the offer is a very reasonable one and should be accepted: it would be foolish to reject it (though, invariably, it may be worth seeking more, but if no increase is forthcoming, the offer should be accepted).

It is, of course, incumbent on the lawyers to give the most objective advice possible and to set aside their financial interests in the outcome. Indeed, advising acceptance of too low a settlement will be professional misconduct and amount to negligence. Where there is a CFA, it is necessary to remind the client of the lawyers' financial interest in settlement in order that the former can properly assess the advice he is getting. If the client is unwilling to accept the advice given in respect of settlement figures, and insists on holding out for a higher sum, then it may well be appropriate to advise obtaining an independent opinion from another counsel on a straight fee basis.

If the Claimant wishes to reject the offer, it is essential to emphasise the risks of losing or of achieving less than the offer. In every case, it is vital to give a realistic assessment of the prospects. Bearing in mind that many Claimants would prefer their lawyers to make the decision for them, it must be stressed that acceptance is the Claimant's personal decision.

Because the rejection of an offer by the client may well have an adverse effect on a conditional fee arrangement, the full consequences of this must be explained in detail – and reported to the after the event insurers (and, of course, confirmed subsequently in writing to both client and insurers).

The advice must be neither over-optimistic or the converse; it must be realistic. Many lawyers formulate a 'bottom line', ie the level below which the Claimant will definitely not be advised to settle. The authors believe that such an approach should not be applied too dogmatically, since new factors emerge continuously as the trial approaches. The personality of the judge is often not known until the night before, and may change on the morning of the trial if the judge allocated is part heard or has emergency business which causes the case to be transferred elsewhere. Witnesses may fail to materialise or may bring powerful new evidence. New documents may appear and be admitted. Arguments advanced by the other side may suddenly be found to be far more telling than was originally assessed.

Negotiations with insurance companies have been dealt with in Chapter 13, and skilled personal injury lawyers will know the characteristics of the leading insurance companies and often of the individuals within them, with whom they frequently deal. Likewise, the approach of Defendants' solicitors and counsel is likely to be familiar. Generally speaking, the closer the case gets to trial the more likely the insurance company is to be guided by the advice of its counsel. A settlement before the delivery of the brief to the Defendant's counsel may be an attractive saving. As a consequence of the pre-trial conference it may be useful to approach the other side for further negotiations. This may be done through solicitors or through counsel, depending on which tactic is thought to be the more likely to be most productive (see Chapter 13 on Negotiations).

IMMEDIATELY PRIOR TO TRIAL

The solicitor must ensure that all the witnesses are at court. Where the trial is to be listed at short notice, a great deal of urgent telephoning has to be done.

For the advocate, the obvious preparations need to be made. The facts and the documents must be mastered. Skeleton arguments are increasingly required and, though not usually appropriate in a straightforward personal injury case, should be considered even if not ordered. It may instead, be thought helpful to prepare a brief 'note of opening' or similar aide memoire for the judge. This may be particularly useful in fast track cases where the judge may well dispense with an opening statement, but will not refuse to accept a written note. Consideration must be given to how the documents are to be introduced and, if by witnesses, their witness statements should be annotated by the advocate at the relevant point as reminders in the course of examination-in-chief. Authorities (ie reports of the cases to be referred to) on any points of law should be sorted out and a list (and usually, new photocopies of the cases) provided to the court and the other side's counsel. Authorities on quantum derived from *Kemp and Kemp*, vol 2 (which includes the Judicial Studies Board's *Guidelines for Damages in Personal Injury Claims*) need not be notified until the morning of trial, since in a personal injury case it may be assumed that the other side and the judge will have these volumes with them. Any authorities on quantum which are not in *Kemp and Kemp* should be notified and photocopies taken to court – such as *Halsbury's Monthly Update*, *Personal Injuries Quantum Reports*, *Current Law* or *Personal and Medical Injuries Law Letter*. The schedule of damages and counter schedule must be understood and all possible permutations of the calculations considered. The weak and strong points in the damages claim should be noted and the interest calculations performed.

The advocate must also get on top of the arguments and calculations in relation to costs in case of a summary assessment of costs.

Leading counsel often try to settle a case over the telephone the day before trial. This is less frequent among juniors. An approach to the other side over the telephone needs careful thought, since an indication of weakness may diminish any likely offer. A pretext may be useful.

CHAPTER 23

The Trial

If a case actually makes it to trial, the conduct of the hearing will vary depending upon whether it is in the small claims, fast track or multi track. Pursuant to the overriding objectives the level of formality increases depending upon the level of track.[1] Representation is different from a litigant in person having a lay adviser (known as a McKenzie friend), which they are entitled to, as of right, for hearings in open court but only as a matter of discretion for hearings in chambers.[2]

THE CONDUCT OF A HEARING IN A SMALL CLAIMS TRACK CASE

The court can adopt any method of proceeding at a hearing that it considers to be fair. Hearings will be informal and therefore it is unlikely that advocates will have to be robed. The strict rules of evidence do not apply. The court need not take evidence on oath. Cross-examination can be limited. The court must give reasons for its decision but provided the central reasons for the decision are noted they can be as brief and simple as the nature of the case allows.[3]

THE CONDUCT OF A HEARING IN A FAST TRACK AND MULTI TRACK CASE

Between the rules and accompanying practice directions in the procedure for fast track and multi track hearings, there is very little formal difference.

The fast track

Generally speaking the fast track hearing will inevitably be more intense. The court will have given previous directions pursuant to the listing questionnaire which will

---

[1] Lay representation will not normally be permitted in the county court: see *Milne v Kennedy* (1999) Times, 11 February.
[2] *R v Bow County Court, ex p Pelling* [1999] 1 WLR 1807.
[3] Rule 27.8 and PD, paras 5.4 and 5.5.

give a timetable for the hearing. This need not be adhered to, but it is a guide. The judge will probably have read the papers before the hearing and will be anxious to get on with the case and is unlikely, due to the time constraints to allow the parties further time for negotiations. As the issues are likely to be less complicated than in multi track cases it is more likely that the judge will dispense with an opening address. At the end of the case the court will normally summarily assess the costs of the claim. This in itself can take a considerable amount of time. Where a trial is not finished on a day for which it was listed the judge will normally sit on the next day to complete it.[4] See generally multi track (below).

The multi track

The main technical difference between the practice directions for the conduct of a multi track and fast track trial is the recognition that a multi track trial will normally require the court to sit on consecutive court days and more often than not, both sides will call their own expert evidence if the experts have been unable to reach agreement.[5]

Whether the trial takes place in the county court or the High Court, it is the solicitor's job to organise the witnesses outside court, make sure the Claimant feels as relaxed as possible and deal with any outstanding matters with the solicitor on the other side. Mathematical calculations relating to the various heads of damages (subject to liability) are often agreed with the other side's solicitors even at this late stage. It is outside court on the first day of the trial that offers or further offers of settlement are frequently made in multi track cases, less often in fast track cases. For these reasons, it is almost invariably essential that the solicitor running a multi track case attends on the first day. Thereafter, it may be possible to leave the case in the hands of a capable assistant whilst remaining available at the end of a phone. Whoever represents the firm will, nowadays, always have a mobile phone at court and advocates too are wise to carry one (though telephones, of course, should be switched off whilst in the courtroom!).

PRE-TRIAL PREPARATION

Consideration should be given to providing the court with as much assistance as possible. There will have been a direction for lodging bundles and skeleton arguments and it may be helpful in a complex case to provide at least a summary of the case, identifying core documents or parts of documents, lists of issues (agreed if possible), glossary of terms, *dramatis personae* and, if there are numerous bundles, core bundles.[6]

Outside the court

The advocate's role at this stage is also, first and foremost, to put the Claimant at ease. If expert or lay witnesses have been called for the first morning, then they will

---

[4]   PD2 Part 28, para 8.
[5]   PD, Part 29, para 10.
[6]   PD (Miscellaneous Provisions Relating to Hearings) CPR 29 and *St Alban's Court Ltd v Daldorch Estates Ltd* (1999) Times, 24 May.

need to be greeted, and a brief explanation of the process given to them. It is then wise to speak to the Defendant's advocate. There is always something to discuss, photographs or documents to be agreed, mathematical computations to be resolved, medical witnesses to be interposed in the normal course of evidence in order to release them as soon as is convenient, and so on. Contact of this kind makes it easier for the Defendant's advocate to make a further offer to settle. Except in rare cases, no weakness is necessarily implied in asking the Defendant's advocate if s/he intends to make an offer. It should, however, be a golden rule that the Claimant's advocate never makes the first offer to the other side (see Chapter 13 on Negotiations).

Any offer from the Defendant's advocate must be taken back and discussed fully with the client. Advice must be given. The client must not be put under pressure and as much time as is necessary should be taken.

In multi track cases, the judge's clerk should be kept informed of the course of negotiations and the judge should be asked for more time before it is needed. Judges often get irritated if they are not kept informed of the needs of the parties for time for negotiation and discussion. The judge must not be told anything about the nature of the negotiations that are taking place, only that time is needed for discussion and the estimate of the amount of time. If more time is required it should be asked for. It is invariably granted.

However presented, the first offer is often an opening bid. Occasionally, it really is the final offer. In spite of the inducements to negotiate inherent in the CPR, first offers will still be made by Defendants at the door of the court. Any offer will be accompanied, invariably by an oral explanation from the Defendant's advocate of how s/he sees the case and, in particular, the weaknesses of the Claimant's arguments on liability and on quantum. These arguments should be attentively listened to, then related back to the client and weighed carefully. While it is fruitless for advocates to argue out the case between themselves, it may well be worthwhile to point out some of the weaknesses of the Defendant's case and/or the strengths of the Claimant's case. This may lay the groundwork for inducing a higher subsequent offer from the Defendant.

There is little more that can be usefully said about the conduct of negotiations, since these are very much a matter of personality and experience and depend so much on the circumstances of the particular case. It is, however, the authors' view that no offer should be accepted unless the lawyers are certain that this is the highest and final offer from the Defendant.

When an offer has been made and considered by the Claimant and it is decided to reject it, the advocate should go back to the Defendant's advocate and explain the reason for rejection and the basis on which the case is capable of settlement. In some cases, this may involve putting a figure to the Defendant's advocate. If negotiations appear to be hopeless, further time should not be wasted, the discussions should be discontinued and the case taken into court. Some Defendants' advocates appear to have a personal rule that they will not make their final offer until everybody is in their seat awaiting the entrance of the judge.

During much of the time spent in negotiations at the door of the court, it is useful (with the consent of the other side) to ask the judge to re-read the most relevant documents such as medical reports and other expert reports, indicating which are agreed and which are not.

Barristers can now speak to lay witnesses in exceptional circumstances.[7] They have always been entitled to speak to expert witnesses outside court and should do so to make clear any points which need clarification and to ensure that nothing new has affected the reports provided.

In court

Court dress in the county and High Courts

Queen's Counsel wear a short wig and a silk, or stuff gown over a court coat and bands. Junior Counsel wear a short wig and stuff gown with bands. Solicitors, who are acting as the advocate, wear a black stuff gown with bands, but no wig.[8]

The court

The rules now provide that at the case management conference the court can direct that the case be tried in front of a judge who specialises in that type of claim, although in practice, this is rare.[9] The court can even transfer a case to another court due to availability or non-availability of a judge specialising in the type of claim in question.[10]

Part 29 deals with the conduct of trial succinctly:

'Unless the trial judge otherwise directs, the trial will be conducted in accordance with any order previously made.'[11]

The practice direction as might be expected gives more detail. At the listing hearing there may be directions about the conduct of the trial, for example how time is to be allocated to particular issues, on which any expert in a particular field will be heard, and so on.

The trial judge has total discretion to adopt the timetable previously given or to set an alternative timetable.[12] Once the trial of a multi track claim has begun, the judge will normally sit on consecutive court days until it has been concluded.[13] The court has the power to exclude evidence but this must be exercised in support of dealing justly with the case.[14]

---

7   In civil cases, barristers are now entitled to talk to lay witnesses, provided that the barrister must not (i) put the witness under any pressure to provide other than a truthful account of the evidence; or (ii) rehearse, practice or coach a witness in relation to the evidence or the way in which s/he should give it (Code of Conduct of the Bar of England and Wales, 1 October 1998, para 608).
8   See *Practice Direction (Court Dress)* [1994] 1 WLR 1056.
9   PD, para 9.
10   Rule 30.3(2)(c).
11   Rule 29.9.
12   PD 10.3.
13   PD 10.6.
14   *Grobbelaar v Sun Newspapers Ltd* (1999) Times, 12 August.

The court has jurisdiction to strike out a defence at trial where the Defendant has failed to comply with procedures and directions of the court.[15]

Assessment of damages hearings

Assessment of damages hearings deal with quantum only. Thus matters discussed in this chapter concerning quantum are also relevant to these hearings. A Defendant can raise any point going to quantification of damages, provided it is not inconsistent with any issue either settled by agreement or by judgment on liability.[16]

Opening speeches

If the case is fought the format of the proceedings is relatively standardised.[17] The trial judge will generally have read the papers in the trial bundle and may dispense with an opening address.[18] If there is an opening speech by the Claimant's advocate, it should describe the circumstances leading up to the accident and the accident itself, shortly, clearly and without ambiguity. Any photographs and plans should be introduced and used and every effort made to convey the atmosphere in which the accident took place. For example, in a work accident taking place in a deafening iron foundry, the noise and hurly-burly must be discreetly communicated to the judge, who may not immediately be sensitive to it in the quiet calm of the court room. In the past the pleadings usually had little importance at trial, except as a basis for the Defendant's advocate to cross-examine the Claimant on inconsistencies between his/her account and the pleadings. Since the CPR, there may be significant matters in the defence statement of case because of the cards on the table requirements. The obligation to plead positively may mean that there is as much revealed by what is not in the defence as is evident by way of admission. At the least the issues in the trial will be much clearer from the defence than in the past. The opening statement will always draw out the issues arising from the defence statement of case. Nowadays the judge will expect to be told which issues have been agreed, which have become irrelevant and no longer require decision, and precisely which issues remain outstanding and, in relation to each such, what the competing contentions are.

The pain, suffering and loss of amenity should be described in concise terms and it is often helpful to give a series of numbered headings to the different ways in which the accident has affected and continues to affect the Claimant. The judge will usually have read the medical reports but it is worth drawing his/her attention to particular sentences or passages which are relied upon by the Claimant. The judge should be taken through the schedule and counter schedule of damages, and the areas of agreement and the scope of disagreement under each head should be indicated. It is not usual in the opening speech to indicate submissions on quantum unless there are

---

[15]   *Garner v Stonestreet* (1999) Times, 28 May.
[16]   *Turner v Toleman* (15 January 1999, unreported), but approved by the Court of Appeal in *Lunnun v Singh* [1999] 31 LS Gaz R 36.
[17]   The trial judge may give directions as to which party shall begin, the order of speeches at trial, and, in actions tried without a jury, dispense with opening speeches: RSC Order 35, rule 7(1); CCR Order 21, rule 5A.
[18]   PD 10.2.

particular reasons for this, for example, to get the judge used to the idea that what appears to be a trivial accident is in fact a very expensive one.

The opening speech will conclude by dealing with any 'housekeeping' matters such as procedural disputes which require resolution (for example, over the admission of a document), and the timetable for the trial and the order of witnesses. If there is any danger of the trial overrunning its allocated time the judge may wish to consider limitations of time for examination, cross examination and re-examination of witnesses, or require written rather than oral submissions at the close. Both advocates must be ready to deal with such matters.

The advocate must be aware that any assurances given to the court will bind the client even if given negligently.[19]

Witnesses

The court will have given directions as to the issues upon which it requires evidence, the nature of the evidence required and the way in which the evidence is to be placed before the court.[20] Since the CPR, it has the power to exclude admissible evidence.[21] Before a witness can be called to give evidence, s/he must have provided a witness statement complying with the practice direction[22] which has been served in time,[23] or a witness summary must have been provided complying with rule 32.9 or the court otherwise must give permission.[24]

Subject to any directions as to the order of issues or witnesses or the allocation of time in the trial, the advocate for the Claimant will call the witnesses permitted by the court in the order which is thought to be most effective.[25] Almost invariably, the Claimant gives evidence first, although there may be good reasons for calling witnesses in a different order. An exception would be, for instance, a split trial on liability where primary liability was admitted and the only issue was contributory negligence with the onus on the Defendant to establish such a defence. Often, medical or indeed other experts may be given on a 'back to back' basis, with like experts for each side interposed in the course of other witnesses' evidence in order to release them. The interposition of witnesses should be agreed only if it will not damage the Claimant's case.

A witness statement will stand as the evidence-in-chief[26] of the witness in the box so that the advocate calling the witness need do no more than ask the witness to give his/her name and address and to identify his/her statement(s). The advocate should nonetheless examine the witness on those parts of his/her evidence which advocate

---

[19]   *Worldwide Corpn Ltd v Marconi Communications Ltd* (1999) Times, 7 July.
[20]   Rule 32.1(1).
[21]   Rule 32.1(2).
[22]   Rule 32.8.
[23]   Rule 32.10.
[24]   Rule 32.10.
[25]   For evidence by video link, see p XXX.
[26]   Rule 32.5(2). In certain rare circumstances, the court has the power to direct that a witness statement or part of it is not open to inspection during the trial. Otherwise, the witness statement will stand as the evidence-in-chief of the witness and be open to inspection (rule 32.13).

wishes to bring out. This is partly to get the witness acclimatised to giving evidence and partly to give the judge a chance to assess the witness. It may also be to update some matter in the witness statement, or explain some complexity or possible ambiguity, or to introduce in a more favourable way a particular matter on which the witness will be cross-examined. The court does not have to give permission to 'amplify' the witness statement in this way. It will only do so if there is 'good reason'.[27] Explaining a difficult point and bringing a particular relevant matter up to date will be good reasons, the others may not be! Unless the accident is trivial, the judge will almost certainly be prepared to hear him as to the circumstances of the accident and on his injuries and disabilities in consequence.

An expert's report should be put in evidence at the beginning of the maker's examination-in-chief or as the court otherwise directs.[28]

A report by a joint expert should be the evidence in the case on the issues covered and generally there should be no need for the report to be amplified or tested by way of cross-examination or examination-in-chief.[29] If a witness's statement has been served by a Civil Evidence Act notice and s/he is called to give evidence, the witness still has to give evidence-in-chief before the statement can be admitted, unless the court orders otherwise.[30] It is now possible not to call a witness yet still have his/her evidence admitted as hearsay evidence.[31] If a party does not call a witness whose witness statement has been disclosed and does not put it in as hearsay, any other party may put it in as hearsay.[32]

Cross-examination

The court may limit cross-examination but will tend to do so only if the advocate is straying into areas which the court considers irrelevant for its determination of the issues.[33] Insofar as it does, it will tend either to limit the issues to be explored or the time to be spent with a particular witness. In short, to keep the cross-examination concise and relevant. The cross-examination of the Claimant should be noted carefully. This will expose the main lines of the defence, if they are not already clear. If cross-examination by the Defendant is inconsistent with the Defendant's statement of case, objection should be taken. If amendment to the defence is sought and permitted and takes the Claimant by surprise an adjournment may be granted.[34] It is, of course, not possible to seek the Claimant's instructions while he is giving evidence. However, the solicitor may take instructions from other witnesses about matters raised in the course of cross-examination so that the advocate can consider dealing with such matters in the examination-in-chief of subsequent witnesses, rather than leaving it to the Defendant's cross-examination. With good witnesses, significant

---

[27]   Rule 32.5(3)(a) and (b).
[28]   See RSC Order 39, rule 43.
[29]   *Peet v Mid-Kent Healthcare Trust* [2001] 1 WLR 210.
[30]   Civil Evidence Act 1968, s 2(2)(b); rule 32.2(3).
[31]   Rules 32.5(1) and 33.
[32]   Rule 32.5(5).
[33]   Rule 32.1(3).
[34]   See, for example, *Bagnall v Hartlepool Borough Council* [1995] PIQR P1.

issues in the case are often more effectively left to cross-examination, rather than examination-in-chief.

As the case continues, consideration should continually be given to not calling available witnesses. If evidence given by the Claimant is unchallenged or his answers on some matters clearly convinced the judge in an unshakeable way, then to call further evidence on that particular point may only risk undoing what has been established.

Re-examination should be as short as possible and in many cases can be avoided altogether. Most judges regard re-examination as an unnecessary irritation.

When all the Claimant's witnesses have been called, the advocate should check to ensure that all documents relied on have been introduced in evidence by witnesses or else are agreed documents which have been put before the court.

After closing the Claimant's case, the advocate should be ready for the possibility of the Defendant deciding to call no evidence. This is a not infrequent tactic in personal injury trials, usually employed because Defendants realise that their witnesses are likely to make their case worse, not better. The effect is that the Claimant's advocate must make his/her closing submissions first, before the Defendant. If time is really needed to prepare these, the judge should be asked for a few minutes.

The trial judge, under the new CPR, may allow the Defendant to make a submission of no case to answer at the close of the Claimant's case. The general rule is that the trial judge should not permit a Defendant to make such a submission unless he elects to rely on the submission alone and whatever the outcome, he will call no evidence on his own.[35] The reason being that if an appeal follows and is successful, it will be necessary to have a re-trial. Accordingly, although the trial judge is not obliged to put the Defendant to an election, the judge must do so with great caution. If the Defendant makes such an election, the issue for the judge is whether or not the Claimant has established his case by the evidence called on the balance of probabilities.

In the usual case, the defence calls witnesses and the Claimant's advocate's task is to cross-examine. It is for the Defendant to prove that the terms in which the Claimant's alleged condition was described in the claim form did not correspond with the evidence of the Claimant's expert.[36] Cross-examination is very much a matter of personal style but the authors' view is that it should be directed only to essential matters, which by then will have become very clear. It should not waste time, neither should it be unnecessarily aggressive, to avoid arousing the judge's sympathies for the Defendant's witnesses. It can cover every aspect of or go beyond a witness statement whether or not the matter was referred to in chief.[37] Cross-examination must, of course, be relevant.

The cross-examination of doctors and experts requires a great deal of preparation. The Claimant's relevant doctors and experts should be in court, available to give immediate instructions to the advocate whilst he/she cross-examines the Defendant's experts. The experienced personal injury practitioner will be aware of those doctors

---

[35]   *Boyce v Wyatt Engineering* (2002) Times, 6 September; *Miller v Crawley* [2002] EWCA Civ 1100.
[36]   *Edwards v Peter Black Healthcare (Southern) Ltd* (1999) Times, 28 May.
[37]   Rule 32.11.

who customarily give evidence only for Defendants and make frequent allegations of malingering. Armed with material from colleagues in the Personal Injury Bar Association, it can be dramatically useful to cross-examine to this effect.

Closing speeches

At the close of the defence case, if the defence has called evidence, the Defendant's advocate will make the first closing submissions. The Claimant's closing submissions should put the Claimant's case not simply shadow the Defendant's submissions. The points should be made shortly and there is no need to review the whole case or all the evidence. The judge will have grasped the critical issues and may indeed indicate the specific issues on which s/he would like to hear the Claimant's submissions.

Judgment, costs and leave to appeal

After judgment, if the Claimant wins, the advocate must ask for an order for judgment for the Claimant in the sum of so many pounds, together with interest[38] totalling so many pounds. Judgments are nowadays payable forthwith so that a period for payment is not needed in the order unless the paying party is seeking longer than 14 days for payment. It is common to give the Defendant up to 28 days to pay.

If there is any money paid into court, the order should be 'that the sum in court should be paid out to the Claimant's solicitors in partial satisfaction and any interest thereon accruing until judgment should be paid out to the Defendant's solicitors and any interest thereafter to the Claimant's solicitors'.

The Claimant's advocate should then ask for an order for the Claimant's costs. There will, of course, be an argument if the damages awarded are less than any amount paid into court. There may be arguments relating to contribution between Defendants.[39]

Costs are always at the discretion of the court. By virtue of CPR, r 44.3(2), the general rule is that the unsuccessful party will pay the costs of the successful party. However, in deciding what order to make about costs, the court must now have regard to all the circumstances (rule 44.3(4)) including:

(i) the conduct of all the parties;
(ii) whether a party has succeeded on part of his case, even if he has not been wholly successful; and
(iii) any payment into court or admissible offer to settle made by a party whether in accordance with Part 36 or not.

The conduct of the parties includes conduct before as well as during the proceedings and in particular, the extent to which the parties followed the relevant pre-action protocol; whether it was reasonable for a party to raise or pursue a particular allegation or issue; the manner in which a party has pursued or defended his case or issue and whether a Claimant who has succeeded in his claim in whole or in part exaggerated

---

[38]   If the plaintiff has failed to prosecute the case properly, the court can deduct interest for the number of years delay: *Spittle v Bunney* [1988] 3 All ER 1031.

[39]   In exceptional cases, costs may be awarded against a non-party: *Symphony Group plc v Hodgson* [1994] QB 179.

his claim (rule 44.3(5)). Practitioners are referred to Chapter 14 on ADR which emphasises the court's recent approach to unreasonable refusal to agree to mediation.

There is a range of orders the court can make, from an order that a party pay only a proportion of another party's costs, a stated amount, costs from or until a certain date or costs limited to certain issues or parts of proceedings (CPR, r 44.3(6)).

The court now envisages far more partial orders for costs which more accurately reflect the level of success achieved by the receiving party.[40] The court will adopt a more issue-based approach rather than merely depriving costs because a party behaved unreasonably. In the context of the personal injury action, most issues remain comparatively self-contained and it is less likely that a large body of the trial will relate to an issue that it transpires does not determine the end result one way or another. Of course, a party who accepts a Part 36 payment late becomes from that date the unsuccessful party. However, if that arose because of, for example, late service of evidence by the other party, there would be grounds for going behind the general rule.

In a publicly-funded case, the Claimant's advocate should ask for a legal services funding assessment of the Claimant's costs.[41] If a legal aid case is lost, the Defendant can be granted an order for costs against the Claimant, but in legal aid cases the words 'such assessment to be adjourned generally until further order from the court' are usually added.[42] The Defendant will then be able to enforce costs only where the Claimant subsequently comes into a large amount of money. This is popularly referred to as a 'football pools order'. Where the Claimant has paid a contribution into the fund, Defendants can ask for a sum equivalent to that amount to be paid to them by way of costs, provided that their costs are equal to or greater than that sum. This happens only rarely.[43]

Where the case is privately funded, the Defendant is usually awarded costs against the Claimant if the claim has failed. In certain circumstances costs can be awarded against legal representatives or a non-party.[44]

The advocate will raise any interim orders on costs which are reserved or outstanding and any issue on costs in relation to expert evidence. The trial judge may summarily assess costs in accordance with rule 44.7 and the practice direction accompanying it. Counsel must be on top of the figures and the arguments to sustain them.

If the case is unsuccessful,[45] an application for permission to appeal (see Chapter 26 on Appeals) should be considered. Best practice is, if in doubt: seek permission; as much as anything because this gives an additional opportunity to seek permission

---

[40]   *AEI Rediffusion Music Ltd v Phonographic Performance Ltd* [1999] 1 WLR 1507.

[41]   Where one party is legally aided, a court can, at an interlocutory stage of proceedings, order costs in favour of the other party but directing that those costs be set off either against any damages or costs to which the legally aided party had or could in future become entitled in the action: *Lockley v National Blood Transfusion Service* [1992] 1 WLR 492.

[42]   By reason of the Legal Aid Act 1988, s 17.

[43]   Exceptionally, costs can be awarded against the Legal Aid Board on certain conditions: see the Legal Aid Act 1988, s 18.

[44]   *McFarlane v EE Caledonia Ltd (No 2)* [1995] 1 WLR 366.

[45]   In order to justify an appeal on costs alone, the Court of Appeal must be able to say that the judge had not exercised his discretion or had not exercised that discretion judicially: *UK Petroleum Products Ltd v Reg Smith and Sons (Cheadle) Ltd* (1991) Times, 30 October.

before having to seek permission from the appeal court. An order for those costs to be paid by the lawyers may well be sought. The vast majority of hearings are now tape recorded. Accordingly, it is not generally necessary to invite the court to make a note of particular parts of evidence or a particular point of law. If the Defendant asks for leave to appeal and asks for a stay of execution, the Claimant should argue for a suspended order such as 'a stay of execution for 28 days or if notice of appeal is lodged within 28 days, until Appeal'.

Any application for a wasted costs order should be made expeditiously and before the judge who heard the substantive proceedings. The applicant should be mindful of the principle of proportionality.[46]

The court can award an interim payment of costs pending their detailed assessment (rule 44.3(8)). In general an interim order will be made for a lesser amount than would normally be expected. In exercising its discretion, the court has to take into account all the circumstances, such as:

(i) prospects of appeal;

(ii) the relative financial position of the parties;

(iii) the parties' conduct; and

(iv) the court's overriding objective to deal with cases justly.[47]

46   *Re Merc Property Ltd* (1999) Times, 19 May.
47   *Mars UK Ltd v Teknowledge Ltd (No 2)* (1999) Times, 8 July.

CHAPTER 24

Costs

This chapter deals with costs as they relate to personal injury claims in particular.

It is essential for practitioners to be alive to issues relating to costs – not only at the end of the case, but from the very outset. Practice directions require the successful party to serve with the bill of costs a 'short but adequate written explanation of any agreement or arrangement between solicitor and client which effects the costs claimed' and must attach to the court copy of the bill a full copy of any written agreement or arrangement between solicitor and client which effects the costs claimed. Accordingly, it is vital that such an agreement is executed properly at the outset of the case.

The court has the power and will expect to make a summary assessment of costs at the end of trial in a fast track case and in all other hearings less than one day. It will generally assess the costs of interim hearings during the course of the claim. At two of the important points in the litigation process, the case allocation questionnaire and the listing questionnaire the solicitor is expected to give an accurate assessment of costs expended to date and estimate the costs of proceeding with the litigation to its conclusion. Although the general rule that an unsuccessful party will be ordered to pay the costs of a successful party still applies, the rules under the CPR 1999 encourage the court to consider a whole range of alternative orders to be made.

Costs have always been in the discretion of the court. However, by rule 44.3(4) and (5), in deciding what, if any, order should be made the court is now required to take into account matters such as the conduct of the parties (including whether pre-action protocols have been complied with) and the question of proportionality – the amount of costs incurred in relation to the value of the claim – in coming to its decision.

One purpose of the rules is to discourage what the court will see as unreasonable and tardy behaviour by costs penalties. An excessively adversarial approach risks adverse costs orders; whether or not that party wins the claim.

The provisions in relation to costs are covered in CPR Parts 43–48, principally Parts 44 (general rules as to costs), 46 (fast track trial costs) and 47 (procedure for detailed assessment of costs and default provisions). Part 48 includes provisions relating to, amongst other things, costs where money is payable by or to a child or patient, pre-commencement orders, conditional fees, wasted costs orders and the basis of detailed assessment of solicitor and client costs, together with the assessment procedure itself. There is an associated Costs Supplementing Parts 43 to 48 of the Civil Procedure Rules practice direction together with a specific practice direction relating to each of Parts 43–48.

THE GENERAL RULES

The general rule remains that the unsuccessful party will be ordered to pay the costs of the successful party. However, it is specifically provided under rule 44.3(2) that the court may make a different order. The court therefore has a complete discretion as to whether costs are payable and by whom, the amount and when they are to be paid. The provisions of rule 44.3(4) state:

'(4) In deciding what order (if any) to make about costs, the court must have regard to all the circumstances, including–
(a) the conduct of all the parties;
(b) whether a party has succeeded on part of its case, even if he has not been wholly successful; and
(c) any payment into court or admissible offer to settle made by a party which is drawn to the court's attention (whether or not made in accordance with the pre-April 2007 provisions contained in Part 36).'

(Part 36 contains further provisions about how the court's discretion is to be exercised where a payment into court or an offer has been made under that Part.)

'(5) The conduct of the parties includes–
(a) conduct before, as well as during, the proceedings, and in particular the extent to which the parties followed any relevant pre-action protocol;
(b) whether it was reasonable for a party to raise, pursue or contest a particular allegation or issue;
(c) the manner in which a party has pursued or defended his case or a particular allegation or issue;
(d) whether a Claimant who has succeeded in his claim, in whole or in part, exaggerated his claim.

(6) The orders which the court may make under this rule include an order that a party must pay–
(a) a proportion of another party's costs;
(b) a stated amount in respect of another party's costs;
(c) costs from or until a certain date only;
(d) costs incurred before proceedings have begun;
(e) costs relating to particular steps taken in the proceedings;
(f) costs relating only to a distinct part of the proceedings; and
(g) interest on costs from or until a certain date, including a date before judgment.

(7) Where the court would otherwise consider making an order under paragraph (6)(f), it must instead, if practicable, make an order under paragraph (6)(a) or (c).'

It follows that the orders for costs are designed to be more issue based and to truly reflect the positions between the parties. A party who fights a case on a broad range of issues cannot automatically expect to recover all its costs when it in fact goes on to succeed on one issue only. The court is now entitled to take into account whether a party has succeeded on part of the case only and whether the other party has been reasonable in raising or contesting a particular allegation. For instance, in a case where the Claimant succeeded on some issues, but failed on or abandoned others, those costs were to be disallowed on detailed assessment as costs unreasonably incurred in the litigation.[1] Unreasonable conduct is no longer the prerequisite for disallowing costs. However, a Claimant who pursues what the court ultimately decides to be an exaggerated and inflated claim must expect costs penalties. Practitioners are referred to Chapter 14 on Mediation for comment on the costs consequences of failing to agree to a request for alternative dispute resolution.

Where there are multiple Defendants and the action has succeeded against one, but failed against the other, the court may in its discretion order the unsuccessful Defendant to pay the costs of the successful Defendant direct (know as a *Sanderson* order)[2] or order the Claimant to pay the successful Defendant's costs and then allow him to add such costs to his own and recover them from the unsuccessful Defendant (know as a *Bullock* order)[3]. The former is generally adopted unless the unsuccessful Defendant is insolvent. However, before considering either order, the court must first be satisfied that the Claimant was reasonable in joining both Defendants. A reasonable doubt as to which Defendant may be liable is usually sufficient.

Where a Defendant is successful at the final hearing against a publicly funded Claimant, the general order is for the Claimant to pay the costs of the Defendant to be assessed if not agreed, but for the determination of the Claimant's liability to pay those costs to be postponed generally until the court orders otherwise. The reality is that the Defendant will not seek to recover its costs unless the Claimant is known to come into a sufficient sum of money to meet the costs. However, where the Defendant is successful at an interim hearing against a publicly funded Claimant who is likely to go on and succeed at trial, the Defendant will commonly seek a *Lockley* order,[4] namely, that the Defendant's costs are not to be enforced against the Claimant save by way of set-off against such damages or costs as the Claimant may recover.

Costs have historically been paid on either the standard basis or indemnity basis. On the standard basis the court would allow a reasonable amount for all costs reasonably incurred. Any doubt about reasonableness was resolved in favour of the paying party. On the indemnity basis, the costs were allowed unless they were of an unreasonable amount or had been unreasonably incurred, any doubt being resolved in favour of the receiving party.

The standard basis will apply unless stated otherwise, but if no order is made as to costs no costs will be recoverable. However, a proportionality test for the assessment of costs on a standard basis is introduced under rule 44.4(2) and 44.5(1). The requirement of proportionality now applies as a two-stage test: a global approach

---

[1]   *Shirley v Caswell* [2000] Lloyd's Rep PN 955.
[2]   After *Sanderson v Blyth Theatre Co* [1903] 2 KB 533.
[3]   After *Bullock v London General Omnibus* [1907] 1 KB 264.
[4]   After *Lockley v National Blood Transfusion Service* [1992] 1 WLR 492.

and an item by item approach. The global approach will indicate whether the total sum claimed is or appears to be disproportionate having regard to the factors set out under rule 44.5(3). If the costs as a whole are not disproportionate, then all that is normally required is that each item should have been reasonably incurred and the costs for that time should be reasonable. If on the other hand the costs as a whole appear disproportionate then the court will need to be satisfied that the work in relation to each item was necessary and if necessary, that the costs was reasonable.[5] In effect, the preliminary judgment of proportionality determines the manner of the detailed assessment, but does not determine the final sum payable. If the global approach suggests that the costs are disproportionate, the receiving party is put to a stringent test of necessity and reasonableness of each item.[6]

In deciding the amount of the costs, the factors which must be taken into account (rule 44.5(3)) include the conduct of the parties, before and during the proceedings, the efforts made, if any to resolve the dispute, the value of the claim, the importance of the matter, complexity, skill, time spent on the case and the area where the work was conducted.

Rule 35.4(4) gives the court an express power to limit the amount that a party may recover with regard to expert's fees. In fast track cases therefore not only will the number of expert witnesses be limited, but their fees will also be subject to scrutiny. Proportionality issues are likely to be fundamental.

SUMMARY ASSESSMENT

The general rule is that the court should make a summary assessment of costs:
(i)   at the conclusion of the trial of a case that has been dealt with on the fast track, in which case the costs of the whole claim should be summarily assessed;
(ii) at the conclusion of any other hearing which has lasted not more than one day, in which case the order will deal with the costs of the application or matter (ie most interim hearings);
(iii) in hearings in the Court of Appeal which involve contested directions hearings, applications for permission to appeal at which the respondent is present, dismissal list hearings, appeals from case management decisions and appeals listed for one day or less.

The general rule will only not apply if there is good reason, for example, where the paying party shows substantial grounds for disputing the sum claimed or there is insufficient court time available to deal with the question of costs (see PD, rule 44.7, para 13.2). The parties are required to prepare and serve upon each other a statement of costs in the form of a statement. The statement must be filed at the court and served not less than 24 hours before the hearing at which the assessment will take place. The assessed costs will be payable within 14 days of the order unless stated otherwise. A summary assessment cannot be made where the receiving party is in receipt of legal aid (the practice direction does not prevent an order being made against a legally aided paying party, but any order cannot be enforced without leave

---

5   *Home Office v Lownds* [2002] 1 WLR 2450.
6   *Giambrone v JMC Holidays* (2003) Times, 20 May.

in accordance with s 17 of the Legal Aid Act), nor can it be made against a party under a legal disability (child or patient).

A practical problem arising from this is as follows: in the fast track there are fixed trial costs; there is (generally) no allowance made for the costs of the solicitor to attend trial where he or she instructs a barrister to represent the Claimant. Costs will be assessed at the conclusion of the claim. This means that the barrister will have to deal with, and argue for, the solicitor's costs. The Bar's experience in dealing with solicitor's costs is very limited indeed; in practice it is likely to be the most junior member of the bar that will be instructed to attend on a fast track trial (the fixed fees are very limited – see later). The reality is that summary assessment is a rough and ready process. The solicitor must therefore be careful to ensure that the barrister has as much detail as possible relating to the items claimed and also should, wherever possible, comment on the other side's costs to assist the barrister in identifying the grounds for challenging the costs. Alternatively an agreement might be best reached with the other side in advance since the figures have to be supplied in advance in any event (see below).

As it is always open to the court to award costs in any event against a party (even where the application itself asks for costs in cause) the person attending any interim hearing must attend with detailed updated costs figures and be prepared for any argument on costs. Furthermore, the costs of preparing for and attending at the hearing must be available. Best practice will be to complete form 1 for every interim hearing.

Once the court has made an order for summary assessment it will be only in the most exceptional circumstances that it can revisit its own order.[3]

PROCEDURAL REQUIREMENTS

The practice direction states that a party who intends to apply for a 'costs in any event' order must supply every other party with a brief summary statement of the amount of the costs of the application.

The provisions do not apply where costs have been agreed by the parties. In all cases, it is better to attempt to agree costs prior to the hearing if possible. This will both cut down time and the uncertainty of what the District Judge or High Court Master may order. Further, it is possible to agree that payment of the costs is left to the conclusion of the claim. An agreement at the beginning of a claim that no costs be paid – generally – until the end of the claim should work to both parties' advantage in a lot of claims.

Where it is not possible to reach such agreement, and the form 1 must be completed, it must state the amount and nature of disbursements (other than counsel's fees), profit costs and counsel's fees in respect of the hearing. Where VAT is claimed it must be separately shown. If an hourly rate is to be applied to costs the statement must specify the number of hours, rate per hour and grade of fee earner. If not, an explanation must be provided for the basis of calculation.

A failure to complete form 1 may be taken that the party is not seeking an order for costs. In this case, none will be made or recoverable!

The form must be signed by the party or her legal representative and served on the other side no less than 24 hours before the date fixed for the hearing.

Cost details as the case proceeds

Details of the costs to date and likely future costs must be given at the case allocation questionnaire stage and the listing questionnaire stage. The parties are likely to be held to the rates claimed, and the general level of costs specified at those stages unless exceptional circumstances arise. For this reason, it is probably good practice – in the larger value and more complex cases – for a costs draftsman to draw up an assessment of costs at these stages. Under the new rules a claim may be made for the reasonable costs of preparing and checking the bill of costs.

Detailed assessment replaced 'taxation' after 26 April 1999. The proceedings are commenced by serving on the paying party notice of commencement (form 5 of Schedule of Costs Forms) together with a copy of the bill, experts' and counsel's fee notes, written evidence as to any other disbursements exceeding £250.00 and form 252 which replaced the old statement of parties.

If the points at dispute are capable of being copied onto a computer disk (which most now are) and the paying party requests it, a copy must be supplied free of charge within seven days!

The lodging fees are now considerably reduced; for orders for costs made before 26 April 1999 there is no change, but for orders for costs made on or after 26 April 1999 the fee (at the time of writing) for a detailed assessment is £120 in the county court and £160 in the High Court.

Time limits by which detailed assessment proceedings must be commenced

The general rule (rule 47.7) is that notice of commencement must be served within three months after the date of judgment or final order, or three months after the date when the right to costs arose, for example, acceptance of a Part 36 offer to settle or following a payment into court. Commencement after the three-month time limit can result in all or part of interest payable being disallowed (rule 47.8). The court must not impose any other sanction unless misconduct is shown.

Points of dispute (rule 47.9) must be served by the paying party within 21 days after the date of service of the notice of commencement. If served late, the paying party may not make any further representations without the court's permission (rule 47.9) and if not served within the requisite time the receiving party can apply for a default costs certificate. Any reply to points of dispute must also be served within 21 days.

Once points of dispute are served the receiving party has a maximum of three months from the expiry of the three month period for serving notice of commencement (under rule 47.7 or as directed by the court) to file a request for a detailed assessment hearing (rule 47.14). The sanction for failure to do so is to disallow all or part of the costs payable. A request for an interim costs certificate can also be made at this time, for example if there is likely to be a considerable delay in obtaining a hearing date for detailed assessment. If the request is filed late, but before the paying party has lodged an application the only sanction is to disallow all or part of the interest payable. The court will give at least 14 days' notice of the time and place of the detailed assessment hearing.

The practice direction to rule 47.14, para 43 contains a list of documents which are required to be submitted with the bill. They must be arranged in accordance with practice direction to rule 47, para 4.13 and must be received by the court not less than seven, but no more than 14 days before the date of the assessment hearing. Once the hearing has ended it is the responsibility of the receiving party to remove the papers filed in support.

After the assessment hearing the bill must be completed in accordance with rule 47.16 (see the relevant practice direction) and filed within 14 days together with receipted fee notes and accounts in respect of all disbursements except those which do not exceed £500 certified as having been paid. No final costs certificate will be issued until all relevant court fees have been paid.

If costs are settled before the hearing the receiving party must give notice to the court immediately by fax.

The general rule is that the receiving party is entitled to the costs of the assessment proceedings. However, the court may make a different order in which case regard must be had to all the circumstances including the conduct of the parties, the amount by which the bill has been reduced and the reasonableness of claiming or disputing any aspect of the bill.

A written offer to settle costs 'without prejudice save as to costs of the detailed assessment hearing' will be taken into account providing that it was made reasonably promptly after notice of commencement or points of dispute served. The court must not be told of the offer until the question of costs falls to be decided.

The practice direction indicates that if an offer to settle is to be made to the paying party it should be served within 14 days of service of points of dispute.

Appeals in relation to costs

Appeals are dealt with, but permission to appeal is not required when the assessment has been conducted by an authorised court officer (Part 47, PD 20), or if the appeal is against a decision of a costs judge (former taxing master) or district judge to impose a wasted costs order or sanction for misconduct on a legal representative. Otherwise permission is required in accordance with the appeals procedure set out in Part 52 (see Chapter 27).

The appeal takes the form of a re-hearing if against a court officer's decision, otherwise the appeal is a review of the decision below and will only be allowed if the decision of the lower court was wrong or unjust because of a serious procedural or other irregularity in the proceedings in the lower court. A further right of appeal lies to a High Court or circuit judge.

Costs under the fast track

Lord Woolf's original intention was to fix all fast track costs. This met with significant opposition and, for the time being at least, the proposals have been shelved apart from the costs of the advocate's fast track trial costs which are fixed as follows:

Value of claim	Amount of fast track costs which the court may award
Up to £3,000	£350
More than £3,000, but not more than £10,000	£500
More than £10,000	£750

The sum of £250 may be allowed where a solicitor attends with counsel, but only if the court considers that attendance was necessary.

If the court deems attendance unnecessary it seems unlikely that the solicitor will be able to recover such costs on a solicitor and own client basis unless the solicitor has specific and clear instructions from the client that she should attend with counsel.

Costs where money is payable by or to a child or patient

In relation to costs the general rule is that the court must order a detailed assessment of solicitor/own client costs and assess any costs payable to a child or patient unless a default costs order has been issued (Part 48.5(2)). The rule is designed to protect money belonging to a child or patient.

The practice direction to rule 48 specifies circumstances in which an assessment of costs will not be required. This is essentially where either costs have been agreed or assessed summarily, the solicitor has waived the right to claim further costs, or where an insurer or other person will be meeting any solicitor/own client liability for costs. Otherwise the solicitor can only render a bill to a client who is a child or patient for the amount which the court specifies in the order.

Costs in relation to pre-commencement orders for disclosure (rule 48.1)

The well established rule is preserved by the CPR, namely that the costs of these applications are awarded against the applicant (whether successful or not). However the new rules also provide that the court may make a different order, having regard to all the circumstances, including whether any relevant pre-action protocol has been complied with and the extent to which it was reasonable for the application to be opposed. In such circumstances, the court will deprive that party of its costs of the application, rather than the costs of providing the disclosure itself.

Solicitor's duty to notify client

Where a solicitor is acting for a client against whom a costs order is made and the client is not present when the order is made the solicitor is under a duty (rule 44.2) to notify the client of the order in writing no later than seven days after receiving notice of the order. The practice direction to rule 44.2 also requires that the solicitor must explain why the order came to be made.

Powers in relation to misconduct

The court has the power under rule 44.14 to disallow all or part of the assessed costs, or order the party at fault or his legal representative to pay costs where it appears to the court that the conduct of the party or his legal representative before or during the proceedings which gave rise to the assessment was unreasonable or improper. This power is in addition to the court's power to make a wasted costs order set out below.

Before making an order the court must give the party or legal representative a reasonable opportunity to attend a hearing to give reasons why it should not make such an order.

Where the court makes such an order against a legally represented party who is not present the solicitor has a duty to notify the client in writing within seven days after receiving notice of the order. No specific sanction for breach of this requirement is mentioned in the rules, but the court can require the solicitor to produce evidence that s/he took reasonable steps to comply.

WASTED COSTS ORDERS

The court's powers to make wasted costs provisions are set out in s 51(6) of the Supreme Court Act 1981. CPR Part 48.7 and s 53 of the Costs practice direction provide further directions as to the manner in which the court should deal with such applications.

Section 51 of the Supreme Court Act provides that wasted costs means any costs incurred by a party:
(i)   as a result of any improper, unreasonable or negligent act or omission on the part of any legal or other representative; or
(ii) which in the light of any such act or omission occurring after they were incurred, the court considers it unreasonable to expect that party to pay.

In *Ridehalgh v Horsefield*, the Court of Appeal held that when a wasted costs order was contemplated, the court should adopt a three-stage test:
(i)   had the legal representative of whom complaint was made acted improperly unreasonably or negligently?
(ii) if so, did such conduct cause the applicant to incur unnecessary costs?
(iii) if so, was it, in all the circumstances, just to order the legal representative to compensate the applicant for the whole or part of the relevant costs?

'Improper' covers (but is not confined to) conduct which would ordinarily be held to justify disbarment, striking off, suspension from practice or other serious professional penalty. It includes conduct which would be regarded as improper according to the consensus of professional (including judicial) opinion, whether or not it violates the letter of a professional code.

'Unreasonable' describes conduct which is vexatious, for example, designed to harass the other side rather than advance the resolution of the case, and it makes no difference that the conduct was the product of excessive zeal and not of an improper motive. The acid test is whether the conduct permits of a reasonable explanation.

'Negligent' should be understood in an non-technical way to denote failure to act with the competence reasonably expected of ordinary members of the profession. Negligence must be proved.

A legal representative is not to be held to have acted improperly, unreasonably or negligently simply because s/he put forward, on instruction, a claim or defence that was bound to fail. It is incumbent on the court to bear prominently in mind the peculiar vulnerability of legal representatives acting for assisted persons. It is only when all allowances have been made and an advocate's conduct of court proceedings was quite plainly unjustifiable that it would be appropriate to make a wasted costs order.

At the initial stage, the court should not automatically invite the legal representative to show cause. The costs of the inquiry as compared with the costs of the claim are a relevant consideration. A causal link between the conduct complained of and the costs incurred is essential. After inquiry and hearing the representative, an order to show cause should not be made unless an apparently strong prima facie case has been made out. The burden of proof is not on the legal representative to exculpate him or herself.

Even if the court is then satisfied that the legal representative has acted improperly, unreasonably or negligently so as to waste costs, it is not bound to make an order, but it will have to give sustainable reasons for not doing so.

The question of wasted costs is normally left to the conclusion of the claim. Applicants must bear in mind the principle of proportionality. It is not proportionate for the court to spend more time on wasted costs proceedings than had been expended on the substantive proceedings.[7]

SOLICITOR AND OWN CLIENT COSTS

A client in contentious proceedings who is unhappy with his/her bill has the right to a solicitor/own client assessment under Part III of the Solicitor's Act 1974. Notice of this must be contained within the bill itself. If the client requests a Part 3 assessment the solicitor must serve a breakdown of costs within 28 days of the order for costs to be assessed. The client must then serve points of dispute within 14 days, with any reply to be served within 14 days thereafter. A hearing date can be requested by either party after points of dispute have been served, but no later than three months of the order for costs to be assessed.

Costs are assessed on the indemnity basis, ie allowed unless they are of an unreasonable amount or have been unreasonably incurred. Costs are presumed (rule 48.8(2)) to have been unreasonably incurred if of an unusual nature or amount and where the solicitor did not tell the client that they might not be recovered from the

[7]   *Re Merc Property Ltd* (1999) Times, 19 May.

other party even if the case were successful. A solicitor must therefore inform the client in writing before steps are taken to incur either unusual expenditure, such as the cost of an accident investigator's report, or a particularly expensive disbursement, otherwise the risk is that the disbursement will not be allowed either on an inter parties or solicitor and own client basis and the solicitor will end up paying for it through a reduction in her profit costs.

CONDITIONAL FEES

In order to limit the prejudicial effect of disclosing full details of funding arrangements at an early stage, the rules provide that the court will not assess any additional liability until the conclusion of the proceedings to which the funding arrangement relates (rule 44.3A). At that stage, the court will either make a summary assessment of all the costs including the uplift, or make an order for detailed assessment of the additional liability (44.3(2)). Where the court carries out a summary assessment, the judge should state separately the amount allowed in respect of the solicitors' charges, counsels' fees and disbursements.

Where the court has assessed solicitor/own client costs, either summarily or by way of a detailed assessment the client may apply (under rule 48.9) for assessment of either the base costs (to which the percentage success fee is applied) or the success fee, or both. Base costs are assessed under the indemnity principle, subject to the presumptions contained in rule 48.8(2) (see above).

The court has the power to reduce the success fee (ie the 'percentage increase') where it considers it to be disproportionate, having regard to all relevant factors as they would have reasonably appeared to the solicitor/counsel to be when the conditional fee agreement was entered into (rule 48.9(5)). There is a wealth of case law attached to whether or not a success fee is reasonable (see, for example, *Callery v Gray (No 1)*,[8] *Halloran v Delaney*,[9] *Bensusan v Freedman*[10] and *Re Claims Direct Test Cases*)[11] and, in particular, the procedure for lodging documentation with the court in preparation for detailed assessment – the solicitor dealing with her own costs should take particular care to liaise with the costs draftsperson drawing when proceeding to detailed assessment, to ensure that she does not fall foul of the rules.

As noted in Chapter 6 on Case funding, the court has stated that it is sensible for the Claimant's legal team to agree a two-stage success fee at the outset of proceedings. Road traffic accident claims will now recover no greater a success fee then 12.5% uplift if the claim settles before trial lifting to 100%. This followed on from the decision in *Callery v Gray*[12] where a split uplift of 100% reduced to 5% was mooted as appropriate before sufficient actuarial research had been carried out.

---

[8]   [2001] 1 WLR 2112, CA; [2002] 1 WLR 2000, HL.
[9]   [2003] 1 WLR 28, CA.
[10]   (20 September 2001, unreported), SCCO.
[11]   [2003] EWCA Civ 136.
[12]   [2001] 1 WLR 2112, CA; [2002] 1 WLR 2000, HL.

CHAPTER 25

Handling the Award

The receipt of a substantial sum of money by award or settlement requires forethought. For nearly every Claimant, this lump sum will be a 'once and forever' award, and is intended to compensate them for any continuing needs for life. Most Claimants have little or no experience of handling large sums of money and little concept of financial planning.

Claims for personal injuries are typically compensated by means of a judgment for a single lump sum. The lump sum is intended to represent fair and reasonable compensation for all past and future losses. It is inevitably speculative and in the case of a large award, requires the Claimant to carefully invest the money to produce an annual return over an uncertain life expectancy. If the Claimant lives longer than the average life expectancy, he or she may find that damages are insufficient to cover his needs. Unforeseen future price rises – and in particular the costs of care – may unexpectedly increase costs out of all proportion with inflation; or a prognosis may in fact transpire to have been overly optimistic, with far more extensive needs than was anticipated. From the Defendant's point of view, the obverse may happen and the Claimant may die shortly after the settlement or trial.

Prior to April 2005, the only way that a party could enter into an agreement to pay all or part of an award by way of a lift annuity was by way of a structured settlement. Put simply, a structured settlement – provided it was properly constituted – was a tax-free annuity paid for life. However, neither party to the litigation could insist on a structured settlement and in practice very few insurance companies wanted to pay out an indexed-linked sum for an uncertain period of time.

On 1 April 2005, the periodical payments order provisions of the Courts Act 2003 – which amended the Damages Act 1996 – came into force. The CPR were amended and now provides under Part 41 and its corresponding practice direction for periodical payment orders.

PERIODICAL PAYMENTS

In a compensation claim of value, the parties, including the court, have a duty to consider whether or not all or part of any award for future losses should be paid by way of periodical payments. The rules state that the court shall have regard to all the circumstances of the case and in particular the form of award which best meets the Claimant's needs, having regard to the factors set out in the practice direction. The practice direction states at PD 41B, para 1 that the factors which the court shall have regard to include the scale of the annual payments taking into account any deduction for contributory negligence, both parties' preferences and financial advice obtained in consideration of whether an award for periodical payments is considered. So whilst the court retains the power to order a periodical payment in respect of future losses, in practice, it is unlikely to do so in the face of the parties' opposition.

Whilst the rules give no specific guidance on what sums are likely to be considered substantial enough to warrant a periodical payment order, there are various indicators of when a periodical payment should be considered: where there are substantial continuing care needs, where there is uncertainly over life expectancy and when awards for payments were made under a structured settlement award, it was unlikely that such an award would be made for a sum smaller then £500K. It is suggested that the terms of reference for where a periodical payment award is made is not what the lump sum award would be, but what the annual sum by way of loss is.

Before ordering a periodical payment award, the court must be satisfied that the method of funding is secure (CPR, r 41.9(1)). Further, that the proposed method of funding can be maintained for the duration of the award and that this method will, in fact, meet the level of payment ordered by the court (PD 41B, para 3).

Where the court awards damages in the form of periodical payments, the order must specify the annual amount awarded, how each payment is to be made during the year and at what intervals, the amount awarded for the future in terms of loss of earnings and other income and in terms of care and medical costs and other recurring or capital costs (CPR, r 41.8).

The court must approve any periodical payment order for a child or person under a disability.

At least the following should be available to the Claimant's advisers before a settlement is reached:
(i)   a detailed opinion of counsel, assessing the value of the claim and its constituent elements on a conventional basis, and the appropriate lump sum figure or bracket for settlement on that basis. Careful consideration of the Claimant's life expectancy based on the medical opinions should be included;
(ii) a report by accountants or other financial experts as to the fiscal and investment advantages to the Claimant of the periodical payment proposed, with particular regard to the life expectancy of the Claimant and the likely future costs of care;
(iii) a draft of the form of agreement proposed;
(iv) material to satisfy the court that there are sufficient funds available outside the periodical provisions to meet any foreseeable capital needs of the Claimant, whether by means of a lump sum element in the settlement or by reason of other resources available to the Claimant;
(v)   material to satisfy the court that the agreement involves a 'reasonably secure' arrangement This will include orders where payments are protected by the

Financial Services Compensation Scheme and orders against government departments where there is ministerial guarantee.

Advantages of periodical payments

The major advantage is that the Claimant is in a substantially more secure position than if a single lump sum were paid. The payments are guaranteed for life and may be increased for inflation (by the Retail Prices Index or, as is now likely to be the case, in respect of earnings and care costs, ASHE 6115).[1] As the Claimant receives only the set periodical amount, there is less chance of either wasting the money or being taken advantage of by family or friends. This is a particularly strong argument in cases concerning a Claimant who, although not considered a patient, has been injured in such a way so as to become more impressionable or dependent or in cases where the life expectancy is uncertain. Another major plus is that the periodical payments are tax free (although it may have implications on the Claimant's entitlement to income support). Further, it is socially desirable to give catastrophically injured Claimants a guaranteed income for life.

Disadvantages of periodical payments

Even though, at first glance, the system appears to be advantageous to both sides, certain disadvantages still exist. The beneficial point of security has the down side of inflexibility. Once the capital sum is used to buy the annuity, it cannot be recovered. Therefore, if the Claimant dies, no further payments can be received (beyond those guaranteed), but, more importantly, if the Claimant requires a lump sum for a special purchase, it cannot be obtained (unlike the conventional system where the Claimant controls the capital to use as he wishes).

Furthermore, a discount may be demanded by the insurers to agree to a periodical payment order.

Finally, though the conventional award is assessed on the basis of a net income of 2.5% pa, a clever, well-advised or lucky Claimant can of course obtain much more than this. There are a series of cases proceeding at present to challenge the normal discount rate applicable to care claims.

INDEPENDENT ADVICE

Those who lack capacity may recover damages to reflect the likely costs of managing their award which would not otherwise have been incurred.[2] Those costs include Court of Protection fees and the cost of appointing a professional trustee or deputy under the Mental Capacity Act 2005. However, damages are irrecoverable for the cost of investment advice which is presumed to have been taken into account by the Lord Chancellor in setting the discount rate at 2.5%.[3]

[1]   *Tameside & Gollop Acute Services NHS Trust v Thompstone* [2008] EWCA Civ 5.
[2]   *Rialis v Mitchell* (1984) Times, 17 July.
[3]   *Page v Plymouth Hospitals NHS Trust* [2004] EWHC 1154; *Eagle v Chambers* [2004] EWCA Civ 1033.

In respect of Claimants who have capacity, arguments have recently been advanced in the more catastrophic cases that such Claimants require some assistance managing their daily affairs, such as assistance setting up a trust to protect the Claimant.[4]

TAX

No tax is payable on an award for damages for personal injuries or death.[5] Where a Claimant loses only part of his/her income, that part is always 'the top slice' when assessing liability for tax and so calculating the net loss.[6]

The income produced by investing the capital (as opposed to receiving periodic payments – see above) is liable to tax and, if the Claimant's award is substantial, it increases the Claimant's post-trial tax liability. The court should take this into account in assessing the Claimant's future loss, but only in exceptional cases, where justice requires, is a special allowance made.[7]

INVESTMENTS

Where the damages are substantial, the client may need assistance in deciding how to invest the money. The regulations regarding investment advice have become increasingly rigorous in recent years and, for a solicitor even to contemplate giving that advice, the firm must be regulated by the Law Society in the conduct of investment business.

Because of the complexities and risks of investment, unless the firm specialises in this subject, it is wisest to avoid giving the client specific investment advice. The best course of action is to state that financial advice ought to be obtained and to refer the client, in the first place, to his bank or building society manager. Even recommending named accountants or financial advisers involves the solicitor in the slight risk of a negligence action if the client receives bad advice, because it may be said that the solicitor should have investigated the adviser's competence more thoroughly.

Following the decision in *Wells v Wells*, management of the Claimant's investment will be more difficult to recover as a head of damage in itself because the multipliers are based upon investment with index-linked government securities. However, transaction costs will be recoverable.

INCOME SUPPORT AND TRUSTS

An award of damages may affect clients who are in receipt of income support, which is the major non-contributory means-tested social security benefit payable in the

---

[4]   For example, *Ure v Ure* (unreported, July 2007), but unsuccessfully argued in *A (by her litigation friend H) v Powys Health Board* [2007] EWHC 2996.

[5]   Income and Corporation Taxes Act 1988, ss 148 and 188; *British Transport Commission v Gourley* [1956] AC 185.

[6]   *Lyndale Fashion Manufacturers v Rich* [1973] 1 WLR 73.

[7]   *Taylor v O'Connor* [1971] AC 115 at 129 per Lord Reid; *Hodgson v Trapp* [1989] AC 807.

UK. Entitlement depends, among other things, on the income and capital resources of the Claimant and his/her partner. The Claimant is not entitled to income support if his/her capital[8] exceeds a prescribed amount (£16,000 for the Claimant and his/her partner).[9] There is a tariff income to be taken into account for capital between £6,000 and £16,000.[10] An award of damages or a settlement is treated as capital, and so the client and his/her family may find the entitlement to income support reduced[11] if the value of damages or settlement is between £3,000 and £8,000, or extinguished if the value exceeds £8,000. If the Claimant loses income support, s/he also loses entitlement to full housing benefit and maximum council tax benefit and (while that operated) community charge benefit.

This problem can be overcome by holding the money on trust. If a personal injury award or settlement is placed on trust for the Claimant, the capital value of such a trust is not taken into account in assessing the Claimant's capital although the income from damages in a trust fund is taken into account in determining a person's means.[12] The Claimant is not treated as having deprived him/herself of such capital.[13] If a Claimant's award is under the control of the Court of Protection (whether by way of a trust fund or otherwise), neither the capital or income are taken into account.[14]

As with periodical payment awards, it is a prerequisite that the money is not first paid to the Claimant or solicitor and is paid straight into the trust fund. The trust can be simple. Independent trustees must be appointed. The trust should give the trustees power to advance capital in their absolute discretion from time to time (unspecified). Payments out of the trust by the trustees, if voluntary and not made at regular intervals, should be treated as capital payments and not income.[15] Therefore, payments made, for example, for a holiday or a wheelchair should not disentitle the Claimant. As each payment depends on its own circumstances, it is difficult to advise whether a particular payment will be treated as income or capital. As a rule of thumb, payments will not be allowed (ie will be treated as income) if their effect is to top up the income of the Claimant from income support or other benefits. There is, however, a disregard of the first £10 per week of income paid from such a trust.

Drafting a trust should only be entrusted to a solicitor or counsel familiar with trusts in this setting. Such drafting would be outside the range of specialisation of most personal injury counsel.

---

[8]   This includes capital of the Claimant's partner, child or dependent young person: Income Support (General) Regulations 1987, reg 23(1).
[9]   Social Security (Miscellaneous Amendments) (No 2) Regulations 2005.
[10]   Income Support (General) Regulations 1987, reg 53 as amended by the Social Security (Miscellaneous Amendments) (No 2) Regulations 2005.
[11]   Since the establishment of the Compensation Recovery Unit, the DSS will know about all the Claimants who are claiming benefit prior to the settlement of their claims.
[12]   Income Support (General) Regulations 1987, SI 1987/1967, reg 46(2) and Sch 10, para 12. *Bell v Todd* [2002] PIQR 107.
[13]   Income Support (General) Regulations 1987, SI 1987/1967, reg 51(2)(b).
[14]   See [1996] 3 JSSL D136. *Ryan v Liverpool HA* [2002] Lloyd's Rep Med 23.
[15]   Income Support (General) Regulations 1987, reg 48(9).

Chapter 26

Appeals

This chapter explains the procedures for making appeals. The procedure for appealing is governed by CPR Part 52.

FUNDING

The first question is whether the appeal can be funded. In private or trade union funded cases, discussions should be held with the client and, where appropriate, the union, as to whether the benefits of an appeal are likely to outweigh the costs.

In a publicly-funded case, an application must be made to the Legal Services Commission. The certificate does not cover counsel's opinion or indeed any work on an appeal. The Commission should, therefore, be asked to authorise an opinion from counsel and the solicitor should set out the reasons why an appeal is thought appropriate. If counsel's advice is positive, the Commission should then be asked to extend the certificate to fund the appeal as soon as possible. A certificate to appeal, or an amendment to an existing certificate, can be obtained from the area director very quickly.[1]

There are time limits, set out below, for lodging an appeal. Often, if a solicitor waits for the granting of public funding before setting down the notice, the case will be out of time. The registrar of appeals may or may not consider the time needed for obtaining legal services funding a good enough reason to waive the time limit. It is, therefore, better to draft, serve and set down the notice within the appropriate period. It can always be withdrawn.

SLIP RULE

If the error which needs to be reversed is a mere accidental slip in drawing the order or judgment, application should be made to the master or judge who made the order under the 'slip rule' for it to be corrected.[2] The provision is designed to correct

---

[1] *Legal Aid Handbook*, 1998/99, Notes for Guidance, para 4-01.
[2] CPR, r 40.12.

typographical errors or genuine slips, but cannot be used to correct any error of substance or by way of an attempt to get the court to add to its original order because a party forgot to ask for it.

The court also has an inherent power to rectify a Tomlin Order (made on the staying of an action on agreed terms scheduled to the order) where the order mistakenly did not reflect the agreement correctly.[3]

TO WHOM IS THE APPEAL MADE?

The hierarchy of appeals is set out in Table 1 of para 2A.1 of the practice direction to Part 52 and should be consulted if an appeal is to be made. The general rule is that an appeal lies to the next level of judge in the court hierarchy. Accordingly, small claims court trials, fast track trials and unallocated trials before a District Judge, as well as all applications before the District Judge, will be appealed to the Circuit Judge in the county court. If it is a county court judge who hears a small claims court case, fast track case, unallocated claim or application, the route of appeal is to a single judge of the High Court. The same applies to all decisions which are not final decisions made by a Master in the High Court or District Judge sitting in a District Registry. Appeals from decisions of a High Court Judge or Deputy High Court Judge will, of course, be to the Court of Appeal.

The normal route of appeal will not be followed where a District Judge or Circuit Judge in the county court or Master or District Judge in the High Court gives a final decision in a multi track claim (unless it is a decision only on the detailed assessment of costs).[4] In such a case, an appeal lies directly to the Court of Appeal. If the case has not been allocated to the multi track, then this exception does not apply, even if the judge regarded the claim as suitable for the multi track and would have allocated it had he appreciated that allocation was so important.[5] The meaning of 'final decision' means a decision of the court that 'would finally determine (subject to any possible appeal or detailed assessment of costs) the entire proceedings whichever way the court decided the issue before it'.[6] However, decisions made on an application to strike out or for summary judgment are not final decisions for the purposes of determining the appropriate route of appeal. Accordingly, a case management decision, grant or refusal of interim relief, a summary judgment or the striking out of a claim are not final decisions for this purpose. By way of contrast, a decision at the end of a split trial on liability would be classed a final decision.[7]

Where the lower court or the appeal court considers that an appeal would raise an important point of principle or practice or there is some other compelling reason for the Court of Appeal to hear it, it may order the appeal to be transferred to the Court of Appeal (rule 52.14). This leapfrog provision should be used sparingly and in any case of doubt, should be referred to the Master of the Rolls for consideration.[8]

---

3   *Islam v Askar* [1994] 42 LS Gaz R 38.
4   *Dooley v Parker* [2002] ECWA Civ 1188.
5   *Clark (Inspector of Taxes) v Perks* [2000] 1 WLR 17.
6   Paragraph 2(c) of art 1 of the Access to Justice (Destination of Appeals) Order 2000.
7   See rule 52, PD 2A.2.
8   *Clark (Inspector of Taxes) v Perks* [2000] 1 WLR 17.

PERMISSION

An appellant or respondent requires permission to appeal where the appeal is against a decision of a judge in a county court or the High Court. (rule 52.3). The application may be made either to the lower court at the hearing which will be subject to appeal or to the appeal court in an appeal notice (rule 52.3(2)). However, if the appeal is to the Court of Appeal from a decision which has already been appealed, permission is always required from the Court of Appeal (rule 52.13(1)).

It is good practice to seek permission from the lower court first, giving 'two bites at the cherry' as a further application for permission may be made to the appeal court even where the lower court refuses permission. Whilst in the vast majority of cases it will be refused, it is clearly advantageous to the appellant if it be the case to have already obtained permission. This will not only remove any uncertainty of permission being refused at a later date, but could be of assistance to any negotiations prior to appeal. Furthermore, it is important to bear in mind that the judge at first instance will be fully aware of the issues and the application will take minimal time. It involves no additional cost.

Where the judge at first instance refuses, the appeal court will generally deal with the application on paper, but in a special case, may request an oral hearing. If permission is refused, that party can apply for an oral hearing provided the request is filed within seven days after permission has been refused.[9] It will usually be attended by one party only. In fact, the role of respondents is expressly limited and they should only file submissions at this stage if they contend that the appeal would not meet the relevant threshold requirements or there is some material inaccuracy in the papers.[10]

If both courts refuse permission, there is no third right of appeal against the refusal of permission.

Permission may only be given where the court considers:
(i) that the appeal would have a real prospect of success; or
(ii) that there is some other compelling reason why the appeal should be heard (Part 52.3(6)).

The first test is similar to the test on summary judgment or setting aside a default judgment (see Chapter 18). There must be a realistic as opposed to a fanciful prospect of success.[11] The meaning of the second ground is more difficult, as it implies that an appeal might be allowed when it has no prospect of success. In reality, this will apply to cases of public importance or where the court considers that the law requires clarifying. Alternatively, it may be applied where the court has a binding authority on itself and disposes of the matter rapidly to allow an appeal to a higher court.[12]

An order giving permission may limit the issues to be heard or make the appeal subject to conditions.

---

9   Rule 52.3(4). This time limit can be extended *Slot v Isaac* [2002] EWCA 481.
10   *Jolly v Jay* [2002] EWCA Civ 277.
11   *Tanfern Ltd v Cameron-MacDonald (Practice Note)* [2000] 1 WLR 1311.
12   This course was adopted by the Court of Appeal in *Beedell v West Ferry Printers Ltd* (2001) Times, 5 April.

APPEAL AGAINST CASE MANAGEMENT DECISIONS

Permission to appeal against case management decisions will be more critically assessed. PD 29 para 4.4 and 4.5 provide that in considering giving permission against such decisions, the court must take into account the significance of the appeal, the likely costs, the delay or disruption which would be entailed and whether the issue could more conveniently be determined at or after trial.

ONE APPEAL ONLY THE NORM

Part 52.13 provides that permission is required from the Court of Appeal for any appeal to that court from a decision that has already been appealed. The Court of Appeal will not give permission unless it considers that:
(i)   the appeal would raise an important point of principle or practice; or
(ii) there is some other compelling reason for the Court of Appeal to hear it.

The Court of Appeal has emphasised that it will no longer be possible to pursue a second appeal to the Court of Appeal merely because the appeal is properly arguable or had a real prospect of success.[13] On the meaning of 'some other compelling reason', the Court of Appeal has stated that, generally (but not always), the starting point will almost always be the prospect of success which must be very high, but even then it will not necessarily be sufficient for permission to be granted.[14]

NOTICE OF APPEAL

As noted above, where permission is still required, it must be requested in the appellant's notice. The notice itself should be filed within 21 days of the date of the decision unless the lower court directs otherwise (rule 52.4). It should be served on the respondent as soon as practicable and not later than seven days after it is filed.

It follows that a party that wishes to appeal a decision must act quickly. Time runs on the date when the judge below makes his decision, not on the date when the order reflecting that decision is drawn up.[15] The rules favour finality. If an extension of time is needed and it has not been sought from the lower court, an application will need to be made to the appeal court pursuant to rule 52.6. It cannot be agreed between the parties.

The notice must be in Form N161. The grounds of appeal should set out clearly why it is said that the decision of the lower court is wrong or why it is unjust because of a serious procedural or other irregularity (rule 52.11(3)).

The notice must be accompanied by a skeleton argument, usually in a separate document accompanying the notice. If not practicable, the skeleton argument must be served within 14 days of filing the notice. Care should be taken to draft this very carefully. It goes without saying that Part 36 offers or payments should not be

---

[13]   *Tanfern Ltd v Cameron-MacDonald (Practice Note)* [2000] 1 WLR 1311 and *Clark (Inspector of Taxes) v Perks* [2000] 1 WLR 17.
[14]   *Uphill v BRB (Residuary) Ltd* [2005] 1 WLR 2070.
[15]   *Sayers v Clarke Walker* [2002] 1 WLR 3095.

mentioned unless they are relevant to the substance of the appeal (rule 52.12). The skeleton argument should contain a numbered list of points spanning no more than few sentences which define and confine the areas of controversy. Each point should be followed by references to any documentation on which the appellant proposes to rely. Where appropriate, a list of persons, glossaries, technical terms, chronology, and/or authorities should be appended (52 PD 5.10).

The appellant must lodge with the Appeal notice the documents set out in PD 5.6. These include:
(i) a copy of the appellant's notice for the court and the respondent;
(ii) a copy of any skeleton argument;
(iii) a sealed copy of the order being appealed;
(iv) an order giving or refusing permission to appeal and the reasons given;
(v) a witness statement or affidavit in support of any application;
(vi) a bundle of documents in support of the appeal considered necessary to enable the court to reach its decision;
(vii) a suitable record of the reasons for judgment of the lower court. This should be an approved transcript if officially recorded. If not officially recorded, a written judgment endorsed by the judge's signature; a note of judgment approved by the judge; or an advocate's note of judgment (Part 52 PD 5.12).

Special provisions relate to small claims. In those circumstances, the notice must be accompanied by:
(i) a sealed copy of the order being appealed;
(ii) an order giving or refusing permission to appeal, together with a copy of the reasons for that decision;
(iii) a suitable record of the reasons for judgment of the lower court.

Any other documents are discretionary.

In a case where permission has yet to be given and is required, then upon that permission being granted, the above documents must be served on the respondents within seven days of receiving permission (52 PD 6.1).

RESPONDENT'S NOTICE

The respondent may file and serve a respondent's notice. This is mandatory if the respondent wishes to cross-appeal or to ask the appeal court to uphold the decision below, but for different reasons (rule 52.5). Again, if appropriate, permission to appeal must be sought in the notice.

The respondent's notice must be served 14 days after it was served with notice that the appeal will proceed (ie either from the notice if permission has been given or is not required, or from the date that the court gave permission if later (rule 52.5)). It must also be served seven days after it was filed.

In all cases where the respondent proposes to address the court, it should file a skeleton argument (PD 7.6). A respondent who files a respondent's notice, but does not include a skeleton argument within that notice, must file and serve his skeleton argument within 14 days. If no respondent's notice is served, the skeleton argument must be filed and served at least seven days before the appeal hearing (52 PD 7.7).

EXPEDITION

In exceptional circumstances an appeal may be expedited. The principles governing this were set out in *Unilever v Chefaro Ltd (Practice Note).*[16] Some appeals are so urgent that justice can only be done if the appeal is heard either immediately or at least within days of judgment. A very serious or distressing personal injury case is treated as requiring an immediate appeal.[17] Further, the courts recognise the need to try and arrange an expedited hearing where it appears that without such expedition:

(i)   a party will lose his/her livelihood, business, home or suffer irreparable loss or extraordinary hardship;
(ii) the appeal would become futile;
(iii) further cases will be delayed as they turn on the decision;
(iv) practice will continue to be diverged until decision; or
(v)   there would be serious detriment to public administration or to the best interests of the public.

Without the presence of one or more of these criteria, a court will not normally grant expedition.

STAY OF EXECUTION

If an application for stay of any order or decision of the lower court pending appeal is necessary, it should be made with the application for permission to appeal. Permission to appeal does not operate as a stay of proceedings[18] and, therefore, an application must be made specifically to the court which made the order appealed from or to the Court of Appeal.

APPLICATION TO STRIKE OUT THE MERITS

This should only be considered if the appeal has no reasonable prospect of success and is being brought to obtain some collateral advantage or where the application, if successful, would achieve a substantial saving of court time.[19]

THE APPEAL

The appeal court has power (rule 52.10) to:

(i)   affirm, set aside or vary any order or judgment made or given by the lower court;
(ii) refer any claim or issue for determination by the lower court;
(iii) order a new trial or hearing;
(iv) make orders for the payment of interest;
(v)   make a costs order.

The appeal is not a re-hearing, but a review of the decision of the lower court unless a practice direction provides otherwise or it is in the interests of justice (rule 52.11).

16   [1995] 1 WLR 243.
17   *Practice Direction (Court of Appeal: hear-by dates)* [1998] 1 WLR 1699, CA.
18   CPR Part 52.7.
19   CPR Part 52.9.

The normal practice is to review. This inevitably makes an appeal more difficult from any exercise of discretion and gives far greater importance to the decision of the lower court than was previously the case under the old rules. The court will allow an appeal when the decision of the lower court was (rule 52.11):

(i) wrong; or

(ii) unjust because of a serious procedural or other irregularity in the proceedings in the lower court.

No further guidance is given in the rules. However, a decision will be wrong if the lower court erred in law, in fact or in the exercise of its discretion. As to what constitutes a sufficient error, the court will only interfere when they consider that the judge at first instance 'exceeded the generous ambit within which a reasonable disagreement is possible'.[20]

It will be rare that ground (ii) is established. There must not only be a serious procedural error or irregularity, but it must make the decision unjust. A recent example is where the judge failed to give reasons for preferring the expert evidence of one party to that of the other, although the judge might take the opportunity at the permission stage to give additional reasons for his decision.[21]

FRESH EVIDENCE

Unless it orders otherwise, the court will not receive evidence which was not before the lower court (rule 52.11(2)). The rules do not restrict the circumstances to special grounds, but, in practice, this is required. The court will have regard to the criteria applicable under the old rules, namely, whether:

(i) the evidence could not have been obtained with reasonable diligence for use at the trial;

(ii) the evidence would probably have an important influence on the result of the case, though it need not be decisive;

(iii) it is credible.[22]

SPECIAL PROVISIONS APPLYING TO THE COURT OF APPEAL

Enquiries concerning the setting down of appeals or applications or about other Court of Appeal procedural matters should be made to the Civil Appeals Office Registry (Royal Courts of Justice, room E307; telephone 020 7947 7882 and 020 7947 6533).Cases filed in the Court of Appeal will be given a reference number. Unlike the county court, the Civil Appeals Office will not serve documents.

Listing

The Civil Appeals List of the Court of Appeal is divided into:

---

20   See *Tanfern Ltd v Cameron-MacDonald (Practice Note)* [2000] 1 WLR 1311, para 32.
21   *English v Emery Reimbold & Stick* [2002] 1 WLR 2409.
22   *Hertfordshire Investments Ltd v Bubb* [2000] 1 WLR 2318; *Hamilton v Al Fayed* (2001) Times, 25 January.

(i) 'the applications list' for applications for permission to appeal and other applications;
(ii) 'the appeals list' for cases where permission has been given or appeal lies without permission being required;
(iii) 'the expedited list';
(iv) 'the stand-out list', for appeals which for good reason are not ready to proceed and have been struck out by judicial direction;
(v) 'the fixtures list' where a hearing date for the appeal is fixed in advance;
(vi) 'the second fixtures list' where a hearing date is arranged in advance on the express basis that the list will only be heard if a gap occurs in the list;
(vii) 'the short-warned list' for cases which the court considers may be ready for hearing within a half day's notice or 48 hours' notice.

The Court of Appeal will send an appeal questionnaire to the appellant that notifies him of the date of the hearing or listing window. It must be completed within 14 days, giving the advocate's time estimate, confirmation that a transcript is being ordered if not already provided and confirmation that appeal bundles are being prepared (52 PD 6.4 and 6.5).

The hearing

In most cases, the court will have read the notice of appeal, any respondent's notice, the judgment, and any skeleton arguments. At the beginning of the hearing, the presiding Lord Justice will usually state what other documents or authorities have also been read. Counsel is notified if any opening is required. Counsel for the appellant is otherwise expected to proceed immediately to the ground of appeal which is in the forefront of the appellant's case. In citing authorities which have been pre-read, counsel should go to the passage in the judgment where the principle relied on is found. Similarly, counsel should refer to the notes of evidence outlined in the skeleton argument and, so far as possible, avoid reading the evidence at length. In considering quantum, the court will not generally examine the party's physical condition.[23]

Solicitor and counsel are under a duty to warn the client that the procedure may appear shorter than expected, but that their case has been just as fully considered. This is an important point. Whereas the full hearing before a county court judge may have been difficult for the client to follow, the Court of Appeal proceedings are totally baffling for most people.

If the appeal is successful, the order for costs of the court below will usually be reversed and costs will include interest, usually from the date of the original judgment.[24]

Dismissal of appeals by consent

Save where the proceedings involve a child or patient, an appellant can withdraw an appeal by requesting an order that his application or appeal be dismissed. It must

---

[23] *Stevens v William Nash Ltd* [1966] 1 WLR 1550.
[24] *Kuwait Airways Corpn v Iraqi Airways Co (No 3)* (1994) Times, 19 February, CA.

contain a statement that the appellant is not a child or patient. It will usually be granted on terms that the costs are paid by the appellant.

If the appellant wishes costs to be dealt with on different terms, a joint consent from the respondent must be obtained (52 PD 12.2–4).

Where a child or protected person is involved, settlements require court approval. A copy of the proposed order signed by the parties' solicitors should be sent to the appeal court together with an opinion from the advocate on behalf of the child (52 PD 13.3). In the case of a protected person, any relevant reports prepared for the Court of Protection should also be filed.

COSTS

Costs are likely to be assessed summarily in the following instances:
(i)   contested directions hearings;
(ii) applications for permission to appeal at which the respondent is present;
(iii) dismissal list hearings in the Court of Appeal in which the respondent is present;
(iv) appeals from case management decisions;
(v)   appeals listed for one day or less (52 PD 14.1).

Accordingly, parties attending on such appeals should be prepared to deal with the summary assessment.

PART 36 OFFERS/PAYMENTS

A Part 36 offer or payment made in the first instance hearing will not apply to the appeal. Accordingly, if a party wishes to protect its position on costs, it should make a fresh Part 36 offer or payment.

APPEALS FROM THE COURT OF APPEAL

Appeal to the House of Lords lies only with leave of the Court of Appeal or the House of Lords.[25] An application must first be made to the Court of Appeal. If leave is refused, a petition for leave to appeal may be presented to the House of Lords. Procedure on appeal to the House of Lords is found in the 'Blue Book' which is available from the Judicial Office of the House of Lords. It is also set out in vol 2 of the *White Book* at section 4A.

The application to the Court of Appeal for leave should be made at the hearing of the appeal. If not, the application should be lodged with the registrar of civil appeals. It should include the title of the action, the name of the applicant, the date of the order of the Court of Appeal and a brief statement of the grounds. The written application is referred to the Lord Justices who heard the appeal and an order is drawn up. If further comment is required, the matter is dealt with inter parties in open court. If leave is refused, application may be made to the House of Lords, by petition, within one month from the date on which the order appealed from was made.[26]

25   Administration of Justice (Appeals) Act 1934, s 1.
26   See further the *White Book*, 1999, vol 2, para 19A.

Once more, appeals to the House of Lords are permitted only on a point of law of public importance. Thus, personal injury cases go to the House of Lords only where some principle of the law concerned with liability or on the assessment of damages is at issue.[27] Personal injury cases in the House of Lords are, therefore, very rare.

Once leave to appeal is granted, the House of Lords has a discretion to hear an appeal where there is an issue involving a public authority even though there is no longer a lis to be decided. This discretion is exercised with caution and only where there is good reason in the public interest for doing so.[28]

---

[27] When the Court of Appeal has drawn the same inferences from the facts as the tribunal of first instance (whether or not the facts are in dispute), the House of Lords cannot substitute its own inferences unless it can be shown that both courts were plainly wrong: *Hicks v Chief Constable of South Yorkshire Police* [1992] 1 PIQR P433.

[28] *R v Secretary of State for the Home Department, ex p Salem* [1999] 1 AC 450.

PART III

Special Problems

CHAPTER 27

Limitation of Actions

This chapter outlines the basic information in relation to the time limits for suing in a personal injury action and summarises the relevant provisions of the Limitation Act 1980. For a full treatment of the problems of limitation, see Nelson-Jones and Burton, *Personal Injury Limitation Law* (Tottel, 2nd edn).[1]

The definition of personal injury is wide enough to cover all proceedings, whether in tort or contract or under statute, in which a claim is made for personal injuries, save for claims involving trespass to the person, false imprisonment, malicious prosecution or defamation. It does not, for example, extend to a claim for damages against a solicitor for professional negligence by causing a personal injury action to be struck out,[2] but would if the negligent mishandling of the case caused clinical depression.[3] Again, it would not apply to a claim by an employee against an employer for failure to advise on the benefits that he was entitled to upon suffering personal injury during the course of his employment.[4]

THE TIME LIMIT

Proceedings are started when the court issues a claim form on the request of the Claimant and the date of commencement is the date entered on the form by the court.[5] The Limitation Act 1980 provides that, in any action claiming damages for negligence, nuisance or breach of statutory duty which consists of, or includes, a claim for damages in respect of personal injuries to the Claimant or any other person, the time limit for the issue of proceedings is three years from: the date on which the cause of action accrued,[6] or if later, from the 'date of knowledge' (see below) of the person injured.[7] Following the recent decision in *A v Hoare*,[8] it now also applies if

[1] See also Law Commission Consultation Paper No 151 'Limitation of Action'.
[2] *Hopkins v MacKenzie* [1995] 6 Med LR 26.
[3] *Bennett v Greenland Houchen* [1998] PNLR 458.
[4] *Gould v Leeds* (1999) Times, 14 May.
[5] CPR, r 7.2.
[6] The day of the accident does not count: *Marren v Dawson Bentley & Co Ltd* [1961] 2 QB 135.
[7] Limitation Act 1980, s 11(4).
[8] [2008] UKHL 6.

the injury was caused by a trespass to the person.[9] It is crucial to establish the dates when the cause of action accrued and the date of knowledge at the first interview.[10]

If the person injured dies during the three-year period, the cause of action survives for the benefit of his estate under the Law Reform (Miscellaneous Provisions) Act 1934 and for his dependants under the Fatal Accidents Act 1976 – provided the cause of action has not been otherwise barred (for example, struck out) – for three years from the date of death, or the date of the personal representative's or dependant's 'knowledge', whichever is the later. Where the person dies outside the three-year period (and the claim under the Fatal Accidents Act is not otherwise barred), the court may exercise its discretion under the Limitation Act 1980, s 33 to disapply the limitation period.

DATE OF ACCRUAL OF THE CAUSE OF ACTION

This is usually relatively straightforward. The act or omission which is alleged to constitute negligence must be identified. However, as a cause of action does not arise until there is both breach of duty and some injury/damage, the date that the alleged breach of duty caused the injury must be ascertained. For instance, in a failed sterilisation case, the cause of action arises with the unwanted pregnancy and not the procedure itself. It gets more complicated when there are several acts or omissions. They should be distilled down to the essential action that caused injury.

DATE OF KNOWLEDGE

Section 14(1) of the 1980 Act specifies the 'date of knowledge' of the Claimant as the date on which he knew the following (see further below):

(i)   that the injury was significant;
(ii)   that the injury was attributable in whole or in part to the act or omission which is alleged to constitute negligence;
(iii)   the identity of the Defendant; and
(iv)   if the act or omission is alleged to have been that of someone who is not the Defendant, the identity of that person and the facts bringing about the liability of the Defendant.

The knowledge of these facts can either be actual or constructive (ie the Claimant ought to have known).

The date of knowledge runs from the date the Claimant first acquired knowledge of the causally relevant facts essential to the cause of action. It is not the date the Claimant acquires knowledge that the act or omission was in fact actionable.[11]

---

9   Overturning the decision in *Stubbings v Webb* [1993] AC 498.
10   *Thompson v Brown Construction (Ebbw Vale) Ltd* [1981] 1 WLR 744; *Donovan v Gwentoys Ltd* [1990] 1 WLR 472.
11   *Saxby v Morgan* [1997] PIQR P531.

SIGNIFICANT INJURY

For the purposes of s 14(1)(a), a 'significant injury' is defined by s 14(2) as one which the Claimant would reasonably have considered sufficiently serious to justify instituting proceedings for damages against a Defendant who did not dispute liability and was able to satisfy any judgment. Section 14(3) then goes on to provide that for the purposes of defining whether the Claimant had such knowledge, one should take into account not only his actual knowledge, but also imputed or constructive knowledge which he might reasonably have been expected to acquire from facts observable or ascertainable to him or from facts ascertainable by him with the help of medical or other appropriate expert advice which it is reasonable for him to seek.

The threshold of a 'significant injury' is therefore very low. It is a question of the quantum of the injury and not of any evaluation a Claimant makes as to its cause, nature or unusualness.[12] It is always difficult for a Claimant bringing proceedings at a later date to say that his injury is significant now, but was not at the time unless there has been a marked deterioration.[13]

The House of Lords in *A v Hoare* confirmed that the test itself is entirely impersonal; not whether the Claimant himself would have considered the injury sufficiently serious to justify proceedings, but whether he would 'reasonably' have done so. Lord Hoffmann stated at para 34:

> 'You ask what the Claimant knew about the injury he had suffered, you add any knowledge about the injury which may be imputed to him under s 14(3) and you then ask whether a reasonable person with that knowledge would have considered the injury sufficiently serious to justify his instituting proceedings for damages against a Defendant who did not dispute liability and was able to satisfy a judgment.
>
> 35. It follows that I cannot accept that one must consider whether someone "with the plaintiff's intelligence" would have been reasonable if he did not regard the injury as sufficiently serious. That seems to me to destroy the effect of the word "reasonably". Judges should not have to grapple with the notion of the reasonable unintelligent person. One you have ascertained what the Claimant knew and what he should be treated as having known, the actual Claimant drops out of the picture.'

An injury only need be relatively minor for a Claimant to reasonably consider bringing an action which cannot fail. Time begins to run even if the injury is later diagnosed as even more serious.[14]

This can lead to problems of forcing a Claimant to proceed early and further injury becoming apparent after a settlement is made.[15] Provisional damages should be employed in such cases.

12   *Dobbie v Medway Health Authority* [1994] 1 WLR 1234 at 1241 per Bingham MR.
13   See, for example, *Norton v Corus UK Ltd* [2006] EWCA Civ 1630.
14   *Miller v London Electrical Manufacturing Co Ltd* [1976] 2 Lloyd's Rep 284.
15   For example, *Bristow v Grout* (1987) Times, 9 November, CA.

ATTRIBUTABILITY

Under s 14(1)(a), the Claimant must not only have knowledge, actual or constructive, that the injury in question was significant, but also, under s 14(1)(b), that:

> 'The injury was attributable to the act or omission which is alleged to constitute negligence, nuisance of breach of duty.'

The subsection goes on to state that the Claimant's ignorance that, as a matter of law, the facts would have given him a cause of action is irrelevant. It is the Claimant's knowledge of the facts that governs the commencement date. Ignorance of the law is irrelevant to this question (even where the Claimant has received incorrect advice about the legal position), although it will be relevant to the s 33 discretion. He does not need to know that he has a possible cause of action (ie fault) provided he has knowledge in broad terms of the facts on which it was based (ie causation).[16]

The Claimant must have knowledge of the essence of the act or omission to which any injury is attributable[17] and time will not run if this knowledge is so vague and general that the Claimant cannot fairly be expected to know what or who to investigate, or if what the Claimant believes is entirely misconceived.[18]

In *Spargo v North Essex District Health Authority*,[19] Brooke LJ considered the meaning of 'attributable' and the question of what qualifies as 'actual knowledge' and stated that the following principles could be derived from the decisions on s 14(1)(b):

> '(1) The knowledge required to satisfy s 14(1)(b) is a broad knowledge of the essence of the causally relevant act or omission to which the injury is attributable;
>
> (2) "attributable" in this context means "capable of being attributed to" in the sense of a real possibility;
>
> (3) a Claimant has the requisite knowledge when she knows enough to make it reasonable for her to begin to investigate whether or not she has a case against the Defendant. Another way of putting this is to say that she will have such knowledge if she so firmly believes that her condition is capable of being attributed to an act or omission which she can identify (in broad terms) that she goes to a solicitor to seek advice about making a claim for compensation;
>
> (4) on the other hand, she will not have the requisite knowledge if she thinks she knows the acts or omissions she should investigate, but in fact is barking up the wrong tree; or if her knowledge of what the Defendant did or did not do is so vague or general that she cannot fairly be expected to know what she should investigate; or if her state of mind is such that she thinks her condition is capable of being attributed to the act or omission alleged to constitute negligence, but she is not sure about this, and would need to check with an expert before she could be properly said to know what it was.'

---

[16]   *Whitfield v North Durham HA* [1995] 6 Med LR 32.
[17]   *Nash v Eli Lilly & Co* [1993] 1 WLR 782.
[18]   *Broadley v Guy Clapham & Co* [1994] 4 All ER 439.
[19]   [1997] PIQR P235.

However, as noted below under 'constructive knowledge', any subjective element under s 14(1) is wholly tempered by what the Claimant acting reasonably ought to have known under s 14(3).

OMISSIONS

In cases where the Claimant is alleging an omission as giving rise to the cause of action, he will not have actual knowledge of the omission until he knew what it was that had been omitted.[20]

IDENTITY

Under s 14(1)(c), the Claimant must also have knowledge of the identity of the Defendant before time begins to run. The obvious case is where the Claimant cannot reasonably have been expected to trace or identify a Defendant or, in some circumstances, know the name of his employer because it was one of a number of limited companies all with similar names and the name of the wrong one was entered on his contract of employment.[21]

CONSTRUCTIVE KNOWLEDGE

Notwithstanding the considerations under s 14(1), s 14(3) extends knowledge to include that which a Claimant might reasonably have been expected to acquire (constructive knowledge) from facts observable or ascertainable by him or from facts ascertainable by him with the help of medical or other expert advice which it is reasonable for him to seek. However, s 14(3) goes on to qualify the position by stating that a person shall not be fixed under the subsection with knowledge of a fact ascertainable only with the help of expert advice so long as he has taken all reasonable steps to obtain (and, where appropriate, to act on) that advice.

As noted above, following the House of Lords decision in *A v Hoare*, this issue is now firmly determined on an objective basis. It turns on what the Claimant ought reasonably to have done. This was emphasised again by Lord Hoffmann in the decision of *Adams (FC) v Bracknell Forest Borough Council*[22] who stated that the introduction of s 33 enabled the court to bring subjective issues relevant to a particular Claimant into play at that juncture rather than under s 14. At para 47, he stated:

'... I do not see how [the Claimant's] particular character or intelligence can be relevant. In my opinion, s 14(3) requires one to assume that a person who is aware that he has suffered a personal injury, serious enough to be something about which he would go and see a solicitor if he knew he had a claim, will be sufficiently curious about the causes of the injury to seek whatever expert advice is appropriate.'

20   *Smith v Lancashire Health Authority* [1995] PIQR P514.
21   *Simpson v Norwest Holst Southern Ltd* [1980] 1 WLR 968. Applied in *Cressey v Timm & Son Ltd* [2005] EWCA 763.
22   [2005] 1 AC 76.

The judges went on to consider that where the Claimant has a disability, but has capacity (in that case, severe untreated dyslexia), the test of constructive knowledge was an objective test based on the reasonable actions of a Claimant with a similar disability, but disregarding specific characteristics of that Claimant.

The Claimant is further fixed with constructive knowledge which his solicitors ought to have acquired.[23]

BEYOND THE TIME LIMIT

Deliberate concealment

If the Claimant can show that one of the Defendant's servants or agents has deliberately concealed any fact relevant to the right of action then this has the effect of delaying the commencement of the primary limitation period until the date the Claimant had discovered the concealment.[24]

An action may be brought, without the permission of the court, after the expiry of the limitation period. It is up to Defendants to raise the limitation defence.[25] Almost invariably they do so. Nevertheless, it is usual not to mention any limitation problem in the statement of case, but to wait to see if it is raised in the defence and, if so, respond by way of a reply (see Chapter 17).

Persons under a legal disability

Persons regarded as being under a legal disability are exempt from the time limit.[26] This is dealt with in more detail in Chapter 29.

The three-year period begins to run for such potential Claimants only from the age of majority of a child or, for protected persons, when they no longer lack capacity.

If a disability occurs after the cause of action has accrued, it does not interfere with the three-year period.[27] However, the court is directed to have regard to the duration of any such disability in considering disapplication of the time limit.[28]

EXTENDING THE TIME LIMIT – S 33[29]

In personal injury cases, the court has an equitable discretion under the Limitation Act 1980, s 33 to 'disapply' the limitation period. The discretion is wholly unfettered

---

[23]   *Henderson v Temple Pier Co Ltd* [1999] 1 WLR 1540 and *Copeland v Smith* (1999) Times, 20 October.
[24]   *Mortgage Corpn v Alexander Johnson* (1999) Times, 22 September.
[25]   *Dismore v Milton* [1938] 3 All ER 762, CA.
[26]   *Turner v Malcolm* (1992) 15 BMLR 40; (1992) 136 Sol Jo LB 236. In exceptional circumstances, where under the inherent jurisdiction of the court there is found to be an abuse of the process, a plaintiff who is under a disability can have his or her claim struck out even though the limitation period has not expired: *Hogg v Hamilton and Northumberland Health Authority* [1992] PIQR P387, CA.
[27]   *Purnell v Roche* [1927] 2 Ch 142.
[28]   Limitation Act 1980, s 33(3)(d).
[29]   See A Biglani, 'Limitation in Medical Negligence Cases Part II: how the court's discretion is exercised under s 33 of the Limitation Act 1980' (1997) JPIL 159.

and the question of proportionality is now important in the exercise of any discretion. The probable amount of an award is likely to be an important factor to consider.[30] In considering whether to extend the time limit imposed by s 11, the court weighs the prejudice to the Claimant and Defendant and has regard to all the circumstances of the individual case, in particular to the following:

(i)   the length of and reason for the delay on the part of the Claimant. This is judged entirely on a subjective basis and there is no actual requirement that the reasons are reasonable.[31] Even a relatively short delay must be explained by the Claimant.[32] It is here that the court takes into account the subjective characteristics of the individual Claimant, not under s 14. Further, in view of the less favourable construction of s 14(1) and (2) that has been applied in *A v Hoare*, the Lords recognised that the favourable factors which were previously taken into account in reaching a conclusion under s 14 should now be applied when exercising a discretion under s 33;[33]

(ii)   the effect of the delay on the cogency of the evidence. There is a risk, therefore, that a Defendant may avoid liability by destroying evidence;[34]

(iii)   the conduct of the Defendant. Any prejudice found to exist to the Defendant by the delay will be discounted if the Defendant has wilfully destroyed evidence.[35] Further, the court will take a harsh view of the Defendant purposely delaying any litigation;

(iv)   the duration of any disability to the Claimant arising after the accrual of the cause of action. 'Disability' is given the same meaning under s 33 as under s 38 (see above). The court therefore has a discretion to grant extension even if the disability is after the initial time began to run;[36]

(v)   the extent to which the Claimant has acted promptly and reasonably once actual knowledge is in place;

(vi)   the steps taken to obtain medical, legal or other expert advice and the nature of such advice. A Claimant cannot escape the s 11 time limit by showing he has been incorrectly advised. However, this would be taken into account under s 33.[37] It is no longer good law to state that the failings of the Claimant's solicitor cannot be held against the Claimant as the Claimant must bear responsibility for the delay whether it is caused by his own default or that of his solicitor.[38]

The onus is on the Claimant to satisfy the court that the discretion should be exercised to disapply the time limit.[39] A summary of further principles derived from the case law is as follows:

---

[30]   *Adams (FC) v Bracknell Forest Borough Council* [2005] 1 AC 76 at para 55 per Lord Hoffmann in approving the dicta in *Robinson v St Helens MBC* [2003] PIQR P128.
[31]   *Coad v Cornwall and Scilly Isles Health Authority* [1997] 1 WLR 189.
[32]   *Ramsden v Lee* [1992] 2 All ER 204.
[33]   *A v Hoare* [2008] UKHL 6 at para 70 per Lord Carswell.
[34]   *Conry v Simpson* [1983] 3 All ER 369.
[35]   See *Hammond v West Lancashire Health Authority* [1998] 14 LS Gaz R 23.
[36]   *Thomas v Plaistow* [1997] PIQR P540.
[37]   *Das v Ganju* (1999) 48 BMLR 83, CA – case allowed to proceed five years outside the primary limitation period due to misleading and wrong advice of lawyers.
[38]   *Horton v Sadler* [2006] 2 WLR 1346 at para 53 per Lord Carswell.
[39]   *Crocker v British Coal Corpn* (1995) 29 BMLR 159.

(i)   the ultimate prospects of success are relevant, although care must be taken in so doing at an interlocutory stage (per *Davis v Jacobs*);[40]

(ii)   the ability to have a fair trial is relevant;

(iii)   loss of the limitation defence is of little importance. What is of importance is the effect of the delay on the Defendant's ability to defend (*Hartley v Birmingham City DC*);[41]

(iv)   the faults of the Claimant's solicitor are not to be visited on the Claimant (*Steeds v Peverel Management Services Ltd*);[42]

(v)   the Claimant will inevitably suffer some prejudice if he has to pursue a professional negligence claim against his solicitor (*Hartley v Birmingham City DC*);[43]

(vi)   the test under s 33(3)(a) is a subjective and not objective test; accordingly, whether it is reasonable or not is irrelevant (*Coad v Cornwall and Isles of Scilly HA*);[44] the delay relates to the delay between the expiry of limitation and issue, not from the accident (*Steeds v Peverel Management Services Ltd*);[45]

(vii)   under s 33(3)(b) cogency is directed to the degree to which either party is prejudiced in the presentation of the claim or defence because the evidence is either no longer available or has been adversely affected by the passage of time; again, it relates to post-limitation delay (*Steeds*);

(viii) s 33(3)(c) relates to the conduct of the Defendant after the cause of action arose;

(ix)   s 33(3)(d) is related to a person's disability as a child or patient, rather than physical disability (*Yates v Thakeham Tiles Ltd*);[46]

(x)   s 33(3)(e) is an objective test. The person whose conduct is relevant is the Claimant's and not his advisers (per *Davis* above).

The application to disapply the limitation period can be dealt with at an interlocutory stage by a master or a district judge,[47] or at a preliminary hearing either before or at the trial.[48] In practice, Defendants usually apply at an interlocutory stage to stay the action on the ground that it is out of time. The Claimant should then respond by making an application at the same time to have the limitation period disapplied under s 33. This requires a supporting verified witness statement setting out the facts relied on. Such an application may be made in addition to the prior argument that, on the facts, the limitation period has not expired (because, for example, the date of knowledge brings the issue of proceedings within three years). The court is directed to have regard to 'all the circumstances of the case'.[49]

It is usually to the Claimant's advantage to delay such a hearing, at least until discovery has been completed. It is not generally advisable to delay such a hearing until trial,

---

[40]   [1999] Lloyd's Rep Med 72.
[41]   [1992] 2 All ER 212.
[42]   (30 March 2001, unreported).
[43]   [1992] 2 All ER 212.
[44]   [1997] 8 Med LR 154.
[45]   (30 March 2001, unreported).
[46]   [1995] PIQR 135.
[47]   RSC Ord 32, r 9A.
[48]   *Buck v English Electric Co Ltd* [1977] 1 WLR 806.
[49]   *Donovan v Gwentoys Ltd* [1990] 1 WLR 472. Exercise of the discretion conferred by s 33 is very difficult to appeal. See *Yates v Thakeham Tiles Ltd* [1995] PIQR P135.

when no costs will be saved and the Claimant's negotiating position will be weakened by the possibility of losing on limitation, as well as by the usual risks of litigation.

If there is a long time gap between the date of accrual of the cause of action and the Claimant's date of knowledge, the court will be less likely to exercise its discretion if the three year period has not been complied with even if the case is only just out of time.[50]

If proceedings are issued, but not served within time on the Defendant, further proceedings for the same cause of action against the same Defendant will no longer be struck out and the claimant will have to apply under s 33 for the Limitation Period to be disapplied.[51]

SPECIAL TIME LIMITS

Practitioners can potentially be caught out by distinct time provisions applicable to discrete areas of practice. A brief summary of the most common are as follows:

(i)   criminal injuries compensation claims: two years;

(ii) Foreign Limitation Periods Act 1984: the provisions must be read in conjunction with ss 11 and 12 of the Private International Law (Miscellaneous Provisions) Act 1995. Those provisions provide that for a cause of action involving personal injury, the law of the country where the person was when he sustained injury is the applicable law unless displaced under s 12. Accordingly, a Claimant who is knocked down by a car in India is likely to be subject to Indian limitation periods unless good reason applies to the contrary. Good reason may be, for instance, that both the Claimant and the Defendant were English;[52]

(iii) Maritime Conventions Act 1911: two-year time limit for actions arising out of the collision of vessels (not where the Claimant sustains injuries as a result of the fault of persons on the ship); there is a discretion to extend, but it tends to be more strictly applied than under s 33 of the Limitation Act 1980;

(iv) international carriage by air, applied by the Carriage by Air Act 1961: two years from the date of arrival at destination or from the date on which the aircraft ought to have arrived;

(v)   international carriage by sea, applied by the Merchant Shipping Act 1979: two years from the date of disembarkation (or planned disembarkation) for death or personal injury to a passenger caused by the fault or neglect of the carrier, his servants or agents. It can be extended to three years in the case of deliberate concealment of facts or where a Claimant is under a disability;

(vi) International Transport Conventions Act 1983: three years subject to an absolute limit of five years in respect of claims for personal injury or death caused to a passenger as a result of an accident connected with internal carriage by rail;

(vii) Consumer Protection Act 1987: for such claims, s 11A of the Limitation Act 1980 creates a 10-year long stop running from the time when the Defendant

---

50   See *Price v United Engineering Steels Ltd* [1998] PIQR P407.
51   *Horton v Sadler* [2006] 2 WLR 1346.
52   *Edmunds v Simmonds* [2001] PIQR 296.

supplies the defective product to another. A product is supplied when it is taken out of the manufacturing process operated by the producer and enters a marketing process in the form in which it is offered to the public in order to be used or consumed.[53] After that 10-year period, the right of action is extinguished. There is no s 33 discretion to disapply the 10-year long stop (s 33(1A)(a)). Further, it overrides the normal disability provisions under s 28 of the Limitation Act (s 28(7));

(viii) s 7(5) of the Human Rights Act 1998 provides that proceedings for breach by a public authority of a person's Convention rights under the Human Rights Act 1998 must be brought within one year from the date on which the act complained of took place or such longer period as the court considers equitable having regard to all the circumstances;

(ix) contribution between tortfeasors is covered by s 10 of the Limitation Act 1980. It is two years from the date when the right to contribution accrued, namely, if when the judgment or award is given or if the claim is settled with or without and an admission of liability, when the amount to be paid has been agreed (s 10(3)), even if embodied in a later consent order.[54]

[53]   *O'Bryne v Sanofi Pasteur MSD Ltd* [2008] PIQR P3.
[54]   *Knight v Rochdale Healthcare NHS Trust* [2004] 1 WLR 371.

CHAPTER 28

Fatal Accidents

Since 1983, running a fatal accident case has been little more complicated than an ordinary personal injury case. Establishing quantum of damages, however, is more complex and its intricacies are thoroughly dealt with in the sister volume to this book, *Personal Injury Schedules, Calculating Damages* (2nd edn). The first part of this chapter sets out a brief working summary on both liability and quantum.

LIABILITY

The evidence on liability in fatal cases is gathered in much the same way as in an ordinary case. The difference is that there is usually no evidence from the victim. In some cases, such as those where the victim had a disease, he may have consulted the solicitor prior to death. If so, notice will need to be served stating that the deceased's statement or proof is to be relied upon as hearsay evidence (Civil Evidence Act 1995).[1] This emphasises the vital importance of preparing a full and adequate proof of evidence at the outset of every case and getting the client to correct, date and sign it.

There is often one additional important source of evidence in fatal cases and that is an inquest. Where an inquest is held, the solicitor or counsel should attend, having given notice to the coroner's officer, both to take the fullest possible note of evidence and to ensure that, as far as possible, questions helpful to the claim are asked. After the inquest, the coroner's notes should be obtained, as should copies of all statements and photographs. The ground should be laid for obtaining these by personal introduction to the coroner's officer at the inquest. The costs of the inquest will be recoverable if the civil action which follows is successful.[2]

Other causes of action should be considered. For instance, the survivors may have personal causes of action because they were passengers in the car, or perhaps because they sustained psychological shock and injury by seeing or learning of the deceased's

---

[1]   However, for proceedings commenced prior to 31 January 1996 (ie the date of commencement of the 1995 Act), notice will have to be served to admit the statement as evidence (Civil Evidence Act 1968).
[2]   *Stewart v Medway NHS Trust* (6 April 2004, unreported), Supreme Courts Costs Office, Master O'Hare.

injuries and death, under the principle in *McLoughlin v O'Brian.*[3] Such personal injury claims can be combined with those for the fatal accident claim. The form of pleading a fatal case is exemplified at Appendix C.

Contributory negligence, of course, applies to fatal cases just as to others,[4] so does the possibility of obtaining interim payments.[5] In cases where children are likely to be the beneficiaries, any settlement must be approved by a Master or the judge.

In a fatal accident case, the victim's family may require a great deal of care and attention because of the trauma of their loss. In these cases, even more than the ordinary personal injury case, the solicitor must keep in close touch throughout the conduct of the litigation.

DAMAGES

For deaths occurring after 1 January 1983, there are two kinds of claim: under the Law Reform (Miscellaneous Provisions) Act 1934, and under the Fatal Accidents Act 1976 (both as amended). Claims in respect of deaths prior to 1 January 1983 are not considered in this book.

Law Reform Act

Under the Law Reform (Miscellaneous Provisions) Act 1934, the deceased's estate inherits the deceased's right to sue in respect of the cause of death. In effect, it is the equivalent of a personal injury claim seeking to recover damages sustained by the deceased between the time of his accident and his death. If death was instantaneous or virtually instantaneous, there will probably be no claim by the estate under the Act. Any recovery under the Law Reform Act which duplicates a head of recovery in respect of the same beneficiary under the Fatal Accidents Act 1976 is deducted from it.

Usually the litigation is commenced, after death, by the administrator or executor on behalf of the estate. If the litigation was commenced by a client who dies, it is an easy matter to amend the statement of case to substitute those acting on behalf of the estate as Claimants in place of the deceased.[6] In order to conduct the litigation on behalf of the estate, the executors must obtain probate in the usual way and administrators must obtain letters of administration. The essential facts relating to these matters must be expressly stated in the claim form and ancillary documents.

There are four heads of claim under the Law Reform Act.

First, special damages, ie loss of earnings of the deceased and damage and loss to property occurring from the date of the cause of action until the date of death, but not future loss of earnings. Such damages are subject to a deduction in respect of

3   [1983] 1 AC 410.
4   Law Reform (Contributory Negligence) Act 1945, s 1(1) and the Fatal Accidents Act (FAA) 1976, s 5.
5   The affidavit in support must give the statutory particulars required by the FAA 1976, s 2(4).
6   The personal representatives should usually make a without notice application to the Master or District Judge for an order to continue the litigation.

any joint living expenses of the deceased.[7] Other typical items will be costs of care, medical expenses and travel expenses. The cost of obtaining letters of administration or probate can be claimed.

Secondly, pain, suffering and loss of amenity sustained by the deceased between the date of the cause of action and death. In the case of immediate death or immediate loss of consciousness followed by death, there will be no or negligible[8] recovery under this head. In some accident cases, the period of suffering prior to death may be relatively short. In disease cases, there may be months or years of increasing incapacity or ill health prior to death.

Thirdly, damages for the deceased's awareness, if any, that his life has been shortened and his knowledge to the effect on his family.

The final head of damages is for funeral expenses which can also be brought under the Fatal Accidents Act 1976.

Fatal Accidents Act 1976

Under the Fatal Accidents Act, the claim is brought by the dependants of the deceased for loss of support. Only one action can be brought for all the dependants (s 2) and a solicitor acting for the Claimant/dependant has a duty to ensure that all potential Claimants are joined into the action, otherwise they are shut out for ever.[9] The dependants are:

(i)   wife or husband or former wife or husband;
(ii)   civil partner of the deceased;
(iii) any person living with the deceased in the same household for at least two years before that date and was living with the deceased as the husband or wife or civil partner of the deceased. With regard to this provision, a distinction is drawn between wanting and intending to live in the same household and actually doing so. Mere sharing of shopping expenses is not enough;[10]
(iv)   any parent of the deceased;
(v)   any person who was treated by the deceased as a parent;
(vi)   any child or other descendant of the deceased;
(vii) any person who was treated by the deceased as a child of the family;
(viii) any person who is the issue of a brother, sister, uncle or aunt of the deceased.

A child born after the death, but *en ventre sa mere* at the time of injury which caused the death is a dependent,[11] but a stillborn baby is not included.

The claim under the Fatal Accidents Act is for the following three heads: first, there is the value of the financial and/or services dependency (see below), secondly, there are the funeral expenses and, thirdly, damages are recoverable in respect of bereavement sustained by a surviving spouse, the parents of a legitimate child or the

---

7   *Phipps v Brooks Dry Cleaning Services Ltd* [1996] PIQR Q100.
8   In *Davies v Hawes, Kemp & Kemp*, vol 3, M2B032, Ogden J awarded £750 for pain and suffering when the deceased did not regain consciousness between the accident and death.
9   *Avery v London and NE Rly Co* [1938] AC 606.
10 *Kotke v Saffarini* [2005] 2 FLR 517.
11 *The George v Richard* (1871) LR 3 A & E 466.

mother of an illegitimate child. Bereavement is assessed at £7,500 for causes of action accruing before 1 April 2002 and £10,000 to 31 December 2007.[12] From 1 January 2008, the sum has been increased to £11,800.[13] Bereavement damages are recoverable for the death of each child under 18 years at the time of death.[14] If there is more than one bereaved, the sum is shared. It is arguable that interest at the higher special damages rate is payable on bereavement damages.[15]

One further head of loss which has now become standard, even though it is a backdoor bereavement award, is the claim for the loss of a particular care and affection of a spouse or parent. Typically, it is awarded for the children or husband for loss of the services of a wife or mother. Awards tend to vary between £3,500 to £5,000.[16]

DEPENDENCY

The dependency in a Fatal Accidents Act case consists of past loss from the date of death to trial and future loss from the date of trial onwards. It is assessed mathematically by establishing a multiplicand and a multiplier, as in an ordinary personal injury case (see Chapter 21). The principles specific to fatal accidents are set out below.

Multiplicands

Financial dependency

The multiplicand is the annual value of the dependency. Nowadays, this is generally assessed in the ordinary case as two-thirds of annual net income for a deceased breadwinner leaving a spouse and no children and as three-quarters for a deceased leaving a spouse and two children.[17] Wage increases between the time of death and trial should be taken into account, together with promotional prospects. The annual income can include state benefits which are lost.[18] Credit is given for any residual earning capacity on the part of the survivor. For instance, where both a husband and wife with no children were earning at the time of death, the formula would be:

[Deceased husband's salary + surviving wife's salary] x 2/3 less wife's salary.[19]

If both spouses were earning and there were children, the formula would be adjusted as follows:

[Deceased husband's salary + surviving wife's salary] x 75% less wife's salary.

---

[12] Damages for Bereavement (Variation of Sum) (England and Wales) Orders 1990 and 2002.
[13] Damages for Bereavement (Variation of Sum) (England and Wales) Order 2007.
[14] *Doleman v Deakin* (1990) Times, 30 January, [1990] 13 LS Gaz 43.
[15] *Khan v Duncan* (19 March 1989, unreported), Popplewell J.
[16] *Bordin v St Mary's NHS Trust* [2000] Lloyd's Rep Med 287; *H v S* [2003] QB 965.
[17] *Harris v Empress Motors Ltd* [1984] 1 WLR 212 at 216. The courts will do so in an appropriate case, such as a high earning individual who would have spent more on himself or a young childless widow: *Owen v Martin* [1992] PIQR Q151.
[18] *Cox v Hockenhull* [2000] 1 WLR 750.
[19] *Coward v Comex Houlder Diving* (unreported).

However, these proportions can be and are varied in particular cases displaying particular features, and the Claimant's lawyers should be alert to exploit variations from these usual situations which may allow a higher proportion of dependency. Another method of checking the value of the dependency is to take the deceased's annual income and deduct from it the 'living expenses' spent exclusively on his/her own maintenance. However, this latter and more detailed approach is rarely adopted or favoured by the courts.

Services dependency

The value of the dependency may be greater than the loss of the relevant proportion of the deceased's annual income,[20] since the deceased may have provided services. These services may include DIY maintenance of the home, maintenance of the car, maintenance of the garden, produce from an allotment, child care, domestic cleaning and so on. The loss of these services needs to be valued commercially for the future, even though some or all may have been provided voluntarily by neighbours or relatives up to trial. Particular consideration should be given to cases involving the loss of a child's mother. The fact that a substitute is found is irrelevant.[21] Any benefits accrued because of the death are disregarded under the Fatal Accidents Act 1976, s 4. Furthermore, the prospects of re-marriage (rather than separation or divorce) are ignored. The consideration of these costs is similar to that in a non-fatal case.

These various heads of loss, expressed as multiplicands, each require application of an appropriate multiplier.

Multipliers[22]

The multiplier is assessed from the date of death, rather than from the date of trial (thus being different from the ordinary personal injury case).[23] The number of pre-trial years for which special damages are awarded should then be deducted to produce the multiplier for future loss. Damages recoverable for loss attributable to the period between death and trial will bear interest, whereas damages attributable to future loss will not. The approach to multipliers (apart from the fact that they are taken from the date of death rather than the date of accident) is much the same as in a non-fatal case.[24]

The multiplier for loss of earnings is usually taken to reflect the deceased's likely years of earning up until the anticipated date of retirement. However, the possibility of further earnings after the date of retirement should be considered, particularly for a deceased who had a job with an early retirement age or a deceased who was fit and had skills easily exercisable after retirement.

---

[20]   The income may arise entirely from state benefits. What matters is what the Claimant has lost as a result of the deceased's death, not the source of the income: see *Cox v Hockenhull* [1999] 3 All ER 577.
[21]   See *R v CICB, ex p Kavanagh* [1998] 2 FLR 1071.
[22]   See *Corbett v Barking Health Authority* [1991] 2 QB 408.
[23]   *White v ESAB Group (UK) Ltd* [2002] PIQR Q76.
[24]   NB, following *Wells v Wells* [1999] 1 AC 345, the multiplier is assessed on the basis of a 3% pa return.

A loss or diminution of pension by reason of the accident or ill health, which would have been sustained after retirement by a deceased who died prior to retirement, is recoverable, though the calculation is usually not easy.

The multipliers for the various services provided by the deceased may each have different figures to reflect the fact that the deceased would have been likely to have ceased providing them at different points in his life. Precise instructions should be taken about each of these matters to establish the deceased's plans and abilities prior to death.

All these losses necessarily relate to the deceased's age at death. The deceased's life expectancy is the base factor from which each multiplier is established.

The great difficulty in making predictions for the very young or those who had not established themselves in a trade, profession or education is exacerbated because the victim is dead. In such cases, evidence should be sought from school teachers, relatives, employers, authoritative friends (such as religious leaders, scout masters, etc) and others who may give worthwhile predictive evidence based on their knowledge of the deceased.

Calculations of future loss of earnings cannot take into account increases in earnings because of inflation,[25] but the claim can and should take into account likely increases in real income attributable to promotion or advancement.[26] Again, this is made more difficult by the absence of evidence from the deceased. Therefore, investigations should be made of evidence likely to demonstrate that the deceased would have been promoted at various stages. Having established the overall multiplier for lost income, the multiplier can then be divided into separate periods with a separate multiplicand for each, to reflect increased earnings by reason of promotion for each period within the overall multiplier.

Just as different multipliers are taken for different losses sustained by the dependants, so too different multipliers may be applied where the dependency may change over the years. If the deceased was single at the time of death, but was likely to have married and had children, then a reasonable estimate should be made of the dates of those events. Likewise any prospect of divorce should be considered.[27] The overall multiplier should be divided accordingly and applied to the differing rates of dependency throughout those differing periods within the overall multiplier. Likewise, for example, if the dependant is likely to leave home and get a job, the multiplier for that dependant may be reduced to that time scale.

DEDUCTIONS AND APPORTIONMENT

From the losses sustainable under both the Law Reform Act and the Fatal Accidents Act, no deductions are to be made for money which has accrued, or will or may accrue, to any person from his estate as a result of death.[28] Therefore, any beneficial

[25]   *Lim Poh Choo v Camden and Islington Area Health Authority* [1980] AC 174.
[26]   *Malone v Rowan* [1984] 3 All ER 402.
[27]   *Martin v Owen* (1992) Times, 21 May; *Dalziel v Donald* (20 October 2000, unreported).
[28]   Administration of Justice Act 1982, s 2.

pensions or insurance money received as a consequence of the death are not deductible,[29] nor are non-financial benefits such as services provided.[30]

Where an award is made to a surviving adult and to children, it must be apportioned. There are no rules of apportionment except that most of the damages is generally paid to the surviving parent. This is done on the basis that the parent will use it to look after the children, and little is given to each of the children, though the younger will be given more than the elder because their expectation of life is greater. A worked example of a fatal accident schedule of damages is given at Appendix C to demonstrate some of these principles.

---

[29] Fatal Accidents Act 1976, s 4; *Wood v Bentall Simplex Ltd* [1992] PIQR P332; and *Stanley v Saddique* [1992] 1 QB 1 at 10.
[30] *Stanley v Saddique* [1992] 1 QB 1.

CHAPTER 29

Claimants Under a Legal Disability

People who do not have full legal capacity include all young people under the age of 18 (children) or protected parties. A person is a protected party if he lacks capacity to conduct proceedings within the meaning of the Mental Capacity Act 2005. The Act came into force on 1 October 2007 and the Act's new definition of capacity is in line with existing common law tests and does not replace them.[1]

The Act is accompanied by a Code of Practice. At para 4.4, it states:

'An assessment of a person's capacity must be based on their ability to make a specific decision at the time it needs to be made, and not on their ability to make decisions in general.'

The Act adopts the former common law position under s 1. It provides that:

'(2) A person must be assumed to have capacity unless it is established that he lacks capacity.

(3) A person is not to be treated as unable to make a decision unless all practicable steps to help him to do so have been taken without success.

(4) A person is not to be treated as unable to make a decision merely because he makes an unwise decision.

(5) An act done, or decision made, under this Act for or on a person who lacks capacity must be done or made in his best interests.

(6) Before the act is done, or the decision is made, regard must be had to whether the purpose for which it is needed can be as effectively achieved in a way that is less restrictive of the person's rights and freedom of action.'

In going on to define whether a person lacks capacity, in s 2 of the Act, it states:

'(1) For the purposes of this Act, a person lacks capacity in relation to a matter if at the material time he is unable to make a decision for himself in relation to the matter because of an impairment of, or a disturbance in the functioning of, the mind or brain.

---

[1]   Paragraph 4.33 of the Code of Practice made under the Act.

(2) It does not matter whether the impairment or disturbance is permanent or temporary.'

The issue is determined on the balance of probabilities. Under s 3, a person is deemed unable to make a decision for himself if he is unable:

'(1) (a) To understand the information relevant to the decision, (b) to retain that information, (c) to use or weigh that information as part of the process of making the decision, or (d) to communicate his decision (whether by talking, using sign language or any other means).

(2) A person is not to be regarded as unable to understand the information relevant to a decision if he is able to understand an explanation of it given to him in a way that is appropriate to his circumstances.

(3) The fact that a person is able to retain the information relevant to a decision for a short period only does not prevent him from being regarded as able to make the decision.

(4) The information relevant to a decision includes information about the reasonably foreseeable consequences of (a) deciding one way or another, or (b) failing to make a decision.'

In determining whether a person is a protected party within the 2005 Act, a judge must be satisfied that an incapacity exists and needs to see medical reports to that effect as the statutory assumption of capacity can only be displaced by evidence proving to the contrary. Nevertheless, whilst a judge will undoubtedly be guided by medical opinion, generally from a psychiatrist, it is for the court to determine the issue. This cannot be overemphasised, as a person treated as a protected party is deprived of the right to sue or defend in his own name and his right to compromise litigation on his own behalf is withdrawn. The fact that an individual may not understand how best to invest their money in the open market does not render them a protected party. This is an important principle based on the idea that a person should not be deprived of autonomy unless that course is necessary. Autonomy includes the right to make unwise decisions. If a person was under a disability on the day that the right of action accrued, then time does not begin to run and the person can bring proceedings up to three years (in a personal injury action) from the date when he ceases to be under a disability.[2]

The rules relating to children and patients can be found in CPR Part 21 and its associated Children and Protected Parties practice direction. Proceedings may not be brought by persons under a legal disability except under the aegis of their 'litigation friend'. This is usually the person's parent, but may be any adult willing to act or, in the case of a protected party, a deputy appointed by the Court of Protection under the 2005 Act. Any step taken before a child or protected person has a litigation friend has no effect unless the court orders otherwise (rule 21.3(4)). Rule 21.4(3) imposes on the litigation friend the duty fairly and competently to conduct proceedings on behalf of a child or patient. He must have no interest in the proceedings adverse to that of the child or patient and all steps and the decisions he

---

[2]   Limitation Act 1980, s 28(1) and *Turner v Malcolm* (1992) 15 BMLR 40, 136 Sol Jo LB 236, CA, where it was decided that a brain-injured plaintiff could not have his writ struck out for delay. See also *Headford v Bristol and District Health Authority* [1995] PIQR P180.

takes in the proceedings must be taken for the benefit of the child or patient. Further, where they are acting on behalf of Claimants, they must undertake to pay any costs which the child or protected party may be ordered to pay in relation to the proceedings, subject to any right he may have to be repaid from the assets of the child or protected party. The court retains the power to terminate the litigation friend's appointment and appoint a new one in substitution (rule 21.7). For instance, this might arise if the litigation friend was not acting in the best interests of the child. If no other party were suitable, the court may seek assistance from the Official Solicitor.

After the appointment of a litigation friend, the title of the proceedings becomes 'AB (a child by CD, his litigation friend)'. If the child is conducting proceedings on his own behalf, he should be referred to as 'AB (a child)'. A protected party is named in the title of the proceedings as 'AB (a protected party by CD, his litigation friend)'.

It is possible for the court to make an order that a child conduct proceedings on its own behalf (rule 21.2(3)), but it is most unlikely that the court would make such an order in a personal injury claim for damages, even if the child was approaching the age of majority. However, once the child reaches age 18, by operation of rule 21.9(1), the appointment of a litigation friend ceases. By way of contrast, a court order is needed to cease the appointment when a party ceases to be a protected party.

The litigation friend may be appointed without court order or by order of the court and his appointment can be substituted or terminated by an order of the court. If proceedings have been commenced and the Claimant becomes a patient, an application must be made by a solicitor to the court for the appointment of a person to be the litigation friend.

The object of having a litigation friend is not only to ensure that decisions are made in the proceedings by somebody with competence, but also to give security for the costs to the Defendant, subject to any right the latter may have to be repaid from the assets of the child or patient.

Legal Services Funding is presently available for children whose own resources and income are assessed, rather than that of their parents.[3] Legal Services Funding is presently available for patients in the same way as for all other adults and the certificate is granted to the patient by way of the litigation friend.

PRINCIPLES

Issuing proceedings

When appointed without court order, the litigation friend must file a 'certificate of suitability' in form N235. This confirms that (as required by rule 21.4(3)) the litigation friend considers himself suitable and confirms that he knows the child is a child or the protected party is a protected party (PD 2.2). In the case of a protected party, the litigation friend must state the grounds of his belief that the Claimant is a protected party, referring to any medical opinion if necessary. The litigation friend must state that he can fairly and competently conduct proceedings and has no adverse interest

---

[3] Civil Legal Aid (Assessment of Resources) (Amendment) Regulations 1990, reg 4(2).

to the Claimant, and the litigation friend must confirm that he will pay any costs ordered against the child or protected party. The certificate must be filed, together with a certificate of service of it, when the claim form is issued. The certificate must also be served, together with supporting medical opinion, on the person in whose care the child or protected party resides – if that person is not the litigation friend (PD 2.4). There is a provision that an objection can be made to the appointment of the litigation friend (rule 21.7 and PD 4).

A deputy appointed by the Court of Protection under the 2005 Act on behalf of a protected party must file an official copy of the order.

When a litigation friend is appointed by court order (for example, when proceedings are issued and the Claimant becomes a protected party), the court must be satisfied (rule 21.6, PD 3) that the proposal complies with the criteria set out above. Where the application is made on behalf of the Official Solicitor a provision must be made for the payment of his charges.

When a child reaches the age of 18 or a protected party recovers (rule 21.9 and PD 4), he must serve on the other parties to the proceedings, and file with the court a notice stating he has reached full age or has recovered (the latter supported by a medical report)[4] stating that the litigation friend's appointment has ceased, giving an address for service and stating whether or not he intends to carry on with his claim. If he intends to carry on, then the proceedings will be amended to show, in the case of a child[5] say 'AB (formerly a child but now of full age)'. If the litigation friend does not want to continue to act, he must file a notice saying so. If he does not, then he remains liable for the costs until the notice is filed.

In practice, if the litigation friend does not want to act, or there is no person to act, application should be made to the Official Solicitor to fulfil the role.

Statutory limitations

One important feature in a child's case is that the statutory limitation period begins only when the child reaches the age of 18. For example, a child who has an accident on its 11th birthday has ten years from that date within which to commence proceedings. The limitation period for a protected party is also extended until recovery.[6]

Service

Special provisions apply for service of documents on children and protected parties (CPR, r 6.6). Unless the court orders to the contrary, service of the claim form on a child who is not also a protected party will be on one of the child's parents or guardians or, if there is none, the person with whom the child resides. For a protected party, service is on the person authorised to have conduct of proceedings in the name of

---

4   If the patient's affairs were under the control of the Court of Protection, a copy of the order discharging the receiver.
5   There is no equivalent for a former patient.
6   Limitation Act 1980, s 28.

the protected party or an adult with whom the protected party resides or in whose care he is. Other documents are served on the litigation friend.

Default judgments

A default judgment can only be made on an application (ie not as an administrative act) when the action is against a child or protected party (rule 12.10).

Interim payments

No interim payment should be accepted or used on behalf of a child or protected party without the consent and approval of the court (rule 21.10).

Part 36 payments into court

Leave is required to accept a payment into court if the Claimant is under a disability, otherwise it will not be valid.

Settlements

No child's or patient's case, no matter how small, may be settled without the authority of a court order (rule 21.10 and PD 5). This applies whether the child or protected party is the Claimant or Defendant. In the absence of court approval, the settlement will not be binding on the child or protected party. Application is made by the Part 8 procedure if proceedings have not yet begun and the claim must include the terms of settlement attached in a draft consent order (form N292), details of whether liability is admitted or not, the age of the child/protected party, the litigation friend's approval and a copy of any financial advice relating to the proposed settlement. Medical reports and schedules should be served. In all but the clearest case, counsel's opinion on the merits of the settlement or compromise must be obtained (PD 5.2).

Where the settlement is in respect of a protected party and is less than £30,000, it may be retained in court and invested in the same way as the fund of a child. However, where it exceeds £30,000, unless a person with authority as the attorney under a registered enduring power of attorney/lasting power of attorney or deputy appointed by the Court of Protection has been appointed to administer or manage the fund, the order approving the settlement will contain a direction to the litigation friend to apply to the Court of Protection for the appointment of a deputy and the fund will thereafter be dealt with as directed by the Court of Protection (PD.10(2)). Settlement or compromise applications are normally heard by a Master in the High Court or District Judge. However, where there is a large complex claim, it is likely that the matter will continue to be reserved to a judge.

Practice and procedure

In the High Court, applications for approval of settlement are made to Masters and appointments are made in their own private rooms. If the application is to a judge, the matter is heard in chambers. The procedure is paralleled in the county court. If the claim is a simple one and the evidence is very clear, counsel's opinion is not needed (21 PD, para 5.2 (1)). In reality, such opinion should not be dispensed with if the settlement is over £1,000.

At the settlement hearing, the Claimant's solicitor should have the summons, a copy of CFO form 320 completed on the first side, a copy of the infant's birth certificate, any pleadings, if liability is disputed, evidence relating to liability, medical reports, the schedule of damages and supporting documentation, consent of the litigation friend and the approval of the settlement by the litigation friend.

If liability is in dispute, the court must be told the extent to which this can be established by evidence. Where counsel has advised, the opinion should be shown to the Master (but not the other side), as should relevant police reports, memoranda of convictions, accident reports, witness statements and so on, ie all the available material to establish liability (see above).

When considering quantum, the court should be shown the medical evidence (which should be up to date, as if at trial) dealing with pain, suffering and loss of amenity. Infant Claimants or patients usually need not attend, but if cosmetic injuries are sustained or if the case is complex, the Master may require their attendance. The litigation friend should attend.

The test to be satisfied in order for the court to give its approval to a settlement for a child or patient is not set out in the CPR or practice direction, but may be assumed to be (as in the past) whether the settlement is a reasonable one and for the benefit of the infant or protected party, having regard to all the circumstances of the case. If the court is not satisfied, the application may be adjourned to give the parties further opportunity to negotiate.

If the settlement is approved, the order will direct by and to whom and in what amounts the money is to be paid and how the money is to be applied or otherwise dealt with (rule 21.11 and PD 9 and 10). The procedure should have been explained to the litigation friend in advance.

Payment out (PD 11) of moneys in court should be sought for expenditure incurred properly by the litigation friend. The Claimant's money will be invested until he is old enough or becomes capable of managing his own affairs (as the case may be) save for necessary expenditure to sustain the Claimant whilst under a disability. The approval of settlement is an appropriate moment to ask for payment out for any immediate expenses for the Claimant such as for an educational course, or a bicycle for the child.

Where an award for damages is made after a trial, the trial judge will direct the money to be paid into court and placed into the special investment account until further investment directions have been given and direct the litigation friend to make an application to a Master or District Judge for further investment directions with a fixed date within 28 days of the date of the trial (PD 9.3). The application is made by filing with the court a completed CFO form 320 and any evidence which the litigation friend wishes the court to consider in relation to investment of the sums. In the High Court, such application is sent to Room E16 (Masters' Support Unit). If the sum is very small, the court may order the sum to be paid direct to the litigation friend to be put into a building society account for the child's use rather than into court (PD 9.7).

Where money is to be transferred to the Court of Protection (PD 10), then a CFO 200 form must be completed. If the Claimant has Legal Services Funding, then the relevant undertaking in respect of the statutory charge must be filed with the Legal Services Commission who will then advise the Court Funds Office of the sum enabling them to transfer the balance to the Court of Protection. Where the settlement is in the High Court, form CFO 200 is completed and presented for authorisation on behalf of a child in the Masters' Support Unit, Room E16 and in the case of a protected party, in the Judgment and Orders Section in the Action Department, Room E17. The money will be available for the infant to take out at the age of 18 or for the patient when s/he is no longer subject to disability.

The litigation friend must be told clearly and in writing what exactly will happen to the money once it is invested. When the money remains in court (either for a child or patient) then the litigation friend should apply to the Master or District Judge when payments are needed out of the fund. When the child reaches 18 years old, he should apply directly to the court for payment out to him (PD 105).

COSTS

In cases where the settlement is approved by a Master, the usual order is to direct costs to be assessed on the standard basis, with the Claimant's solicitor waiving any further costs. In more complicated cases, the Defendant may agree or be ordered to pay on an indemnity basis.

The litigation friend is liable to pay costs of an unsuccessful application or an unnecessary, frivolous or vexatious one. Where an order for costs is made against a litigation friend of a publicly-funded child or protected party, the latter has the benefit of the Legal Aid Act 1988, s 17(1). The costs ordered will not exceed the amount which is reasonable, having regard to the resources of the parties and their conduct. The means of the litigation friend are deemed to be the means of the infant or protected party.[7]

---

[7]   Civil Legal Aid (General) Regulations 1989, reg 133.

CHAPTER 30

Disease Cases

There is no fundamental difference between a personal injury case which results in a traumatic injury and one which results in a disease. However, many diseases are the result of prolonged exposure to some hazard. Such prolonged exposure is usually found in the work environment, but more and more cases are being taken on behalf of clients made ill by their living environment which has been polluted by some nearby enterprise.

Where the disease is the result of momentary exposure, the case is really no different to run than an ordinary accident case, except that specialised expertise may need to be brought in to prove causation, if there is room for doubt as to the nature of the disease and its attribution to the incident. See Chapter 16 on pleading disease cases.

PROLONGED EXPOSURE

The real problems in disease work arise in prolonged exposure cases. This is usually found in the industrial context. Such cases are complicated and should not be undertaken lightly by an inexperienced practitioner. Evidence to support the Claimant about the conditions which it is alleged gave rise to the illness many years before may be difficult to obtain. The system of work which involved the causative exposure may have been commonplace at the time. There may be problems over limitation with arguments over the 'date of knowledge', and the court's discretion under the Limitation Act 1980, s 33 may have to be relied on. Causation may be difficult where the client is an employee who worked for a number of employers in the same trade and was exposed by each to the factors giving rise to the disease, or if a number of factors apart from the work (or other) environment may arguably be causative of the disease or of its symptoms (for example, lung disease to which smoking may have contributed).

Experts are needed to demonstrate what a reasonable employer would have considered to be a safe system of work at the various periods of exposure and to establish the level of knowledge of a hazard arising from the system which was available to the employer (or polluter) at the various periods. Expert medical evidence is required to show that the disease was caused by the exposure. Some diseases are notoriously difficult to demonstrate in a living patient, particularly where the condition may be overlaid by other conditions (for example, asbestosis or pneumoconiosis, particularly if overlaid by emphysema). One client complaining of a progressive disease caused by exposure to some hazard often indicates that there may be other victims and the solicitor should investigate this.

A detailed examination of this subject is beyond the scope of this book, but examples of such diseases are: leukaemia from living near nuclear installations; heavy metal poisoning from eating fish or drinking water polluted by escapes from toxic waste treatment plants or dumps; noise-induced deafness from working near machines; asthma and welder's lung from welding operations; pneumoconiosis from mining in silica-bearing rocks or working in iron and steel foundries which use silica sand for mouldings; work-related upper limb disorders in journalists, secretaries and other operators of word processors and in chicken trussers; dermatitis in woodworkers and others; headaches and constipation in workers with solvents; vibration white finger in workers with vibrating tools such as drills and grinders; asbestosis and mesothelioma in laggers and building workers.

COLLECTING EVIDENCE

It is essential to draw on the huge body of knowledge and expertise which has been built up on many industrial diseases, the processes which give rise to them, and the means by which their incidence can be avoided or minimised. Contact may be made with the Association of Personal Injury Lawyers (see Useful Addresses) as well as Hazards and the HSE. The medical profession, of course, is a repository for much knowledge and a useful starting place is *Hunter's Diseases of Occupations*,[1] and the library of the Royal Society of Medicine (for members). Appropriate expert witnesses will be essential.

The first step is to establish a full history of the client's exposure to the causative hazard. There must be a complete chronology of his working history, showing the nature of the work, the place of work, the name and address of the employer(s), the names and addresses of any potential witnesses, and a full description of the work undertaken by the Claimant and others. The chemicals, dust, fumes and processes giving rise to the hazard must be described in detail. The duration and intensity of exposure must be examined. The manufacturer of machines and substances should be identified as far as possible.

All warnings given by all possible Defendants and all instructions, advice and information must be fully particularised, the giver of each identified and the absence of such warnings and information noted. The presence or absence of pre-exposure tests for susceptibility must be investigated. Demonstrations, training, or other guidance on how to perform the work safely must be considered. All possible forms of protection, by containing the hazard and/or the plaintiff, need to be investigated. After advice from experts, this is one area which is likely to require further investigation when the solicitor is fully appraised of the safety measures available to

---

[1]   (9th edn, 2000) Arnold.

a reasonable Defendant in the various periods of exposure. The attitude of the Defendant to health and safety matters should be dealt with in detail. All relevant complaints must be logged and complainants identified. All previous occurrences of contraction of the disease must likewise be explored. General practitioner and hospital records for the client must be obtained and his consent for this given immediately. All available literature must be gathered by the solicitor, particularly from the Health and Safety Executive.

Disclosure in such cases must be pursued rigorously. This concerns not only substances, machines and systems, but also the Defendant's potential sources of prior knowledge. Records should be obtained from the Department of Health and discovery sought from the Health and Safety Executive. The relevant experts, both on the conditions giving rise to the contraction of the disease and on the disease in the plaintiff, must be instructed early and their advice sought on other steps and investigations which the solicitor should carry out. There will often be major battles over the Defendant's 'date of knowledge', ie the date from which a reasonable Defendant in the position of the Defendant, would have known of the risk, and the date such an employer would have taken precautions. This may be tried as a preliminary issue.

In recent years, multi-party litigation on behalf of large groups of employees of the same employer have led to the establishment of sophisticated 'handling arrangements' for assessing Claimants and paying out on a fixed tariff. The schemes apply to the workers (and former workers) in particular industries who have contracted particular diseases. It is necessary to prove only the existence of the disease or disability. Some schemes include a loss of earnings element, others are restricted to a one-off lump sum. There is, for example, a chest diseases scheme and also a vibration white finger scheme for former mine workers. There are deafness schemes for those who worked in the engineering and shipbuilding industries and for railway guards and shunters. Solicitors concerned with industrial diseases need to be familiar with these handling arrangement schemes (which are outside the scope of this book). They must weigh up with the client whether, bearing in mind the level of disability, the strength of the case on causation, and the prospects of proving negligence or breach of statutory duty, it is more beneficial to claim under the relevant scheme or pursue a claim for damages (if such is possible – many handling arrangements schemes involve a practice direction on court orders staying similar actions outside the scheme).

PRE-ACTION PROTOCOL FOR ILLNESS AND DISEASE CASES

A separate protocol covers all personal injury claims where the injury is not the result of an accident, but takes the form of an illness or disease. It acknowledges that such claims are generally not suitable for fast track procedures even though the value of the claim is under £15,000. It extends beyond disease cases in the workplace to cover exposure through the occupation of premises or the use of products.

The protocol recognises that, in appropriate cases, the potential Claimant may obtain occupational records, including health records and personnel records, before sending a letter of claim. A suggested wording is appended at Annex A1 to the protocol. The records should be provided within a maximum of 40 days of the request at no cost. If the potential Defendant has difficulty in providing within that time, details should be given of what is being done to resolve it with a reasonable time limit for so doing. If it fails to do so, the potential Claimant may apply for pre-action disclosure, with provision for costs sanctions for unreasonable delay.

Where a decision is made to make a claim, two copies of a letter of claim should be sent with sufficient information to substantiate a realistic claim. One copy is for the Defendant and one to be passed on to the insurers. The letter must contain a clear summary of the facts on which the claim is based including details of the illness alleged and the main allegations of fault. It should give details of the condition and prognosis and financial loss in outline form. Notification of the funding arrangement should be given if the claim is being pursued under a CFA. The standard format of the letter of claim is set out in Annex B to the protocol. The letter of claim should contain a chronology of relevant events and identify any relevant documents. It should also state whether a claim is being made against any other potential Defendant.

The Defendant should send an acknowledgment of the letter of claim within 21 calendar days of the date of posting of the letter of claim identifying the insurer (if any) who will be dealing with the claim. Otherwise, the Claimant will be entitled to issue proceedings. Once an acknowledgment is sent, the Defendant has three months from that time to provide a reasoned answer to the claim. If it is not practical to do so within that time, it should indicate the difficulties and outline the further time needed. If reasonable justification is given, an extension should be granted.

On the issue of experts, the protocol specifically recognises that, in disease cases, opinions will be needed from experts on knowledge, fault, causation, condition and prognosis and that it may be unrealistic for such reports to be obtained jointly. In particular, in many cases, the Claimant may need to obtain such evidence before service of the letter of claim.

Prior to issue of proceedings, the protocol states that it will be usual for all parties to disclose those expert reports relating to liability and causation upon which they propose to rely and the Claimant should delay issuing for 21 days from disclosure to enable settlement if possible.

If, due to the imminent expiry of limitation, the Claimant has to issue before the protocol has been complied with, the court should consider whether to order a stay to enable compliance with the protocol.

MESOTHELIOMA CASES

Special procedural provisions now apply to mesothelioma cases by virtue of the practice direction supplementing CPR, r 3.1. In such cases, the claim form and every statement of case must be marked with the title 'living mesothelioma claim' or 'fatal mesothelioma claim'. Any practitioner dealing with such a case will need to make specific reference to such a claim which provides different urgent procedures for dealing with cases where Claimants have a severely limited life expectancy. It also imposes a specific show cause procedure in which the Defendant must identify the evidence and legal arguments that give the Defendant a real prospect of success on any or all issues of liability. In particular, at the first case management conference, unless there is good reason not to, the Defendant must show cause as to why a judgment on liability should not be made and a standard interim payment on account of damages, costs and disbursements should not be made (Annex A to rule 3.1, para 6.1).

CHAPTER 31

Claims for Injury Caused by Stress at Work

Since 1994 and the case of *Walker v Northumberland County Council*,[1] claims for injury caused by stress at work (stress claims) have been possible. They can be distinguished from 'nervous shock' claims because they do not generally arise out of a traumatic event.

THE TYPES OF CLAIM AND EVIDENCE

Most claims cover a considerable period of time over which the Claimant criticises his or her system of work. Thus it is important to get to grips with the facts and issues that are material at an early stage. In these types of cases, particular care should be taken with the witness statement. It is an unfortunate characteristic that stress Claimants are often obsessed by what has happened to them and find it cathartic to write at length, sometimes giving their life history. It can then take considerable time and be disproportionate to the amount of costs involved to go through this evidence with the Claimant in order to sort out the real issues. It is thus important to ensure that the witness statement is taken at the first interview or soon thereafter.

Usually, after a general discussion, it is possible to sort out the essence of what the Claimant alleges to have been the breach of duty. This may be the general system of work or specific circumstances or both. Care must be taken to get sufficient details of the essence of the complaint without going into details of non-essential matters.

The essence of the case is to identify what caused the Claimant injury, whether those causes were occupational and if so, why injury ought to have been foreseeable, and whether those causes should have been prevented. The witness statement should address:
(i)   the system/incidents giving rise to the injury;
(ii) any complaints about the above and in particular complaints of injury being or likely to be caused thereby;
(iii) any periods of sickness relating to the above and in particular a description of the illness on sickness certificates;

[1]   [1995] 1 All ER 737.

(iv)   was the work generally that the Claimant was required to do known to be stressful?

(v)   was the work that the Claimant was being required to do one that had caused injury to others at the Claimant's place of work? If so, give details as in (iii) above;

(vi)   was there anything about the Claimant that ought to have put the Defendant on notice that he was at risk of sustaining psychiatric injury?

Attempts should be made at the first interview to answer all these questions. In particular, the last one. Often, a Claimant is the last person to expect to suffer injury. However, if it can be shown that the risk of injury was plain to a reasonable employer, then the Claimant satisfies the common law requirement that triggers a duty of care requiring steps to be taken to reduce the risk of injury.[2] First, breakdown cases are the most difficult cases to prove. Cogent evidence will be required. This evidence has to be objective and preferably independent. Claimants' perceptions may not always be capable of proof in practice!

The types of cases that give rise to stress claims are multifarious. The most common are that of bullying and/or harassment at work (employer/employee conflict). In appropriate circumstances, this might involve a claim to the Employment Tribunal for race, sex or disability discrimination.[3]

Bullying claims are arguably more likely to cause foreseeable injury due to the personal aspect that this type of pressure can have. It is more stressful being targeted by someone or by a group.

WHAT IS THE DIFFERENCE BETWEEN BULLYING AND HARASSMENT?

The courts have so far failed to distinguish between the type of behaviour that constitutes bullying and harassment. However, in Protection From Harassment Act 1997 cases, it is now clear that the harassment has to be of the character that is arguably criminal. It is less clear how the jurisprudence of harassment under discrimination legislation affects the position.

The questions to be determined at common law when considering whether alleged bullying or harassment (he did not differentiate) give rise to potential vicarious liability in negligence were addressed by Gray J in *Barlow v Borough of Broxbourne*.[4] His analysis is to be found at para 16 of his judgment:

'(i)   Whether the Claimant has established that the conduct complained of in the particulars of claim took place and, if so, whether it amounted to bullying or harassment in the ordinary connotation of those terms. In addressing this question, it is the cumulative effect of the conduct which has to be considered rather than the individual incidents relied on;

---

[2]   *Hatton v Sutherland* [2002] 2 All ER 1.

[3]   Since the decision in *Sherrif v Klyne Tugs (Lowestoft) Ltd* (1999) Times, 8 July, it is clear that the Employment Tribunal has jurisdiction to deal with claims for personal injury arising out of sex, race or disability discrimination.

[4]   [2003] EWHC 50, QB.

(ii) did the person or persons involved in the victimisation or bullying know or ought they reasonably to have known that their conduct might cause the Claimant harm;

(iii) would they, by the exercise of reasonable care, have taken steps which would have avoided that harm; and

(iv) were their actions so connected with their employment as to render the Defendant vicariously responsible for them.'

The direct liability of the employer for bullying or harassment of his or her employees was considered by Owen J in *Green v DB Group Services (UK) Ltd.*[5] He stated at para 10:

'(i) Did the Claimant's managers and/or members of the HR department know or ought they reasonably to have known that the Claimant was being subjected to the conduct complained of;

(ii) did they know or ought they reasonably to have known that such conduct might cause the Claimant psychiatric injury;

(iii) could they, by the exercise of reasonable care, have taken steps which would have avoided such injury.'

PROTECTION FROM HARASSMENT ACT 1997

Section 1 of the Protection From Harassment Act 1997 provides that:

'(1) A person must not pursue a course of conduct –
   (a) which amounts to harassment of another; and
   (b) which he knows or ought to know amounts to harassment of the other;
   ...

(2) For the purposes of this section, a person whose course of conduct is in question ought to know that it amounts to or involves harassment of another if a reasonable person in possession of the same information would think the course of conduct amounted to or involved harassment of the other.'

By s 3, a breach of s 1 may be the subject of a claim in civil proceedings, and on such a claim:

'... damages may be awarded for (among other things) any anxiety caused by the harassment and any financial loss resulting from the harassment.'

Section 7 provides that:

'(2) References to harassing a person including alarming the person or causing the person distress.

(3) A "course of conduct" must involve –
   (a) in the case of conduct in relation to a single person ... conduct on at least two occasions in relation to that person;
   ...

(4) Conduct includes speech.'

---

[5]   [2006] EWHC 1898, QB.

The relevant sections of the Act were the subject of the decision of the Court of Appeal in *Majrowski v Guy's & St Thomas's NHS Trust*.[6] There were two limbs to the decision, both of direct relevance. First, the Court of Appeal held that vicarious liability was not confined to common law claims and that an employer could be vicariously liable under s 3 of the Act for harassment by an employee in breach of s 1. That limb of the decision was the subject of appeal to the House of Lords[7] in which the opinions of the House were given on 12 July 2006 and the decision of the Court of Appeal was upheld.

The second limb of the decision of the Court of Appeal in *Majrowski*, which was not the subject of the appeal to the House of Lords, was directed to the meaning of 'harassment' within the Act. At para 82 of the judgment, May LJ cited the following passage from the judgment of Lord Phillips of Worth Maltravers MR in *Thomas v News Group Newspapers Ltd*:[8]

> 'The Act does not attempt to find the type of conduct which is capable of constituting harassment. "Harassment" is, however, a word which has a meaning which is generally understood. It describes conduct targeted at an individual which is calculated to produce the consequences described in s 7 and which is oppressive and unreasonable.'

May LJ then continued:

> 'Thus, in my view, although s 7(2) provides that harassing a person includes causing the person distress, the fact that a person suffers distress is not by itself enough to show that the cause of the distress was harassment. The conduct has also to be calculated, in an objective sense, to cause distress and has to be oppressive and unreasonable. It has to be conduct which the perpetrator knows or ought to know amounts to harassment, and conduct which a reasonable person would think amounted to harassment. What amounts to harassment is, as Lord Phillips said, generally understood. Such general understanding would not lead to a conclusion that all forms of conduct, however reasonable, would amount to harassment simply because they cause distress.'

The Court of Appeal has recently considered *Majrowski* and attempted to give guidance on what is harassment under the 1997 Act (*Conn v Sunderland County Council*).

To constitute harassment within the meaning of the Act, there must have been conduct:
(i)   occurring on at least two occasions;
(ii)   targeted at the Claimant;
(iii)   calculated in an objective sense to cause distress;
(iv)   which is objectively judged to be oppressive and unreasonable; and
(v)   of such gravity to justify the sanction of the criminal law.

What crosses the boundary to 'oppressive' may well depend on the circumstances. What may not be harassment in a factory may be in a hospital. The decision is arguably wrongly decided because the Court of Appeal:

---

6   [2005] QB 848.
7   [2006] UKHL 34.
8   [2002] EMLR 78 at para 30.

(a)   by concentrating upon each incident in isolation did not appear to appreciated that the Act requires an analysis of the 'course of conduct.' It is the totality of the conduct not the individual incidents that needs to be considered. Indeed so does the common law. (See the dicta of Gray J in the *Barlow* case, above)

(b)   were not referred to a decision of the Scottish Outer House which considered the same point and reached a different conclusion: *Roberton v Scottish Ministers* [2007] CSOH 186. Lord Emslie stated: '...Criminality is ...explicitly a consequence, rather than a prerequisite, of civil harassment under section 1(1)...'

(c)   were not referred to a decision of the Divisional Court: *R v DPP* (2001) Times, 20 February. This case decided that: '... words or conduct ostensibly directed to something or someone other than the person it was alleded was caused to be put in fear of violence did not, because so directed, fall outside conduct which could support a conviction.'

LEGAL DEVELOPMENTS IN STRESS AT WORK CASES

Breach of statutory duty

Management of Health and Safety at Work Regulations 1999

The Management of Health and Safety at Work and Fire Precautions (Workplace) (Amendment) Regulations 2003, SI 2003/2457 provide for civil liability for management of health and safety at work cases after 27 October 2003.

Regulation 3 requires employers to carry out a suitable and sufficient risk assessment so as to comply with other statutory duties. This includes health and safety regulations such as the Management of Health and Safety at Work Regulations 1999. Regulation 4 requires something to be done about any identified hazards.

Regulation 4 recites the general principles of prevention. These principles are new to English law. They represent a sequential approach to the provision of health and safety:

(i)   avoid risks;

(ii)   evaluate the risks which cannot be avoided;

(iii)   combat the risks at source;

(iv)   adapt the work to the individual, especially as regards the design of work places, the choice of work equipment and the choice of working and production methods, with a view, in particular, to alleviating monotonous work and work at a predetermined work rate and to reducing their effect on health;

(v)   adapt to technical progress;

(vi)   replacing the dangerous by the non-dangerous or the less dangerous;

(vii) develop a coherent overall prevention policy which covers technology, organisation of work, working conditions, social relationships and the influence of factors related to the working environment;

(viii) give collective protective measures priority over individual protective measures;

(ix)   give appropriate instructions to workers.

Relevant issues

The questions that should now be asked for all types of injury occurring after 27 October 2003 are:

(i)   what preventative steps should a suitable and sufficient risk assessment for injury (including psychological)[9] have identified prior to the date of injury?

(ii)   were these preventative steps taken?

(iii)   if not, would those steps have made any difference to the Claimant's injuries? If so, there is a causative breach of statutory duty and foreseeability is irrelevant.

Practical developments in the HSE guidance since Hatton

The literature considered by the Court of Appeal in *Hatton* dated back to 1997.

It did not contain any detailed guidance for managers as to what they should do to manage the workplace so as to avoid occupational stress, as opposed to pressure. The Health & Safety Executive ('HSE') guidance now recognises that all occupational stress should be avoided, as opposed to pressure, which can be productive.

How should stress be managed?

The HSE[10] has advised that stress should be treated like any other occupational health risk. An employer's risk assessment should include the risks of psychological as well as physical injury.

Employer's must carry out a risk assessment pursuant to the Management of Health and Safety at Work Regulations 1999, reg 3. Prior to undertaking or reviewing the risk assessment, the employer is required to carry out a systematic general examination of the effect of their undertaking, their work activities and the general condition of the premises.[11] The risk assessment is carried out to identify the risks to health and safety. It should identify how the risks arise and how they impact on those affected.[12] This requires the employer to consult extensively with the workforce to find out if stress is a problem in the workplace.[13] The approved Code of Practice requires the risk assessment to be 'suitable and sufficient'.[14] This means that employers are expected to take reasonable steps to help themselves identify risks, for example, by looking at appropriate sources of information such as relevant legislation, appropriate guidance (which includes the HSE guidance and sector-specific guidance), reading the trade press or seeking advice from competent sources.[15]

---

[9]   The Framework Directive and the Management of Health and Safety at Work Regulations 1999 do apply to psychiatric injury. See Ramsey J in *Sayers v Cambridge County Council* [2006] EWHC 2029 at para 312.

[10]   'Stress at Work: a Guide for Employers' (1995, HSG 116).

[11]   ACOP, para 9.

[12]   ACOP, para 10.

[13]   'Tackling Work-Related Stress: a Manager's Guide to Improving and Maintaining Employee Health and Well-Being' (2001, HSG 218) paras 24–38.

[14]   Regulation 3(1).

[15]   ACOP, para 13(b).

In practice, the risk assessment needs to be practical and take account of the views of employees and their safety representatives.[16] The employer should follow the principles laid out in the HSE's publication 'Five Steps to Risk Assessment'.[17]

The five steps are:
(i)   identify the hazards;
(ii)   decide who might be harmed and how;
(iii)   evaluate the risk by:
    (a)   identifying what action is already being taken;
    (b)   deciding whether it is enough; and
    (c)   if it is not, deciding what more needs to be done;
(iv)   record the significant findings of the assessment; and
(v)   review the assessment at appropriate intervals.

The risk assessment should ensure all aspects of the work activity are reviewed, including routine and non-routine activities.[18] This should take place every six months, but if this is too frequent, at least annually.[19]

The guidelines for the management of occupational stress are generic. They are common to most jobs. Employers should have a health and safety policy. This ought to refer to the risk of occupational stress and the system that an employer has in place for reporting and managing it.

How important is the question of risk assessment?

In *Griffiths v Vauxhall Motors*,[20] Clark LJ (as he then was) stated in response to a submission that a risk assessment may have made no difference:

> 'The whole point of a proper risk assessment is that an investigation is carried out in order to identify whether the particular operation gives rise to any risk to safety and, if so, what is the extent of that risk, which of course includes the extent of any risk of injury, and what can and should be done to minimise or eradicate the risk.'[21]

Risk assessment and foreseeability

It is likely that Defendants will argue that the ACOP notes that employers are not expected to anticipate risks that were 'not foreseeable'.[22]

It is clear from the guidance 'Tackling Work-Related Stress' (see below) that the question of foreseeability should only be considered after the employer has undertaken the first three of the five steps to risk assessment, ie they have taken

---

16   ACOP, para 15.
17   HSE Books (INDG 163 (rev1)), ISBN 0 7176 1565 0.
18   ACOP para 18(b).
19   'Tackling Work-Related Stress: a Manager's Guide to Improving and Maintaining Employee Health and Well-Being' (2001, HSG 218) paras 91–92.
20   [2003] EWCA Civ 412.
21   This was a negligence case, not a claim for breach of statutory duty, but the quote is relevant.
22   ACOP, para 13(b).

steps to find out if there is a hazard, identified the individuals who might be affected and evaluated the risk. If there is no significant risk worth recording, then the employer does not have to do so, neither does it have to take preventative steps.[23]

'Tackling Work-Related Stress: a Manager's Guide to Improving and Maintaining Employee Health and Well-Being'

This is the latest HSE guidance on stress (2001, HSG 218). It recommends employers evaluate the risk of occupational stress by reference to the following seven risk factors:

(i)   culture;
(ii)   demands;
(iii) control;
(iv)   relationships;
(v)   change;
(vi)   role;
(vii) support, training and factors unique to the individual.

These risk factors are often present in one form or another in stress cases.

Culture

An organisation has a positive culture when:

(i)   work-related stress and health issues are treated seriously and the organisation responds positively to any concerns;
(ii)   there is good, open communication between employees and between employees and management;
(iii) staff are consulted and, where possible, able to participate in decisions that may affect them;
(iv)   staff are supported emotionally and practically;
(v)   staff 'buy into' their work, ie they are undertaking the tasks because they understand what they are trying to achieve and are proud of their achievements for personal and organisational reasons;
(vi)   problems are recognised and solved promptly;
(vii) working long hours is not encouraged; and
(viii) staff are not encouraged to take work home.

Demands

DEMANDS: WORK OVERLOAD

Work overload can occur when a person is allocated a great deal of work, but insufficient resources (in terms of ability, staff, time or equipment) to cope with it. There are two types of work overload. Quantitative overload is having too much

---

[23]   ACOP, para 23.

work to do in the time available. Qualitative overload is work that is too difficult for the employee to do, possibly because it is a new area and they have not received appropriate training, they do not have the intellectual or physical capacity to do the work or they have been set an impossible task (regardless of resources or ability).

Workers faced with work overload may try to cope by working excessive hours, which may lead to health problems and problems outside work. Working excessive hours can lead to fatigue, which in turn can impact on performance, creating a 'vicious circle' of more time and effort being put into the work with less being achieved.

Working at a fast pace and the need to resolve conflicting priorities is associated with a higher risk of psychiatric disorder, poor physical fitness or illness. An example is several people giving the same person large amounts of work with short deadlines.

DEMANDS: CAPABILITY AND CAPACITY

Reference is made to the ACOP, para 80 which states:

'When allocating work to employees, employers should ensure that the demands of the job do not exceed the employees' ability to carry out the work without risk to themselves or others … Employers should review their employees' capabilities to carry out their work, as necessary.'

This includes making sure that employees' mental health is not put at risk through work they are required to do. This is potentially the most important requirement in the prevention of occupational stress.

DEMANDS: WORK UNDERLOAD

Job underload, associated with repetitive, routine, boring and under-stimulating work, can lead to occupational stress.

DEMANDS: PHYSICAL ENVIRONMENT

Aspects of the physical environment that can affect employees include noise, vibration, temperature, ventilation, humidity, lighting and hygiene.

DEMANDS: PSYCHOSOCIAL ENVIRONMENT (VIOLENCE)

Employers should assess the risk of violence to staff. They are reminded to report any act of violence which results in incapacity for normal work for three or more days.[24] Violence is defined as:

'Any incident in which an employee is abused, threatened or assaulted by a member of the public in circumstances arising out of the course of his or her employment.'

---

[24]   Reporting of Injuries, Disease and Dangerous Occurrences Regulations 1995.

Control

Control is the amount of say the individual has in how their work is carried out. It helps if people have some control over their work.

Relationships

There are two particular aspects of relationships that could lead to work-related stress: bullying and harassment.

Harassment is taken to mean unwanted conduct based on sex (including transgender status), race, colour, religion, nationality, ethnic or national origin or disability that affects the dignity of people at work.

Bullying is taken to mean persistent unacceptable behaviour (or a single, grossly unacceptable act) by one or more individuals working in the organisation against one or more employees. This behaviour is perceived by the person experiencing it to be offensive, abusive, intimidating, malicious, insulting or involving an abuse of power. It includes:

(i)   verbal abuse (including shouting or swearing);
(ii)   insubordination;
(iii)   victimisation, humiliation or ridicule;
(iv)   libel, slander or malicious gossip;
(v)   spying, pestering or other inappropriate intrusive questioning particularly into personal or domestic life;
(vi)   setting impossible or arbitrary objectives or deadlines;
(vii)   excessive supervision;
(viii) unjustified fault finding;
(ix)   withholding information that the employee has a reasonable expectation of being given, exclusion from meetings that the employee has a reasonable expectation of attending or other forms of unreasonable ignoring of the employee;
(x)   refusing without reasonable cause reasonable requests for leave or training; or
(xi)   maliciously preventing career development.

Change

Poor management of change can leave individuals feeling anxious about their employment status and reporting work-related stress.

Role

There are two potentially stressful areas associated with a person's role in an organisation. They are 'role conflict' and 'role ambiguity'.

Role conflict exists when an individual is torn by conflicting job demands or by doing things that he or she does not really want to do, or which the individual does not believe are part of their job. (That's why trainees complain about regularly being asked to photocopy, make the tea or run personal errands.)

Role ambiguity arises when individuals do not have a clear picture about their work objectives, their co-workers' expectations of them and the scope and responsibilities of their job. Often, this ambiguity results from a supervisor who has not adequately explained what is required of them or because the job has changed without being acknowledged in the job description.

Support, training and factors unique to the individual

Every employer should provide adequate health and safety training.[25] The HSE also recommends that members of staff receive sufficient training to undertake the core functions of their jobs. Staff should feel 'competent and comfortable doing their jobs'. Employers should not try to train staff to become 'stress resistant'.

When work has not been completed to the standard required, constructive and supportive advice should be provided. Not simply a reprimand.

Employers are urged to take account of the 'make up' of their team. Some members may thrive on working to tight deadlines, other may like to plan their work so that they know what they have to do and when. Employers should try, as far as possible, to cater for these individual differences by talking to staff as a team.

OTHER DEVELOPMENTS

'Real Solutions, Real People: a Managers' Guide to Tackling Work-Related Stress'[26]

This consists of a guide pack, published by the HSE in 2003, intended to provide guidance for managers so that solutions can be developed in the workplace for occupational stress identified in their risk assessment. This has to be read in addition to the guidance on tackling work-related stress published in 2001 by the HSE, which concentrates on identifying the risk of occupational stress through the risk assessment process.

'The Management Standards'[27]

This was published by the HSE in November 2004 and does not replace the HSE's existing stress guidance documents 'Tackling Work-Related Stress' (HSG 218) and 'Real Solutions, Real People'.

It provides further practical information, advice and tools for employers on how to assess the risk from work-related stress in an organisation. Only six risk factors have to be actively assessed. The risk factor of the 'culture of the organisation' is a matter that should be identified when assessing the other risk factors (see 'Tackling Work-Related Stress' above).

---

[25] Management of Health and Safety at Work Regulations 1999, reg 3.
[26] ISBN 0 7176 2767 5.
[27] Http://www.hse.gov.uk/stress/standards/index.htm.

It has a proforma stress policy which can be downloaded from the HSE website (http://www.hse.gov.uk/stress/index.htm). There is a questionnaire for staff which can be evaluated using the toolkit provided to establish whether the organisation has a 'stress problem'.

'Guidance on Bullying'

HR departments should also be aware of the guidance produced by the the Chartered Institute of Personnel and Development. Its 'Guidance on Harassment' was issued in May 1997 and revised in March 2006. The 'Guidance on Bullying' was published in April 2005. Both are available at www.cipd.co.uk.

Table 1 of the 'Guidance on Bullying' looks at different ways of tackling poorly-performing teams and distinguishing between strong management and bullying behaviour.

Table 1: differences between strong management and bullying behaviour when tackling poorly-performing teams

Addressing poor performance in teams	Strong management	Bullying
Identifying the performance issue	Involves looking at all the potential reasons for poor performance, for example, people, systems, training and equipment	No attempt to identify the nature or source of the poor performance
Seeking the views of the team or individual to identify the cause of the unacceptable level of performance	The team takes part in looking for the source of the problems in performance and helps the manager to identify solutions for the whole team	No discussion of the cause of the performance deficit or opportunities for the team members to discuss their difficulties
Agreeing new standards of performance with all team members	Involves setting and agreeing standards of performance and behaviour for each team member and the manager	Imposing new standards without a team discussion on appropriate standards of performance or behaviour
Agreeing the method and timing of monitoring/auditing team performance	Wherever possible, the team or team member takes part in the monitoring process. The outcome of the monitoring is openly discussed	Without agreeing standards, the monitoring can occur at any time and can involve areas that are unexpected by team members

Addressing poor performance in teams	Strong management	Bullying
Failure to achieve the standards of performance is dealt with as a performance-improvement issue	Opportunities are taken to identify individuals who are struggling and support is provided. Where individuals are unwilling to comply with the agreed performance-improvement process, disciplinary actions may be taken	Individuals who fail to achieve the standards of performance are put under pressure to conform. This may include ridicule, criticism, shouting, withholding of benefits, demotion, teasing or sarcasm
Recognising positive contributions	Recognises and rewards improvements in performance, attitudes and behaviour	With no monitoring, it is impossible to recognise where there have been positive contributions. Rewards and recognition are therefore arbitrary and open to acts of favouritism

Healthy conflict and bullying

A certain amount of competition is normal and important in working life. However, bullying is different from normal conflicts because it involves unfair and unethical behaviour that causes extreme distress and disruption to the individual, group and ultimately the whole organisation. The World Health Organisation produced a guide in 2003 to raise awareness of bullying and psychological harassment at work in which it charts the contrasts between healthy conflicts and bullying situations (Table 2).

Table 2: differences between healthy conflict and bullying situations

Healthy conflicts	Bullying situations
Clear roles and tasks	Role ambiguity
Collaborative relations	Unco-operative behaviour/boycott
Common and shared objectives	Lack of foresight
Explicit inter-personal relations	Ambiguous inter-personal relations
Healthy organisations	Organisational flaws
Ethical behaviour	Unethical activities
Occasional clashes and confrontation	Long-lasting and systematic disputes
Open and frank strategies	Equivocal strategies
Open conflict and discussion	Covert actions and denial of conflict
Straightforward communication	Oblique and evasive communication

One of the most important ways to distinguish between healthy conflicts and destructive situations that may lead to bullying is to identify the type of issue involved. Conflicts can be related to an issue, idea or task, or to a personal value or belief. The resolution of issue-related conflicts are generally easier to achieve than a conflict related to strongly-held values or beliefs.

Issue-related conflict

For example, a work group may have a conflict in deciding what strategy to pursue or how to allocate responsibilities. These conflicts can have a fruitful outcome if managed correctly. Problem-solving approaches allow participants vigorously to debate the issues involved and come to a creative solution.

Personal conflict

Personal conflict involves issues that threaten the individual's identity or values system and are characterised by intensely negative inter-personal clashes. The types of issues involved in personal conflict are commonly viewed as non-negotiable. It is therefore much more difficult to deal with personal conflict than issue-related conflict.

The Hatton practical propositions

The following practical propositions in *Hatton* on liability[28] now require further consideration in the light of the developments discussed above.

Proposition 2: the threshold question is whether this kind of harm to this particular employee was reasonably foreseeable: an injury to health (as distinct from occupational stress) which is attributable to stress at work (as distinct from other factors)

At common law, before an employer has to do anything, the employer has to foresee that the Claimant (as opposed to anyone else) was going to suffer a psychiatric injury (as opposed to stress) caused by work (as opposed to other factors). This is very difficult to prove in practice. Most employers have little understanding of psychiatric causation. Understandably, the courts have been reluctant, after the event, to criticise an employer who fails to spot an impending breakdown. This has meant, in practice, that someone can be on the verge of a nervous breakdown before their behaviour displays signs that are plain to a reasonable employer.[29] By then, it may be too late to do anything about it.

Thus, arguably, the *Hatton* propositions encourage employers to remain ignorant of the psychology of work, lest they be taken to have sufficient knowledge to make them liable because they should have foreseen the consequences. This, arguably,

---

[28]   Practical propositions 15 and 16 deal with quantum matters. No 15 should be challenged for different reasons that cannot be dealt with in this book.

[29]   I explained some of the causes of stress in my article 'Stress Cases: Foreseeability and Breach' (2001) JPIL, issue 1/01, p 5.

encourages a diminution in standards: a 'rush to the bottom'. This contrasts with the intention of the Framework Directive and the HSE which is to improve standards of health and safety.

The question to be asked for Claimants injured after 27 October 2003 is whether a risk assessment (which has to take place at least every six months for the first year and thereafter reviewed annually) would have identified occupational stress (as opposed to injury) at work and whether the Claimant should have been identified by the assessment as a person who could be harmed. Stress is the hazard that needs to be risk assessed. This will require consultation with the employee. The guidance[30] specifically refers employers to their statutory duty to consult employees (non-unionised) or their health and safety representative (unionised) about their health and safety in good time as required by the Safety Representatives and Safety Committees Regulations 1977 and the Health and Safety (Consultation with Employees) Regulations 1996. The guidance[31] advises that doing the following may help an employer to get ready to undertake the assessment:

(i)   talk to all your staff about work-related stress and explain that you want to identify if there is a problem in your unit;

(ii)   explain that you are setting up a group to help you (which includes trade union/ employee representatives, your unit's health and safety officer (if you have one), one or more supervisors or managers in your unit to co-ordinate action and, if available, someone from your occupational health service);

(iii) share what you are trying to achieve with staff and then the group and explain that the first step is to undertake a risk assessment;

(iv)   ask the group to undertake the assessment using the five steps listed in para 22 (the five steps to risk assessment);

(v)   agree a date by when you want to see the key findings of the risk assessment.

This is arguably a 'sea change' from what is required in *Hatton* and what currently happens in most places of work. This should change if the courts enforce the current HSE guidance set out above. The guidance follows the steps in 'five steps to risk assessment', ie, first, an employer has to take pro-active steps to identify in broad terms if they have a stress problem.

Step 1 of the guidance is entitled 'identify the hazard'. It gives examples of several methods by which an employer has to look for and identify whether or not stress is a hazard in the workplace. These include quantitative methods (performance appraisal, focus groups, managing attendance, staff turnover and questionnaires) and qualitative methods (sickness absence and productivity data). Employers are advised not to rely upon just one method of measuring work-related stress, but are urged to formulate an overall picture.[32]

The seven risk factors are set out above under the heading 'Tackling Work-Related Stress'. Each risk factor needs to be addressed. A typical stress case usually involves a combination of these factors.

---

[30]   Paragraph 20.
[31]   Paragraph 19.
[32]   Paragraph 20.

If the risk assessment does identify occupational stress as a hazard, the employer has to comply with the principles of prevention to reduce the risk before it gives rise to injury. Therefore, under the statute, the employer has to be pro-active.

Proposition 3: foreseeability depends upon what the employer knows (or ought reasonably to know) about the individual employee

Because of the nature of a mental disorder, it is harder to foresee than a physical injury, but may be easier to foresee in a known individual than in the population at large. An employer is usually entitled to assume that the employee can withstand the normal pressures of the job unless he knows of some particular problem or vulnerability.

An employer ought reasonably to comply with the statutory duty to carry out a risk assessment. This, for the reasons given in proposition 2 above, involves consulting the employee about what he or she considers stressful. Unscrupulous employers can no longer turn a blind eye to their staff's suffering and deny all knowledge when they go off sick.

The HSE statistics for 2004/2005[33] show that 420,000 people in the UK believed that work-related stress was making them ill. Approximately 6,500 suffered from a work-related breakdown.

Proposition 4: the test is the same whatever the employment: there are no occupations which should be regarded as intrinsically dangerous to mental health

A risk assessment may identify certain sectors as being particularly at risk, for example, scenes of crimes officers.

Proposition 5: factors likely to be relevant in answering the threshold question

These include:
(i)   the nature and extent of the work done by the employee. Is the workload much more than is normal for the particular job? Is the work particularly intellectually or emotionally demanding for this employee? Are demands being made of this employee unreasonable when compared with the demands made of others in the same or comparable jobs or are there signs that others doing this job are suffering harmful levels of stress? Is there an abnormal level of sickness or absenteeism in the same job or the same department?
(ii)   signs from the employee of impending harm to health. Has he a particular problem or vulnerability? Has he already suffered from illness attributable to stress at work? Have there recently been frequent or prolonged absences which are uncharacteristic of him? Is there reason to think that these are attributable to stress at work, for example, because of complaints or warnings from him or others?

---

[33]   Http://www.hse.gov.uk/statistics/causdis/stress.htm.

This has, arguably, now been superseded by 'Tackling Work-Related Stress'[34] published in May 2001. A risk assessment should not only look at these factors, but others that may identify a risk. The HSE has also published specific guidance for new and expectant mothers[35] and violence at work.[36] Each work sector also has its own guidance.[37]

Proposition 6: the employer is generally entitled to take what it is told by its employee at face value unless it has good reason to think to the contrary

The employer does not generally have to make searching enquiries of the employee or seek permission to make further enquiries of his medical advisers.

If the employer does comply with the guidance 'Tackling Work-Related Stress', ie provides an organisational culture where employees feel they can explain that they are suffering from stress without fear of victimisation, where they have been properly trained in stress awareness so that they can recognise it in themselves and the employer has taken pro-active steps to consult them and the resultant risk assessment has not shown any significant risk of injury due to occupational stress because the Claimant has not disclosed his or her feelings, then this proposition remains valid, but a great deal more is now required of employers than just asking an employee if they are or have been suffering from stress.

Proposition 7: to trigger a duty to take steps, the indications of impending harm to health arising from stress at work must be plain enough for any reasonable employer to realise that it should do something about it

The duty to take steps is now triggered when the risk identifies stress as a hazard. The risk assessment may identify a duty to take steps long before it can be argued that it should have been plain enough for a reasonable employer to do something about it. Defendants often argue that:

(i)   *Hatton* requires the employee to complain not only about the stress they are experiencing, but also the fact that it is affecting their health before any duty is triggered at common law;[38]

(ii)   until then, it cannot be said that it is plain to a reasonable employer that injury, as opposed to stress, will occur;

(iii)   this is a prerequisite to a duty to do anything.

This argument fails to take account of:

(i)   the commercial reality of the situation in that many employees may be afraid to speak out because they fear losing their jobs or missing out on promotion prospects;

(ii)   the medical reality of the situation in that in some cases the last person to know that there is a problem is the employee concerned.

---

34   See above.
35   Http://www.hse.gov.uk/mothers/index.htm.
36   'Violence at Work: a Guide for Employers' (1999, INDG 69): http://www.hse.gov.uk/violence/index.htm.
37   Http://www.hse.gov.uk/stress/experience.htm.
38   This is, for reasons given above, not sustainable.

'Tackling Work-Related Stress', for the reasons given above, does take these factors into account. For the risk of injury to be so high that it is plain to a reasonable manager (who is not a psychiatrist and may not have been trained in what signs to look out for to spot occupation stress) means that it is only the most obvious cases where an employer will be held liable at common law. The statutory position now requires employers to take a pro-active approach to stress prevention.

Proposition 8: the employer is only in breach of duty if it has failed to take the steps which are reasonable in the circumstances, bearing in mind the magnitude of the risk

The principles of prevention set out the sequence and the principles that must be applied by an employer whilst taking the preventative and protective measures required in order to deal with the hazard of stress identified by the risk assessment.

The employer has to start off by considering ways of avoiding the risk altogether. If the risk cannot be avoided, it should be combated at source rather than by applying palliative measures. Wherever possible, the work has to be adapted to the individual and so on.

These steps are preventative and designed to avoid the possibility of injury arising. The Regulations require that this process be undertaken long before mental symptoms (lack of sleep, anxiety attacks, loss of concentration, etc) and questions of foreseeability of injury arise in any particular case. If the risk assessment has been performed and preventative and protective measures undertaken, there would be no question of negligence.

The principles of prevention arguably require an employer to take steps which it would not be reasonable for it to take at common law on the grounds of costs. Health and safety questions should not be subordinated to questions of economic considerations alone.

Proposition 9: the size and scope of the employer's operation, its resources and the demands it faces are relevant in deciding what is reasonable; these include the interests of other employees and the need to treat them fairly, for example, in any redistribution of duties

This proposition is reflected in the Framework Directive. The duty upon small and medium-sized organisations (fewer than 50 people) is less than larger organisations. The guidance of the HSE reflects this distinction. The guidance for employers of fewer than 50 staff is set out in 'Help on Work-Related Stress: a Short Guide' (INDG 281) published in August 1998. It is in question and answer form and identifies work-related stressors as:
(i)   doing the job;
(ii)   responsibilities;
(iii)   relationships;
(iv)   balancing work and home;
(v)   working conditions;
(vi)   management attitudes.

It then gives practical advice on what managers can do. It highlights that stress is bad, whilst pressure can be good.

Proposition 10: an employer can only reasonably be expected to take steps which are likely to do some good; the court is likely to need expert evidence on this

The risk assessment ought to identify what steps should have been taken. In the absence of such an assessment, the court will need to hear expert evidence upon when it should have taken place or been reviewed, what it would have consisted of and what hazards it should have identified and what preventative steps it should have recommended.

The HSE guidance 'Real Solutions, Real People' (2003) and 'The Management Standards' (2004) also provide useful material to judge what steps should have been taken.

Proposition 11: an employer who offers a confidential advice service, with referral to appropriate counselling or treatment services, is unlikely to be found in breach of duty

The Management of Health and Safety at Work Regulations 1999, ACOP, para 30(c) emphasises the statutory requirement is to 'combat risks at source', rather than taking palliative measures. Counselling and advice are 'palliative measures' and therefore providing such a service in the absence of preventative steps should not be a defence to a claim of breach of reg 4. This approach has been followed recently on the common sense basis 'that counselling cannot help in an overwork case' in *INTEL Incorporation Ltd v Daw*.[39]

Proposition 12: if the only reasonable and effective step would have been to dismiss or demote the employee, the employer will not be in breach of duty in allowing a willing employee to continue in the job

If the employee is not capable of performing the tasks required, there may also be a breach of reg 13 of the Management of Health and Safety at Work Regulations 1999. A risk assessment may identify an employee as incapable of doing the job even with proper training, for example, having been over-promoted. In such circumstances, if the employee cannot cope and is risking his/her health and safety, then following the principles of prevention, may, in exceptional circumstances, require the employee to be returned to his or her previous job or sacked on the grounds of capability. This is preferable to doing nothing and letting the employee have a nervous breakdown with all the consequences that flow from that.

Proposition 13: in all cases, therefore, it is necessary to identify the steps which the employer both could and should have taken before finding it in breach of duty

The breach of statutory duty is the failure to carry out a suitable and sufficient risk assessment and take preventative steps as required by the Management of Health and

[39]   [2007] 2 All ER 126.

Safety at Work Regulations 1999, regs 3 and 4. The HSE guidance 'Tackling Work-Related Stress' (2001), 'Real Solutions, Real People' (2003) and 'The Management Standards' (2004) also provide useful material to judge what steps should have been taken.

Proposition 14: the Claimant must show that that breach of duty has caused or materially contributed to the harm suffered; it is not enough to show that occupational stress has caused the harm

It is enough to show that occupational stress materially contributed to the harm if a suitable and sufficient risk assessment should have identified preventative steps that were not taken to avoid the harm suffered.[40]

CAUSATION

Causation can be a major problem in stress claims. It must be shown, upon reliable psychiatric evidence that the workplace stress as opposed to other non-occupational stresses caused or materially contributed to the psychiatric injury. At the time of writing it is not clear how the courts will approach the material contribution tests with respect to stress claims. It is likely that they will be cynical. Thus where the Claimant has a psychiatric history the court might attribute all the injuries to this rather than finding that the occupational stress materially contributed to (ie caused) the injury. Thus cases where Claimants have any history of psychiatric problems are going to be very difficult. The psychiatrist should be specifically instructed to review the Claimant's medical and personal history (for example, a recent death in the family) with a view to ensuring that all other possible causes of psychiatric injury are considered. There is often scope for psychiatrists to disagree on causation in these types of cases whilst both giving a responsible medical opinion. The final decision is obviously a matter for the court, but it is important that the Claimant's psychiatrist considers all possible causes so that a proper view can be taken on the prospects of success before significant costs are incurred.

Even if the court is satisfied that the work materially contributed to the injury, it will still have to consider whether damages should be apportioned to take into account other causes.[41]

LIMITATION

Limitation issues often arise. It is important to identify the date when the Claimant first suffered a significant injury. This is arguably the first visit to the GP complaining about stress and anxiety especially if the Claimant was prescribed medication and/or signed off sick for a significant period of time. Judges will vary in their approach to this issue. Much will depend on the judge's assessment of the Claimant. Once the Claimant has been injured, it may be possible to show that s/he lacked capacity to

---

[40]   Management of Health and Safety at Work Regulations 1999, regs 3 and 4.
[41]   *Hatton v Sutherland* [2002] 2 All ER 1.

bring proceedings for a period of time following the injury. Psychiatric evidence will be required on this point. Tactically, it may be better not to claim for 'significant injuries' that have occurred prior to the first real breakdown, but to use them as evidence of foreseeability of that injury. This is provided that medical evidence supports the case on causation, ie had the employer acted reasonably and solved the problem in time, it would have avoided the injury. Judges are less likely to be persuaded to exercise discretion under s 33 of the Limitation Act 1980 in this kind of case because they often involve recollection of events which are not documented and of systems of work that span considerable periods of time. Thus, the Defendants are likely to be able to show that they have been prejudiced by any delay due to the impairment of the recollection of witnesses.

CHAPTER 32

Liability for Products and Premises

PRODUCT LIABILITY

The principles of litigation for injuries caused by defective products are the same as for other personal injury cases. However, the Defendants and the causes of action are difficult and require a brief consideration. This chapter contains a summary of the legal provisions affecting liability for defective products. Since this book does not deal with medical negligence, there is no discussion of special statutory provisions dealing with liability for medical products.

Breach of contract and negligence

An action may be brought by the buyer of defective goods against the seller. Statute has implied terms protective of consumers into contracts for the supply of goods and services: the Sale of Goods Act 1979 governs products supplied for money and the Supply of Goods and Services Act 1982 applies to services. In both statutes, the implied terms are the same.[1] The goods have to be of satisfactory quality, that is, they must 'meet the standard that a reasonable person would regard as satisfactory, taking account of any description of the goods, the price (if relevant) and all other relevant circumstances' (s 14(2A) of the Sale of Goods Act 1979). Liability is strict.[2] However, the provisions do not apply to defects specifically notified to the buyer or to any that inspection by the buyer ought to have revealed (s 14(2C)(a) and (b)). The Sale of Goods Act 1979, s 14(3) provides that goods must also be reasonably fit for the purpose for which they are bought. The Unfair Contract Terms Act 1977, ss 6(1) and 7(3A) prevents a retailer who sells to a consumer from excluding liability under the 1979 and 1982 Acts.

Actions under the Acts have a number of advantages over claims in negligence as there is no need to prove fault, only defectiveness. Further, no distinction is drawn between dangerous and ineffective goods. Nevertheless, in spite of the contractual

---

[1] Sale of Goods Act 1979, s 14 and the Supply of Goods and Services Act 1982, s 4.
[2] Sale of Goods Act 1979, s 14(2); Supply of Goods and Services Act 1982, s 4(2) and the Supply of Goods (Implied Terms) Act 1973, s 10 (hire purchase agreements).

provisions, negligence remains the principal means of recovering compensation for injury sustained from defective products. The principles are stated in *Donoghue v Stevenson*[3] – the snail in the ginger beer bottle case, known to all law students. The law here is so extensive, well known and thoroughly dealt with in other textbooks that the application of the law of negligence to product liability cases will not be considered here.

Consumer Protection Act 1987

The principles to be found in the Consumer Protection Act 1987 do, however, require mention (see Chapter 16 for pleading the Act). The important feature of the Act is that defectiveness, not fault, is the criterion for recovery.

Products made after 1 March 1988 are subject to the provisions of the Consumer Protection Act 1987, introduced following the European Product Liability Directive.[4] The Act does not apply to agricultural produce or game that has not undergone an industrial process. Part I of the statute provides a cause of action in personal injury claims. The Act must be construed to comply with the directive, but the directive has no effect on common law liability or other statutory provisions.

The Act creates liability for producers of goods causing 'damage', ie death, personal injury or any loss of or damage to any property, including land. The minimum damages that can be claimed are £275. The damage is regarded as having occurred at the earliest time at which a person with an interest in the property had knowledge of the material facts about the loss or damage. The three-year limitation period for personal injury and death apply equally to actions under the Act, subject to minor variations.[5] Actions for damage to property are limited to a 10-year long stop and no extension is possible.[6] The remaining part of this section explains the main provisions of the Act.

Where injury is caused, wholly or partly by a defective product, the following persons may be liable without proof of negligence and if two or more are involved they will share liability jointly and severally; the producers of the product; any persons who, by putting their name on the product, have held themselves out to be the producers of that product; and any persons who have imported the product into an EC member state in order to supply it to another in the course of business.[7]

The supplier of the product is liable for the fatality or injury if the following action has been taken. First, the person who suffered the injury has requested the supplier to identify one or more of the above persons (whether they are still in existence or not). Secondly, that request has been made within a reasonable period after the incident occurred and at a time when it was not reasonably practicable for the injured person to identify all those persons. Thirdly, the supplier has failed, within a reasonable

[3]   [1932] AC 562, HL.
[4]   85/374/EEC.
[5]   Limitation Act 1980, ss 11A(4), (5), 12, 14(1A), 33(1).
[6]   Limitation Act 1980, ss 11A(3), 33(1A).
[7]   Consumer Protection Act 1987, s 2(2).

period after receiving the request, either to comply with the request or to identify the person who supplied the product.[8]

A product is defective if the safety of the product is not such as 'persons generally are entitled to expect'.[9] This includes the safety of products comprised in that product. It extends to protect against risks of damage to property, as well as risks of death or personal injury. Knowledge of previous accidents is not an ingredient necessary to a finding that a defect was present.[10] Further, it is important to note that defects can be of different kinds. Something may be inherently dangerous, or dangerous without a warning, but safe with it.[11]

What 'persons generally are entitled to expect' depends on the circumstances of each case and involves consideration of: the manner in which, and the purposes for which, the product has been marketed, its getup, the use of any mark in relation to the product and any instructions for, or warnings with respect to, doing or refraining from doing anything with or in relation to the product; what might reasonably be expected to be done with, or in relation to, the product (this includes misuse to which the product may be put); and the time when the product was supplied by its producer to a customer. For instance, it was recently held in relation to a failed condom that no-one had ever said that a method of contraception would be 100% effective. Fractures happen by chance. There was no evidence of a weakness in the system of testing used and the condoms were manufactured to the standard required.[12] In another case, it was held that sufficient unambiguous instructions on the box directing the consumer to the detailed leaflet inside which contained appropriate warnings was sufficient.[13]

Section 4 provides certain statutory defences. The onus of proof is on the Defendant to show:

(i)   that the defect is attributable to compliance with any requirement imposed by or under any enactment or with any Community obligation; or
(ii) that the Defendant did not at any time supply the product to another; or
(iii) that the following conditions are satisfied, that is to say:
    (a)   the only supply of the product to another by the Defendant was otherwise than in the course of a business of that person; and
    (b)   that s 2(2) above does not apply to that person, or applies to him by virtue only of things done otherwise than with a view to profit; or
(iv) that the defect did not exist in the product at the relevant time; or
(v)   that the state of scientific and technical knowledge at the relevant time was not such that a producer of products of the same description as the product in question might be expected to have discovered the defect if it had existed in his products while they were under his control;[14] or

8   Consumer Protection Act 1987, s 2(3).
9   Consumer Protection Act 1987, s 3(1).
10   *Abouzaid v Mothercare (UK) Ltd* (31 December 2000, unreported).
11   Consumer Protection Act 1987, s 3(2).
12   *Richardson v LRC Products Ltd* (2 February 2000, unreported).
13   *Worsley v Tambrands Ltd* [2000] PIQR P95.
14   Records of accidents does not come within the category of 'scientific and technical knowledge', per *Abouzaid*.

(vi)   that the defect:
  (a)   constituted a defect in a product ('the subsequent product') in which the product in question had been comprised; and
  (b)   was wholly attributable to the design of the subsequent product or to compliance by the producer of the product in question with instructions given by the producer of the subsequent product.

Damages will not be awarded for injury or fatalities caused by property not ordinarily intended for private use, occupation or consumption, or property not intended by the injured or deceased person to be for his own private use, occupation or consumption.[15] Private use is not defined, but this Act is of little benefit for accidents at work, in respect of which the Employer's Liability (Defective Equipment) Act 1969 is relevant.

Employers' Liability (Defective Equipment) Act 1969

Employers are liable for personal injuries sustained by their employees in the course of their employment, caused by defective equipment. The latter must be provided by the employer (including public authorities), for the purposes of the employer's business. The defect must be attributable, wholly or partly, to the fault of a third party, whether identified or not. If all these elements are proved or admitted, the employer is liable, regardless of fault. Equipment has been defined to include any plant and machinery, vehicle, aircraft and clothing. It has also been held to include a ship[16] and a flagstone.[17] The equipment must be defective, not just unsuitable or inadequate. For example, soap provided at work that was materially more of an irritant than other soaps and caused dermatitis was held to be defective.[18] See Chapter 16 on pleading the Act.

LIABILITY FOR DEFECTIVE PREMISES

People injured by the defective state of premises may have an action in negligence. They may also be able to sue under one of the other statutes or regulations which apply to accidents at work, such as the Workplace (Health, Safety and Welfare) Regulations 1992.

The Occupiers' Liability Act 1957 may also assist, although in general the occupiers' liability under the Act is no more onerous than it ever was under common law.[19] Liability arises to lawful visitors, who may be invitees or licensees under s 1(2) of the Act, persons entering premises under contractual rights under s 5(1) (for example, workmen), or persons entering under general legal rights, rather than by personal or implied permission of the occupier, under s 2(6) (for example, firefighters). The question 'who is the occupier?', so as to determine the proper Defendant, is not always easy to answer. The 'control test' is helpful, but not always conclusive. In

---

[15]   Consumer Protection Act 1987, s 5(3).
[16]   *Coltman v Bibby Tankers Ltd, The Derbyshire* [1988] AC 276.
[17]   *Knowles v Liverpool City Council* [1994] PIQR P8, HL.
[18]   *Ralston v Greater Glasgow Health Board* 1987 SLT 386.
[19]   *Cole v Davis-Gilbert* [2007] EWCA Civ 396.

each case, an occupier must be entitled to control at least part of the premises, and must have done something by way of control or established a right of control. There may be more than one occupier of premises at any one time.

The occupier of premises owes the common duty of care to all visitors. That is such 'as in all the circumstances of the case is reasonable to see that the visitor will be reasonably safe in using the premises for the purposes for which he is invited or permitted ... to be there'.[20] The liability is limited to dangers due to the state of the premises, rather than the activity on the premises.[21] The character of the visitor in question is relevant to the standard of care owed to him/her.[22] Thus, a child[23] or blind person requires a greater standard of care. Warnings will not absolve an occupier of liability unless the warning was enough to enable the visitor to be reasonably safe or would not have made any difference.[24] Further, where the danger is caused due to the faulty execution of any work of construction, maintenance or repair by an independent contractor employed by the occupier, the occupier will not escape liability unless he was reasonable in delegating the work to the contractor and he took reasonable steps to ensure that the contractor was competent and the work properly done.[25]

No duty is owed in respect of dangers which are entirely obvious to a reasonable visitor. This was emphasised strongly in *Tomlinson v Congleton Borough Council*, a case in which a swimmer injured by swimming in a lake was denied recovery.[26] In respect of obvious dangers, the Defendant will now most probably also rely upon the provisions of s 1 of the Compensation Act 2006 which provides:

> 'A court, considering a claim in negligence or breach of statutory duty, may, in determining whether the Defendant should have taken particular steps to meet a standard of care ... have regard to whether a requirement to take those steps might (a) prevent a desirable activity from being undertaken at all ... or (b) discourage persons from undertaking functions in connection with a desirable activity.'

Furthermore, a Defendant will always be able to argue that a visitor willingly accepting a risk is not entitled to succeed under the Act (s 2(5)). However, it is very rare that a court will find that a Claimant had sufficient knowledge of the risk truly to consent to it, particularly if his action was reasonable in the circumstances.

Whereas the 1957 Act covers the liability of an occupier to lawful visitors to a premises, the position of a trespasser is covered by the Occupier's Liability Act 1984. Under that Act, an occupier has a duty of care, reasonable in all the circumstances, to protect anyone whom the occupier has reasonable grounds to believe may come into the vicinity of a danger on the premises. For the trespasser to establish liability, he must first establish that the occupier knew or ought to know of

---

[20] Occupiers' Liability Act 1957, s 2(1).
[21] See, for example, *Tomlinson v Congleton BC* [2004] 1 AC 46.
[22] Occupiers' Liability Act 1957, s 2(2).
[23] Section 2(3)(a) specifically states that an occupier must be prepared for children to be less careful than adults.
[24] Occupiers' Liability Act 1957, s 2(4).
[25] Occupiers' Liability Act 1957, s 2(4)(b).
[26] [2004] 1 AC 46.

the existence of a danger on his land, secondly, that a trespasser is likely to come in its vicinity and thirdly, that the risk is one against which the occupier could reasonably be expected to offer some protection.[27]

In addition to the 1957 Act, there is the Defective Premises Act 1972. Section 3 relates to a landlord's liability for defects existing at the time a lease was entered into for work of construction, repair, maintenance or demolition. Section 4 relates to defects arising during the currency of the lease or licence if the landlord knows or ought in all the circumstances to have known of the defect. It is a general test of negligence.[28] This Act also imposes a duty on, among others, architects and engineers who undertake work for, or in connection with, the provision of a dwelling to carry out their work in a professional manner so that the house is fit for habitation.[29] The Act does not apply to houses constructed under the National House Building Council scheme. The limitation period is six years from the time when the building is completed, unless further work is carried out later.[30]

There may, of course, be a claim in contract as well as negligence if the claim relates to a housing disrepair claim between the tenant and landlord. A specific pre-action protocol applies to such claims.

Liability in nuisance and under the principle of *Rylands v Fletcher*[31] should also be considered in relevant cases. The reader is referred to the standard textbooks on these subjects.

[27]   Occupiers' Liability Act 1984, s 1(3).
[28]   *Sykes v Harry* [2001] QB 1014.
[29]   Defective Premises Act 1972, s 1(1).
[30]   Defective Premises Act 1972, s 1(5).
[31]   (1868) LR 3 HL 330.

CHAPTER 33

Motor Drivers and Owners

Road traffic accidents are familiar and frequent sources of personal injury litigation. This chapter briefly describes compensation payable by drivers and owners of vehicles involved in such accidents. See Chapter 16 on pleading such cases.

The Road Traffic Act 1988, s 143 requires the drivers of motor vehicles to be insured against their liability to third parties and the owner of a vehicle is liable if s/he causes or permits a driver to drive the vehicle without insurance against third party risks.[1] Problems arise sometimes in spite of these laws. These may be where the insured's insurance company denies liability under the policy or security (for example, a cover note), the driver was not insured, the driver cannot be traced or the insured's insurance company is in liquidation. These situations are dealt with below.[2]

INVESTIGATING THE INSURANCE

The solicitor must first try to find out if the Defendant driver or vehicle was covered by an insurance policy or security. From 19 January 2003, the place to start is the Motor Insurance Information Centre (tel: 0845 165 2800; www.miic.org.uk). The Centre contains a list of all vehicles normally based in the UK and the names and addresses of the registered keepers and insurance policies for the vehicles. Information will be supplied where there has been an accident in the UK or involving a UK vehicle in another EEA state[3] and the request (made in writing) is received by the Centre within no more than seven years of the accident and contains sufficient information to identify the vehicle.[4] Where the police have been involved, they may have served a form HORT 1 which requires, among other things, the production of the driver's insurance details. This information should be obtained from the police.

---

[1]   *Monk v Warbey* [1935] 1 KB 75.
[2]   More detailed consideration can be found in *Bingham and Berryman's Motor Claims Cases* (Butterworths, 11th edn, 2000).
[3]   A state that is a contracting party to the agreement on the European Economic Area, May 1992 as adjusted in 1993.
[4]   Motor Vehicles (Compulsory Insurance) (Information Centre and Compensation Body) Regulations 2003, SI 2003/37.

The Road Traffic Act 1988, s 154 requires drivers to give particulars of their insurance certificate or security if required. If there is no certificate, the driver must include the name of the insurer, the policy number, the vehicle covered and the period of cover. It is an offence to fail to comply with such a request or to give a false reply without reasonable excuse. If the driver was not insured, or liability is not covered by the terms of the policy, or the person will not give this information, the solicitor should contact the Motor Insurers Bureau ('MIB').

SUING AN INSURED DRIVER

Once it is established that the driver had an insurance policy in existence, the solicitor must give notice to the insurance company within seven days following the commencement of proceedings against the driver. The solicitor should then proceed with the action against the driver in the usual way. Where the identified driver was uninsured, but there was a policy in force in relation to the car, under s 151(5) of the RTA 1988, the insurer who issued the Certificate must (subject to limited exceptions) satisfy the judgment even though the insurer is entitled to avoid or cancel the indemnity because of some breach of condition. Proceedings are again commenced against the driver with notice being given to the relevant insurer before or within seven days of commencement.

REFUSAL TO PAY BY INSURERS

If the insurers refuse to pay any damages awarded against a driver who appears to be insured by them, proceedings may then be brought directly against the insurance company under the Road Traffic Act 1988, s 151 for recovery of the judgment debt. This requires: the appropriate notice to have been given;[5] that the judgment is in relation to damage covered by compulsory insurance under the Road Traffic Act 1988, s 145, ie death or bodily injury to the third party; that liability is covered by the terms of the policy or security; that the policy has not been validly cancelled; that the claim is for less than £250,000; and that the insurance company has not obtained a declaration of entitlement to avoid. It is of course only in small cases that it would be advantageous to enforce judgment against the driver personally, rather than pursue the insurers.

MOTOR INSURERS BUREAU

All authorised insurers are required to be members of the MIB. The bureau is not itself an insurance company and exists to compensate persons who have been injured by uninsured drivers (the first agreement), untraced drivers (the second agreement), or foreign motorists visiting Britain, or where the insured's insurance company has become insolvent.

---

[5]   The insurance company has to plead the absence of notice as a defence: *Baker v Provident Accident and White Cross Insurance Co Ltd* [1939] 2 All ER 690.

UNINSURED DRIVERS

For accidents before 1 October 1999, where the negligent driver was uninsured or the identity of the insurer cannot be ascertained, notice of bringing proceedings must be given to the MIB by a 'section 151 notice' (under the Road Traffic Act 1988, s 151), within seven days following the commencement of proceedings. Because of delays in postal service it is better to issue and serve in person in an uninsured driver case, as the MIB is strict and will refuse to accept proceedings if the 'section 151 notice' is not served within the time limits. Proof of service is therefore crucial.[6] If the driver had some form of contract of insurance with an identified insurance company, the notice is served on the insurer.[7]

The notice must be accompanied by a copy of the claim form. The Claimant should issue and serve the summons by post and send a copy to the MIB. Otherwise, the court will not be able to return a copy within seven days. The MIB prefers service by fax.[8]

For accidents which occur after 1 October 1999, the notice, completed application form (if appropriate) and all documentation must be received by the MIB no later than 14 days after the date of commencement of proceedings (clause 9(1) and (2)(a)). Notice will only be sufficient if given by fax or registered or recorded delivery to the MIB's registered office.

Exceptions to the 1999 agreement relate to:
(i)   Crown vehicles;
(ii)   vehicles which are not required to be covered by a contract of insurance;
(iii)   a vehicle in which there was no insurance in force and the Claimant knew or ought to have known that was the case;[9]
(iv)   a claim in which the cause of action or judgment has been assigned or subrogated;
(v)   claims where the Claimant was voluntarily in the vehicle and either before or during the journey, could reasonably be expected to have alighted from the vehicle because he knew or ought to have known that it had been stolen, or was being used without insurance, or was being used in the course of a crime or escape from lawful apprehension.[10] [11]

For these cases, there is no relief under the agreement. Further potential pitfalls for the unwary under the 1999 agreement are:

---

6   *Stinton v Stinton* [1993] PIQR P135.
7   First agreement, para 5(1)(a).
8   Notes for the Guidance of Victims of Road Traffic Accidents Supplemental Agreement, 13 August 1999.
9   This has been given a narrow interpretation (mere negligence or carelessness is not enough: knowledge or being wilfully blind will entitle the MIB to avoid): *White v White & MIB* [2001] 1 WLR 481.
10   The wording of the agreement relates to a Claimant knowing that he was in an uninsured vehicle. Ironically, where the individual being carried in the vehicle dies in the accident, the agreement does not preclude a claim brought by the dependent of that deceased bringing the claim, as they are not a Claimant who knew that the driver was uninsured: *Phillips (as a representative of the estate of Neville Phillips, deceased) v Rafiq and MIB* [2007] 1 WLR 1351.
11   The issue of consent is not determined at the commencement of the journey and can be withdrawn at any stage during the journey provided it is unequivocal: *Pickett v MIB* [2004] 1 WLR 2450.

(i)   the liability is not covered by the compulsory insurance requirements relating to vehicles;[12]

(ii)   the injury was caused by an intentional act on the part of the Defendant;[13]

(iii)   failure 'as soon as reasonably practicable' to make a request for insurance information from the driver and if not provided, make a formal complaint to a police officer and make other diligent steps to obtain the insurance details of the driver (Clause 13);

(iv)   failure to make an application in the proper form (Clause 7.1);

(v)   failure to give notice of commencement of proceedings within 14 days of commencement to give with the requisite documentation (claim form, particulars of claim, copy of any insurance, correspondence between the Claimant and Defendant);

(vi)   failure to serve notice of the date of service on the MIB within seven days after the Claimant receives notification from the court that the proceedings have been served or within seven days of the deemed date of service;

(vii)   failure to serve on the MIB notice within seven days of receipt of a defence or any amendment to the particulars of claim including schedules, or setting down for trial or a trial date;

(viii) if the driver has disappeared, failure to obtain an order for substituted service on the MIB pursuant to CPR, r 6.8;[14]

(ix)   35 days' notice before entering judgment. However, in most cases the MIB will be joined as a second Defendant;

(x)   the driver gave a false name and address. In such a case, the appropriate application is under the Untraced Driver's Agreement;[15]

(xi)   failure to apply to the MIB within three years of the date of the incident.

If a Claimant has failed to give timely notice of her claim to the MIB and the MIB was not prepared to overlook the fact, there is no reason in principle against the Claimant discontinuing those proceedings and commencing a fresh action in which a timely notice is then given.[16]

An injured party or the estate of a deceased party (but not a knowingly uninsured passenger)[17] will be compensated by the MIB where a judgment has been obtained in the United Kingdom for damages, costs and interest, resulting from a road traffic accident. Thus, damages for pain, suffering and loss of amenity are recoverable, as are damages for lost employment. Property claims for over £300[18] may be recoverable.

Where an insurance contract exists, the insurer concerned will usually act as agent for the MIB. If no policy exists, the bureau may appoint an insurance company to act as agent. The MIB may waive the requirement of obtaining judgment. Under the old rules, interim payments were not obtainable against the MIB. This position has now changed[19] and it is possible to recover an interim payment from the MIB.

---

[12]   *Lees v MIB* [1952] QBD 511.
[13]   *Hardy v MIB* [1964] 2 All ER 742.
[14]   *Gurtner v Circuit* [1968] 2 QB 587.
[15]   *Clarke v Vedel* [1979] RTR 26.
[16]   *Richardson v Watson* [2007] PIQR P18.
[17]   *Stinton v Stinton* [1993] PIQR P135.
[18]   By the 1999 agreement. The sum by the 1988 agreement is £175.
[19]   Rule 25.7(2)(l).

UNTRACED MOTORISTS

Where the problem is that the negligent driver cannot be traced, so his/her insurers cannot be discovered, an application[20] to the MIB must be made in writing within three years from the date of the event giving rise to the death or injury. The agreement makes no special exception for the time limit that children have to bring a claim, although it was recently held that the failure to do so gave rise to an exposure to liability on the part of the Secretary of State for Transport.[21] The MIB will nominate an insurance company to handle the case. Payment is made for fatality or bodily injury to any person caused by, or arising out of the use of, a motor vehicle on a road in Great Britain.[22] It has to be shown that, on the balance of probabilities, the untraced driver was responsible. The applicant must assist the MIB as reasonably required in carrying out its investigation. An appeal may be made against the decision of the MIB, provided that the applicant gives notice within six months from the date of receipt of the notice of decision. Under the MIB agreement, the MIB cannot be sued in disputes over such claims.[23] Nonetheless, the injured person is well advised to appoint an experienced personal injury solicitor to look after his or her interest. As always, the insurance company will be looking to escape as cheaply as possible. The claim needs to be maximised and tough negotiations may be involved.

FOREIGN MOTORISTS/FOREIGN ACCIDENTS

Where someone has been killed or injured by a foreign motorist in the United Kingdom, the driver's name, registration number of the vehicle, and details of the green card should be given to the MIB as soon as practicable. The bureau will deal with the claim and proceed against the foreign insurance company.

Where an injured party is resident in the UK and an accident occurred in an EEA state other than the UK and the offending vehicle is normally based outside the UK in an EEA state, the injured party may make a claim for compensation from the MIB provided that:

(i) the injured party has claimed compensation from the vehicle insurer or insurer's claim representatives and no reasoned reply has been received within three months; and

(ii) the insurer has failed to appoint a claims representative in the UK and the injured party has not claimed compensation directly from that insurer.[24]

Similar provisions apply where the vehicle or insurer abroad are not identified and it has not been possible to identify the vehicle or insurer.

The European Court of Justice has now also ruled that an injured person can sue an overseas (EU) insurer in the courts of the injured party's domicile.[25]

---

20 Under Sch 2 to the agreement.
21 *Byrne (a child by his litigation friend, Julie Byrne) v MIB and Secretary of State for Transport* [2007] EWHC 1268, QB.
22 Second agreement, para 1(1)(c).
23 *Persson v London Country Buses* [1974] 1 WLR 569.
24 Motor Vehicles (Compulsory Insurance) (Information Centre and Compensation Body) Regulations 2003, reg 7.
25 *FBTO Schadeverzekeringen NV v Jack Odenbreit* (Case C-463/06).

Claims against a motorist who is a member of a visiting foreign military force should be made to the Ministry of Defence.[26]

---

[26]   Visiting Forces Act 1952, s 9(2); and see *Littrell v USA (No 2)* [1995] 1 WLR 82.

CHAPTER 34

Criminal Injuries

It is a basic feature of personal injury (or indeed, any) litigation that the claim is pointless if the Defendant is unable to pay even if the Claimant is successful. Therefore, for this reason, it is very rarely worth bringing a civil action against an uninsured attacker. The assailant will rarely have the means to pay the damages awarded.

However, the Criminal Injuries Compensation Scheme has now been in operation for 40 years. By this scheme, the state makes unique financial provisions for the compensation of victims of crimes against the person in certain specified situations (see below). Where a claim is made under the scheme, it is usually because the Defendant is not worth suing. However, that is not always the case and a worker may claim under the scheme for injury caused by crime which he may claim in a personal injury claim was something his employer could and should have prevented. Bringing a claim made under the scheme may be a useful way of obtaining, in effect, an interim payment.

There cannot be double recovery, however, and damages or settlement in a civil suit must be paid over to the extent necessary to reimburse the scheme, and if the scheme award post-dates the damages or settlement, the former will be reduced to take account of the latter.

The operation of the scheme was altered in both form and constitution by the Criminal Injuries Compensation Act 1995. This empowered the Secretary of State for the Home Office to replace the non-statutory 'old' scheme with a 'new' legislative scheme.

The 1996 scheme came into operation on 1 April 1996 and all claims made between that date and 31 March 2001 are covered by the 1996 scheme. Claims made on or after 1 April 2001 are now covered by the 2001 scheme. Copies of the scheme and guide to the scheme can be obtained on the CICA's website at www.cica.gov.uk. There are still some claims outstanding for applications received prior to 1 April 1996. These are referred to falling under the 'old scheme'.

THE 1996 SCHEME

The Home Secretary for the Home Department failed, in 1995, to revise the old scheme. It was held in *R v Secretary of State for the Home Department, ex p Fire Brigades Union*[1] that it was unlawful for the proposed new scheme to be implemented as it contradicted the Criminal Justice Act 1988 which gave statutory backing to the old scheme. However, the Criminal Injuries Compensation Act 1995 was hastily enacted which repealed[2] the relevant provisions of the Criminal Justice Act 1988 and ss 1–6 gave the Secretary of State express power to create a new scheme. This power was exercised and the new scheme was set down on 12 December 1995. The new scheme applies to all applications received on or after 1 April 1996 (para 1 of the new scheme).[3]

The scheme is administered by the Criminal Injuries Compensation Authority ('the Authority'), which is a non-departmental public body. The Authority is made up of claims officers who deal with the applications and adjudicators who work on the appeals. Appeals are decided on by a Criminal Injury Compensation Appeal Panel made up of adjudicators.

The old scheme was formerly administered by the Criminal Injury Compensation Board ('the Board'). The Board ceased to exist on 1 April 2000 and all existing claims under the old scheme were transferred to the Authority, but continue to be dealt with as though they were old scheme applications.

INITIAL APPLICATION

All applications made after 1 April 2001 will be dealt with under the 2001 scheme.

The application must be made in writing on a form issued by the Authority (para 18). There are two separate forms available, one for personal injury claims and one in fatal injury cases. The form requires details of the incident, injuries, the offence committed, the reporting of the crime, treatment received, any loss of earnings or special expenses and any particulars of previous applications. It is the role of the claims officer to investigate the claim. This will include verifying details with the police as to the reporting of the crime, the outcome of the investigation and the applicant's own background. The claims officer may also require the applicant to submit to a medical examination (para 21). However, it is not the duty of the claims officer to seek out evidence. It is for the applicant to make out a case and for the officer to act on only that information provided. It is not practical for the Authority to have a duty to improve the applicant's case.[4]

Following these investigations, it is for the officer to decide the level of award.[5]

---

[1]   [1995] 2 AC 315.
[2]   Section 12.
[3]   The actual date of injury is irrelevant for the purposes of deciding which scheme applies.
[4]   See *R v CICB, ex p Milton* [1997] PIQR P74.
[5]   Paragraph 3 states that claims officers 'will be responsible for deciding in accordance with the scheme what award (if any) should be made in individual cases'.

Eligibility

The injury

For an applicant to be compensated, the personal injury must be a 'criminal injury'. Paragraph 8 sets out this as an injury sustained (in Great Britain) directly attributable to:

(i)   a crime of violence;

(ii)   an offence of trespass on a railway; or

(iii)   the apprehension (or attempt) of an offender, the prevention of an offence or in the aiding of a police officer in such.

An attempt to define a crime of violence was made in *R v CICB, ex p Webb*.[6] It is one in which the definition of the crime itself involves either direct infliction of force on the victim, or at the very least a hostile act towards the victim. In cases involving a sexual crime, an applicant's consent to events (provided it is 'real consent') is an important factor to be taken into account in considering if those events amounted to a 'crime of violence'.[7] Submission to a crime is not the same thing as consent.[8] Arson is stated as a violent crime, but an injury inflicted by a vehicle is not a criminal injury unless the injury is deemed to have been intentional (para 11).

A personal injury is defined in much the same way as at common law. Paragraph 9 defines personal injury as including physical injury (including fatality), mental injury and disease. However, compensation is only awarded for mental injury alone in the following circumstances:

(i)   the applicant was put in reasonable fear of immediate physical harm;

(ii)   the applicant had a close relationship of love and affection with another who sustained a criminal injury, the applicant was present at the incident or the immediate aftermath and the close relationship still exists (unless a fatality);

(iii)   the crime is a sexual offence; or

(iv)   the applicant was employed in the business of the railway and witnessed an injury caused by trespass on a railway line.

The claims officer must adopt a common sense approach to the term 'directly attributable to a criminal injury'. The use of the word 'directly', however, does indicate a partial restriction.[9]

The victim

The Authority will entertain an application from any person sustaining a criminal injury. However, the scheme operates certain restrictions relating to the conduct and identity of the applicant which entitle the officer to withhold or reduce an award; in particular, where:

6   [1986] QB 184 at 195.
7   See *R v CICAP, ex p A* [2001] 2 WLR 1452 and *R v CICAP, ex p JE* [2003] EWCA Civ 234.
8   *R v CICAP, ex p JE* [2003] EWCA Civ 234. See also *R (on the application of CD) v CICAP* [2004] EWHC 1674 (Admin).
9   See *R v CICB, ex p Kent and Milne* [1998] PIQR Q98.

(i)   the applicant failed to take reasonable steps to inform the police of the crime or failed to co-operate and assist the police in their investigation of the crime or the Authority in their investigation of the application (para 13(a)–(c)). The guide to the scheme emphasises that the victim must report the incident personally unless prevented by injury. All relevant circumstances must be reported. Deliberately leaving out any important information will result in rejection of an application. The incident must be reported as soon as possible. Furthermore, telling employers, trade union officials or social workers rather than the police will not usually be sufficient except in special circumstances. Failure to co-operate with the Authority includes, for example, refusal to undergo a medical examination without good reason, failing to respond to requests for information or making false statements about the incidents or injuries;

(ii)   the conduct of the applicant or his character as shown by criminal convictions makes any full award inappropriate[10] (para 13(d) and (e)). Examples are where the injury was caused in a fight which the victim had voluntarily agreed to take part in, even if the fight turned out to be more serious than expected; or the victim struck the first blow, regardless of the extent of retaliation, or the victim used aggressive language or provocative gestures. When considering conduct under para 13(d), a claims officer may withhold or reduce the award where excessive consumption of alcohol or the use of drugs contributed to the circumstances of the injury. The Authority can and will consider the convictions of the applicant prior to and subsequent to the injury, but before the final award. They will ignore spent convictions. The system is based on penalty points with the more recent conviction and the more serious offences attracting more points. Ten or more points will result in no award (practitioners are referred to the table in the guide). The purpose behind the scheme should not be undermined by those involved in criminal activity receiving money from the public purse;[11] or

(iii) at the time of the injury, the victim and the assailant were living in the same household as members of the same family, the award is withheld unless:
    (a)   the assailant has been prosecuted or the claims officer is satisfied a good reason exists as to why not; and
    (b)   the applicant and assailant no longer live together and it is not foreseen that they will in the future (para 17).

Both restrictions (i) and (ii) above apply also to the non-victim applicant in a fatal case (para 15).

A final proviso is that the claims officer will only make an award where there is no likelihood that an assailant would benefit if an award is made or, where the applicant was under 18 at the time of determination, it would not be against his interest for an award to be made (para 16).

---

[10]   The award should be reduced if the injury is partly the fault of the applicant, *R v CICB, ex p Gambles* [1994] PIQR P314. NB, the Authority is under no duty to take special account of an applicant's good character: *R v CICB, ex p Cook* [1996] 1 WLR 1037.

[11]   *R v CICB, ex p Thomas* [1995] PIQR P99 and *R v CICB, ex p Moore* [1999] 2 All ER 90, which decided that the Board is master of its own procedure and a single member can remit a case back to the full Board other than on the Claimant's application. The Board must give reasons.

Limitations

The claim must be submitted as soon as possible after the incident, but no later than two years (three years under the old scheme). However, the claims officer may waive the time limit if it is in the interest of justice to do so (para 18).[12] If s/he does not do so, reasons should be given.

The value of the claim may not exceed a total of £500,000 in respect of the same injuries (para 24). This may be considerably less than what can be obtained at common law. Conversely, the injury must be sufficiently serious to qualify for the minimum amount payable (para 25). This is currently £1,000 (see below, the minimum was £750 under the old scheme).

An application under the scheme will not be entertained if an application was previously made under any other scheme.

THE AWARD

General damages

The major change imposed by the 1996 scheme and maintained under the 2001 scheme is in the calculation of compensation for the injury itself. Under the old scheme, the calculation of general damages is much the same as at common law whereby the Authority had a discretion to award the value they thought appropriate in the case taking into account the wide range of considerations associated with general damages for personal injury at common law.[13]

It was the attempt to remove this discretion which was the major hurdle for the Secretary of State in the *ex p Fire Brigade* case[14] and which necessitated parliamentary intervention.

The new scheme operates on a tariff basis, stating a set value for an identifiable injury. The tariff lists an extensive range of possible injuries (in considerable detail) and specifies a level regarding the seriousness. This level is numbered 1 to 25 and has a corresponding value under the 2001 scheme of:

Levels of compensation	Compensation
Level 1	£1,000
Level 2	£1,250
Level 3	£1,500
Level 4	£1,750
Level 5	£2,000

---

12   *X v CICB* (1999) Times, 5 July.
13   For example, pain, suffering and loss of amenity, similar awards reported in *Kemp*, etc.
14   [1995] 2 AC 513.

Levels of compensation	Compensation
Level 6	£2,500
Level 7	£3,300
Level 8	£3,800
Level 9	£4,400
Level 10	£5,500
Level 11	£6,600
Level 12	£8,200
Level 13	£11,000
Level 14	£13,500
Level 15	£16,500
Level 16	£19,000
Level 17	£22,000
Level 18	£27,000
Level 19	£33,000
Level 20	£44,000
Level 21	£55,000
Level 22	£82,000
Level 23	£110,000
Level 24	£175,000
Level 25	£250,000

Within the list, only two injuries are specified as level 25 (ie £250,000). These are quadriplegia/tetraplegia (paralysis of all four limbs) and extremely serious, permanent brain damage (with no effective control of functions). All other injuries range from £1,000 to £175,000 (the majority obviously being at the lower level), for example:

(i)   level 1 (£1,000): blurred vision lasting 6–13 weeks or tinnitus lasting 6–13 weeks;
(ii) level 10 (£5,500): injury to tongue leaving moderately impaired speech;
(iii) level 15 (£16,500): loss of smell and taste;
(iv) level 20 (£44,000): uncontrolled epilepsy or total deafness.

Where an applicant has suffered minor injuries which, by themselves, do not reach level 1, he may nevertheless receive compensation if there are three separate minor injuries. The effects of one must last at least six weeks and require two visits to a doctor. Minor injuries include cuts, severe and widespread bruising, bloody nose, lost fingernails, etc. A combination of at least three is placed at level 1 (£1,000).

If an applicant has sustained multiple, classified injuries, then the award under the 2001 scheme is evaluated as follows (para 27):
(i)   the tariff amount for the highest rated injury, plus
(i)   30% of the next highest rated, plus
(iii)   15% of the third highest rated description of injury.

Where an injury is sustained which is not classified and the claims officer deems it serious enough for at least a level 1 award, then the injury is referred to the Secretary of State (para 28).

Loss of earnings

The evaluation of loss of earnings has also changed under the new scheme. Under the old scheme, loss is limited to one-and-a-half times the gross UK average. However, paras 30–34 (together with a general guide to the scheme) deals with the loss under the new schemes.

No compensation is recoverable for the first 28 weeks.[15] Thereafter, the applicant is entitled to his net loss of earnings and this may include future loss calculated on the basis of a multiplier/multiplicand.

Care

If the applicant is incapacitated in some form for over 28 weeks, additional compensation may be awarded (para 35(d)) for the reasonable costs falling on the victim for special equipment required, the adaptation of accommodation and the cost of care (either residential or at home).

Further, the loss of or damage to a physical aid where the damage attributable to the incident may be recovered (para 35(a)), along with costs associated with National Health Service treatment (para 35(b)) and the cost of private health treatment when this is reasonable (para 35(c)).

Fatal cases

The only application the estate of the victim may make is for the costs of a funeral (para 37).

However, certain dependants may make an application as a 'qualifying Claimant'. Paragraph 38 limits these to the spouse (or co-habitee of over two years), a parent or a child of the deceased. The dependency calculation is similar to the principles of the Fatal Accidents Act 1976.

---

[15]   Intended to remove double recovery for statutory sick pay.

A financial dependency is calculated as loss of earnings (para 40). A child receives a further award at level 5 (£2,000) per year for loss of parental service, based on a multiplier until adulthood (para 42). Further, a qualifying Claimant receives a tariff amount as bereavement. If there is only one Claimant, the award is level 13 (£11,000) or if there are more than one, each receives a level 10 (£5,500) award.

Even if, prior to death, the victim applied and succeeded in a claim, the qualifying Claimant can still claim as long as death is caused by the injury (para 43).

DEDUCTIONS

Collateral benefits gained from the injury are deducted. The only exception, in effect, are privately financed insurance[16] and charitable payments.[17]

In particular, any compensation the applicant was able to recover directly from the assailant should be deducted (para 48(c)), whether by way of civil proceedings, settlement or compensation orders in criminal proceedings.

A payment made by the Authority does not disentitle a subsequent action against the assailant. Indeed, it is for the public good as any sum recovered must be used to repay the Authority.[18]

Any award or settlement in a civil suit must be paid to the Authority to the extent necessary to reimburse it.

A substantive difference between claims brought in the CICA and an ordinary personal injury action is that the Panel will deduct not only past state benefits that have been received against a relevant head of loss, but also anticipated future benefits.

REVIEW AND APPEAL

Review (paras 58–60)

If the applicant is dissatisfied with the decision or any award, he may apply for a review within 90 days of the decision. This must be made in writing on a form obtained from the Authority, supported by reasons. The review is simply a re-evaluation of the award by a different and more senior claims officer. The applicant may also supply any further information thought relevant.

Appeal against review decisions (paras 61–71)

The decision of the review is sent to the applicant and an application form for appeal is included. If the applicant wishes to appeal, the form must be returned within 30 days of the review decision under the 1996 scheme and 90 days under the 2001 scheme. In exceptional circumstances, the time limits can be waived (para 62).

16   *Bradburn v Great Western Rly Co* (1874) LR 10 Exch 1.
17   *Redpath v Belfast and County Down Rly* [1947] NI 167.
18   *Oldham v Sharples* [1997] PIQR Q82.

Any appeal concerning the time limits or a re-opening of the case (see below) is dealt with by the Chairman of the Authority.

Any appeal concerning the award either goes to an oral hearing or to an adjudicator (this is decided by a member of the Authority). If an appeal is sent to an adjudicator, s/he may personally consider the appeal unless:

(i)   it has been deemed not serious enough for level 1 award; or
(ii)   there is a dispute of a material fact or conclusion;

in which case, the adjudicator *must* refer the appeal to an oral hearing.

Old scheme

Under the old scheme (pre-April 1996), the applicant may apply for an oral hearing within three months of the initial decision. An oral hearing will be granted in three situations:

(i)   an award was refused because it was below the £750 minimum, but it appears an award of this level could be made;
(ii)   the award should be higher; or
(iii)   there is a dispute of material fact or conclusion or the decision was wrong in law or principle.

The decision as to whether an oral hearing is granted is made by a single member of the board and if it is deemed likely to fail, it is reviewed by not less than two other members. The application is also refused where it is decided that, were any disputed facts or conclusions decided in the applicant's favour, it would nevertheless make no difference to any final decision.

Oral hearing (paras 72–78)

Where an appeal is referred for determination on an oral hearing, the application is considered afresh with the burden of proof resting on the applicant. The hearing will take place before at least two adjudicators. The evidence should be checked to see if further evidence on eligibility or medical evidence is required. The hearing itself takes place in private. The CICA is represented by an advocate and the applicant may either represent himself or be represented. The procedure is flexible and, in less complicated cases, is usually semi-inquisitorial. If the case is complicated, however, the panel may be asked to adopt a more adversarial procedure.

The applicant will give evidence in chief and then be cross-examined by the Authority/ Board advocate before, finally, the panel asking any outstanding questions. The applicant (or his advocate if represented) is given an opportunity to ask questions of the panel. The applicant is given 21 days' written notice of the hearing date and may be represented at the hearing. The Panel consists of at least two adjudicators (para 72) and these must not include any member who previously considered the application (except for the adjudicator who simply referred it to an oral hearing). Under the old scheme, the Panel consisted of three members of the Board.

The decision of the oral hearing is final and the only recourse for the applicant is to apply for judicial review with all its pitfalls and difficulties.

The principles of *res judicata* and abuse of process do not apply to the Authority.[19] The principles applied under the old scheme as to deciding whether damages should be re-assessed are similar to those used by the Court of Appeal. Quantum will not be altered unless it is considered that the initial judgment proceeded on a wholly erroneous estimate, ie if a significantly different award is appropriate.[20] Therefore, it is wise to cite relevant cases on quantum as in civil personal injury trials.

As the new scheme operates a strict tariff, relevant cases of quantum are not necessary. However, relevant cases on level of injury may be useful.

It should be noted (and the client made aware) that the hearings are, in practice, remarkably quick. The client should not be left with the feeling that he has not been given a fair hearing.

It should also be noted that the panel (under the new scheme) has greater powers to withhold expenses and/or reduce any award previously offered if the request for a hearing is considered frivolous. Therefore, a client should be fully informed of his chances.

Re-opening the case

If the applicant's medical condition materially changes from that at the assessment, the case may be re-opened if it would be an injustice for the original evaluation to stand (para 56). This will not be done over two years after the final decision unless a claims officer is satisfied that no extensive enquiries are necessary.

[19]   *Re G (A Minor)* (1992) Times, 18 June.
[20]   *Wilson v Pilley* [1957] 1 WLR 1138.

PART IV

Appendices

Proofs and Witness Statements

A   Witness proof

PROOF OF JOHN SMITH OF 15 HIGH STREET, HAXBY, YORK

1   I am a teacher, born on 3 February 1959. National Insurance number YZ 321999. I am married and have two children aged three and 15 months.

2   I work in the English department of Monkthorpe School, Manor Lane, York and I am on scale 2. I have worked for this comprehensive school since 1989 and teach children from 11 up to 'A' level standard.

3   While the school is only 25 years old there have been major structural problems due, apparently, to subsidence. The Johnson Building, where most of the English teaching is carried out, was out of bounds for perhaps three months over the last two years while they tried to rectify the problem. The last time it was closed was at Christmas 2001 when the headteacher, Ms Graham, told us the problems had been resolved.

4   In September 2007 I noticed that cracks were beginning to appear in the walls in the classroom where I do most of my teaching, room 3A. I complained twice to Mr George, the head of the English department, once toward the end of October in the staff room and again about a fortnight later while we were both on playground duty. On both occasions he just shrugged and ignored me. I then came across Ms Graham, only a couple of days later just outside her office. I think this was on Friday 16 November. I told her about the problem and she said she would see what she could do. I was told by Ms Shepherd, deputy head of English, that the school had been inspected by the education authority maintenance department during the Christmas holidays. She is not prepared to be involved in my case, however.

5   On Monday 10 December 2007 at about 10am I was teaching year 8 and I went to lean against the wall, next to the window overlooking the playing fields. In doing so a part of the wall suddenly gave way, and I fell out through the hole onto the playing field. If it were not for the fact that I fell into the sand of the adjacent infants' sand pit, my injuries would have been far worse as I had fallen some 15 feet from the first floor level.

6   I was immediately taken to the casualty department of York Hospital in Main Road, York (my no is RD 132567) where I was diagnosed as suffering from a

fractured femur of the left leg. I also had sustained grazing and bruising to my left thigh and arm.

7   My left leg was put into plaster, I was discharged late that afternoon and have been seen another four times since then in out-patients. The consultant, Mr Jones, has told me that I should come out of the plaster at the end of January 2008.

8   I lost no wages and have received no benefits during my time off work so far. I will inform my solicitor if the position changes. My National Insurance number is YZ 321999.

9   The expenses I have incurred to date are as follows:

Damaged trousers bought from M & S in June 2007   £66.00
Travelling expenses to and from hospital, four-and-a-half
      return trips at £8 return   £36.00
Excess on insurance for cancelled holiday   £50.00
Total   £152.00

10   The holiday was booked for my wife and me to go to Paris after Christmas, while my parents looked after the children.

11   The injury has not only stopped me doing work around the house, putting an additional burden on my wife, but has stopped me playing in my Sunday league football team and attending my evening class in pottery. It has proved very difficult and embarrassing to have sexual intercourse with my wife and this has caused some tension between us. It ruined Christmas.

12   I confirm that I do not have the benefit of any legal expense insurance; nor am I in a Union that will fund the legal expenses associated with running a claim for compensation.

(signed)   (dated)

I have initialled all changes I have made to the above.

(Proof taken on 14 March 2008 by Mary Doyle)

B   Witness statement for exchange

This is the first statement of John Smith

Initials of J Smith

There are no exhibits

Dated this 10th day of July 2003

IN THE YORK COUNTY COURT CASE NUMBER

JOHN SMITH
Claimant

v

MONKTHORPE EDUCATION AUTHORITY
Defendant

WITNESS STATEMENT OF JOHN SMITH

Statement of John Smith of 15 High Street, Haxby, York YK7 3Z

1   I am a teacher, born on 3 February 1959. National Insurance number YZ 321999. I am married and have two children aged three and 15 months. I am the Claimant in these proceedings and the statement is made from my own knowledge.

2   I work in the English department of Monkthorpe School, Manor Lane, York and I am on scale 2. I have worked for this comprehensive school since 1989 and teach children from 11 up to 'A' level standard.

3   While the school is only 25 years old there have been major structural problems due, apparently, to subsidence. The Johnson Building where most of the English teaching is carried out was out of bounds for perhaps three months over the last two years while they tried to rectify the problem. The last time it was closed was in Christmas 2001, when the headteacher, Ms Graham, told us the problems had been resolved.

4   In September 2007 I noticed that cracks were beginning to appear in the walls in the classroom where I do most of my teaching, room 3A. I complained twice to Mr George, the head of the English department, once toward the end of January in the staff room and again about a fortnight later while we were both on playground duty. On both occasions he just shrugged and ignored me. I then came across Ms Graham, only a couple of days later just outside her office. I think this was on Friday 16 November 2007. I told her about the problem and she said she would see what she could do.

5   On Monday 10 December 2002 at about 10am I was teaching year 8 and I went to lean against the wall, next to the window overlooking the playing fields. In doing so a part of the wall suddenly gave way, and I fell out through the hole onto the playing field. If it were not for the fact that I fell into the sand of the adjacent infants sand pit, my injuries would have been far worse as I had fallen some 15 feet from the first floor level.

6   I was immediately taken to the casualty department of York Hospital in Main Road, York (my no is RD 132567) where I was diagnosed as suffering from a fractured femur of the left leg. I also had sustained grazing and bruising to my left thigh and arm.

7   My left leg was put into plaster, I was discharged late that afternoon and was seen another four times since then in out-patients. The consultant, Mr Jones, told me that I should come out of the plaster at the end of January 2008, but it was actually removed during the second week of February 2008. I was given a walking stick and told that I would be able to weight bear on my leg fully as soon as I felt able to. I was referred for physiotherapy, but there was a long NHS waiting list and I was told that I would have to wait for at least five weeks before I could be seen. I wanted to recover quickly and I therefore decided that I would pay privately for this treatment and I underwent 10 physiotherapy sessions at 'The Physio-Well' – a private physiotherapy clinic at 1 Minor Road, York. Each session cost £50.00.

8   The fracture was terribly painful at first and I had to take a lot of painkillers and was kept awake for most of the night. After a few days, the pain stopped, but I still found it difficult to sleep at night because I would get cramps in my leg and could not move about easily. I could not get in and out of the bath without help and I felt constantly dirty because I could not wash properly. It was a great relief getting out of the plaster and for a few weeks I felt quite vulnerable and unstable as I had to get used to walking again with a stick. I used the stick for about four weeks and have not used it since.

9   I think that I have now recovered almost fully. However, my leg still aches when it is cold or wet. I have been discharged from hospital care. I don't think too much about the accident anymore, but for about six months following the accident I had nightmares during which I would fall off a tall building and I would wake up with a start with my heart thumping. I cannot remember having had nighmares before the accident.

10   I worry about developing arthritis in the future and whether this fracture will affect me when I get older.

11   I returned to work in the Summer term of 2008. As a result of this accident I lost no wages and have received no state benefits. I refer to my schedule of loss and damage which was served with proceedings in this matter for details

of my financial losses. I confirm that I have lost the sums specified in that schedule.

12   My wife and I were going on holiday to Paris for three days after Christmas 2007 while my parents looked after the children. This holiday had to be cancelled because of my injuries. It was very disappointing to both of us. In addition, Christmas was ruined because I was in plaster and I was unable to help my wife with the preparations and shopping. While I was in plaster I was unable to pick up and play with my young children and this upset me.

13   The injury not only stopped me doing work around the house, putting an additional burden on my wife, but has stopped me playing in my Sunday league football team and attending my evening class in pottery. Until the plaster was removed from my leg it proved very difficult and embarrassing to have sexual intercourse with my wife and this has caused some tension between us.

I believe that the facts stated in this witness statement are true.

(signed)   (dated)

Specimen Correspondence

B1   Letter before initial interview

Dear Mr Smith,

Further to your telephone conversation with this office, I write to confirm your appointment to see me on Thursday 8 March 2007at 3.30pm. The appointment is likely to last about an hour.

I would be grateful if you would bring with you the following:

(i)   all the documents you have which relate in any way to the accident;

(ii)   details of your employment (including wage slips and contract of employment);

(iii)   details you have from the DSS (if you have been claiming benefits);

(iv)   anything else which relates to your injuries such as out-patient's card and the name, address and phone number of your doctor, etc;

(v)   details of your National Insurance number;

(vi)   proof of your identify for the purposes of complying with the money laundering regulations,your birth certificate or passport and/or driving licence together with a household utility bill will suffice;

(vii) copies of your household insurance policy and/or other insurance documents that may carry legal expense insurance to cover the investigation into your claim.

The first meeting is free and at that meeting we will discuss future financing of your case. There is no longer any public funding for claims such as yours, but you should not worry about funding your case as my firm operates a 'no win no fee' scheme with insurance cover and we may well be able to offer to run your claim under such a scheme if we think that the merits of the case are strong enough. I will explain the outline of the scheme to you when we meet. However, I would be grateful if you would consider, before we meet, whether or not you have any insurance that will meet your legal expenses. You may well have such cover within your household contents insurance or if you are a member of a trade union, or professional body, they may well be willing to fund the legal investigation into your claim.

A plan is enclosed showing the location of the office and I look forward to meeting you. I would be very grateful if you could telephone me if you run into any difficulty in keeping the appointment at 3.30pm.

Yours sincerely,

William Roberts

For Leigh, Gall & Ayed

B2   Letter after initial interview

Dear Mr Borne,

Personal Injury Claim

Thank you for instructing me to act for you and I confirm that you have instructed me to pursue a claim against your employers Broco-mix Limited following your accident on 7 September 2003 and, in accordance with the procedures recommended by the Law Society on client care, set out our terms of business.

I am a Solicitor. I shall carry out most of the work in this matter personally under the supervision of my Department Head Katy Mallett. You can contact me at the above address and telephone number. If I am not available you are always most welcome to contact my secretary Marjority Grimes who will be pleased to take a message for you. If you are unhappy with any aspect of mine, or my firm's service to you, you may raise the matter with Marjority who has responsibility for your case.

In the event that you are unhappy with Majority's resolution of any complaint you may make, you may complain to the Office for the Supervision of Solicitors and I have enclosed copies of the following leaflets:

Can we help? (the Office for the Supervision of Solicitors)

How I intend to progress your claim

You will remember when we met that I explained that in order to succeed in a claim for compensation you have to show the following:
(i)   that you are owed a duty of care by those who caused or helped cause the injury;
(ii)   that this duty was breached;
(iii)   that you have suffered injury as a result of that breach, the extent of the injury, and that the extent of the injury is sufficient to justify bringing a claim on a costs/benefit ratio basis (ie that the costs of litigating do not outweigh the likely award that the court will make).

To do this, we will gather in the evidence that supports the accident itself by writing to your employers and asking them to disclose to us the accident reports and other supportive documentation. These documents deal with the liability issues arising and in respect of injury and causation. We will need to gather in your clinical notes and instruct an independent expert (or experts) to read the same and provide medical confirmation on the issues of injury, causation, condition and prognosis for the future.

Following these investigations, I will also be in a better position to advise you as to the potential value of the claim. This will depend on the nature of your injuries, and the extent to which these have caused you out of pocket expenses, such as loss of earnings.

Timescale

Please note that if we have to issue court proceedings, this must be done within three years of the accident or event which caused the injury. In your case proceedings would need to be issued within that time limit. We will advise you should this step become necessary, but your accident was on 8 September 2003 your claim will become time barred on 8 September 2006.

Our Charges

My firm's current charge out rate is set out below. Each year we review charges on the 1 April and we will notify you in writing should our charges change:

Grade 1 – Partner	£ ... per hour
Grade 2 – Assistant Solicitor/Legal Executive	£ ... per hour
Grade 3 – Trainee Solicitor/Trainee Legal Executive	£ ... per hour
Paralegal	£ ... per hour

All the above figures are subject to VAT.

Letters and telephone calls are charged as units of time, ie six minutes represents 1 unit of time. Please note that the rates do not include the expenses of the case (ie fees for experts).

Please note that I will write to you every six months giving you details of your costs and telling you of any circumstances that may change my view of your overall costs estimate.

Please also note that if I become aware of circumstances that may make me change my view on the sense of you continuing to pursue your claim; if, for example, the costs of pursuit overwhelm the likely benefit of doing so, I will let you know.

Costs

I am recommending to my 'no win no fee' committee that we enter into a 'no win no fee' agreement with you to protect you from costs. I will write under separate cover concerning this agreement.

Chargeable hours

It is difficult to estimate how many hours of work will be necessary to complete the matter, but, however the claim is funded, I am obliged by my professional rules to give you an idea of the likely cost of pursuing your claim to completion. At present, on the information before me, it appears that you have a valuable claim which will require a lot of medical evidence to support the severity of your injuries. My best estimate of the overall costs of a fully fought trial on liability and value is that the costs are likely to be:

Investigation stage to the point of issue of proceedings   £3,000 plus VAT
Post investigation stage to four weeks prior to trial   £8,000 plus VAT
The trial   £2,000 plus VAT

My total legal costs, including legal expenses (medical fees and court fees), are likely to be in the region of £13,000 plus VAT. This estimate may change as the matter proceeds and it becomes clearer how much time is likely to be needed.

Finally, I enclose two copies of this letter; would you please sign and return one copy to me in the enclosed stamped addressed envelope to confirm that you agree to and accept our conditions of retention.

Yours sincerely,

B3 Letter sending proof of evidence

Dear Mr Smith,

Please find enclosed a copy of the 'proof of evidence' that I have written for you, following our discussions at the meeting on Monday. I would be grateful if you would read it through carefully and make and initial any amendments or alterations that you feel are necessary and then sign it at the foot of the proof. Please return it to me in the enclosed stamped addressed envelope. I also enclose a duplicate copy which you can keep.

This is a proof of evidence and not the statement that we will disclose in court proceedings to the Defendant in due course. However, it is important that you check through the proof carefully as this will form the basis for various legal documents and may also be sent to various experts and counsel. If therefore there are any inaccuracies they must be corrected now. I look forward to receiving the proof returned, duly signed.

Yours sincerely,

B4   Letter outlining case plan

Dear Mr Smith,

I write to set out how I intend to proceed with your case. I confirm that your claim is one where the matter is likely to proceed in the 'multi track' for claims worth in excess of £15,000 and the steps to be taken are as follows:

(i)   gather in the medical reports on your injuries and this may involve joint medical examinations with the Defendants to your claim should they accept the experts that I propose to use. We discussed this in detail when we met;

(ii)   gather in information on actual and projected financial losses to draft the schedule of special damage and financial losses;

(iii) consider whether it is necessary to obtain other expert reports from perhaps an accident reconstruction expert and, if necessary, obtain these reports;

(iv)   I will then consider whether or not your claim is capable of early settlement and if so, make arrangements to see you to discuss making an offer to the Defendants to accept a certain amount of money to settle the claim. No offer will be made without your participation and instruction. If the claim is not capable of settlement, or the offer is not accepted;

(v)   I will then draft the court documentation or send the papers to a barrister expert in accident litigation for the court documentation to be drafted;

(vi)   issue a Claim Form in the High Court and serve the court documentation on the Defendant to your action. The court rules require that this documentation is served with supporting medical evidence and the schedule of financial loss;

(vii) receive the defence and at this point the court will take over management of the matter and serve an Allocation Questionnaire and I will attempt to agree directions for the progress of matters towards trial with the Defendants. If they cannot be agreed, the court will order directions.

The matter will then progress towards a trial date set by the court. In the time between the issue of proceedings and the trial date the medical and other expert evidence will need to be updated and exchanged with the Defendants.

If necessary, I will ask counsel to advise in the case, either in writing or in a meeting, on the claim's value and merits. At this point counsel will let us know what else he or she thinks needs to be done before trial.

I will of course send you copies of all relevant documents as they are received and I will ask you to comment on them.

Please note that we cannot proceed to trial until and unless we can get a firm medical prognosis and we cannot accurately value a claim until we know the extent of the damage. The above plan may need to be modified (with the approval of the court if proceedings are issued) as we proceed in the light of circumstances which may arise. In some cases where evidence is complicated for whatever reason, I may have to ask counsel to advise on more than one occasion. In other cases, I do not have to ask counsel to advise at all.

At present, I estimate we should reach trial in about 18 months provided no major problems arise.

In due course, please confirm that you have received this plan and approve its contents. If there are any aspects of it that you do not understand, or any questions you wish to raise on it, just ask me. It is generally best if we communicate by letter, and delays will be avoided if you respond as quickly as possible to my letters. I will try to do the same. If you need to see me to discuss something, my secretary will be happy to arrange an appointment for you to come to the office or, if this is impracticable, I could come to see you. If an emergency arises, please do not hesitate to phone me.

Yours sincerely,

B5   Letter advising 'no case'

Dear Mr Brown,

I have now had an opportunity to consider fully your case and have taken on board everything that you told me at the meeting on Monday 12 November 2007 together with all the documents that you sent on to me.

Having considered all the evidence I am sorry to have to inform you that I take the view that there is no realistic prospect of pursuing a successful claim in your case.

The reason for my opinion is that the part of the pavement where you fell is unlikely to be considered sufficiently dangerous for the council to be held liable. As I mentioned to you at the meeting, the courts consider a difference in height of less than one inch as being acceptable. In your case the defect was at best a quarter of an inch as you told me and as the photographs you sent me seem to confirm.

I will therefore be filing your papers and can confirm that there is no charge for this advice or for our initial discussion.

Finally, I must warn you that if you do intend to pursue the claim, despite my advice, proceedings must be issued by Tuesday 9 December 2008 This is three years from the date of the accident. A claim commenced after that date is very likely to be struck out for not coming within the statutory three-year limitation period.

I am sorry once again that my advice is not more optimistic. If you want to discuss any of the above please do not hesitate to write or phone my secretary to make an appointment with me. I return to you the documents and photographs you provided to me.

Yours sincerely,

B6   Letter sending medical report

Dear Mr Maloney,

I have now received the expert's report from Mr Doctor and enclose a copy. I would be grateful if you could read through the report carefully. Please provide me with any comments you would care to make, including a note of any inaccuracies and any part of the report you do not agree with.

(WHERE THERE HAS BEEN A JOINT INSTRUCTION)

As you know, this report was prepared jointly with the Insurers of the Defendant to your claim. A copy of the report has been sent directly to them, and they will be aware of its contents. When I hear from you with your comments I will put them on notice of any inaccuracies that you point out.

You will see that Mr Doctor says that your fracture is serious and that it will be some time before a full prognosis (ie, a forecast of how the fracture will turn out and what effect it will have on your life) can be made.

He recommends that he sees you again in nine months' time and I have put this in my diary and will write to him for an appointment nearer that time. I would like your confirmation that this is in order.

While we wait for that further medical report I shall be continuing to progress the other aspects of your case.

Yours sincerely,

B7   Letter advising making a Part 36 offer to settle a claim

Dear Mr Maloney,

I enclose:

(i)   copy of the second and final medical report of Mr Doctor dated 3 December 2007;

(ii)   schedule of your financial loss as per your instructions.

I have considered carefully the evidence in your claim. It is clear that Mr Doctor considers that your fracture has now fully healed and I note that you have told him that your problems are, more or less, resolved. I note that you have no further financial losses and I think that the matter is capable of settlement now.

I therefore recommend that we write to the Insurers for the man who knocked you off your bicycle and make a formal offer of a sum of money to settle your claim. We can do this before we issue proceedings in the court, and if the Insurers do not respond to the offer, or make a counteroffer that is unacceptable, then we can issue proceedings without further delay.

The strength of making an offer to settle your claim is

(i)   the case will be settled now, which of course would be very good news for you;

(ii)   that if the Defendants do not respond or make an offer that is less that we request, and at trial the judge orders them to pay more then the offer we have made, the court may order the Defendants to pay a higher rate of interest on both the award made and on the costs of pursuing the award, than that normally ordered to be paid.

The offer should be made on a 'without prejudice' basis; this means that it cannot be referred to in correspondence with the court and we cannot be held to it if we choose to withdraw it. However, the normal effect of making an offer is that it 'sets an upper limit' to the claim. Having made an offer to settle your claim, the Defendants will never, unless your position changes drastically, offer you more then the amount we have asked for. For this reason, our offer needs to be carefully thought out.

There should follow a careful consideration of the clients particular claim; separated out into headings dealing with:

(i)   liability; strengths and weaknesses;
(ii)   contribution; the likely finding of any;
(iii)   damages; general with case/Judicial Studies guidelines and special damages – the strengths and weaknesses of each head on the schedule.

You will see from the above that I think that you have a good claim, with an overwhelming chance that you would succeed if the matter went to trial. I do not think that you should accept any percentage for contributory negligence. I think that the likely bracket of general damages is between £6,500–£8,000. Your special damage schedule totals £5,300 and I think it perfectly reasonable for us to expect to recover a sum of £4,300 as I expect that we will have to accept a percentage discount for the age of the items lost. You received no state benefits as a result of this accident and so nothing falls to be repaid in this respect.

My advice is that we should write to the Defendants and make an offer to settle the claim for the sum of £14,500. This gives us a little room for discount should they wish to attempt to negotiate downwards. If the Defendants make an offer that is acceptable to you, then they will pay your reasonable costs. I would remind you that reasonable costs do not always mean all costs and I would refer you to the costs letter that I sent to you when you first instructed me. *Further, you will remember that I am advising you as a 'no win no fee' client with the benefit of after the event insurance, and that there will be a success fee payable on the costs of the award. Again, I refer you to the costs letter on this point.*

This is a serious step to take in the proceedings, and I would be grateful if you would consider this letter carefully, and let me know whether or not you wish to accept my advice. If you wish to come to see me to discuss the matter, please do not hesitate to telephone my secretary and make an appointment. In any event, I will need your signed authority to make an offer to settle and I enclose a short standard form of authority together with a stamped addressed envelope for you to return to me in the event that you wish to proceed.

I look forward to hearing from you.

Yours sincerely,

B8   Authority from client to make Part 36 offer

I JOSEPH MALONEY confirm that I have read your letter to me of 11 December 2007 carefully. I understand the letter and that you advise me to make an offer to settle my claim in the sum of £14,500 to the Defendants, and I instruct you to take this step.

Signed

Dated

B9 Letter seeking client's authority to issue proceedings

Dear Mr Maloney,

(As you know, I wrote to the Insurers and made an offer to settle your claim. I received no response to this offer and I therefore consider that we ought to issue proceedings to force the Insurers to properly consider and settle your claim).

I have prepared the necessary documentation to commence legal proceedings against the Defendants. I enclose a copy of the Particulars of Claim which forms part of the documentation that will be sent to the court for issuing. It sets out your case in legal language and I would be grateful if you would read it through and confirm that there are no factual inaccuracies in it.

I also enclose a copy of the schedule that I have prepared of your financial losses. Again, please would you confirm that you are in agreement with the claim as set out in the schedule.

When I issue proceedings, I intend to rely on the medical report of Mr J A Doctor. You have already seen and confirmed to me that this report is accurate.

I confirm that I have considered the funding position prior to issue of proceedings and that I have taken any necessary steps to ensure that *your After the Event Insurers* are content with the matter going ahead.

The issuing and commencement of proceedings is the start of the formal court process and although we have discussed the position I would be grateful if you would write, confirming that you are in agreement that we should start the legal proceedings.

If you have any queries please do not hesitate to contact me at the office.

Yours sincerely,

B10   Letter re: Part 36 payment into court or offer

Dear Mr Maloney,

I have just received notification from the Defendants that they have paid the sum of £9,000 into court. You will remember that before we issued proceedings, we made an offer of £14,500 to settle your claim. The Defendants failed to respond to our offer to settle and so we had to issue proceedings.

The significance of the payment in is, as I explained at our meeting last week, that you have until 13 September to decide whether to accept the offer (that is, 21 days from the receipt of the notice of payment). If you accept the offer the Defendants will pay their own and nearly all my costs.

If you do not accept the payment in by 13 September and the case then goes to trial, and if you are awarded a sum equal to or less than that paid into court, it is highly likely that the court will order you to pay the Defendants' costs from the date of the last day upon which you could accept the sum in court/offer to settle – that is the 22 December 2007 up until the end of the case. My best estimate is that this could quite easily come to £5,000 or £6,000 plus VAT, though it could conceivably be more.

However, my advice is still that your claim is worth between £11,000 and £14,000 and I remain of the view that you are much more likely to win than to lose.

It is always difficult to advise clients on settlement when there is a small margin between that which is offered and that which I think that a claim is actually worth. However, in your claim I am confident that we will recover more then the sum paid into court should the matter proceed to trial and I therefore advise you to refuse the offer.

You are, of course, free to accept or refuse my advice. Should you wish the matter to end now, you can accept the money paid into court and that will be an end to the matter.

If you want to discuss the matter please do not hesitate to phone me at the office or to arrange an appointment with my secretary to come in and see me.

Yours sincerely,

B11   Letter confirming accepted offer

Dear Mr Maloney,

I am pleased to say that, following our discussions, the Defendants' insurers have now agreed to pay to you the sum of £12,500 which you authorised me to accept on the phone yesterday in settlement of your claim. We are now in the process of having an order issued by the court to that effect and I should be in receipt of the cheque within the next two or three weeks.

As I have informed you, I will be able to send you £9,000 at this stage until the costs position has been determined. It is certainly possible that I may be able to reach agreement with the Defendants on costs which would mean that you would be entitled to the full balance of the monies due to you. If, however, it is impossible to reach agreement with the Defendants, it may be a good few months before the courts have gone through the costs in a process known as 'detailed assessment' which will determine how much has to be paid by the Defendants and how much by yourself. You will be entitled to attend that assessment and I will let you know the hearing date as soon as we have it, if that is the case.

Conditional fee clients

Under the terms of our insurance agreement, and the contract we have signed, I confirm that I will charge you no contribution towards your legal costs. I will therefore forward to you the total amount of your compensation as soon as I receive the same.

I will keep you informed of progress.

Yours sincerely,

B12   Pre-protocol letter – letter of notice of possible claim

To: Mr A Heart
The Rockery
Granchester
Berks

Dear Sir

Re Our client Mrs Jemima Brooks
123 The Boundings, Ipswich, IP3 1QF
Date of birth 3 March 1954
NI number; FI/123/GHO
Unemployed

We are instructed by the above named to investigate a possible claim against yourself for your possible negligence in connection with certain building work that you undertook to her property during the months of May and June 2007.

We write to put you on notice that our client, by way of a Litigation Friend, may make a claim against you for compensation for the significant head injuries she suffered when an unattached oak beam in her living room fell on her head during the storms of September 2007.

Our client is severely brain injured and at present resident on Laurel Ward in Ipswich General Hospital. She is unable to communicate verbally and her prognosis is poor.

Would you please pass this letter on to your Insurers to put them on notice of a possible claim against you, and would you please write to confirm both receipt of this letter and to provide us with details of your Insurers' name, address and policy reference number.

Yours faithfully,

B13   Road traffic accident protocol letter

Mr J B Knockhouse
123 Brightwater Road
Cardiff

Dear Sir

Re Our client: Ms Rose Jones of 16 Albany Road, Cardiff CB1 2RJ
Date of birth 31 January 1960
National Insurance number YZ 223991B.
Employed by Huge Gaskets Ltd of 13 New Industrial Estate, Greenbelt, Kent.
Employee number 1234

We are instructed by the above named to claim damages in connection with a road traffic accident which took place on 6 October 2007.

Our client was driving her Volvo motor car, registration number H232 MLN, along Albany Road, Cardiff in a southerly direction when a Vauxhall Nova motor car, registration number G192 KNV, which we believe to have been owned and driven by yourself, came straight out of Dartmouth Road and hit our client's vehicle in the middle nearside.

The reason why we are alleging fault is that you were turning from a minor road into a major road and were under a duty to give way to the traffic on Albany Road. You failed to give way to our client and turned into the path of her car causing this accident.

As a result of the accident our client sustained whiplash injuries to her neck and shoulders.

Our client is employed as a gasket maker and was unable to work for three weeks following the accident. Her approximately weekly income is £225 per week net.

We are obtaining a copy of the police report on this accident and will let you have a copy of the same upon your undertaking to meet half the fee.

We enclose a copy of the pre-accident personal injury protocol standard disclosure list for fast track disclosure in road traffic accident claims. We require disclosure of documents A (i) – (ii) which we consider to be relevant to this action.

We understand that you are insured with Murkeybooks Insurance Company under policy number 1234/567A. We attach a copy of this letter for you to forward to them, and confirm we have also sent them a copy direct.

Finally we expect an acknowledgment of this letter within 21 days by yourself or your insurers.

Yours faithfully,

B14 Initial letter to the other side in work accident case

Dear Sir/Madam,

Re: James Maloney of 31 Dean Street, London, SE5
Date of birth 30 January 1965
NI number: YZ 220991B

We are instructed by the above-named in respect of an accident at work which occurred on 13 May 2008. Our client is employed by your company as a fitter and his works number is B16143.

The accident occurred at your factory in Rason Road, Sutton at about 10am. The accident occurred when the pipe he was preparing gave way, falling on top of him.

The reason why we are alleging fault is that our client had warned you via his forman Mr Jim Drain, on several prior occasions that the system of work he was being asked to operate could lead to an accident of this nature. Despite warnings, Mr Drain insisted that the pipe mechanism was strong enough to bear our client's weight which has proved not to be the case.

As a result of the accident our client sustained a broken collar bone and bruising.

As you will know, our client was away from work for 4 weeks following this accident during which you did not pay him.

Please provide us with details of his earnings on a week by week, gross and net basis, for the six months prior to this accident so that we can quantify our client's loss of earnings claim.

We enclose a copy of the pre-accident personal injury protocol standard disclosure list for fast track disclosure in workplace claims. We require disclosure of documents * – * which we consider to be relevant to this action.

We understand that you are insured with The Strongiron Insurance Company under policy number 134/67A. We attach a copy of this letter for you to forward to them, and confirm we have also sent them a copy direct.

Finally we expect an acknowledgment of this letter within 21 days by yourselves or your insurers.

Yours faithfully,

B15   Initial letter to other side in tripping case

Dear Sir/Madam,

Re: Helen Hartigan of 15 Flowers Close, Hitchin
Date of birth 29 January 1930
NI number YZ 22099 1B
Pensioner

We are instructed by the above named in respect of an accident which occurred on 7 June 2008. Our client was walking along the London Road, Hitchin in a northerly direction when, outside number 17, she tripped and fell over a paving stone which we understand to be your responsibility.

We have been to the scene of the accident and have measured the defect in the pavement which is clearly raised well over one inch of the stones surrounding it. In these circumstances we consider that you are in breach of your duty to ensure that the path was safe for people walking along it and that you are liable to compensate our client for your failure.

As a result of the accident our client sustained a broken hip. She is a pensioner and has suffered no loss of earnings as a result of this accident.

We enclose a copy of the pre-accident personal injury protocol standard disclosure list for Highway Tripping Accidents. We require disclosure of documents * --* which we consider to be relevant to this action.

We understand that you are insured with The Geneva Insurance Company under policy number 100767A. We attach a copy of this letter for you to forward to them, and confirm we have also sent them a copy direct.

Finally we expect an acknowledgment of this letter within 21 days by yourselves or your insurers.

Yours faithfully,

Bl6   Letter to insurers re: joint medical expert instruction

Dear Sir/Madam,

Re: Helen Hartigan of 15 Flowers Close, Hitchin.
Accident 7 June 2008. – London Road, Hitchin

Thank you for your letter of 7 May last and for confirming that you are the relevant insurers in this matter. We acknowledge receipt of the documents disclosed as part of the pre-action protocols and thank you for copies of the same.

We wish now to obtain an opinion from a medical expert on our client. We confirm that we are gathering in her medical records, both GP and Hospital and we put forward the following names of experts we consider suitable to examine and report on her:

Mr A B Grant FRCS
123 The Downlands
Burford
Hitchin HG1 2FR

Mrs R S Wattle FRCS
The Experts Chambers
45 High Street
Hitchin HG2 19P.

We remind that you that under the protocol you have 14 days in which to object to the instruction of one of the above experts. If you object kindly put forward names of your choice so that we may consider the matter further. If we do not hear from you within the 14 day time limit we will continue to instruct one of the above experts and may not then be entitled to rely on your own expert orthopaedic evidence.

Further, if you are happy to instruct one of the above experts, will you bear half the cost of the report?

We look forward to hearing from you.

Yours faithfully,

B17   Letter to Insurers re: joint medical expert instruction – questions to the expert where the insurers have instructed

Dear Sir/Madam,

Re: Helen Hartigan of 15 Flowers Close, Hitchin.
Accident 7 June 2008. - London Road, Hitchin

Further to our previous correspondence in this matter. You will remember that you instructed Mrs R S Wattle FRCS as a joint expert to see our client Helen Hartigan.

Mrs Wattle has now seen our client and forwarded to us a copy of her report. There is one minor inaccuracy.

1.   At paragraph 4 on page 2, she states that Miss Hartigan fell heavily and bruised the right side of her face. This is an inaccuracy as we are sure that you will note from the photographs of the bruising we have sent to you already.

We have read the same carefully and would be grateful if you would put the following questions to her:

3.   Mrs Wattle refers under the prognosis section to the possiblity of the pins being removed from the fracture site. However, she fails to give a likely timescale for this.

Question: what is the likely timescale for the removal of the pins?
Question: what is the likely cost of removing the pins in the private patient sector?
Question: what are the possible advantages of removing the pins?
Question: what are the possible disadvantages of removing the pins?

We look forward to receiving Mrs Wattle's reply to the above queston.

Yours faithfully,

B18 Request to police for accident report

The Superintendent,
Process section.
Ref MD/GILL/9829

Dear Sir/Madam,

Re: Road traffic accident on 13 October 2007 at Chestnut Close, Canterbury.

We are instructed on behalf of Peter Gill of 13 Mall Lane, Canterbury in connection with the above street accident. The two vehicles involved in the accident were a Honda Accord, registration number B219 AFC, owned and driven by Mr Gill, and a Rover 2000.

We understand that the police have investigated the circumstances of this accident and intend to take no further action. The police report is therefore available for disclosure and we enclose a remittance of £60 and should be obliged if you would forward a copy of the police report and statements.

(If proceedings are pending or have been concluded we would be grateful if you would inform us of the name and address of the Defendant, any charges laid against him/her, the hearing date, the court, the outcome if any, and details of the Defendant's insurers).

This action is likely to be the subject of a civil court claim so we ask that the original report is not destroyed until after the conclusion of our client's litigation. We would be grateful if you would confirm this.

Yours faithfully,

B19   Request to interview police officer

Dear Sir/Madam,

Johnson v Patel

Thank you for sending on the police report dated September 2007. We have now had a chance to read through the report and in the light of the contents thereof we would like to interview PC 132 Rose on behalf of our client Patricia Q Johnson of 17A Balham Drive, London SE17.

We enclose the interview fee and would be grateful if you would let us know through whom the arrangements should be made for the interview.

Yours faithfully,

B20   Obtaining defendant's details from police

Dear Sir/Madam,

Re: Joan Deans of 3 St John's Crescent, Portsmouth.

Further to your letter dated 18 January 2004 informing us that the police report is not yet available, we would be grateful if you would provide us with the name, address, vehicle registration and insurance details of the driver of the vehicle that hit our client.

Yours faithfully,

B21   The protocol letter of instruction to medical expert

Dear Sir

Re:
Date of birth
Address
Telephone number
Date of accident

We are acting for the above named in connection with injuries received in an accident which occurred on the above date. The main injuries appear to have been ***.

We should be obliged if you would examine our client and let us have a full and detailed report dealing with any relevant pre-accident medical history, the injuries sustained, treatment received and present condition, dealing in particular with the capacity for work and giving a prognosis.

It is central to our assessment of the extent of our client's injuries to establish the extent and duration of any continuing disability. Accordingly, in the prognosis section we would ask you to specifically comment on any areas of continuing complaint or disability or impact on daily living. If there is such continuing disability you should comment upon the level of suffering or inconvenience caused and, if you are able, give your view as to when or if the complaint or disability is likely to resolve.

Please send our client an appointment direct for this purpose. Should you be able to offer a cancellation appointment please contact our client direct. We confirm we will be responsible for your reasonable fees.

We are obtaining the notes and records from our client's GP and hospital attended and will forward them to you when they are to hand please request the GP and hospital records direct and advise that any invoice for the provision of these records should be forwarded to us.

In order to comply with court rules we should be grateful if you would insert above your signature a statement that the contents are true to the best of your knowledge and belief.

In order to avoid further correspondence we can confirm that on the evidence we have there is no reason to suspect we may be pursuing a claim against the hospital or its staff.

We look forward to receiving your report within **** weeks. If you will not be able to prepare your report within this period please telephone us upon receipt of these instructions.

When acknowledging these instructions it would assist if you could give an estimate as to the likely time scale for the provision of your report and also an indication as to your fee.

Yours faithfully,

B22   Letter to medical records officer

Dear Sir/Madam,

Re: Gay Bone of 4 Joseph's Avenue, Deal, Kent. Hospital no 34512/HY.

We are instructed by the above-named in respect of an accident which occurred on 13 January 2008. Immediately following the accident our client, who had sustained a fractured pelvis and right tibia, was admitted to your hospital for treatment.

Our client was kept in your hospital for four days and was then seen regularly in your out-patient department.

We have asked Mr Jones, a consultant orthopaedic surgeon of 35 Harley Street, London, W1 to provide us with an independent medical report in relation to these injuries.

Would you please forward to us a full set of all of the records that you are holding on our client. Would you also please ask your x-ray department to forward to us a copy of the schedule of x-rays held so that we can confirm with Mr Jones which x-rays he requires sight of in order to properly advise.

We shall of course be responsible for any reasonable copying and postage fees to the maximum of £50. We confirm we have no instructions to take any proceedings against your authority. Finally, we enclose an authority from our client for you to release the records.

Yours faithfully,

B23   Authority to release medical records

Re: Hospital no 23456/78.

Dear Sir/Madam,

I write to authorise you to make available a set of my medical records and 'X-rays to my solicitors, Messrs Grey & White of 13 Time Square, High Wycombe, under reference MD/HUMPHRIES/98914 relating to the treatment I received following my accident on 5 December 2007.

I am grateful to you for your assistance.

Yours sincerely,

Beverly Humphries

Solicitors' reference MD/HUMPHRIES/98914

Note: This letter should be typed on plain paper with the client's address in the top right-hand corner.

B24   Request for final medical report

Dear Ms Johnston,

Re: Michael Williams of 6 Belfast Road, Barry.

Thank you for kindly providing us with your interim report of 2 September last year on this case. The case is now issued in the county court and the trial date is fixed for 3 November next. *You will not be required to attend trial as the court has ordered that expert evidence be given by written report alone.*

The court has ordered that final medical evidence be served by 4 July; in order that the judge can arrive at a fair and reasonable decision on Mr Williams' medical problems we need a final report from you.

I would be grateful if you could send our client an early appointment for examination and would ask you to provide us with a report dealing particularly with the present position and the prognosis. If you still think an operation may be necessary at some time in the future, could you kindly estimate the cost at today's value, and give us your best estimate of when the deterioration might occur and when thereafter an operation might be advisable. I appreciate how difficult these estimations are, but the court is required to make them.

In preparing your report I would be grateful if you would pay especial attention to the client's employment prospects and any future disabilities that are likely to affect his work position, social life or health.

I will of course be responsible for your reasonable fees and I look forward to receiving your report in due course.

Finally, if you think that you cannot report by the date requested, please let me know at once so that I can explain the problems to the court and ask for an extension of time in which to serve the further evidence.

Yours sincerely,

B25   Notification to expert witness of hearing date where oral evidence is allowed

Dear Mr Peters,

Re: John Paul of Grate Street, Grantham.

We have now received notification that the trial date has been listed for 5 May 2008 at the Grantham County Court at 4 High Street, Grantham. The case has been listed for two days and we are likely to need you to give evidence on the first day.

Please note that it is my standard practice to issue and serve a witness summons on experts. If, for some reason, you do not consider it appropriate for me to serve you with a witness summons, please contact me directly

It is certainly possible that the Defendants will agree your evidence prior to the hearing, or indeed that the case will settle. I would however be grateful if you would note this date in your diary to ensure that you are free to attend the court if necessary. If you have any problems with the particular date I have mentioned, it may be possible to have your evidence taken on the other day of the trial. I would however be grateful if you could notify me of this straight away.

I confirm that we will be responsible for your reasonable fees in appearing at the hearing, together with any preparation fee. If you impose a late cancellation charge in the event of the case settling before trial, please let me have the details forthwith so that I can put the Defendants on notice.

I would be grateful if you would acknowledge receipt of this letter and confirm your availability for the hearing.

Yours sincerely,

B26   Request for engineer's report

Dear Sir/Madam,

Re: Laura Green of 3 Fry Rd, Leeds.

We are instructed by the above-named in respect of an accident on 5 March 2007. We write to ask that you prepare a report for us for our use in the court case that has evolved following the accident.

Our client is a machine operator and works for Scrooge plc at their premises, Station Road, Leeds. The company is involved in the making of widgets. On the day of the accident our client was operating her widget-making machine and in pulling the lever to close the hood of the machine the hood fell off and hit her head.

I enclose:
(i)   particulars of claim and defence;
(ii)   witness statements as exchanged;
(iii)   order on directions from which you will see that I must serve expert evidence by *;
(iv)   correspondence with the Defendants from which you will see that they confirm that you may have access to the premises in question.

I would be grateful if you would arrange to inspect the locus in quo with my client and myself, and I ask that you provide us with a report explaining:
(i)   how the accident happened;
(ii)   the likely causes of the accident and your support for the claims of negligence and/or breach of statutory duty as set out in the pleadings.

Please let us know If you consider that any of the allegations are not supportable, let us know as well If there are further allegations that should be made.

Please would you let me have an estimate of your likely costs of reporting – *you will see from the directions order that the court has set a limit upon the costs in relation to your report recoverable from the Defendants in the event that the claim is won. This means that if the costs of your report exceeds that fee, my client will have to pay the difference at the end of the day.*

Yours sincerely,

B27   Request for care expert's report

Dear Ms Smith,

Re: Peter Vincent of 2 Green Street, Lytham.

I am instructed by the above-named in respect of an accident on 4 July 2007. The Defendant to this accident lost control of his motorcar and mounted the pavement hitting my client. My client's lower body was crushed, and he suffered both lower spinal damage and the loss of use of both of his legs. He is now seriously incapacitated, being wheelchair bound. The lower spinal fracture has resulted in a partial paralysis to his lower body and he is doubly incontinent.

I enclose copies of the following to assist you:
1.   Particulars of claim and Defence. Order on directions given by the court.
2.   Full set of GP records.
3.   Set of treating hospital notes.

Medical reports:
4.   Mr J J Jones FRCS – consultant spinal surgeon.
5.   Mrs G Bury – psychiatrist.
6.   Mr R Hancock – consultant in rehabilitation medicine.
7.   Mrs Peters – physiotherapist.
8.   Mr S Shallow – occupational therapist – aids and equipment expert.
9.   Mr P Bunt – prosthetic expert.

Witness statements as exchanged:
10.   The client.
11.   The client's wife Laurel Vincent.

I am awaiting a report from an architect on adapting and modifying the client's present accommodation. I will forward this to you as soon as it is available.

I need a report detailing the amount and extent of care that my client has received in the past, and what care he may need in the future. You will see from the statement of Laurel Vincent that she has had to give up her employment to look after her husband. Part of the problem would appear to be the constant spasms that Mr Vincent suffers as a result of the spinal cord damage (please see the report of M Jones for full details of this) and partly as a result of the psychiatric distress and grave depression that he continues to suffer from which makes him an active suicide risk (please see the report of Mrs Bury for details).

You will see from page 44 of the Hospital notes that a care worker employed by the local authority visited my client at home on 1 June and estimated that he did not need any care provisions apart from those already given by his wife. You will also see from his wife's statement that she is worn out, and stressed by the situation that she finds herself in. Further, she is unable to safely assist her husband in bathing as he is far too heavy for her to get in and out of the bath. The Occupation Therapy report of Mr Shallow recommends the installation of a Closobath and this is being put in hand.

I need you to comment on whether or not the local authority report is realistic. Perhaps you would explain to the court the difficult financial situation that local authorities find themselves in and the pressure on their services and funding constraints.

Would you please comment on whether or not you think that this is a claim where a case manager will need to be employed.

Please would you let me have an estimate of your likely costs of reporting – *you will see from the directions order that the court has set a limit upon the costs in relation to your report recoverable from the Defendants in the event that the claim is won. This means that if the costs of your report exceeds that fee, my client will have to pay the difference at the end of the day.*

I am advising this client with the benefit of legal expense insurance and I will need to get authority from the insurer before incurring your fee; would you therefore please provide me with details of the likely cost of the same before proceeding

You will see that I am under an order to exchange your report by ** next. I would be grateful if you would ensure that the report is with me at least three weeks prior to that date so that I can ensure that my client and other experts can see it before disclosure. I have already telephoned your office to ensure that the timescale is acceptable to you.

If you need any further information, please contact me.

Yours sincerely,

B28 Request for road accident expert's report

Dear Ms Piper,

Re: Timothy Bennet of 4 Peters Gate, Broadway.

I am instructed by the above-named in respect of a road accident that occurred on 8 July 2007. I write to ask that you provide us with a road accident report.

The accident occurred at the junction of Main Road and High Street, Broadway at approximately 10am. On the day of the accident Mr Bennet was walking across the junction, travellingon the north side going from east to west, with the pedestrian lights showing the green man. A Mercedes motor car jumped the lights and knocked him down. You will see from the Police Report that the driver of the vehicle that hit my client alleges that my client was walking from west to east rather then east to west.

I enclose:
(i)   a copy of the pleadings;
(ii)   my client's witness statement;
(iii)   witness statement of independent witness Trevor Brown;
(iv)   the police report;
(v)   a rough sketch plan prepared by my client showing the various positions of the people and vehicles involved in the accident.

I would be grateful if you would prepare an accident report describing your views as to how the accident occurred, where the various people involved in the accident were placed at the time the accident happened and your estimate as to the speed of the various vehicles involved.

Please give your expert opinion about the cause of the accident and any support you can give to the allegations of negligence in the particulars of claim.

You will see that my client suffered, among other injuries, a fracture to his left femur and left lower arm and hand. He suffered gross bruising to the inside of his right leg. I would be grateful if you would confirm whether or not these injuries are consistent with him travelling from east to west rather then the other way around as alleged by the driver.

If you have any doubts regarding the allegations made by counsel in the particulars of claim I would be grateful if you could let me know in a separate letter. If you consider there are any further allegations of negligence please mention them in your report.

You may well want to meet with my client at the scene of the accident and I have warned him that you may be contacting him. His telephone number is 0546-75645.

I look forward to receiving your report and photographs of the locus in quo.

Please would you let me have an estimate of your likely costs of reporting – *you will see from the directions order that the court has set a limit upon the costs in relation to your report recoverable from the Defendants in the event that the claim is won. This means that if the costs of your report exceeds that fee, my client will have to pay the difference at the end of the day (will need to ask the Legal Aid Board for authority to expend the sum in question).*

Yours sincerely,

B29   Request for employment expert's report

Dear Mr Stevens,

Re: John Doors of 13 Southvale, Peterborough.

I am instructed by the above-named in respect of an accident on 25 May 2007. I write to ask that you provide me with an employment report for our use in the ensuing court action that has arisen following the accident.

My client was very severely injured on the day of the accident when the car in which he was a passenger went into the crash barrier on the M1. His injuries are right-sided hemi-plegia and some brain damage as a result of a fracture to his skull.

At the time of the accident my client was working as a car mechanic. His working history up to that time was that he left school at the age of 16 and had worked for three different garages as a mechanic before commencing the current job with Len's Autos, High Road, Peterborough in 1989 when he was aged 23.

I enclose:
(i)   a copy of the pleadings;
(ii)   my client's witness statement;
(iii) witness statement from his previous employer and workmates;
(iv)   medical reports.

You will see from those documents that he has been unable to return to work until now, but that the orthopaedic doctor is saying that he may be able to do a job involving light duties in the near future. The neurologist is more doubtful of the client's capabilities and you will see that the report of the rehabilitation consultant is frankly disparaging. You will see from my client's proof that he is suggesting that he would be interested in doing the following jobs: telephonist, receptionist or filing clerk.

I think that he may need a period of rehabilitation and retraining given the extent of his hemi-plegia. My client is very optimistic and you will see from the neuropsychological report that this is partially due to a small amount of brain injury that my client has suffered in the accident.

I need a thorough assessment of my client's working capabilities and whether or not his expectations and those of his medical advisors are reasonable given his presentation and skills. I also need your assessment of what employment rehabilitation opportunities exist and the cost of the same.

I would be grateful if you would provide a report giving an assessment as to his chances of finding work in these fields and his likely earnings. Would you set out his likely career pattern if the accident had not occurred? I would finally be grateful if you would compare the wages that he would have earned, as against the wages that he is likely to earn.

I have told my client that you may well need to contact him to clarify certain points and his telephone number is 0234-675456. Please ensure that you put in writing any appointment dates both to the client (he forgets things easily, but his partner will ensure she is present on the day) and to me so that I can diarise the appointment.

Please would you let me have an estimate of your likely costs of reporting – *you will see from the directions order that the court has set a limit upon the costs in relation to your report recoverable from the Defendants in the event that the claim is won. This means that if the costs of your report exceeds that fee, my client will have to pay the difference at the end of the day (will need to ask the Legal Aid Board for authority to expend the sum in question).*

Yours sincerely,

B30   Letter to NI people for history of work

Special Section A
DSS Longbenton
Newcastle upon Tyne
NE98 1YZ

Dear Sirs

Re; Joseph Reilly
NI Number – 1234 YY NO

Date of birth 17 August 1965
Address 1 Craven Court, Whitstable, York

We are instructed by the above named in connection with a claim for compensation arising out of an accident on 1 January 2008.

We would be grateful if you would send us a list of the National Insurance contributions that Mr Reilly has made and the employers he has worked for since leaving school to date.

We enclose our cheque in the sum of £27.19, made payable to the contributions agency, and confirm that this request is made in connection with a claim for compensation following a road traffic accident.

We look forward to hearing from you in the near future.

Yours faithfully,

B31　Letter to lay witness with questionnaire

Dear Ms Philips,

Re: My client – Roy Jones of 17 New Road, Ilford, Essex.

I am instructed by the above-named in respect of an accident in which he was hit by a Volvo motor car on 16 September 2007 at 10am. The accident occurred when Mr Jones was walking across the High Road where it joins at the Roundhouse Roundabout, Ilford, Essex. Mr Jones was badly injured in the accident and I am advising him in relation to a possible claim for compensation for these injuries against the driver of the Volvo.

I understand that you were a witness to this accident. I would be most grateful if you would answer the questions raised in the enclosed questionnaire, and draw a sketch plan, if appropriate, on the paper attached.

I enclose a stamped addressed envelope for your reply. I look forward to hearing from you and thank you for your assistance.

Yours sincerely,

B32   Initial questionnaire for Ms Philips

1   Your full name
2   Your address
3   Your telephone number
4   Your date of birth
5   Your job
6   The date of accident
7   The time of accident
8   What was the weather like at the time of the accident?
9   The place where accident occurred
10 Please give a description of exactly what you saw
11 State where you were positioned. (It may assist you to draw a plan of the accident spot and where the various people were stationed. A sheet of paper is enclosed for this purpose.)
12 Please state who you think was to blame for the accident, giving your reasons for your view
13 Please confirm whether you would be prepared to give evidence if this case went to court.

Signature   Date

Ref MD/JONES 917

Note: The questionnaire should be spaced out appropriately to give adequate space for descriptions, reasons, etc.

B33   Request to take detailed statement

Dear Ms Pound,

Re: My client – Roy Jones of 17 New Road, Ilford, Essex.

Further to your kindly providing me with a written statement, it is now clear that this case is likely to proceed and I would like to take a full statement from you to send to the Defendants to the claim and to lodge with the court.

In order for me to do this, I will need to see you. I do not think that the appointment will take any longer then one hour. I am happy either to make arrangements to see you at your home, or perhaps you would like to come to see me at my office if it is more convenient? If you have any travelling expenses or loss of earnings as a result of the time spent with me I will be more than happy to pay those costs. If you do have loss of earnings I would be grateful if you could provide me with either a wage slip or a letter from your employer confirming the amount.

Please would you telephone my secretary to make an appointment at your convenience.

Yours sincerely,

B34 Notification to witness to attend court

Dear Ms Pound,

Re: My client – Roy Jones of 17 New Road, Ilford, Essex.

I write to inform you that the court hearing in this case has now been fixed for 6 October 2008 and this will be heard at the Swindon County Court at 10.30am. The case has been listed for hearing for one day and I would like you to attend the hearing in the afternoon.

I enclose, as is my normal practice, a witness summons together with a cheque in the sum of £70.00 which we understand is a sufficient amount to allow you to travel by public transport from Ilford to Swindon and back, together with a sum sufficient to allow you to purchase refreshment for the day.

The witness summons is a formal document from the court requiring you to attend. I enclose a second copy of the witness summons for you to pass onto your employers; I think that you will find that you will have no difficulty in getting them to allow you to take the day off work so long as you provide them with a copy of this summons. You may claim your loss of a day's pay for attending at court from us, providing you provide me with a formal letter giving details of your losses from your employers. On the day that you are required at court I would be grateful if you could arrive at 9.30 am which will give us the opportunity to have a short discussion prior to your giving evidence.

Yours sincerely,

B35   Request for wage details

Dear Sir/Madam,

Re: Melinda Moyne (Payroll No A79632).

We are instructed by the above-named, an employee of your company, in connection with her road accident on 17 October 2007, as a result of which she sustained serious injuries.

To assist in the preparation of our client's claim for loss of earnings as a result of the accident, we would be obliged for the following information:

(i)   dates of our client's absence(s) from work attributable to the accident;

(ii)   details of her net and gross earnings week by week for the period of 13 weeks prior to the accident; if any of those weeks were untypical please extend the period accordingly;

(iii) details of changes of wage rates or deductions during the period of absence with an estimate of the weekly net and gross earnings that would have been produced thereby;

(iv)   details of gross and net earnings week by week for six weeks from her return to work;

(v)   any sick pay awarded to her, including any which may be refundable to yourselves, should she be successful in her claim. If this is the case please send a copy of the contract of employment or other agreement or document setting out this provision;

(vi)   any other losses in respect of earnings which have resulted or may result from the accident or period off work such as overtime, bonuses, commission, pension contributions and entitlement, etc.

We look forward to receiving the information requested above, and thank you in advance for your co-operation. We confirm that you have no involvement in the claim. A stamped addressed envelope is enclosed for your reply.

Yours faithfully,

B36 Request to Meteorological Office for weather report

Dear Sir/Madam,

Re: George Pervis of 15 Shepherd's Bush, London, W6.

We are instructed by the above-named in relation to a road accident that occurred on 15 January 2008, at approximately 5 am. The accident took place at Shepherd's Bush Roundabout, London, W6.

We are making a claim, on behalf of our client against the driver of the other vehicle involved in the crash and we are keen to know the exact weather conditions, not only at the time of the accident, but also for the preceding 12 hours.

There is an allegation that wind speed played a part in the accident and we would be grateful if you would detail the wind speed at the time of the accident and let us know whether it was in any way unusual.

We would be very grateful if you could supply us with as detailed information as possible for both 14 and 15 January 2008, including a description of the rainfall, cloud cover, and temperature. We shall, of course, be responsible for your reasonable fees.

Yours faithfully,

B37   Request for Health and Safety Executive report

Dear Sir/Madam,

Re: Melissa Jones of 2 Connecticut Close, York.

We are instructed by the above-named in relation to a potential claim against her employers, Bigsby, Brown & Co of 2 High Road, York, following an accident at work on 13 December 2007.

The accident occurred at 2 High Road, York at about 10.15am. Our client was in the process of operating the lathe on which she worked, when a component in the lathe exploded and a piece flew off into her eye.

We understand that an officer from the Executive attended the scene of the accident to carry out an investigation. We would be very grateful if you could provide a statement of your findings together with any other documents relating to the case that relate to the incident. We will of course pay any reasonable fee incurred in producing the information.

If you are unable to send certain documents without the necessary court order, please list the documents in your possession.

Yours faithfully,

B38   Letter to Motor Insurers' Bureau – uninsured driver

Dear Sir/Madam

Re: John Smith of 5 Browning Road, London, E5.

We are instructed by the above-named in relation to a road accident that occurred on 16 November 2007. The accident was, we say, caused by the negligent driving of a motor vehicle driven and owned by Mr Alan Brook of 13 Clapham Street, London SW5. We were first asked to investigate this claim by Mr Smith on 1 December 2007 and on 2 December 2007 we wrote to the Horseferry Road Police – who have control over the area in which this accident took place, to ask for full details of Mr Brook's insurance details. We obtained no reply to that letter and within the dates requisite under the scheme we wrote again to the Police (copies of these letters enclosed) and again received no response to our letter. We believe that Mr Brook was uninsured and in accordance with the terms of the scheme we ask that you accept this claim within the terms of the scheme.

We look forward to hearing from you with the relevant application form in the near future.

Yours faithfully,

B39   Letter to Motor Insurers' Bureau – untraced driver

Dear Sir/Madam

Re: Peter Jones of 10 Manor Road, Hanley, Middlesex.

We are instructed by the above-named who was injured by a hit and run driver in an accident on 18 May 2007. We write to ask that you accept this case under the terms of the 'Untraced Drivers Scheme' and send us the relevant form for notification of the same.

The accident happened in London Road, Hanley. Our client was walking across a pedestrian crossing when the driver of a Golf GTI motor car drove straight across the pedestrian crossing knocking him to the ground. The driver did not stop and neither the client nor any witness took his registration number. We enclose a copy of the letter from the police confirming they have been unable to locate him. We therefore ask that you accept the case under the MIB agreement.

The injuries and losses sustained by our client were as follows: fractured left tibia; cut left ear; bruised left thigh and arm.

We look forward to hearing from you.

Yours faithfully,

B40 Letter to defendant's solicitors disclosing evidence

Dear Sirs

Re: *Maloney v Blunt*

We enclose for disclosure to you copies of the following:
(i)   orthopaedic report prepared by Mr Price FRCS;
(ii)   psychiatric report prepared by Dr Morris;
(iii) schedule of financial loss and supporting receipts;
(iv)   witness statement of Mr D Maloney;
(v)   witness statement of Ms J P Kim;
(vi)   police report.

Kindly acknowledge receipt of the above documentation. We consider that this claim is now capable of resolution and will write to you separately on this point. If the matter cannot be settled, we have advised our client to issue proceedings in the Lowestoft County Court at the expiration of 21 days from service of this letter upon you which we calculate to be 26 March 2008.

Yours faithfully,

B41   Part 36 Offer to settle

Without prejudice except as to costs

Dear Sirs

Re: *Maloney v Blunt*

You will now have received our letter of [date] in which we made full disclosure of the medical evidence, schedule of financial loss, witness statement from both our client and the independent witness, and the police report. You will recall that your client was convicted of the offence of careless driving, a relevant conviction, at the Highbury Magistrates Court last Wednesday in relation to this accident. Our client suffered significant injuries, but fortunately has made a good recovery and accordingly, we consider that this claim is now capable of resolution.

This letter is an offer to settle the above claim before proceedings are commenced. It complies with Part 36 of the Civil Procedure Rules and if it is not accepted, we will ask the court to take this offer into account when making any order as to costs.

The Claimant in this action is prepared to settle her claim for the total sum of £14,500.00 plus her reasonable costs to the date of settlement. This amount is inclusive of interest and benefits repayable to the state under s 1 of the Social Security (Recovery of Benefits) Act 1997 – which we understand to be Nil.

This offer relates to the whole of the claim. It will remain open for 21 days from the date of service, which we calculate to be two days after the date of this letter.

Yours faithfully,

B42   Letter enclosing pleadings

Dear Madam,

Re: *Smith v Bailey*

On behalf of the Claimant, please find enclosed a copy of the letter and documents we have today served on the Defendant in this case. We look forward to receiving the defence within the time set down by the rules.

Yours faithfully,

Note: This letter should be sent to the Defendant's solicitors if they have not yet given notice that they will accept service of the proceedings.

B43   Letter varying time – fast track claim

Dear Sir,

Re: *Deans v Berry*

You will be aware that CPR Part 28.4 states that a party must apply to the court if he wishes to vary the date which the court has fixed for:

(i)   the return of a listing questionnaire under rule 28.5;

(ii)   the trial; or

(iii) the trial period;

or if the variation of any other date would make it necessary to vary the above dates.

You ask us to give you an extension of 14 days in which to serve the expert evidence. The court, in the directions given, have not ordered that no extensions of time should be given.

We do not consider that the extension will vary any of the above dates and accordingly we are content to consent to the extension. We calculate that expert evidence should now be served on 14 March 2008.

Yours faithfully,

B44   Letter varying time – multi track claim

Dear Sir,

Re: *Deans v Berry*

You will be aware that CPR Part 29.5 states that a party must apply to the court if he wishes to vary the date which the court has fixed for:

(i)   a case management conference;
(ii)   a pre trial review;
(iii)   the return of a listing questionnaire under rule 29.6;
(iv)   the trial; or
(v)   the trial period;

or if the variation of any other date would make it necessary to vary the above dates.

You ask us to give you an extension of 28 days in which to serve the expert evidence. The court, in the directions given, have not ordered that no extensions of time should be given.

We do not consider that the extension will vary any of the above dates and accordingly we are content to consent to the extension. We calculate that expert evidence should now be served on 12 March 2008.

Yours faithfully,

B45   Letter enclosing claimant's list of documents – standard disclosure

Dear Madam,

Re: *Herbert v Curry and Co*

In anticipation of being directed by the court to disclose our client's list of documents

Or

In accordance with the order on directions dated *

We enclose for service upon you the Claimant's List of Documents in accordance with the rules relating to standard disclosure under CPR Part 31.

If you wish to inspect any of the above discloseable documents, or if you want copies of the same, kindly give us written notice of which documents you require inspection/ copies of, and confirm that you will pay our reasonable copying costs. We confirm that we will provide inspection facilities/copies of the documents within seven days of your reasonable request.

Kindly acknowledge receipt.

Yours faithfully,

B46 Letter to defendant upon receipt of the allocation questionnaire – fast track claim

Ref MD/HERBERT/91404

Dear Sirs

Re: *Curry v Motors Limited*

You will by now have received the case Allocation Questionnaire from the court and be aware that this must be returned, together with any proposed draft directions by 1 October 2008.

We attach to this letter a copy of the standard Fast Track Directions practice form upon which we have written our suggested directions.

If you are in agreement with our suggestions, please let us know within seven days of receipt of this letter. We will then write to the court with our suggested joint directions hopefully for approval by the District Judge.

Because of the tight timetable in which to return the Questionnaire to the court, it may be better if your reference telephones Ms Jones of this office should any problems arise with our suggested directions, or should you require any discussion over your suggested directions.

Yours faithfully,

B47   Letter to defendant upon receipt of the allocation questionnaire – multi track claim

Dear Sirs

Re: *Curry v Motors Limited*

You will by now have received the case Allocation Questionnaire from the ... this is a very complex claim and we consider that directions are best *given by the Master in a case management hearing –*

OR

–   we consider that it is unnecessary to take up the court's time in a case management hearing and that we can attempt to agree directions subject to the court's approval; accordingly, we enclose a copy of our draft order on directions for your consideration. The directions comply with CPR practice direction on multi track directions. Please let us know if you agree the directions as sought and we will then draw up an order by consent, hopefully for the court's approval.

Yours faithfully,

B48   Letter re: defendant's request for medical examination

Dear Sir/Madam,

Re: *Downs v Elliot*

Further to your letter requesting facilities to have our client examined by Dr Brown, we write to confirm that you may have the facilities provided that you undertake:

(i)   to pay the Claimant's reasonable travellingexpenses and loss of earnings;

(ii)   that Dr Brown has not treated our client previously to yours or his knowledge.

Kindly ask Dr Brown's secretary to send our client an appointment at the following address:

1 Sunnybrook Dean
Bramble Road
Orpington
Kent
KT2 1PQ
Tel: 0123 345 567

Yours faithfully,

B49   Request for facilities for expert

Dear Sir/Madam,

Re: *Gerry v Tunes Ltd*

We write to ask that facilities be granted for us to obtain an expert engineering report on the accident in question. We propose instructing our expert, Mr John Dixon, to examine the locus in quo.

We are quite happy for this inspection to proceed as a joint expert engineering inspection should you wish. If so, please would you confirm that you are happy to meet half of the expense of this expert and we will then send you a copy of our proposed letter of instruction for your consideration.

Please confirm that you are prepared to grant those facilities and we would ask that you notify us of the telephone number of the person through whom the arrangements should be made.

Yours faithfully,

Note: The paragraph in italics is for consideration only.

B50 Letter to defendants on service of listing questionnaires – fast track claim

Dear Sirs

Re: *Brown v Butter*

We have now been served by the court with the Listing Questionnaire in this matter. You will note that it must be returned to the court by 3 March 2008

We enclose our form completed and would be most grateful if you would consider our responses and let us know if you are in agreement with the proposals contained therein and our suggested directions for the trial and the trial timetable of this matter.

Yours faithfully,

B51   Letter to defendants on service of listing questionnaires – multi track claim

Dear Sirs

Re: *Bean v Bone*

We have now been served by the court with the Listing Questionnaire in this matter.

It must be returned to the court by 3 March 2008.

– *we consider that this matter is of such complexity and there have been so many problems in the litigation process to get to this step in the proceedings that it is essential that the court fixes a date for a pre-trial review. Accordingly, we are asking the court to give us a date for such review*

– *we enclose our completed form for your attention. You will be aware that co-operation on the completion of the questionnaire is encouraged by the court. Accordingly, kindly consider our suggestions for further directions and the conduct of the trial in this matter, and complete and return your form to us without delay OR confirm that you have returned your form duly completed to the court and send us a copy of the same.*

Yours faithfully,

B52   Letter regarding trial bundle

Dear Madam,

Re: *Ball v Cox*

In accordance with our order on directions and the order made upon pre-trial review in this matter, please find a draft bundle of documents for use at the court hearing. If you want us to include any other documents please let us know by 3 March 2008, otherwise we will assume that you are content with the bundle as it stands.

Yours faithfully,

B53 Statement of costs following settlement

Without prejudice save as to the costs of detailed assessment

Dear Sir/Madam,

Re: *Evans v Chapman*

Further to the settlement of this action we set out below our costs for possible agreement. We confirm that we advised our client under a 'no win no fee' agreement with the benefit of after the event insurance. We confirm that the charges relate to work undertaken whilst the agreement was in force. We confirm that this is not a claim to which fixed costs relates.

To: taking initial instructions from the client on 1 March 2007. Drafting an intial proof; interviewing in person two witnesses Mrs Brown and Mrs Weathers and preparing statements which were disclosed to you on 3 July 2007. Gathering in and reading the police report, the medical records both hospital and GP, instructing Mr Doctor to prepare both initial and final medical reports, liaising with the client and seeing her on two occasions to prepare a witness statement which was disclosed to you on 3 July 2007. To considering quantum and making a part 36 offer to settle the claim. Including advising the client in person on settlement and the steps involved in final settlement.

Legal Executive involved; FILEX: Hourly rate as specified in agreement £110 per hour

Telephone calls – 30 @ £11.00 per call	£ 330.00
Letters out – 56 @ £11.00 per letter	£ 616.00
Attendances, preparations, etc – 12 hours @ £110.00 per hour	£1320.00
	£2266.00

Success fee on CFA agreement signed date of formal instruction. We confirm all the necessary statutory provisions were complied with upon entry of the agreement. Risk element rate of success fee 75%.

75% of £2266.00	£1,699.50
Total due	£3,965.50
VAT at 17.5%	£693.96
Total	£4,659.46
Disbursements liable for VAT:	
Engineer's fees:	£750
VAT at 17.5%	£131.25
Total	£881.25
Disbursements not liable for VAT:	
Court fees	£120
Police report	£60
Insurance premium fee	£96.50
Medical reports	£250.00
Total	£526.50
Our total costs are therefore	£6067.21

Please let us know if you are prepared to agree these costs or whether we will need to have a formal bill drawn to lodge with the court for detailed assessment.

Yours faithfully,

B54   Draft agenda for experts' meeting

AGENDA FOR MEETING BETWEEN

Dr Brown and Dr Westthorpe

Please answer the following list of questions. If you feel a question is outside your field of expertise, say so in your answer. If the answer is agreed please state that fact. Alternatively, in your answer set out what matters are agreed and where you differ.

Please ensure that all of your answers are given on balance of probabilities (ie more likely than not) rather than in terms of medical certainty:

(i)   what would have been the probable natural history of the Claimant's development of arthritis in any event;

(ii)   what was the relative importance of the accident on 20 June 2007 to this development;

(iii) what would have been the Claimant's ability to work but for the accident? This is to include the type and frequency of work and the length of time it might have continued.

Specimen Schedules of Special Damages

A Schedule of damages appended to particulars of claim

IN THE MAIDSTONE COUNTY COURT   Case No 765

BETWEEN:

JOHN SMITH

Claimant

and

LONG DISTANCE HAULIERS LTD

Defendant

Schedule of damages

Medical treatment	£43.10	
Earnings for 13 wks prior to accident 5.4.01–9.7.01		
Gross pay	£6,227.59	
Tax	£1,154.35	
NIC	£510.25	£1,664.60
	£4,562.99	

= Ave wkly net earnings =
£4,562.99 ÷ 13 =
For period 10.7.01–13.8.01   £351.00

Expected earnings The Claimant was off work for 5 weeks

5 x £351.00 =   £1,755.00

Actual earnings Gross   £820.68

Tax   £66.31

NIC   £59.12   £125.43

                                                                £695.25

Net loss of earnings   £1,059.75

(Interest: to be calculated when date of trial known)

Total Special Damage   £1,102.85

APPENDIX A TO SCHEDULE OF SPECIAL DAMAGE

Pre-accident earnings 5.4.99–9.7.99

Week ending	Gross	Tax	NIC
9.4.01	390.80	66.96	33.80
16.4.01	488.49	89.93	43.57
23.4.01	488.49	89.93	43.57
30.4.01	488.49	89.93	43.57
7.5.01	21.25	nil	nil
21.5.01	586.20	111.90	44.72
28.5.01	488.49	89.93	43.57
4.6.01	391.26	67.06	33.85
11.6.01	578.44	110.01	44.72
18.6.01	576.69	109.91	44.72
25.6.01	561.39	106.19	44.72
2.7.01	645.11	125.45	44.72
9.7.01	522.49	97.25	44.72
	6,227.59	1154.35	510.25

Gross =   6,227.59

Tax =   1,154.35

NIC =   510.25

Net =   4,562.99

= net earnings per week = £351.00

APPENDIX B TO SCHEDULE OF SPECIAL DAMAGE

Post-accident earnings 10.7.01–13.8.01

Week ending	Gross	Tax	NIC
16.7.01	212.77	26.01	16.00
23.7.01	126.75	6.23	7.40
30.7.01	10.50	28.33	nil
6.8.01	185.67	19.78	13.29
13.8.01	284.99	42.62	23.22
Totals	820.68	66.31	59.12

(This excludes damage in respect of:
(i)   pain, suffering and loss of amenity;
(ii)   loss of congenial employment;
(iii) loss of earning capacity;
(iv) interest on the above at 2% pa;

since the service of the Claim Form on 14 November 2002.)

DATED etc

B   Final schedule of damages in serious case

MR PATRICK PYLE

SCHEDULE OF SPECIAL DAMAGE AND FUTURE LOSS

Date of accident: 6 April 2001

Item Number	Head of loss and damage	Sum Claimed
1	**Items lost during the accident** (a) The Claimant's trousers were damaged beyond repair (b) The Claimant's wristwatch was damaged – estimated cost of repair 40.00 65.00	
		105.00
2	**Prescription charges** (a) As a result of the accident the Claimant has had to purchase prescriptions on a regular basis. These are estimated at the sum of £300.00 to date	300.00
3	**Loss of earnings** Before the accident the Claimant was employed as a driver/labourer earning approximately £300 pw gross, £232.50 after deductions for tax and national Insurance. He has not received any pay since 14 April 2001. The gross earnings rate has been increased by 5% from April 2002 and 4% from April 2003.	

Loss of earnings

14.4.01–31.3.02 50 weeks at £232.50 pw net   £11,625.00

1.4.02–31.3.03 52 weeks at £315.00 gross and 239.04 net   £12,430.08

1.4.03–7.1.04 40 weeks at £327.60 gross and £247.70 net   £9,908.00

Total   £33,963.08

4   **Total Special Damages**

Item 1	£105.00	
Item 2	£300.00	
Item 3	£33,963.08	£34, 368.08

5   **Interest on special damages** Interest is claimed at half
the special account rate from 6.4.01 to 7.1.04

6.4.01–31.1.02	301 days at 7.00%	5.79%
01.2.02-7.1.04	706 days at 6.00%	11.61%
	Full rate 17.4%	
	Half rate 8.7%	

£34,368.08 at 8.7%   £2,990.02

Total special damage and interest   £37,358.10

Future loss of earnings

The Claimant has not been able to work since
the accident. If he were working in his old job
he would be earning £17,035.00   = £12,880.40 net pa

The Claimant is now 45 years old. He anticipated
working until he was 65. Thus for the remaining
20 years of working life a multiplier of 17.08 is
appropriate

£12,880.43 net pa x 17.08   = £219,997.74

Because of his injuries the Claimant is permanently disabled

It is possible that the Claimant may be able to work on
a part time basis in light work in the future, following a
retraining course.

The Claimant will therefore give credit for the following:

One year on government retraining programme at £10 pw
above existing benefits. In the Claimant's case these
will be part of the CRU to date of settlement/judgment.
Therefore:

£10 pw for 52 weeks   = £520.00

Assuming light part time work after one year's retraining
programme based on estimated earning levels of £4.00–
£5.00 per hour. Say 18 hours pw at £4.50 per hour = £81.00 pw
or £4,212 pa. Earnings below taxable limit – less NI =
£4,065.36 pa.

The prospects of obtaining such work are not great for a man with
the Claimant's disadvantages.

A multiplier of 9 is therefore appropriate.

£4,065.36 net pa x 9   = £36,588.24

Total deductions = £37,108.24

Therefore total future loss   = <u>£182,889.50</u>

The claim is therefore:

Total special damage and interest   £37,358.10

Total future loss <u>£182,889.50</u>

<u>£220,247.60</u>

C   Schedule of damages for interim payment application where child very severely disabled

IN THE HIGH COURT OF JUSTICE
QUEEN'S BENCH DIVISION

BETWEEN:

ALEXANDRA MOORE

(Infant suing by her Mother and Litigation Friend Avril Moore)

Claimant

and

AVRIL MOORE

Second Claimant

and

SOUTH CENTRAL TRAINS

Defendant

SCHEDULE OF SPECIAL DAMAGE AND FUTURE LOSS SERVED ON BEHALF OF THE CLAIMANT'S CLAIM FOR AN INTERIM PAYMENT

FIRST CLAIMANT

(Throughout this Schedule, the First Claimant is referred to as 'Alexandra', and her mother and Litigation Friend as Mrs Moore.)

1   PARENTAL CARE/SUPERVISION
The claim under this head is as follows:

Additional care:
from 29.4.01 to 31.10.03
(130 weeks) @ 45.5 hrs pw @ £7.20 per hr   £42,558.00

Loss of earnings – *Mrs Moore*
From 1.5.01 to 31.8.01 – (17.5 wks)
Loss of 7 hrs pw @ 5.30 net per hr =   £37.10 net pw

£649.25

Loss of earnings – *Mrs Moore*
From 1.5.01 to 30.4.02 – (1 yr)
Difference between salary as a Research
Scientist and grant as a student because qualification
was delayed by 12 months.
Salary:

£18,950 gross pa less tax and NI gives	£14,585 net pa
Less grant of £4,500	=£10,085.00
Total	£96,559.50

2   MISCELLANEOUS ADDITIONAL EXPENSES

(a) Extra heating costs
      From 1.7.02 to 31.10.03 (70 wks) @ £7 pw   £490.00
      Plus further 3 yrs' costs – 3 x 52 x £7   £1,092.00

(b) Extra washing costs
      From 1.7.02 to 31.10.03 (70 wks) @ £5 pw   £350.00
      Plus further 3 yrs' costs – 3 x 52 x £5   £780.00

Total   £2,712.00

3   TRAVELLING EXPENSES

To and from Queen Mary Hospital from
house in Peterborough – 1.5.01 to 1.7.02
(72 weeks) – average of 3 pw @ 8 miles per
trip @ 36p per mile   £622.08

4   FUTURE CARE

The cost of a nanny would be £13,750.00 pa
which for the next 3 yrs would cost   £41,250.00

The agency costs are:

Temporary relief – 6 wks @ £255 pw for 3 yrs £4,590.00

Cost of taking nanny for 2 wk holiday –
£500 for 3 yrs   £1,500.00

Cost of placing Alexandra in care for 2 wks pa

£250 for 3 yrs   £750.00

£48,090.00

5   HOUSING AND ASSOCIATED COSTS

(Paragraph 10 of the Affidavit)
The claim is for 3% of £150,000 over the
multiplied period of 20 years, being £90,000
together with the expenses of conveyancing
and moving, estimated at £5,000

Total   £95,000

6   AIDS, ADAPTATIONS and SPECIAL EQUIPMENT

(Reference report Jacqueline Webb & Associates of 15 July 03
p&p and VAT not included)
to

Appendix

Page 1	Rifton Adjustable Corner Chair	£310.50
Page 2	Spa Controller Chair	£480.50
Page 3	Tumbleform Deluxe Floor	£104.00
Page 4	Ladderback Chair	£85.00
Page 5	Cut Out table	£211.00
Page 6	Computer Work station	£67.50
Page 7	Home Bed Rails	£80.00
Page 8	Sheffield Potty Seat	£27.20
Page 9	Chailey Toilet Seat	£104.24
Page 10	Chiltern 10 Shower Trolley	£1,050.00
Page 11	Alverna Series 8 Pushchair	£800.00
Page 12	Physioform Wedge	£362.00
Page 13	Prone Standing Frame	£262.11
Page 14	Dell Microcomputer etc	£1,500.00
Page 15	Super Pethna	£405.80
Page 16	Swing and Seat	£115.00
	Boots	£420.00
	Physical appliances	£340.00
	Waterproof sheets	£5.50
	Computer disks	£144.00
	Total	£6,853.55
	+25%	£1,713.53
		£8,566.08

7   TRANSPORT

Cost of Nissan Prairie	£27,215
Less trade-in for present car	£5,000
Estimated running costs per annum £1,500 x 3	£4,500
Total	£26,715

8   TOTAL CLAIM

1	Parental care	£96,599.50
2	Additional expenses	£2,712.00
3	Travelling expenses	£622.08
4	Future care	£48,090.00
5	Housing costs	£95,000.00
6	Aids, adaptations, etc	£8,566.08
7	Transport	£26,715.00
Total		**£278,264.66**

Dated etc

D   Schedule of damages following death of family's breadwinner

IN THE HIGH COURT OF JUSTICE
QUEEN'S BENCH DIVISION

BETWEEN:

LESLEY JOHNSON

(Widow and Administratrix of the Estate of
WINSTON JOHNSON Deceased)

First Claimant

and

NATALIE JOHNSON

Second Claimant

and

NORTHERN TRANSPORT

Defendant

SCHEDULE OF DAMAGES

1   Fatal Accidents Act 1976 claim

a)   The value of the weekly dependency is put at 75%
         of an average net weekly wage of £247.21 (during
         2001 until the deceased's death on 31 December 1998)
         75% of £247.21=   £185.41
         which represents an annual dependency of   £9,941.36

To which must be added £300 pa loss of the
Deceased's services to his family in the form of
produce from the family's allotment which has
now had to be surrendered   £300

Based on the projected increase in the
Deceased's rate of earnings (from 1 January 2002)
and taking into account the effect of changes in the
value of money to the Deceased's projected
contribution (including those items which were
provided as services by the Deceased), a reasonable
percentage increase in the net annual dependency
would be 5% pa

Pre-trial loss of dependency (calculated to trial
on 2 July 2001)
2002 @ £10,435.42 p.a   £10,435.42
2003 @ £10,960.35 p.a   £10,960.35
2004 – 30 wks @ £11,508.37 p.a   £6,639.44
Total   £25,035.21

Discount factor for pre trial damages; see Table A7, page 30
of PNBA Tables, 2002 Edition, is 0.99
Thus pre trial dependency £25,035.21 x 0.99 is   £24,787.86
Plus interest at half the special account rate
over the period, ie 7.73%

applied to £24,784.86   = £1,915.87

Total   £25,926.15

                                                        £26,700.73

b)   Future loss

Based on the age (43 years) and future employment
prospects of the Deceased an appropriate multiplier
would be 16.39 to age 65 from date of trial, less
discount factor see 1a above 0.99 = 16.23

The annual value of the dependency in 2004 is
£11,508.37 (as before)

£11,508.37 x 16.23   £186,780.85

c)   Totals

Pre-trial loss   £26,700.73
Future loss   £186,780.85
Grand total   £213,481.58

d)   Apportionment

i)   The dependency of Leslie Johnson, the Deceased's
        widow, aged 42, is put at:
        65% of total   £138,763.00

ii)	The dependency of Natalie Johnson, aged 12, daughter of the Deceased and the First Claimant is put at: 15% of total to cover full time education to age 23	£32,022.00
	The dependency of Sally Johnson, aged 11, daughter of the Deceased and the First Claimant is put at: 15% of total to cover full time education to age 23	£32,022.00
e)	The dependency of Christopher Rose, the Deceased's son, aged 14, who does not live with the family is put at: 5% of total	£10,674.58
f)	Bereavement of the First Claimant	£7,500.00
	Interest thereon a the full Special Account Rate, ie 15.46% from 31.12.01 to 2.7.04	£1,159.50

2 Law Reform (Miscellaneous Provisions) Act 1934 claim

i) Special damage

a)	Funeral expenses	£1,000.00
	Plus interest at the full special investment account rate 15.46%	£154.60
	Totalling	£1,154.60
b)	Loss of earnings	
	Loss of wages for 4 wks from accident to death 4 x£196.80 = £787.20 Against which credit is given for payment by employer for First Claimant of £790	£0.00

ii) General damages[1]

a)	Awareness that his life had been shortened while conscious prior to death say	£1,500.00
	Pain and suffering from the date of accident to death say	£1,500.00
	Total	£3,000.00
	Interest at 2% between the date of service of Claim Form (10 July 2002) until trial, say 2 yrs	£120.00
	Total	£3,120.00

iii) The total sum awardable under the Law Reform (Miscellaneous Provisions) Act 1934 is

Special damages	£1,206.00
General damages	£3,180.00
Total	£4,424.00

3   Pain and suffering of the First and Second Claimants in *McLoughlin v O'Brian* claims

First Claimant (widow)	£8,000.00
Second Claimant (daughter – Natalie)	£2,500.00
Total	£10,500.00
Plus interest at 2% pa for 2 yrs	£210.00
Total general damages	£10,710.00

DATED etc

---

[1]   It is unusual to quantify the claims for general damages as has been done here under paras 2 and 3. However, where Counsel feels sure of the valuations and where the figures are needed in what appear to be productive negotiation, it may be sensible to set them out to produce a wholly quantifiable claim.

Useful Addresses

Action for Victims of Medical Accidents (AVMA)
44 High Street
Croydon
Surrey
CR0 1YB

Tel: 020 8686 8333

Association of Personal Injury Lawyers (APIL)
33 Pilcher Gate
Nottingham
NG1 1QF

Associaton of Trial Lawyers of America
PO Box 3717
Washington DC 20007
USA

Tel: 0101 202-965 3500

Compensation Recovery Unit (CRU)
Department of Social Security
Reyrolle Building
Hebburn
Tyne & Wear
NE31 1XB

Tel: 0191 201 0500

Criminal Injuries Compensation Authority (CICA)
Tay House
300 Bath Street
Glasgow
G2 4JR

Tel: 0141 331 2726

Fax: 0141 331 2287

Criminal Injuries Compensation Board (CICB)
Morley House
26–30 Holborn Viaduct
London
EC1A 2JQ

Tel: 020 7842 6800

General Council of the Bar
3 Bedford Row
London
WC1R 4DB

Tel: 020 7242 0082

Fax: 020 7831 9217

Health and Safety Executive (HSE)

HSE Books:
PO Box 1999
Sudbury
Suffolk
CO10 6FS

HSE Information Centre:
Broad Lane
Sheffield
S3 7HQ

Tel: 01742 892345

Fax: 01742 892333

Inquest
Ground Floor
Alexandra National House
330 Seven Sisters Road
London
N4 2PJ

Tel: 020 8802 7430

International Paraplegic Claims Service
7 Cross Lane
Preston
Oakham
Rutland
LE15 9NQ

Tel: 01572 85543

Law Society
113 Chancery Lane
London
WC2A 1PL

Tel: 020 7242 1222

Fax: 020 7831 0344

Motor Insurers' Bureau
152 Silbury Boulevard
Central Milton Keynes
MK9 1NB

Tel: 01908 240000

Fax: 01908 671681

National Head Injuries Association
4 King Edward Court
King Edward Street
Nottingham
NG1 1EW

Tel: 0115 924 0800

Spinal Injuries Association
76 St James Lane
London
N10 3DF

Tel: 020 8444 2121

Index